Successful Careers beyond the Lab

There is a major demand for people with scientific training in a wide range of professions based on and maintaining relations with science. However, there is a lack of good first-hand information about alternative career paths to research. From entrepreneurship, industry and the media to government, public relations, activism and teaching, this is a readable guide to science-based skills, lifestyles and career paths.

The ever-narrowing pyramid of opportunities within an academic career structure, or the prospect of a life in the laboratory losing its attraction, mean that many who trained in science and engineering now look for alternative careers. More than thirty role models who began by studying many different disciplines and then succeeded in a wide range of other careers give personal guidance for graduates, postgraduates and early-career scientists in the life sciences, physical sciences and engineering. This book is an entertaining resource for ideas about, and directions into, the many fields which they may not be aware of or may not have considered.

DAVID J. BENNETT is a Senior Member of St Edmund's College, Cambridge, and part natural, part social scientist in both academia and companies. He has long-term experience, activities and interests in the relations between science, industry, government, education, law, the public and the media, and has spent the last twenty-five years running large, international, multidisciplinary, science-based projects.

RICHARD C. JENNINGS is an affiliated research scholar in the Department of History and Philosophy of Science at the University of Cambridge. His research interests are focused on the responsible conduct of research and the ethical uses of science and technology. He is an active member of Scientists for Global Responsibility and has worked with BCS, the Chartered Institute for IT, on a 'Framework for Assessing Ethical Issues in New Technologies'.

Successful Careers beyond the Lab

Edited by

DAVID J. BENNETT
St. Edmunds College, Cambridge

RICHARD C. JENNINGS
Department of History and
Philosophy of Science, University
of Cambridge

CAMBRIDGE
UNIVERSITY PRESS

CAMBRIDGE
UNIVERSITY PRESS

University Printing House, Cambridge CB2 8BS, United Kingdom

One Liberty Plaza, 20th Floor, New York, NY 10006, USA

477 Williamstown Road, Port Melbourne, VIC 3207, Australia

4843/24, 2nd Floor, Ansari Road, Daryaganj, Delhi – 110002, India

79 Anson Road, #06–04/06, Singapore 079906

Cambridge University Press is part of the University of Cambridge.

It furthers the University's mission by disseminating knowledge in the pursuit of education, learning, and research at the highest international levels of excellence.

www.cambridge.org
Information on this title: www.cambridge.org/9781107161054
10.1017/9781316676103

© Cambridge University Press 2017

First published 2017

Printed in the United States of America by Sheridan Books, Inc. in April 2017

A catalogue record for this publication is available from the British Library.

Library of Congress Cataloging-in-Publication Data
Names: Bennett, David J. | Jennings, Richard C.
Title: Successful careers beyond the lab / David Bennett, St. Edmunds College, University of Cambridge, UK, Richard Jennings, Department of History and Philosophy of Science, University of Cambridge, UK.
Description: New York, NY : Cambridge University Press, 2017. | Includes bibliographical references and index.
Identifiers: LCCN 2016042159 | ISBN 9781107161054 (Hardback : alk. paper)
Subjects: LCSH: Science–Vocational guidance. | Science–Vocational guidance–Great Britain.
Classification: LCC Q147 .B455 2017 | DDC 502.3–dc23 LC record available at https://lccn.loc.gov/2016042159

ISBN 978-1-107-16105-4 Hardback
ISBN 978-1-316-61379-5 Paperback

Contents

Contributors

Dr Kat Arney
Freelance science writer and broadcaster, London, UK

Professor Sir Tom Blundell FRS, FMedSci
Emeritus Sir William Dunn Professor of Biochemistry, University of Cambridge, Cambridge, UK

Sir Walter Bodmer FRS, FRCPath
MRC Weatherall Institute of Molecular Medicine, University of Oxford, UK

Nicola Buckley
Associate Director, Centre for Science and Policy, University of Cambridge & formerly Head of Public Engagement, University of Cambridge, Cambridge, UK

Dr Delphine Carron
Regulatory Affairs Manager, Agricultural Biotechnology, Europa-Bio, Brussels, Belgium

Dr David Cleevely CBE FREng
Chair of Advisory Council, Centre for Science and Policy, University of Cambridge, Cambridge, UK

Dr Lori Conlan
Director, Office of Postdoc Services and the Career Services Center, National Institutes of Health, Bethesda, USA

Dr Darrin M. Disley
Entrepreneur, Angel Investor and Enterprise Champion, Cambridge, UK

Professor John Durant
The Mark R. Epstein (Class of 1963) Director, The MIT Museum & Adjunct Professor, The Science, Technology & Society Program, Massachusetts Institute of Technology, Cambridge, MA, USA

Peter Evans
BBC science radio presenter and journalist, London, UK

Ian Harvey
Head of Biology, Hills Road Sixth Form College, Cambridge, UK

Richard Hayhurst
Public relations professional, Richard Hayhurst Associates, Long Marston, Warwickshire, UK

Julie Hill
Associate of Green Alliance, Non-Executive Director and author, Oxford, UK

Professor Jackie Hunter PhD CBE FBPharmacolS FMedSci
Former Chief Executive Officer, Biotechnology and Biological Sciences Research Council (BBSRC), now Chief Executive Officer, Benevolent Bio Ltd, London, UK

Dr Julian Huppert
Scientist and politician. Former MP for Cambridge and now Founding Director, Intellectual Forum, Jesus College, Cambridge UK.

Stephen Isherwood
Chief Executive, Association of Graduate Recruiters, London, UK

Clare Jones
Senior Careers Adviser (Research Staff & PhDs), University of Nottingham, Nottingham, UK

Ermeena Malik
MPhil student, Judge Business School, University of Cambridge, Cambridge, UK

Dr Jonathan Milner
Entrepreneur and co-founder of Abcam Plc, Cambridge, UK

Madhumita Murgia
European Technology Correspondent, The Financial Times, London, UK

Dr Miles Parker OBE CBiol FRSB
Former Deputy Chief Scientific Adviser to the Department for Environment, Food and Rural Affairs, London and now Visiting Research Fellow, Centre for Science and Policy, University of Cambridge, Cambridge, UK

Dr Stuart Parkinson
Executive Director, Scientists for Global Responsibility, Lancaster, UK

Vivienne Parry OBE
Writer and broadcaster, London and Oxfordshire, UK

Tim Radford
Journalist and former letters editor, arts editor, literary editor and science editor of *The Guardian*, London UK

Dr Jasdeep Sandhu
Head of Chief Scientific Adviser's Cabinet, Research and Evidence Division, Department for International Development and Science Policy Fellow, Centre of Science Policy, University of Cambridge, UK

Dr Nick Scott-Ram MBE
Director of Commercial Development, Oxford Academic Health Science Network, Oxford, UK

Dr Chris Smith
Public Understanding of Science Fellow, Institute of Continuing Education, University of Cambridge and Consultant Clinical Virologist, Addenbrooke's Hospital, Cambridge, UK

Robert Stephen
Partner, Olswang LLP, London, UK

Dr Nalayini Thambar
Director of Careers and Employability, University of Nottingham, Nottingham, UK

Dr Philip Webber
Chair, Scientists for Global Responsibility, Non-Executive Director YES Energy Solutions and Research Associate University of Leeds, Leeds, UK

Dr Adam Wright
Former Lead Policy Officer, National Union of Students and now Senior Policy Adviser, The Royal Society, London, UK

Foreword

This volume provides a fascinating introduction to almost thirty successful individuals whose careers have taken them 'beyond the lab'. Most have travelled with no clear intention of being where they are now! Not all started as scientists in their university training! Some of the career paths described would be beyond the experience of academic and career advisors in universities. So here we have a resource that is equally valuable to the graduate scientist, to careers' advisors and to those of us who are concerned that we populate the workforce beyond academia with bright and innovative people with good science training and knowledge of research.

Many contributors to this volume tell of their travels in research ecosystems that bring together academia, start-ups and large companies. For me this is the Cambridge phenomenon, but for others it will be Oxford, Munich, Aarhus and other innovation centres in Europe, or Boston, San Francisco and San Diego in the United States. Such ecosystems are now widely acknowledged to be central to the knowledge economy, and I find them encouraged in São Paolo in Brazil, Shanghai and Beijing in China, in Bangalore in India and elsewhere in the world.

However, David Bennett and Richard Jennings are clear, and my own experience tells me they are right, that successful careers beyond the lab include local government sponsoring science parks and providing skills training; central government providing infrastructure funding and resources for longer-term investment, especially in the current environment; and venture capital and 'angels' providing more risky investment for new ideas about innovation. We are also reminded that successful research investment involves the public, with whom we need to engage and communicate if we are to have their support in taking forward new ideas. For this we need journalists and radio and TV commentators who communicate our science and engineering and facilitate the exchange of knowledge.

I have been lucky to find my passion for basic science sustained over more than fifty years so that I have never really left the lab. Even during the six years that I was a full-time government employee as CEO of a Research Council, I worked early mornings and late nights to produce many papers in basic science. Dorothy Hodgkin had introduced me in the 1960s to the challenge of understanding the architecture and mechanism of proteins, which are central to cell processes. My PhD started in Oxford in 1964, the year that Dorothy was awarded the Nobel Prize for her work on vitamin B12 and penicillin, but when the insulin structure was still expected from the group. Dorothy's multidisciplinary team of scientists included everyone from mathematicians to medics and came from Europe, South America, India, Africa, China and Australia. I soon gave up thoughts of being a full-time modern jazz musician or left-wing politician, to devote most of my time to exploring new methods to solve the insulin structure, a project that Dorothy had started thirty years before. This set me on a journey of developing methods and solving problems in basic molecular, structural and cellular biology that still gets me out of bed at 4 a.m. every morning.

For me this volume of biographical commentaries is a fascinating read. I have met again people whose paths have crossed mine over several decades. As David Cleevely says, networking is central. Indeed, an underlying strength of Dorothy's laboratory was its interactions with many great scientists and their teams, not only those working in the United Kingdom, for example J. D. Bernal, Max Perutz, David Phillips and Francis Crick, but also those visiting from abroad, such as Jim Watson, Siv Ramaseshan and Liang Dongcai. But the network extended to her former student, Margaret Thatcher, who, in the early 1970s when she was Minister of Education, would visit Dorothy in Oxford – even though their political views were far apart. And of course the network included many scientists in industry – mainly from pharma, where Dorothy kept close links. Our team would visit Dorothy's friends and former students in The Wellcome Foundation, Novo and Eli Lilley to discuss our work on insulin and to receive insulin samples. I learnt that knowledge travelled in both directions; new knowledge of value to basic research quite often originates from industry, a fact that surprised many of my college high-table friends in Oxford. Networks of people working in the wider research ecosystem are, not surprisingly, a central theme of this volume.

The contributions on industry and related occupations in this volume are fascinating. I frequently asked myself as I read it through: should I have taken courage in my hands and been more adventurous beyond the lab? After all, Jackie Hunter travelled successfully from academic labs in psychology and pharmacology to neuroscience and Alzheimer's research in Glaxo and SmithKline Beecham (SKB). Jackie became responsible for the GlaxoSmithKline (GSK) science parks and then formed her own open innovation and spinout companies, before becoming CEO of the Biotechnology and Biological Sciences Research Council. Courage to join new ventures has characterised her career development. In contrast, I remained in my academic labs in Sussex, Birkbeck and Cambridge, venturing out to consult with Pfizer, ICI and SKB, in the latter to be entertained by George Poste and Peter Good-fellow, and meeting Jackie for the first time.

David Cleevely took a parallel path from physics and mathematics in academia through British Telecom to found several successful con-sultancies and companies in telecoms and computing. I first met him when he became active in the Cambridge Centre for Science and Policy. I was very impressed when he then co-founded with Jonathan Milner and Tony Kouzarides the successful company Abcam. This was truly a great feat of networking, a convergence of multidisciplinary interests in computing, evolutionary theory and antibody technologies, as Jonathan describes in his chapter.

My own adventures in founding companies started in London in the 1980s with Biofabrika, but flourished only after 1996 when I moved to Cambridge. One needs serial entrepreneurs, large numbers of early career researchers who are willing to move from one company to another every few years, and investors who feel that the idea, the people and the environment are right. Astex, the company I co-founded in 1999 with Harren Jhoti and Chris Abell, was a success that was very much dependent on the research ecosystem and networking in Cam-bridge. It took seventeen years to get ten candidate drugs into clinical trials, and in 2016 its first was ready for approval.

Other adventurers in the world of science found their way into the public sector. My own experience here took me by surprise. Like Julian Huppert, I became involved in local issues, particularly racial integra-tion in Oxford where many immigrants had come from Bangladesh and the West Indies to work in the motor industry. I was elected to the City Council in 1970, focusing on street committees and environmental issues in the town centre – we pedestrianized much of the centre and introduced bus lanes way ahead of their time. Julian recounts how his election to the Cambridge City Council led to similar involvement in local planning, but much more significantly to his election as MP for Cam-bridge. There he was able to make some very significant contributions to science in the United Kingdom, although he recounts the challenges from one MP who advocated alternative medicines and astrology.

Miles Parker started in rock pools, and later worked in the Department of Agriculture and Fishing in Dublin before becoming involved in Whitehall. My own route was a little more circuitous. Having been a Labour City Councillor, I was surprised in 1988 to be invited to join Margaret Thatcher's Advisory Council on Science and Technology that met in 10 Downing Street. Just over two years of very interesting, amicable and positive deliberations were interrupted by the suggestion that I apply for the Head of the Agricultural and Food Research Council. It turned out that the Chair of the Advisory Board of the Research Councils, Sir David Phillips, and Chief Scientific Advisor, Sir Bill Stewart, had other plans, and I soon found myself not only talking with the Ministry of Agriculture, Fisheries and Food (MAFF) but also reorganizing the research. I became founding CEO of the Biotechnology and Biological Sciences Research Council (BBSRC) through which I later met Miles.

This was an interesting time for policy makers, as the implications of Lord Rothschild's 1971 proposals for 'customer-contractor' relationships were still being implemented, the research council institutes were being reorganized and staff reduced, and Margaret Thatcher's definition of 'market failure' as the basic criterion for government funding of research was still being pursued. Basic science survived, but applied science, particularly in government institutes, had a tough time. Miles's chapter shows how challenging such times can be both for scientists in government departments and for research council staff.

As for journalism and the media, Peter Evan's piece provides many insights: the amount of preparation, the impossibility of being an expert in every area and the need to make sure the audience will understand what the interviewee is saying. To find that Peter started as a graduate with an interest in nineteenth-century French poetry was a real revelation. In another chapter Madhumita Murgia recounts the challenges of writing about HIV and the feelings she had in interviewing Donna Mildvan, MD, chief of infectious diseases thirty-six years after she came across one of the first gay men to die of AIDS in Manhattan. And Chris Smith and Kat Arney talk about mixing up music and science as *The Naked Scientists*. All amazing stuff!

Science communication is central to science and, like everything else in the research ecosystem, it is about knowledge exchange. Public engagement remains a challenge for us all. In fact, John Durant describes one of the most exciting experiences I had in public engagement. As we were obtaining a Royal Charter for the Biotechnology and

Biological Sciences Research Council, and deciding on the launch for 1994, John and Simon Joss approached us with the idea of a first consensus conference in the United Kingdom, a more inclusive approach to public engagement and influencing policy. Together with David Bennett who was secretary to the committee that organised the consensus conference on the Danish model, they recruited experts and members of the general public to discuss and to conduct cross-examinations – as John says, 'we were making a tiny piece of history'. As CEO I saw it as a central component of our new research council but, when I later put it to Council, the cost of £80,000 became central, and I failed to get it on the agenda for the long term. Communication and engagement does not come cheap in time or cash, but this kind of approach has to be pursued! I learnt a lot from the consensus conference that was useful when I became Chair of the Royal Commission on Environmental Pollution from 1998 to 2005. But that body along with many other 'quangos' was closed by the recent coalition government, along with many others that brought independent views to government policy making.

This volume has much for all of us involved in science, society and innovation. As President of the UK Science Council over the past four years, I worked with Diana Garnham, our brilliant chief executive during that period, and other members of the organisation that brings together professional societies, to get over to government, business and universities many of the messages that I find here. Most of them are relevant to the broader workforce. They are that most of those trained in science end up well beyond the lab! We know very little about the career paths, and most were not planning to go where they eventually found rewarding occupations. However, these scientists are central to the industries that represent employment of millions of people in the United Kingdom and other advanced economies, as well as those in the public sector in health, environment, agriculture, food, planning, building and so on.

T.L.Blundell

Professor Sir Tom Blundell FRS, FMedSci
Emeritus Sir William Dunn Professor of Biochemistry,
University of Cambridge

Preface

Science today is exciting and hugely important but, like many other human endeavours such as art, sport and politics, it is a Darwinian enterprise. The ever-narrowing pyramid of opportunities in its (especially academic) career structure, the prospect of a life in the laboratory losing its attraction or simply other pursuits becoming more appealing mean that many who originally chose to do science, instead of continuing in the lab, now look for alternative careers – usually based on science. With the difficulties of keeping up in a rapidly developing field for re-entry after child-raising, this is particularly so for women who now make up a large and progressively growing proportion of young scientists.

Intriguingly, one of the authors in this book (Tim Radford) begins by recounting the story of the marsupial mole – a very good example of Darwinian evolutionary theory in action. However emulation is not to be recommended in this case if one is a male as they die after mating because of the stress hormones through over-exertion! But in many other respects the theory is apposite, particularly when it speaks of mutations leading to advantageous adaptations to the large range of alternative ecological niches available. So it is with careers and the almost unlimited range of opportunities available "beyond the lab" – including, for example, an impecunious post-doc becoming a multi-millionaire as another of this book's authors (Dr Jonathan Milner) tells about in his lessons from evolution on how to build a business.

Most young people say they know little or nothing about careers in science. The majority obtain their information largely from family members, teachers and school careers advisors. Later their experience is mainly restricted to their lecturers, senior researchers and professors at university as role models. In the first, introductory chapter to this book university careers advisers Dr Nalayini Thambar and Clare Jones write:

> Undertaking research in a university setting is intensive with strong encouragement to be fully immersed in the subject and the disciplinary community. While career-affirming and critical for those working to make their name, this can create a restricted view of options beyond academia, limit time to explore career alternatives and perhaps, albeit unintentionally, foster a sense that such options are of less value, so that to consider them is to be failing.

As Dr Jasdeep Sandhu, neuroscientist and now Head of the Chief Scientific Adviser's Cabinet in the UK Government's Department for International Development, says in her chapter, many academics have not themselves had or explored other possible careers so do not have broader experience and some university careers offices are limited in guidance on wider careers and how investigation about them can be undertaken. She also speaks of the uncertainties of research funding and the skills needed for obtaining it not being covered during the PhD, the pressure of "publish or perish", the difficulties women face with child-rearing and the subtle influences that affect their careers although there are now incentives for them.

So young scientists are generally poorly prepared and know little of life outside the lab and the almost boundless variety of careers open to them using their scientific knowledge and experience while maintaining links with science. This is in spite of the fact that there is major demand for people with scientific training in numerous other professions based on science and maintaining relations with it. If those individuals – and there are many – do not find such jobs, then both they and those who have funded their scientific education have wasted their investment and, crucially, opportunities for fulfilling rewarding occupations required in the wider world.

There is a need, therefore, for a collection of reliable, succinct, first-hand accounts dealing with the many widely differing opportunities open for 'successful careers beyond the lab' to serve as role models for those who are looking to move on from it. These should be written by experienced people who began their life across many disciplines and explain how they developed other flourishing careers based on science for the rest of their lives. They should provide a readable and readily accessible practical guide for the many brought up in science who neither really know the questions to ask nor, even if they do have some ideas, know the people who can give them personal guidance from their own experiences. There is also a great deal of relevant information now on the internet which should be collected and its availability made more widely known as in the "Further Sources of Information" section at the end of this book.

That was our starting point. We come from very different backgrounds but, as friends and colleagues, we have worked together previously on several books because we found that we complemented each other very well. One of us (David Bennett) is a part natural and, later, part social scientist together with being part academic and, later, part company man. He has spent the last twenty-five years or so running large international, network-based, multidisciplinary projects for the European Commission, UK Research Councils and UK and US foundations. The other (Richard Jennings) has been a philosopher of science for most of his life, lecturing to and supervising countless numbers of students in the Department of History and Philosophy of Science at the University of Cambridge. The students come from the Natural Science Tripos (the framework within which most of the sciences are taught in Cambridge) and become interested in the social, historical and philosophical context of science. Many then go off into a wide range of other professions based on and maintaining their relations with science. It turns out that two of the authors of this book's chapters studied in his department and one was supervised by him personally!

So, based on the thoughts outlined above and with our varied experiences, we prevailed on a number of good people with science related careers who had started off in a wide range of disciplines, the majority in science but a few in the arts and humanities, to tell their life stories as guidance for others who may be interested in doing similarly when they know what is possible. We are truly grateful for the ready willingness of those we approached to undertake the task and their cooperation in producing this book.

We very much hope that in reading their accounts you will see opportunities that you may not have been aware of previously and are encouraged to follow their example. We wish you all the luck in the world – because luck plays a large part and helping

Much of the book consists of a wide variety of fascinating individual stories of people's careers, from each of which there is much to learn. Many careers are not simple linear trajectories. Take Jackie Hunter, for example. She went from psychology and physiology, to a PhD on the pharmacology of rodent sexual behaviour, to Glaxo working on the pharmacology of Alzheimer's disease, to an academic Institute of Neurology, to being a programme manager at the pharmaceutical company SmithKline Beecham (SKB) and, after its merger with Glaxo, various research management positions at GlaxoSmithKline (GSK), including opportunities for involvement in policy decisions at a national level and the development of science parks, to a private commercial consultancy and starting a spinout company, to being CEO of the Biotechnology and Biological Sciences Research Council (BBSRC) and most recently back to industry leading a biotech company. The importance of networking in such a varied career is obvious. Each career move benefits not only from the increased experience of previous positions, but also from the increasing opportunities for networking.

Not all the stories start from science. Tim Radford, for example, went straight from school to be an apprentice journalist, having had no formal academic training, and became one of the UK's foremost science journalists. Peter Evans' first interest at university was in nineteenth-century French poetry and he is now a highly accomplished broadcaster and interviewer. Nicola Buckley moved from history through social anthropology to running science festivals in Cambridge.

Several stories are about science-based entrepreneurs, often in the biotech industry. Here the challenges of managing science and a start-up company are mostly greater than those of the underlying science and technology. You have to be prepared to take the risks and, as Vivienne Parry emphasises, not be afraid of failing, and if you do fail, just try again.

To me, it is rewarding to see, more than 30 years after the Bodmer Royal Society report, how much activity there now is in the public understanding and public engagement of science areas, leading to many employment opportunities. As I wrote in 2010, it is now much less likely that a head of a science laboratory would berate a junior member of his or her group for taking part in public understanding of science (PUS) activities. Indeed, they are encouraged to do so, and nearly all science applications for funding now have to include a plan for public science engagement and communication.

PR, journalism, policy and advocacy, patent law, teaching and politics are all represented in the individual career stories. As a teacher, it must be quite a thrill to meet successful former students whose interests in science were clearly stimulated by your teaching at school.

Julian Huppert urges scientists concerned about public affairs and policy to consider putting themselves forward for election to public office, from local councils to being an MP. He points out that, when he entered the House of Commons, there were only two out of 650 MPs with PhDs in a science subject, of which he was one. He comments further that, with respect to attitudes to science, "There was a decent cohort- maybe around 75 - who got it". How very discouraging that only just over 10% of MPs had a 'decent attitude to science' given that nearly all issues of major importance have some scientific content. Even if not standing as an MP or a local councillor there are many ways to influence policy through involvement with Government select committees, the civil service, relevant NGOs, a variety of think tanks and charities with an obvious mission, including cancer and anti-smoking.

Serendipity is an important feature of many careers, including my own. Be sure to take advantage of unexpected opportunities, 'know thyself' and make sure you enjoy whatever career you choose. There is much stimulating food for thought in this excellent and timely book for those interested in 'alternative' scientific careers.

Sir Walter Bodmer FRCPath, FRS
The Weatherall Institute of Molecular Medicine, University of Oxford

Part I Career Services', Recruiters' and Students' Viewpoints

1

What Type of Scientist Are You?

'I want to work in industry'. In our experience, whether we hear these words from an exhausted first or higher degree science student, final examinations finished or dissertation or thesis submitted; an early career researcher, current funding really ending; or a postdoctoral researcher who returned to academia from industry to further their career prospects, the depth of feeling and a sense of not knowing where to start are palpable. 'Industry' is usually used as shorthand for wanting to follow a career outside academic research, whilst still 'using science' in the jobs that might be out there. Does this sound familiar? Anyone embarking on a scientific research career is aware of the high levels of attrition at every stage of academic progression, so 'working in industry' is an ever-present option that is rarely explored until necessary. In this chapter, the challenge of making such a career move is defined and addressed, so that you can convert the inspiration you find in this book into a strategy for your career success.

RECOGNISING THE CHALLENGE

The Master's degree or PhD pathways have much to commend them, but there are features which do not naturally support career exploration and development beyond the academic route. For example, it is common for students to decide to embark on a PhD during their undergraduate or Master's degree – the decision being made as a result of enjoyment of a final year's research project, developing an interest in an aspect of their course or being 'spotted' as a potential higher-degree student. Such 'triggers' will often override the process of career

Successful Careers beyond the Lab, ed. David Bennett and Richard Jennings.
Published by Cambridge University Press. © Cambridge University Press 2017.

planning and development that is usually undertaken by those students for whom an undergraduate or Master's degree is enough when they consider a range of options, industries and organisations. For a potential research degree student, their trusted advisers are potential supervisors or academic tutors as the choice of research area and availability of funding dominate their decision. Careers services, offering expert, generic careers guidance and connections to organisations across all sectors, tend to be less used by this group of students because, with some legitimacy, they see academics as having more specific knowledge and expertise about the academic career routes. This lack of contact can leave doctoral and post-doctoral researchers with little experience and confidence when it comes to career exploration outside academia, even though they will have gone through some of the same steps when deciding to take a higher degree. They may be so dislocated by the loss of an academic expert to facilitate career change decisions that it may not even occur to them to seek help from career experts within their institution even though careers services and careers advisers are poised to support such career changes. For undergraduate and taught Master's students, especially those who wish to consider alternatives to the academic route, the careers service should be an early port of call so that they can understand their many options, however it can seem counter to the culture within their academic department.

Undertaking research in a university setting is intensive with strong encouragement to be fully immersed in the subject and the disciplinary community. While career-affirming and critical for those working to make their name, this can create a restricted view of options beyond academia, limit time to explore career alternatives and perhaps, albeit unintentionally, foster a sense that such options are of less value, so that to consider them is to be failing. When surrounded by friends and colleagues at various stages of the academic journey, the academic route can seem clearly mapped out, even preordained (despite the unpredictability of funding), while other careers seem more fluid, unpredictable and harder to access. Comparison can also be unhelpful when it comes to individual talents in the context of the wider job market. Scientific research is conducted by highly able people who are judged by their output: this can be an intimidating benchmark which distorts an individual's sense of what they have to offer. One example, of many, is the student who did not consider themselves to have the level of maths required for a software engineering role, despite their recently submitted PhD in the field of electronic engineering. The student's academic base (the Department of Mathematics), while boosting credibility with the hiring company, was an initial hindrance in enabling them to realise that they were more than equipped for the role; their perception of what constituted 'a sound understanding of mathematics' had been skewed by the skills and knowledge of their fellow researchers.

The intensity of the research experience with a focus on precision and accurate output can lead to a lack of recognition of the many skills and experiences which have been developed in the process. This, again, undermines the confidence of those seeking alternative routes as it is harder to see beyond the detailed focus of their key tasks to the abilities and knowledge they could deploy in alternative career settings. A further approach which can undermine confidence occurs if, following on from an undergraduate or Master's degree experience, PhD students themselves, their family or their social circle still consider a researcher to be still 'going to university' rather than going to work. This masks the fact that they are now part of the research, and potentially teaching, businesses of an institute or university, with all the responsibilities and skills which such roles require; and can foster a sense of 'arrested development' resulting in less social confidence and a hesitance to seize opportunities.

In the context of the challenges outlined above, it is easy to see how the prospect of changing career direction, whilst retaining a scientific focus, can seem daunting and unlikely. Yet, as this book shows, it is clearly possible. In our experience, the self-perception fostered by the research experience is the biggest challenge for research scientists seeking to change career and context. Your challenge is to see yourself as others could see you: a professional researcher with highly accredited scientific knowledge and a sought-after qualification. You possess skills in problem solving and critical thinking; you are able to handle and deal with complexity within the problem you are solving and analyse the data or evidence that you generate. You are a flexible, creative and innovative thinker and are able to present your work to a range of audiences, both orally and in writing. These capabilities are valued within organisations across all sectors and used by many doctoral graduates outside academia. The remainder of this chapter suggests ways in which you can start to consider the type of person you are, and find your best fit.

RESEARCHING YOURSELF

The starting point for any sound career decision is to be clear about who you are, what you have to offer and what is important to you in your work, whether that is the skills you use, the values you uphold, the purpose of your role or the place of work in your life. Many people find this process challenging and try to leave it out, jumping straight to considering the job opportunities that are out there. This is an understandable approach, but even with limited time and when feeling the pressure of the end of a degree or contract, stepping back from the intensity and specificity of your degree to consider options from a broader perspective will make a difference to the quality of the decision you make. You will be able to identify and consider the wide range of skills, behaviours and personal characteristics (attributes) that you have gained, and also to reflect on which of them you want to use or develop more in the next phase of your career.

Remember that you are more than your research. Think of the number of times that you may have been asked: 'How is your degree progressing?' Could this contribute to a view of yourself that is limited both by the scope of your degree and by whether or not it has been successful? These limitations are not helpful when you are considering your options and making decisions about your future career. Rather than taking your first degree, Master's degree, PhD, or your research experience as a whole, consider specific tasks and the skills, behaviours and attributes that you deploy when you are at work, or have used in a setting away from work, or when on a placement. Table 1.1 gives an example of how a conference poster presentation can be analysed to identify sub-tasks, skills used, level of competence and outcomes and achievements. As a research task this can differ in apparent rigour from the usual scientific approach as the source data is subjective, derived from you, your personal experience and your interaction with others, rather than external, empirically verified data. In this context, 'measurable evidence' can mean externally verifiable achievements (e.g. subsequent collaborations), supporting descriptive statistics (e.g. Research Excellence Framework (REF) scores, audience numbers), but also potentially unverifiable data, such as comments (i.e. personal communication) made by others. Some words of caution, echoing our tale of the electronic engineer earlier in the chapter; do not judge yourself too harshly by comparing yourself with experts in the field, your supervisor or more senior collaborators. Recognise your own talents and abilities and then use this knowledge to move towards a career decision.

Using a range of key tasks to identify your skills gives you a good basis from which to prioritise the personal characteristics, skills and behaviours that you would like to use in your next career. In your current role, you will be deploying certain skills and personal qualities,

Table 1.1 *Example Analysis – The Poster [1]*

Main Task – Preparation and Presentation of Poster for a Conference

---

Sub-Tasks

1. Reviewed and analysed research material to identify key information to meet conference themes
2. Discussed and agreed ideas and approaches with supervisor
3. Sought advice from post-doc researcher on effective poster styles to allow for a clear and concise presentation of material
4. Prepared draft poster and presentation for research group meeting and received feedback from colleagues
5. Acted on feedback and informal advice from other researchers to improve poster and presentation
6. Liaised with print department, agreed on deadlines for printing and costs
7. At the conference – attended poster session and presented research to delegates

Skills Used/Level of Competence/Outcomes and Achievements

- Analytical skills to identify key themes
- Communication skills – able to rationalise material in order to convey a clear and concise overview of research. Needed also to be able to capture interest of audience quickly. At conference used good oral presentation skills to provide further information by answering questions confidently and knowledgeably.
- Teamwork/collaborative skills – Able to use feedback and advice from colleagues to improve work. Liaison and negotiation skills used with supervisor and with print staff in order to meet deadlines.
- Networking skills – made a number of specific contacts with researchers working in similar areas
- IT skills – improved IT design skills in order to produce poster with good visual impact – now feel more competent with a software package

   Achievements – awarded conference commendation for poster, invited to attend conference next year as a direct result of contact made. Complimented on clear nature of presentation.

   Own assessment – have significantly improved written and oral communication skills. Know that I can identify and analyse information to convey complex ideas in a clear and concise way. Can talk confidently and enthusiastically to a range of people – from senior academics and industrialists to fellow researchers – which has made me feel more confident about defending my work at my viva. Felt more confident to discuss my approach with my supervisor and defend my ideas.

---

because 'that's what researchers do'. and you will deploy them effectively, because that is what is required for success in the role. However, when looking at a change in career direction, it is time well spent to think about which of those skills and attributes you are stronger and weaker at and also those you like and dislike, mapping them out in a two-by-two grid. This decision-making matrix can be used to help you to assess career opportunities as follows.

A focus on the areas of your experience that you have enjoyed, have strengths in or the potential to develop further can allow you to introduce new or reinforce existing career ideas. For example, if you love lab work, are good at it and want to continue to use these precise skills and work in the same type of environment for the next phase of your career, then this heavily defines the type of job which you will be looking for. However, if the reason you like lab work is because of certain key characteristics, such as the precision, the reproducibility or the sense of community, then many other jobs have these characteristics. Or maybe there are certain components of the researcher role that you like. For example, you may have used and developed your computer programming and modelling skills and expertise as part of your higher degree and would prefer to shift the focus of your career to this area of work. This type of self-analysis could also help you to explore more options within areas related to science; for example, you may have developed an interest in the commercialisation of science through assisting with a patent application or undertaking a placement with a company with a focus on commercialisation of scientific discoveries. A next step, in these cases, could be to explore a career as a patent attorney, illustrated in a later chapter in this book, or to investigate roles that will allow you to combine your scientific knowledge, expertise and commercial interests such as are exemplified by the personal accounts given by the authors of other chapters. Identification of the personal characteristics, skills and behaviours, which you like using but don't feel to be particularly good at (remember to judge yourself fairly), can also lead to some 'quick wins' in terms of taking steps to develop your career by gaining more experience or training while in your current role, or by taking a job that acts as a stepping-stone towards the career area that interests you; for example, if you enjoy teaching, a Postgraduate Certification in Education (PGCE) could accredit your natural skill set.

By focussing your analysis on the positive areas of your experience, not only can you generate options and find career clues, but explaining your choice to others can be helped considerably. It will make conversations with your supervisors, family and friends much easier, and, more importantly, it will help you to make informed and realistic job applications. It will help you to generate the evidence base that you need to demonstrate your enthusiasm and commitment to your chosen career path, especially to potential employers.

Steering clear of careers that involve using skills and doing tasks which you dislike and are not your strongest points is obvious, as they are unlikely to realise your potential or the ambitions of the organisation you work for. Most people naturally avoid these career options. However, there is a further direction to your self-analysis that you should conduct, and this is to identify those experiences, tasks and skills that you (or those who work with you) would consider that you do well but that you have not enjoyed, or no longer enjoy as much as you did before. We would caution against moving into areas where you have ability but little enjoyment. This tends to happen where the career area is reassuringly familiar, if uninspiring, and it is common for career-changers to drift into this 'box' even if it does not provide the career satisfaction they seek, particularly if there are other aspects of their life which they need to balance or if they are under pressure to make a career decision. This is understandable, given the sense of disillusionment, disappointment and loss that can accompany a move away from the research path. At first glance, everything else can feel uninspiring by comparison, so it is hard to judge the enjoyment of any other career.

Throughout this process, honesty is critical. Recognising that you are good at, yet dislike, using a particular skill which is fundamental to an academic research career may not be something that you wish to share with your lecturer, tutor or principal investigator. However, it could hold an important clue to the direction your career now takes.

These stages of self-analysis should take you closer to understanding what type of individual you are. It may seem uncomfortable to draw conclusions that suggest an academic research career does not perfectly align with your skills and interests, but that may be a very positive first step. This can particularly be the case given that the requirements of those in an academic research career change dramatically as career progress is made, and time spent on lab-based research recedes. An example of revealing a career clue and acting upon it was the PhD oncology student who had undertaken a lab-based research project but, through analysis of her decision-making matrix, realised how much she enjoyed science communication through participating in poster competitions, research showcase and outreach activities. She utilised this knowledge to explore possible career options using these skills and experiences and moved into science communication roles initially with *Nature* and the Wellcome Trust and now in a university. When she returned to her university to speak about her career, her enjoyment and enthusiasm were evident to all. The next section of this chapter outlines some steps you can take to explore career alternatives.

DEVELOPING CAREER MOMENTUM

Planning and developing your career is an individual task, but it does not have to be a solitary one. Indeed, we would recommend (admittedly with some bias!) that you seek out the careers experts in your university or institute for impartial professional support as you take these important steps. It is not an admission of weakness or a lack of independence to seek help; careers services are designed to help people going through this process and, contrary to popular belief, do not expect to be approached by people who know exactly what they want to do. It is common for opening statements from undergraduates, higher-degree students and (early) career researchers to express concern about not knowing where to look for jobs, that they will not be welcomed by industry or that no-one will want their specialist area of research. There is also an assumption that they will have to start from scratch in a new career area rather than use their existing skills for a more horizontal move.

You will be able to get current and detailed support about how to research job opportunities from your careers experts, but there are some general principles that we can share here. You will find that there are options related to your broader academic background – for example, as a biochemist, biotechnologist or biologist. There will be some roles which have a job title or career area with the word 'research' in it, such as research scientist or research and development biochemist, but of course each company has their own approach to job titles; one company's senior scientist is an equivalent company's research scientist. There are also jobs that draw directly on scientific research skills but do not name them in the title: for example, science consultant, management consultant, patent attorney, policy officer, analyst or data scientist.

Organisations within the science industry are an obvious place to start, from large multinationals to small spin-out organisations. In a range of companies, including pharmaceuticals and fast-moving consumer goods, research skills are key, with a tendency to 'development' rather than 'research'. This may be just the thing if you don't feel that your strength lies in the more abstract and theoretical sides of research. Such roles offer the opportunity to work on a number of projects, but the opportunities to specialise remain – for example, working as a hair biophysicist in a cosmetics company. Away from the science industry, there are more scientifically driven organisations than it might first appear – for example, the mighty global brands which have worked their way into our day-to-day living which rely on advanced data analysis to maintain and develop their businesses.

While it is common to look at what is 'out there' and think in terms of trying to find a forever, perfect or ideal job, such an approach puts a lot of pressure on the next step or decision. A focus on the next phase of your working life will help you to consider the range of options and open up those stepping-stone routes towards your optimal role. For example, the graduate entry route may be the best road into your chosen field, with your research skills, attributes and experiences coming to the fore once you are established within the organisation. Examples of researchers who have made a transition through this route include a chemistry PhD graduate who secured a role as an analyst in an investment bank and a neuroscience PhD graduate now working as a logistics analyst for a large retailer, as well as first-degree graduates who have moved into management consultancy, actuarial training, marketing and fundraising. They are all enjoying their new careers.

It is never too early to start thinking about career alternatives to research. Nor is it ever too late, although if you sense you are delaying the inevitable then you are probably putting additional pressure on yourself by trying to ignore an impending 'crisis point'. This can be avoided by speaking to your careers experts who will be able to allay your fears and help you to develop a plan of action.

At an early stage take responsibility for your own development by making time to find out about training and development opportunities. Does your university, faculty, school or department have a training or employability programme specifically for undergraduates or postgraduates? Identify your own training needs and opportunities and make sure you allocate time for training in your project planning. Do not rely on supervisors or other colleagues to tell you about them, as their priority will not be in broadening your career options. If your university does not offer a specific programme, check out if a learned society or professional institution has similar opportunities.

If you are undecided about a career in industry or academia, keep in touch with the world outside academia. What techniques and skills do employers want? Which sectors and industries are growing? Which are not? Find out about opportunities for work shadowing or work experience through your university, institute or professional institution. These will provide an invaluable insight into different roles and organisations; furthermore, they will help you to have a realistic idea about the options you are considering and to build your professional network and your CV. A simple way of keeping up to date is to continue to analyse job adverts, even when you are not applying for a job. This is likely to require a change of approach: job descriptions for academic research posts require particular knowledge and techniques, and the requirements for post-docs are highly specific. Outside academia, the 'must haves' are not always so hard and fast, and the successful candidate may not have every last requirement listed in a person specification but instead have a particular blend of skill and experience, or strong skills in a particular area, which means they are still the best person for the job. Analysing a few job descriptions with a careers expert may be a useful starting point in adjusting your perception of your suitability for a role. Keep a note of skills and techniques, areas of work and company names. Follow organisations on Twitter and use LinkedIn to keep in touch with the world beyond academia. LinkedIn especially can often be used by people reviewing applications for interview and for appointments to check applicants' credentials.

If you are undertaking collaborative projects with industry or other organisations, let them know that you are interested in finding out about career opportunities with them after your degree. Keep in contact with former colleagues and peers who have moved into industry as you never know when this connection may prove to be beneficial. One post-doctoral researcher discovered this two years after finishing their PhD when they were contacted by their friend, who had since moved into industry. A job had come up in her company and she thought this researcher would be ideally suited.

This is an excellent example of 'Planned Happenstance' [2], the career theory that chance plays a role in everyone's career and that exploratory activities will increase the likelihood of discovering unexpected career opportunities [3]. This theory, borne out many times by experience as is demonstrated by all of the accounts in the following chapters of this book, suggests that you do not have to think of your next move as a permanent, life-defining move, but a positive step that will increase your chances of gaining yet more opportunities. The organisation or area of work where you find your ultimate niche may not yet exist, but you can still prepare yourself for it, gaining experience and growing your skills and reputation along the way. It is often said that the best strategy in life is to maximise the opportunity for happenstance, chance, serendipity, luck – whatever you like to call it – to happen!

For scientists, used to working with clear data and converting an idea into a research proposal, the process of career decision-making can seem unhelpfully vague; there is no list of all the jobs and organisations you could work in, and a lack of consistency between job titles and levels of experience looked for across the sector. But like research, there is a process you can follow to gather evidence (about yourself, then the job market) to help to solve the 'problem' of wishing to move away from your current career trajectory which can be analysed to determine the best course of action. In lieu of a research group, your institutional careers experts will be able to help to provide the discussion and challenge that will hone your ideas, either on a one-to-one basis or in seminars and workshops where you can network with like-minded people who are also considering their careers.

YOUR CAREER, YOUR STRATEGY

At the beginning of this chapter, we outlined the challenges of making a career change away from an academic research environment. Particularly difficult can be a fear of being seen as a failure or having a lack of commitment to the research cause. Attempts to conceal a wish to change career direction can put pressure on an open and honest relationship with a supervisor or principal investigator. Moving away from the patronage of well-known experts in a research area to the perceived opportunism of non-academic careers may feel like a high-risk strategy – sufficiently high-risk to be a foolish move. There is an element of holding your nerve, accepting risk and taking risk to open opportunities. If you continue to explore your own skills and motivations, the options that are open to you will become more concrete. You will feel more confident in your identity as a professional scientist and in your career possibilities.

Try and help yourself by not having too many constraints – for example, in relation to location or by disregarding particular sectors based on hearsay or anecdote. If you have rational and practical reasons for a particular geographical location, consider carefully whether you can extend your search area by undertaking a longer commute, even for a short period. Get to know the local job market, use local business directories to find out more, especially about small to medium-sized enterprises that could be engaged in really interesting cutting-edge work. If you have legitimate and personal objections to working in certain sectors, then of course you should be true to that, but if your decision is based on something you have heard from someone else – for example, 'only failed academics work in R&D in industry', or 'research in industry is second rate' – ask yourself why so many people with first and higher degrees do in fact work in these roles? It is also important that you give serious consideration to other life commitments that you have. Don't assume they are constraints, but do factor them into your thinking now so that you are confident that any steps you take will work for all aspects of your life.

Your career strategy will be inspired by other people's stories, influenced by your circumstances and will be very personal, driven by the type of scientist you are, which may not be the same type as your peers and your speciality or research group. Having a personalised career strategy is also really important in helping you to fulfil your potential and ability, for which you have evidence through your achievements to date. We would not be doing justice to our experience of working with hundreds of scientific career-changers and our roles as career professionals if we did not end by re-emphasizing two clear calls to action. First, as soon as you start to think of moving your career 'beyond the lab', take action by participating in the career development opportunities available through your institute or institution. There won't be a 'sign' that tells you when it is the right time, and no-one will seek you out and organise a bespoke career change for you. Hence the second call; speak to your institutional careers experts. They will focus on your personal circumstances, answer your questions, allay your concerns and help you to make the best use of your time as you consider your change of career.

As common as the opening lines of 'I want to work in industry' and 'I don't know where to start' is the feedback 'I wish I'd spoken to you earlier'. As soon as you have been inspired by some of the stories in this book, we suggest you make a start on the next stage of your career journey. We wish you every success.

REFERENCES

1. Jones, C. (2008) *Identifying and valuing your transferable skills.* In G. Hall & J. Longman (Eds.), *The postgraduate's companion* (pp. 407–416). London: Sage.

2. Krumboltz, J. D. (1996). *A learning theory of career counseling*. In M. L. Savickas & W. Bruce Walsh (Eds.), *Handbook of career counseling theory and practice* (pp. 55–80). Palo Alto, CA: Davies-Black.

3. Mitchell, K. E., Levin, A. S., & Krumboltz, J. D. (1999) 'Planned happenstance: Constructing unexpected career opportunities'. *Journal of Counselling and Development*, 77, 115–124.

2

Researching My Career
From Science to Career Education

I received my PhD in biochemistry and biophysics in 2002. In 2006, I moved "beyond the bench" to focus on career development issues for biomedical trainees. I am currently the Director of the Office of Postdoctoral Services and the Career Services Center in the Intramural Research Program of the National Institutes of Health (NIH). My job is to plan and execute programs to help scientists think and prepare for the variety of careers available to them.

All of our career stories are intertwined with career development theory. As a researcher I want to understand the research, methods and theories behind the theories on how individuals choose a career. There are three theories that I have found helpful. More than a century ago, Parsons, the Harvard sociologist, wrote that individuals need to understand their skills and interests. Additionally he suggested that you need knowledge of career paths and what it takes to be competitive for those jobs [1]. Next, Holland hypothesized in his theory of career choice that individuals seek to match their work environments to their personalities to maximize congruence with their skills (what I have learned or could learn) and interests (what I enjoy doing) [2]. A third seminal career theory developed by [3] Super describes the importance of including work values (what motivates me) in career decisions [3]. To me, the key to successful career choices and job satisfaction is embracing all of these theories. I use these theories today to advise trainees having successfully used them to search for my own career path as I navigated from bench science to science education and administration.

Successful Careers beyond the Lab, ed. David Bennett and Richard Jennings.
Published by Cambridge University Press. © Cambridge University Press 2017.

I loved science in secondary school, decided to major in biochemistry at university and continued on for a doctoral degree in biochemistry/biophysics. My choice made sense from my limited assessment of my skills, interests, and values. I could see that my skills were technical, my interest was science and I valued discovering new things. As I completed my PhD training, however, I realized that while I enjoyed science, something was missing.

Deliberate self-assessment helped me explore my nontechnical skills and I found that those skills were more personally fulfilling. I could formulate and answer a question including setting up the process to get an answer, collecting and analyzing data, and synthesizing the conclusion in the context of previous research. I communicated well as demonstrated by papers, fellowships, poster presentations, and talks. I could defend my ideas. I made inventories of my lab's chemicals and devised numerous standard operating procedures. I taught others, developing strategies and protocols that encouraged each person to grow their personal skill set. As I examined these skills and compared them to my interests I identified a pattern: I was more interested in using my nontechnical skills to manage programs and help others see their potential than in completing technical projects.

Knowledge of these expanded interests mapped on to Holland's career theory. He suggested that an individual's interests and work environments can be coded into six categories as identified by the acronym RIASEC: Realistic (practical, hands-on); Investigative (ideas, thinking); Artistic (art, music, drama, design); Social (people, teamwork); Enterprising (business, leadership); and Conventional (procedures, organization) [2]. A high correlation between the score for an individual and a workplace could suggest a potential career path that will be satisfying. One of my strongest Holland codes was Investigative and an associated career environment was science. So my first career choice to be a scientist would have seemed accurate. However, my original Holland codes pointed to both Investigative (science/research) and Social (people). My scores were equal in these areas so an optimal long-term career path would likely be one that incorporated both of these interests.

Having navigated through skills and interests, I needed to examine my values. Career values are the motivations, goals and beliefs that make us excited to do our jobs. They include intrinsic values (motivation and satisfaction), extrinsic values (physical environment, pay/benefits and titles) and lifestyle values (an intersection of work and life). I valued contributing to the scientific enterprise but I came to realize that this was a narrow definition of my value set. I can now see that I am motivated to work in teams doing a job that varied from day to day and involved contact with people. I wanted intellectual status, management responsibilities, good pay and promotion potential. I did not want to be an entrepreneur and did not need awards or honors. Finally, living in a big city, having time for fun and work and being able to travel are my most pressing lifestyle values.

Now my job is to help postdocs and grad students identify career paths that fit their own skills, interests and values. Parsons suggested that finding a satisfying job requires self-awareness and an understanding of the job, specifically "a knowledge of the requirements, conditions of success, advantages and disadvantages, compensation, opportunities, and prospects in different lines of work" [1, p. 5]. The best way to gather these data is through informational interviewing – talking to individuals in the paths one is considering. Here is what I would say in an informational interview about my current job:

1.   *What is my job like?* I run the Career Services Center and the Office of Postdoctoral Services for the Intramural Research Program of the NIH. We are responsible for more than 5,000 trainees on our campuses, 3,000 of whom are postdocs. My main role is to develop programming that enables our trainees to acquire four core competencies to supplement their research skills. These programs include topics in:
     a) career readiness (exploring careers and creating personal job search strategies);
     b) leadership and management (understanding how to work and lead in a diverse and team-based work environments);
     c) teaching and mentoring (knowledge of pedagogy and mentoring approaches); and
     d) communication (improving written and oral communication skills).

     I run at least one workshop a week across diverse topics, many of which I teach myself. I use the skills I learned as a researcher to understand a new topic, develop and deliver a presentation that fits my audience and evaluate the outcomes to improve future deliveries. I also travel to present these topics at universities and scientific meetings.

     My current job requires much more writing than I had anticipated. The type of writing I do now is quite different from the grant and manuscript writing I struggled with as a grad student and postdoc. I write emails, material for websites, blogs, program descriptions and policy pieces; the nontechnical, often more conversational style suits me.

I provide individual career advice to postdocs and other trainees, sharing resources and directing them to potential connections to help them gather data on possible careers. I also work with trainees on managing difficult situations or conversations such as how to have a conversation with their advisor on their career paths or navigating workplace conflicts. Advising is a learned skill set quite different from those acquired at the bench. The scientist in me wants to solve problems for the trainee. Effective advising requires that I listen, propose options and allow trainees to find their own solutions.

I also participate in various policy discussions regarding postdocs, both here at the NIH and in the postdoc community at large. I have served as a board member for the National Postdoctoral Association, presented about enhancing the postdoc experience at the National Academy of Sciences, participated in national meetings about career planning and advocated for increased access to career development.

Over the years I have taken on managing the Career Services Center within the Office of Intramural Training & Education (OITE) at the NIH. Five career counselors and advisors in our office provide personalized career advice to NIH trainees at all levels. While I have learned career advising skills, these individuals have more career counseling expertise than I do. I now work on understanding management theories and best practices to ensure that my staff have the resources and tools to do their jobs well.

2. *How did I get this job?* As a postdoc, grad student, and undergrad I ran events for my peers and learned that I enjoyed helping others understand career options and building communities. As a postdoc at the Wadsworth Center, the public health laboratory run by the New York State Department of Health, I started a postdoc association to improve the climate on campus for postdocs which allowed me to work with administrators and a team to define the mission and vision of the organization. The postdoc association hosted speakers to highlight biomedical job opportunities exposing me to a range of possibilities and foreshadowing my role as a career advisor. I strategized careers to highlight, identified and hosted speakers, developed a marketing plan to encourage postdocs to attend and executed the events.

I became involved in the National Postdoctoral Association which provided insights into policies and issues important to the national postdoc community. Earlier, as a graduate student at Texas A&M University, I started a "Careers in Science" workshop series and was actively involved in the Biochemistry Graduate Association. I also initiated departmental community-building events to encourage graduate students to take care of their whole selves. Even earlier, as an undergraduate at Michigan State University, I served as a Resident Assistant helping the students in my dormitory build a sense of community and place. These events culminate in what Krumboltz calls "Planned Happenstance," positioning oneself for career success without really planning ahead [4]. In retrospect, career development theories were applicable to my own career story. While I didn't intend it at the time, these activities made me a competitive candidate for career advisor/manager jobs. Following my curiosity and seizing unexpected opportunities positioned me for a career that would make me happy.

Through my network I found an opportunity at the New York Academy of Sciences running their Science Alliance program. The goal of this position was to build career development programming within the scientific community of New York City and beyond. In collaboration with university partners, I ran monthly events on various career preparation topics. In the beginning I brought in outside speakers but as I grew in the role I took over presenting (e.g., the topics included networking, resumé building, and interview skills). I used examples taken straight from research groups about real-world situations to create materials that resonated with my scientist audience. After two years the NIH recruited me to develop their postdoc office. I still present the workshops I developed in New York, but I also have the freedom to master and present new topics. Among these are a leadership series that explores personal preferences and how they work best together (based on the Myers-Briggs Type Indicator personality assessment) [5], managing conflict (using the Thomas-Kilman model for handling conflict) [6], managing and motivating teams and capitalizing on diversity, and a management boot camp for trainees transitioning to their next job.

3.   *Where do I see myself going?* Career planning never ends. I would like to enhance my presence in the national conversation in order

to improve career outcomes of biomedical trainees. For example, my office provides a wealth of career information online including a blog, information about careers, job search guidance and videocasts/YouTube Channel. However, the message that biomedical PhDs have *many* career options has not yet reached every graduate student and postdoc. We still have work to do to ensure positive and successful career outcomes for all young scientists.

I also would like to be involved in providing more leadership and management training to faculty. Most faculty still learn their non-research skills by trial and error having often been immersed in the technical aspects of their work at the expense of developing a more rounded skill set. I hope to modify and further develop for faculty the mentoring, leadership and management modules I have developed for postdocs.

4.   *If you wanted my job, what should you do?* Gain experience organizing events for your university: seminars, journal clubs, career speakers, social events. Learn what's happening in the career development field by getting involved in the National Postdoctoral Association (www.nationalpostdoc.org), the Cambridge, UK–based careers service Vitae (www.vitae.ac.uk/about-us), or your professional society's career activities. Career development for scientists is a fairly new field, so opportunities continue to open up as universities make career development a priority and faculty come to appreciate the value of non-bench careers. Make sure you are taking advantage of opportunities to build your network so when the time comes to make a career transition others know who you are and will advocate on your behalf.

Personally I am still on my career journey but so far the work I have put in to understanding who I am and what I want has me doing exactly what I love – for now. It is important to remember that this is a continuous journey and my skills, values, and interests must be period- ically reevaluated to make certain I am still on the right path. I was never going to be passionate about my work until I took time to ser- iously explore the intersection of what I was good at and what I truly found rewarding. My job now combines my skills, interests and values. I have found a career where I use my two strongest Holland codes every day. I think about how to build career programs by analyzing data and information (Investigative). I work closely with people to help them learn, grow and find their personal career success (Social). As an added bonus I am still working in the scientific enterprise and have a satisfying work/life balance.

If you are making your own career choices you might notice that making a career-related decision is different from how we make a scientific-related decision. Many research problems have well-defined questions and solutions. As a researcher you pick the best measurement methods and application of those methods leads to one answer. Career choices are less clear-cut. You may have multiple career choices but insufficient information to make a selection (How will I know if I like that career better than being a researcher?) Your career decision may lead to multiple conclusions of which you now must pick an optimal (but perhaps not perfect) choice.

One last career theory helps explain this process – Cognitive Information Processing (CIP) [7]. In CIP the three components necessary are self-knowledge (what are your skills, values, and interests), occupational knowledge (what careers exist and how do they match with your self-knowledge) and career decision-making. The CASVE (Communication / Analysis / Synthesis / Valuing / Execution) cycle can help you process career decisions. This approach adds values to the decision-making process:

- Communication helps identify gaps in our career choices. This manifests as tension, such as when many scientists say, "I want to be more than just a researcher but I am not sure what I want to do". For me this came early in my graduate career when I recognized I did not want to be a professor but I had no idea what else was out there.
- Analysis is a step of self-reflection to understand why a gap exists. A good question to ask here is: "What are the reasons why this current path (being a professor) is not desired?" I examined all of the reasons why I had a gap: my confidence level in running a lab and writing grants, the fact that I was part of a dual-career couple with two PhDs and my knowledge that I felt my talents would be better utilized in a career with a direct impact on people.
- Synthesis involves the exploration of potential alternatives, researching career options and doing informational interviews. I looked at many careers: science policy, tech transfer, patent law, industry science, science writing and more. This step also used my extracurricular activities to crystalize potential career choices.
- Valuing prioritizes these alternatives, to ensure that the options will meet your needs. I looked at the list of career options, and

decided that some paths did not use my talents in the way I wanted, others were not people-focused enough and still others did not fit the family lifestyle that I wanted. I chose career advising because it was the best fit for my intrinsic, extrinsic and lifestyle values.

- Finally, Execution creates strategies to obtain a career goal. After I decided that I wanted a career running a postdoc office I became more active in the national postdoc community, networked to enhance potential job opportunities and ensured that my skill set and resumé were attractive to potential employers. For me, the hardest parts of the CASVE cycle came during the Communication phase and the Valuation phase. I understood that I was not happy as a bench scientist but choosing a career that better fitted my values was scary especially since I was at the bench for more than 12 years and there was no guarantee that I would be happier on my new path.

I am often asked if I would do it all over again given the chance – in other words do I regret getting my PhD since I no longer do bench research? The answer is: I absolutely would not have changed a thing. My PhD taught me far more than just science skills. It taught me to gather, synthesize and analyze data and information. It gave me problem-solving skills. I learned to support my ideas by presenting facts to back up my arguments. I learned to persevere and work under pressure. Graduate study gave me the confidence to become an expert in a field starting from a place where I knew nothing. I would not be who I am today without my PhD. I love my career and my career mission: helping others understand how to make their career choices will allow them to love their jobs as well.

ACKNOWLEDGMENT

I would like to thank the staff of the Office of Intramural Training & Education for thoughtful comments on this chapter.

REFERENCES

1. Parsons, F. (1909). *Choosing a vocation*. Boston: Houghton Mifflin.
2. Holland J. L. (1997). *Making vocational choices: A theory of vocational personalities and work environments* (3rd ed.). Odessa, FL: Psychological Assessment Resources.

3. Super, D. E. (1962). The structure of work values in relation to status, achievement, interests, and adjustment. *Journal of Applied Psychology*, 46(4), 231–239.
4. Krumboltz, J. D. (2009). The happenstance learning theory. *Journal of Career Assessment*, 17(2), 135–154.
5. The Myers and Briggs Foundation. *MBTI® Basics*. www.myersbriggs.org/my-mbti-personality-type/mbti-basics/
6. Kilmann Diagnostics *An Overview of the Thomas-Kilmann Conflict Mode Instrument (TKI)*. www.kilmanndiagnostics.com/overview-thomas-kilmann-conflict-mode-instrument-tki
7. Peterson, G. W., Sampson, Jr., J. P., Lenz, J. G., & Reardon, R. C. (2002). A cognitive information processing approach to career problem solving and decision making. In D. Brown (Ed.), *Career Choice and Development* (4th ed., pp. 312–369). San Francisco: Jossey-Bass.

3

Career Enlightenment for the 21st Century

So you know your science; in fact, you have spent many years studying your specialty to great depth. You may know the difference between a strange quark and a bottom quark, can name all 118 elements in the periodic table or know how photosynthesis actually works. But many graduate employers don't care. That they don't care could be a good thing. In the United Kingdom, for example, scientists can train as accountants, lawyers or doctors, or go on to become a famous TV celebrity physicist like Brian Cox.

Let's stick with physicists for a moment because of all graduates they are most likely to be engaged in further study, training or research (34.7% compared to 12.1% for all disciplines) but nearly a fifth are working as business professionals six months after graduation [1]. Only 6% are working as science professionals. The opportunities for scientists beyond the lab are boundless. And opportunity begets choice.

CHOICE

Choice is a wonderful thing. Choice implies freedom and research has shown that people with greater control of their working lives are generally happier in and out of work and make for better employees. Today's graduates have more career options – what to do and where to do it – than any previous generation. But too much choice can present a problem; excess choice can cause psychological distress with somatic symptoms and turn into paralysis.

Successful Careers beyond the Lab, ed. David Bennett and Richard Jennings.
Published by Cambridge University Press. © Cambridge University Press 2017.

'Would you tell me, please, which way I ought to go from here?'
'That depends a good deal on where you want to get to,' said the Cat.
'I don't much care where –' said Alice. 'Then it doesn't matter which way you go,' said the Cat, '– so long as I get somewhere,' Alice added as an explanation. 'Oh, you're sure to do that,' said the Cat, 'if you only walk long enough.' (Lewis Carroll, himself an Oxford mathematician, was dispensing careers guidance in 1865)

I'm going to assume that you are reading this book because you have ambitions: ambitions to create a successful career in your field of choice. But I'm continually surprised by the people I meet who arrived in their current role, often quite a senior one, by serendipitous circumstances – they just took what came along. This is OK if you are happy at your destination; not OK if you are trapped in a job or career you dislike. So my advice is to get some advice.

I studied business. I enjoyed finance and markets and fully intended to train as a management accountant. On graduation I took a temporary job at Coopers and Lybrand in the human resources (HR) department that turned into a permanent job that turned into a secondment into graduate recruitment that turned into, well, the rest of my career to date. At university I did not like studying HR.

Having overseen the recruitment of hundreds of accountants over the years and observed the auditors working in the organisation I run, I now know I wouldn't have made a very good accountant, very probably a rubbish one in fact. If I had worked out where on campus the careers service was perhaps I might have understood myself and my options a little more clearly.

Recent research by the Unite Foundation showed that only 43% of students use their university careers service [2]. And the most common reason students don't use the service? Because they don't know what they want to do. Odd, you may think. But, as I have already said, too much choice can sometimes lead to a paralysis in decision-making. Choosing a career from the thousands upon thousands of options is difficult – especially if one doesn't have much work experience to draw from. In hindsight I think I knew finance wasn't the right route for me. I did not enjoy a summer temp job in a finance department. Application forms for various finance-related graduate programmes sat on my desk as finals approached uncompleted. (Before the Internet, these had to be filled out by hand!)

Choosing a career or employer to me is like choosing a car – but you need to spend a lot more time on it than I did to avoid buying a dud. We have our constraints and preferences that drive our instincts towards a certain type of car or manufacturer. We then consult experts, gather information that needs to be factored into our decision-making and it helps significantly if we can take a test drive. We may like to imagine driving down the Pacific Highway in a Ford Mustang convertible. But drive one every day to the office and the primitive solid rear live axle suspension and slush gearbox may soon make us unhappy.

This is why work experience is so important: it is our opportunity to kick the tyres of a job and test if we'll be happy sitting behind our desk on a rainy Monday morning.

REFLECTION

'Know thyself', said Socrates 2,400 years ago. Because I have made a point of getting feedback through my career and reflecting on what I am good at and what I'm not so good at I have a pretty good idea where my strengths and weaknesses lie. It is important you do the same. I am a strong believer in the principles of positive psychology in the work environment: that we excel by focusing on what we are good at. I rarely consider that weaknesses are development points because I don't always want to focus on what I'm not good at – unless it's a real barrier to the job I must do.

Let me give an example to illustrate. I am not a detail person. This is why I'd have made a lousy accountant. What I am good at is generating ideas, thinking commercially and making sure that strategic goals are not forgotten as project leaders grapple with operational detail. I cannot ignore detail. If I were to skim over our company accounts and ignore the details of our investments, cash flows and forecasts of the organisation would be put at risk. However, if I chose to focus on my detailed deficiencies to the exclusion of all else, I would soon sink into depression.

My pet theory (albeit based on a sample size of one) is that I must enjoy 80% of what I do for a living to put up with the 20% of crap that I don't! Flip the ratios and not only are people fundamentally unhappy at work, they are also unproductive. I once spent three days filing old court papers at the Lord Chancellor's office. I'm pretty sure that if I enjoyed organising I'd have finished the job in two. We are at our best doing what we love to do rather than what we just can do. And the organisations we work for are more productive and successful as a result. This is one reason many employers are adopting 'strengths'-based recruitment techniques pioneered by organisations such as Capp & Co, the career strengths-based specialist.[1]

---

[1] www.cappeu.com/Home

The only reality TV show I positively enjoy is 'Masterchef' – and even then only during the final rounds. The episode where the finalist spent time in the San Sebastian kitchen of three-Michelin Star chef Andoni Luis Aduriz is a master class in passion driving success.

We can overlook where we excel as we devalue what comes easily. Experience is a good guide so reflect on moments when work does not feel like work, moments of flow. Gordon Ramsey, British celebrity chef and restaurateur, loved food so much that in the early stages of his career he saved up all his wages so he could visit London's top restaurants.

Peers, tutors, parents and friends can also be a rich seam of insight. People who know us, who have a view from outside our heads, can often give us insights we overlook. Socrates also famously said 'The unexamined life is not worth living'.

I'm also lucky to be at a stage in my career where I have some say in who works alongside me. Guess what skills I look for in colleagues? You may not have that luxury for a while but you can aim for as close to the 80:20 rule as possible.

TRANSFERABLE SKILLS

At the risk of generalising and stereotyping, there are a number of traits that scientists have brought to the organisations I have worked in over the years (chemists can make good accountants in my experience). These are the transferable skills that many employers, regardless of sector, are interested in:

1. Problem solving: Organisations hire intelligent people because they have problems that need to be solved either for their clients or to function effectively. Scientists solve problems logically.
2. Data analysis: Scientists are used to handling complex data and, in a world where more data has been produced in the last two years than in the history of the human race [3], people who can interpret and make use of data are going to become ever more essential.
3. Evidence-based decision-making: Good decision-making is essential to any successful enterprise. So using data to solve problems and make decisions is an essential skill employers value highly.

I used to think that marketing roles were only really suited for creative types. A marketing director once joked to me that a board colleague had called her the 'director of colouring in'. She then proceeded to demonstrate how graduates couldn't get into her team unless they could analyse complex data sets to assess trends and predict buying habits based on statistical probabilities. You'd be surprised how many industries will value your ability to analyse data.

But numbers are only part of the equation. People who cannot communicate ideas and solutions to others struggle to have impact. I once interviewed a PhD biologist who thought he wanted to be a management consultant. But he was explicit that he didn't want to deal with clients – he just wanted to solve problems. If you can't talk to clients, though, how can you understand their needs? What could be the most innovative, ground-breaking solution for a client is useless if the client doesn't understand it. Working in isolated hierarchies is no longer the norm; open-plan offices and flat organisational structures are. Teamwork skills aren't fluffy human resources criteria used to test how nice people are. Teamwork is about getting things done with and through others as effectively as possible; it's about managing up, negotiating and compromising (or not) with peers. Look at Figures 3.1 and 3.2 (QCF means Qualifications and Credit Framework). How are you developing the granular people skills that employers need?

So you should have gathered by now that intelligence alone is not enough. Intelligent solutions are often forged by hammering out a compromise of time, money and resources available; intelligence has to be applied practically in conjunction with people skills. The very skills listed in Figure 3.1 highlight the broad range of attributes that your ideal employer is seeking.

Some of these skills you can gain in the lab but others you'll develop by putting yourself into any number of activities that will stretch your knowledge, skills and other necessary attributes such as drive and tenacity. Let's use teamwork as an example. Don't make the mistake of demonstrating your people management abilities by explaining at length how you motivated your fellow students through a gruelling piece of coursework. Two problems with these examples. First, every other applicant will have a similar example. Second, the task was compulsory. And let's be honest here, most group work consists of everyone completing their section separately before the 'team' spends hours close to the deadline stitching disparate essays into a coherent whole whilst complaining about the person who didn't show up.

So don't dismiss your time running the college hockey team, or volunteering to teach maths to school kids, or supervising the night shift over summer, or grinding through three days of filing in an office basement – these examples will be evidence to employers that you have

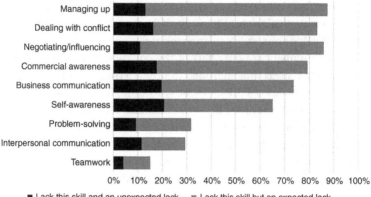

Figure 3.1. Skills lacking by graduate intake. Survey data from the Association of Graduate Recruiters

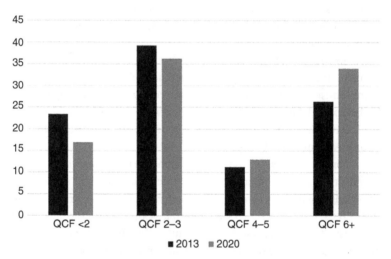

Figure 3.2. Percentage UK demand for qualification by skill level 2013 to 2020. Data from [4], *Supply & Demand for Higher Skills*

the motivation, the people skills and the resilience to match your fabulous intellect.

As Malcom Gladwell explains through numerous examples in his book *David and Goliath*, from lawyers to bankers to Nobel Prize winners, that all you need to succeed is an IQ of 120 [5]. The rest is down to character, happenstance and hard work. As Noel Coward said: 'Thousands of people have talent. .... The one and only thing that counts is staying power'.[2]

CAREER PATHS AS CRAZY PAVING

'There's no such thing as a career path. It's crazy paving and you have to lay it yourself' [6]. When asked, as I often am, what skills employers will need in five or ten years' time, I answer truthfully: "I haven't a clue". Five years ago everyone said coding skills were being made redundant; today they have been added to the shortage occupation list for the United Kingdom [7]. A friend spent years learning the skills of a draughtsman, now he draws with a mouse. Look into any architects office now and you will find that the CAD programme has replaced paper and pen while the A1 drawing boards have been sold to artists on eBay.

In its 2013 report *Tomorrow's Growth*, the Confederation of British Industry (CBI) [8] describe how the hollowing out of middle managers has created an 'hourglass' labour market. Skilled opportunities at the top of the market are matched by an increase in unskilled demand (for example longer lifespans create more need for care assistants) whilst technology reduces middle-layer roles.

Richard and Daniel [9] predict a future where technology will significantly reduce the number of accountants, lawyers and consultants we need as specialist expertise becomes systemised. Google 'robot pharmacists' and you will find a plethora of articles explaining how the majority of a pharmacist's basic work can be automated resulting in improved patient care.

As the CBI explained, this creates a problem for employers and employees: fewer middle managers means fewer rungs on the career ladder on which to learn and continuously develop skills in a linear fashion. Careers become less predictable just like crazy paving.

So how do you prepare for working life in today's world? First, awareness. As Bill Gates said, most people tend to overestimate what they can do in two years, but they usually underestimate what they can do in ten.[3] Committing to lifelong learning, accepting challenges outside our comfort zone and remaining open to new ways of working will enable you to react as the labour market changes. France's taxi drivers may be fighting a strong rearguard action against Uber but only for so

---

[2] www.goodreads.com/quotes/127953-thousands-of-people-have-talent-i-might-as-well-congratulate

[3] www.goodreads.com/quotes/302999-most-people-overestimate-what-they-can-do-in-one-year

long. Frustrated at the lack of responsiveness from engineering curricula, a major global employer I know now seeks general engineering students letting them learn the most current technologies on the job.

Do not let all this uncertainty leave you despondent though. For those willing to develop their skills at the higher levels, demand is only set to increase.

Universities UK, the body that represents the Vice-Chancellors of the United Kingdom's universities, has predicted that the demand for skills of degree level and above is only going to increase [4]. My own organisation found that nearly half of graduate employers did not fill all their vacancies in 2015 [10]. The precise nature of the knowledge, skills and attributes employers will seek may be uncertain but they will be hiring.

Apparently [11], the often quoted 'seven careers in a lifetime' may be an exaggeration for most but cradle-to-grave jobs are no longer the norm. I'm currently on career number three and expect to do at least one more before I retire. Those that do not become complacent about their skills and commit to lifelong learning will have the flexibility to adjust their career trajectories to an increasingly unpredictable labour market.

CONCLUSION

The principles of career management are not as complex as string theory. But every year a significant number of graduate vacancies go unfilled. Align your mix of knowledge, skills and attributes to the career that is right for you and you have the elements required for a successful career. Getting the right job may seem a daunting task fraught with uncertainty. But get the basics right and it could be more straightforward than you think. So, to sum up:

1. Take time to get to know yourself. Reflect on what tasks you are good at, enjoy and can do well even when tired. Then look for an area of work that will let you deploy your talents.
2. Play to your strengths. If you enjoy reading the *Financial Times* over the weekend you will probably enjoy a business career. If the sight of blood makes you faint maybe you shouldn't be a medic. To be successful you need to work hard and you will work hard at anything over a long period of time only if you are passionate about it.
3. Try on the shoes of a prospective employer. Marketing is as much about numbers as it is about creativity. Management

consultants spend considerable periods away from home so you may struggle to commit to a weekly netball match. Do you or don't you want to spend your days in the lab?

And it's OK to make mistakes. My first two career choices were totally wrong for me but I eventually found my niche. Apply your scientific mind to what you want to do with your life. Forty to fifty years in workforce is rather a long time so surely we want to be able to say to ourselves, as James Rebanks does about his work in *The Herdwick Shepherd* in England's Lake District, 'My life has a purpose.' (He is also an Oxford history graduate) [12]

REFERENCES

1. HECSU (2015). What do graduates do?, available at www.hecsu.ac.uk/assets/assets/documents/wdgd_2015.pdf (accessed 13 January 2017)
2. Unite Students (2015). Unite Students Insight Report, available at www.unitestudents.com/about-us/insightreport/2016-full-report (accessed 13 January 2017)
3. Forbes Magazine (September 2015). Big Data: 20 mind-boggling facts everyone must read, available at www.forbes.com/sites/bernardmarr/2015/09/30/big-data-20-mind-boggling-facts-everyone-must-read/#6e85e4c26c1d (accessed 13 January 2017)
4. Universities UK (2015). Supply & demand for higher skills, available at www.universitiesuk.ac.uk/policy-and-analysis/reports/Documents/2015/supply-and-demand-for-higher-level-skills.pdf (accessed 13 January 2017)
5. Gladwell, M. (2014) *David and Goliath: Underdogs, Misfits and the Art of Battling Giants.* Penguin: London.
6. Association of Graduate Recruiters (1995). Skills for graduates in the 21st century, available at www.agr.org.uk/write/Documents/Reports/Skills__for_Graduates_in_the_21st_Century.pdf (accessed 13 January 2017)
7. Computer Weekly (2015, 25 February). Digital Tech Skills Added to Shortage Occupation Lists for UK and Scotland, available at www.computerweekly.com/news/2240241225/Digital-tech-sector-skills-added-to-Shortage-Occupation-List-for-UK-and-Scotland (accessed 13 January 2017)
8. Confederation of British Industry (2013), Tomorrow's Growth, available at http://blogs.bbk.ac.uk/george/2013/08/06/university-business-engagement-the-key-to-tomorrows-growth/ (accessed 13 January 2017)
9. Susskind, R., & Susskind, D. (2015). *The future of the professions: How technology will transform the work of human experts.* Oxford: Oxford University Press.
10. Association of Graduate Recruiters (2015). Annual Salaries and Vacancies Survey 2015, available at www.agr.org.uk/Press-Releases/agr-annual-survey-gender-diversity-a-challenge-in-a-growing-graduate-market#.WHiwsGdvipo (accessed 13 January 2017)
11. Wall Street Journal (2010, 4 September). Seven careers in a lifetime? Think twice, researchers say, available at www.wsj.com/articles/SB10001424052748704206804575468162805877990 (accessed 13 January 2017)
12. Rebanks, J. (2015) *The Illustrated Herdwick Shepherd. Particular Books,* Penguin: London.

4

Doctoral Graduates in Policy and Advocacy

"[A]fter ... doing a PhD and starting to teach politics, I very quickly realized that I hated academia. To get a PhD, you have to find something that no one else has done, possess it, and then build a ring fence of quotations and references around it to protect it. In the 1980s, the academic world was facing uncertainty and because of that becoming increasingly cynical and corrupted. So I decided to leave, but without knowing what to do next." [1]

Doctoral study was never something I really planned on doing. A specific set of circumstances toward the end of my undergraduate degree led me down the doctoral path. It is improbable that such a constellation of events should ever happen again, for which I consider myself deeply fortunate. But it has also left me concerned about the opportunities available to those who study social science at a doctoral level and the type of information (or misinformation) offered about the shadowy world of the PhD. I hope that I can offer some insight to those thinking of utilising their PhD outside of academia, particularly in the exciting world of policy and advocacy.

As an undergraduate, I was a firebrand Marxist; a professor once confessed to me that he had fought the introduction of audio capture of lectures because my comments in his class might be "exploited by agents of the state and media" should I ever gain enough public importance. At the time, it would have been perfectly reasonable for me to have assumed my future would be the product of economic forces. But looking back now, having renounced the economism and class

Successful Careers beyond the Lab, ed. David Bennett and Richard Jennings.
Published by Cambridge University Press. © Cambridge University Press 2017.

essentialism of Marxism, I find it incredible just how important the economy actually was in shaping my career.

It was September 2007, and I was about to begin the final year of my International Relations and Politics degree when I witnessed on BBC News the long queues of anxious savers outside branches of the Northern Rock Building Society. As the emergent financial crisis began to reveal itself, it became clear to me that I would be graduating and entering the labour market at the worst possible time. Record numbers of students were about to dive head-first into a broken economy. Young people's prospects looked bleak and, like most of my friends, I really hadn't any idea what I wanted to do even if I could find a job.

Later that term the head of my department stopped me in the corridor and asked me if I'd thought about doing a PhD. He suggested I put a proposal together as there was some funding available, funding that would cover a Master's degree as well. Four years of income security with a Master's and PhD at the end of it was an absolute dream, especially with the very real prospect of unemployment or underemployment in six months when I graduated.

I was put forward for funding through the ESRC Open Studentship Competition.[1] For several weeks I worked through the clunky, overly bureaucratic application process. The Je-S online submission system[2] was more suited to the teletype machines of the Ministry of Information in Terry Gilliam's film *Brazil*.[3] There were at least a few occasions on which, like the film's main character, I fell into surreal daydream in order to escape the absurdity of Je-S, with its insistence on logging you out every half-hour whether you were in the middle of something or not.

Luckily, the Je-S system has been through several releases since then and is now much more user friendly. However, my experience exemplifies the time and effort required for any successful funding application. I have little doubt that my third-year marks suffered as a result of the time and effort needed to write the perfect proposal, seek advice and chase academics for references and fill in all the supporting information for the electronic submission. But it all seemed worth it when I found out that I had been successful.

Two things in particular were very important to my success in the Open Competition. The first was that I had found an academic to supervise

[1] Economic and Social Research Council.

[2] The UK Research Council's web-based system for grant applications and award administration.

[3] https://en.wikipedia.org/wiki/Brazil_(1985_film).

me and that academic had been willing and more than capable of helping me with my research proposal. We met regularly because he was also supervising my undergraduate dissertation. This also helped later on when starting the PhD because he already had a clear understanding of my proposal, having played his part earlier in the application stage.

Unfortunately, I'd imagine that many students would not be in the same situation, especially if applying to a different university. But having a relationship with your potential supervisor beforehand seems to be incredibly advantageous for both parties – particularly for the student. If you build that relationship early on, you are much more likely to have a good relationship throughout your PhD. You also get to test out the knowledge and capabilities of your supervisor and utilise them to improve your chances of getting funding. Even if this is not possible in the application stage, it is still highly beneficial to have an academic willing and able to help you write an excellent research proposal, particularly for highly competitive funding.

The second important thing was to know two academics who were willing to write excellent references. However, just going to a lecturer because you like them or because they've given you good marks is not necessarily enough. You need to be strategic: you need to try and find academics at the top of their field who would be known and respected by those judging your proposal. I happened to be a member of a study group run by Professor Anthony King, a well-known figure in the study of British politics.[4] He agreed to write me a reference on the strict condition that I was not to read it. I submitted myself to the trust and respect I had for the man, and indeed all of his old-fashioned, idiosyncratic ways.

I admit that I broke this condition, albeit by complete accident (the reference had been scanned and uploaded as an unnamed file in my online application and I happened to open it to see what it was), and feel I owe it to the professor to apologise. Nevertheless, I am incredibly glad that chance happened to force my impropriety because I was so proud of what he'd written about me that I printed it out and put it on the wall above my desk as a reminder of what I was capable of. It still inspires and motivates me today.

LEAVING ACADEMIA BEHIND

One might have expected that, given the opportunistic circumstances that led me to postgraduate research, I had no intention of staying in academia. That wasn't exactly the case. I did all of the things that a doctoral student is

---

[4] www.essex.ac.uk/news/event.aspx?e_id=11697.

told to do in order to make themselves employable in a highly competitive academic marketplace. I published in decent academic journals, I networked at conferences and I took on part-time teaching and research roles. And I took enjoyment from the experience. I was, according to one lecturer in my old department, "a natural academic". Perhaps it was true; but never think that just because you're good at something you have to stick with it. Academia was a natural choice of career but it wasn't my dream.

What mattered the most to me from the moment I became interested in politics, what gave me the most enjoyment and satisfaction, was the thought that I could use my knowledge and skills to tackle social and economic problems. It was highly unlikely, I thought, that I could do this from the lectern or from the pages of political science journals (no matter how important the "impact" of research becomes in the Research Excellence Framework (REF)).[5] Some academics are able to slip through into the policy world and lead double lives; I've met many of them in my time as a policy advisor. But I didn't want to wait twenty years to build up a profile, fighting through the rat race of early career research on fixed-term contracts, slave to the research grant and the REF submission. What I wanted was to be at the coal-face, close to the policymakers, influencing decisions and challenging the conventional wisdom.

I got my wish when I was taken on as a policy adviser at the UK National Union of Students (NUS). In many ways, it was the perfect first job. Education policy is my forte, and working in an organisation with considerable influence and political capital was hugely stimulating.

NUS is part of the "third sector" of the economy which is comprised of non-profit, non-governmental organisations such as charities, think tanks, social enterprises and co-operatives. The third sector relies heavily on highly skilled labour and consumes it at a blistering rate. Several of my colleagues have PhDs or are working part time toward one alongside their job. More and more doctoral graduates from the social sciences are finding a home in the third sector because they are able to provide the right skills and experience for research, policy and advocacy jobs.

It's easy to see why this is the case. In the social sciences, a doctoral student will have a highly advanced knowledge of research methods and the proven ability to use them. They will have developed essential project management skills, juggling their research against various other commitments. Most will have experience in communicating research to wider audiences and be good public speakers, the

---

[5] A system for assessing the quality of research in UK higher education institutions.

result of all those conference presentations and teaching undergraduates. You'll certainly be able to write research proposals, essential for pulling in external funding for projects or for building partnerships with other organisations.

Recently, I left NUS and joined the Royal Society. Each day, I walk past the British Academy which represents the interests of the humanities and social sciences and I go to work for the United Kingdom's national academy for the natural sciences. I think that says a great deal about the growing importance and demand for the skills developed in rigorous social science doctoral programmes. I had expected it to be difficult to obtain a position at the Royal Society because of my lack of a hard science background but having the right skill set for the policy world allows you to be adaptable, to quickly learn new areas of policy and understand the contexts it is employed.

In many cases, doctoral study is as good as three year's work experience for such a role because that's really what it is. Other sectors of employment still haven't caught on to this yet and, consequently, they underestimate the labour value of the doctoral graduate. But as more doctoral graduates enter non-academic work, these unhelpful misunderstandings about the PhD will, hopefully, soon dissipate.

But it isn't just the fact that doctoral-level labour is in demand. The nature of the job and the work environment is attractive. The policy world is certainly as intellectually stimulating as a good social science department and it also has the reward of applying research and knowledge to fundamentally change lives.

There are downsides, of course. Starting salaries vary but are often quite modest, and chances for internal advancement mixed and complicated leading to high staff turnover, but this does mean that plenty of potential opportunities open up elsewhere. Many third-sector organisations also fail to live up to their own progressive values when it comes to the employment terms and conditions of their own staff. As a trade union representative, I discovered this the hard way.

The policy world also remains too white and middle-class. This isn't necessarily the result of organisational bias. Even organisations such as NUS and the Royal Society which are actively seeking to increase the diversity of their workforce may struggle to find applicants from minority groups or from poorer backgrounds because there are simply not enough of them coming out with Master's degrees and doctorates.

This underrepresentation of certain groups in postgraduate study may well stem from the fact that the majority of doctoral students are educated in the United Kingdom's most selective institutions which attract a disproportionate number of white students from privileged socio-economic backgrounds. The most selective institutions also tend to attract more of their own undergraduate students to stay on and do postgraduate study. Research revealed that 94% of undergraduates from highly selective institutions who transition to postgraduate research will stay at a highly selective institution to do so [2]. Therefore, what we see is a replication, and indeed an amplification, of under-representation in doctoral study.

In spite of the constraints and contradictions in my world of work, I would take it over the life of an early career academic which is why I must now turn to discuss the comparison of the academic labour market. As I shall explain, it was not only my interest in making a difference in the policy world that made me leave academia; I also came face to face with some rather nasty realities of UK higher education in the age of marketisation.

THE REALITY OF THE ACADEMIC LABOUR MARKET

I have focused on my own experiences and reasons for leaving higher education to pursue a career in education policy. However, as an adviser in higher education policy I know that it is worth talking more generally about the current trends in employment of doctoral graduates.

The number of teaching and research jobs in UK higher education has slowly increased over the past ten years to cope with the expansion in the number of students. But this has been significantly outstripped by the 40% increase in the number of doctoral graduates over the same period.[6] You don't need to have a PhD in econometrics to work out what that means for the career prospects of postgraduate research students: the academic labour market is becoming far more competitive and a growing number of doctoral graduates fail to secure employment in a UK university.

The majority of postgraduate researchers intend to progress into an academic career when they graduate. In the 2013 Postgraduate Research Experience Survey 58.5% of postgraduate research students said they intended to take up an academic career in higher education; the figure was 65.3% in the social sciences compared to 53.3% in

---

[6] Data from various HESA Statistical First Releases on student qualifier numbers, available at www.hesa.ac.uk/content/view/2077/239/.

science, technology, engineering and mathematics (STEM) subjects and 69.7% in the arts and humanities.[7]

The actual number of doctoral graduates in academic roles is somewhat lower however. In a recent study of the careers of doctoral graduates Vitae found that 38.1% of doctoral graduates from 2006 to 2007 and employed in the United Kingdom were working in either HE research (16.7%) or HE teaching roles (21.4%) in 2010, three years after graduating. This figure rises to 58.7% in the social sciences (44.1% HE teaching and lecturing, 14.6% HE research) [3].

Since 2010 the number of new academic jobs being created in UK universities has shrunk despite a continuing upward trend in the number of doctoral graduates. This is likely to put further pressures on the academic job market for recent graduates and early career researchers.

Moreover, an increasing number of recent doctoral graduates are having to take fixed-term or hourly paid contracts. The 2013 Careers in Research Online Survey found that 92% of academic researchers under 30 were employed on a fixed-term contract and that 82% of first academic contracts were fixed-term [4].

A large number of jobs remain on "atypical" contracts which include hourly paid and fractionalised contracts. We do not know for sure how many of these "atypical" roles exist because some institutions do not provide data of hourly paid staff to the Higher Education Statistics Agency and the number also depends on the date that the staff count is conducted, as many atypical contracts do not run for the full year.

A study for Research Councils UK has highlighted the 'growing insecurity offered by research jobs in higher education' as one of the main reasons for doctoral graduates leaving academia for a non-academic career [5]. In the social sciences we are seeing a drive to force recent doctoral graduates into either research-only or teaching-only academic career pathways which may also act as an incentive to move to a non-academic career.

The 'growing insecurity' in higher education was quite clear to me when I was nearing the end of my PhD. Searching through the academic jobs available in my field, the bulk of them were fixed-term contracts and research-only. I didn't so much mind it being research-only but I wanted some permanency.

---

[7] *Postgraduate Research Experience Survey* (PRES) data provided courtesy of the Higher Education Academy.

I also wanted to settle down, not have to move around the country from job to job especially with my partner working in a permanent role – she would have had to find a new job too! Hopping around different university towns to pick up short-term research jobs is not ideal, as many of my doctoral colleagues are now finding out. One friend who recently obtained her doctorate in international politics, travelled more than 200 miles by train to take up a part-time research job. The job was too short-term to consider relocating so she spent her entire wages on transport just to get the experience. The job basically became an unpaid internship with travel expenses.

More UK students are looking abroad for academic jobs and opportunities are increasing as more courses are being taught in English. But graduates are not always so geographically mobile or willing to relocate to another country to work. I considered the possibility of taking a lectureship in Ireland. The wages may have been lower than in the United Kingdom but my purchasing power, outside of Dublin at least, would have perhaps compensated for that. I also considered a post-doctoral fellowship in Canada which was appealing because of the option of a visa allowing my partner to live and work over there with me. In the end, the logistics of moving to another country became too demanding and my ties to family and friends too important.

In the years since I left, it has only worsened. The University of Warwick seems to be at the pinnacle of this trend toward workforce casualisation. *Teach Higher* was a controversial project at Warwick which involved a university-owned company dealing with the recruitment of hourly paid academic staff. While the university insisted that *Teach Higher* was an "academic services department" and would not lead to the "outsourcing" of academic labour, many believed that it was an attempt to create a casual employment agency for early career academics that could be franchised out across the university sector. Fortunately, after strong opposition from academics, postgraduates, the students' union and trade unions, Warwick disbanded the project [6]. However, its very existence shows that there is an expectation and, for some, the hope that the casual and precarious working conditions in academia are here to stay and that universities are finding novel ways of making this casualisation process more efficient and less transparent and accountable.

Casualisation is just one of many factors that has led to increases in work-related stress and mental health issues amongst academics. The University and College Union (UCU) found that the levels of stress amongst academics have increased in recent years with 48% of UCU members experiencing unacceptable levels of stress at work in 2014, up from 39% in 2012 [7].

Doctoral students will be well aware of these issues as they are being passed down to them before they even get the chance to enter an academic career. Overburdened academics are relying more and more on the labour of doctoral students for teaching and research, and their treatment is far from adequate in most cases. An NUS survey found that postgraduates in part-time teaching roles worked on average of twice the hours that they were paid for with 30% earning less than the minimum wage in real terms and 22% receiving no training whatsoever before being thrown into seminar rooms [8].

The future is far from rosy in academia. Short and precarious employment contracts, ever-increasing workloads and pressures, pay being eroded in real terms, pensions raided – and it is the next generation of doctoral graduates who will feel the brunt of this.

PREPARING FOR LIFE ON THE OUTSIDE

Considering the push and the pull factors explained in the preceding sections, it is not surprising that many doctoral graduates end up outside academia. This is fine so long as there are jobs available which utilise the skills developed in a PhD. In the social sciences there certainly are those jobs because, as I have already mentioned, there are plenty of employers that understand the value of a doctorate. A big problem, however, is the lack of preparation that doctoral students receive for the world outside the university.

After seven solid years at university, it was a frightening experience to leave and immediately enter full-time employment. It would probably be easier for someone who had returned to study for their doctorate after a period in the labour force. But for the significant number of students who transition straight through from their previous studies, it can be hard to acclimatise.

As mentioned earlier, part of this stems from the combination of strong intentions and high expectations of an academic career at the end of the PhD. But this expectation is often fuelled by the lack of information, advice and guidance on alternative career pathways. Supervisors and other academic mentors will often be ill-equipped to offer good advice on non-academic careers and, although there is no harm in actively encouraging doctoral students to consider an academic career and helping them to prepare for it, the pressures and influences exerted by academics can often lead students to concentrate solely on very specific activities for career development that have little value outside of a particular academic discipline.

When I started looking for jobs in public policy I found myself underprepared for what was expected of me. The application process wasn't particularly bad; I was able to articulate clearly what I could bring to a job, highlighting particular aspects of my academic experience to emphasise the right knowledge and skills to match the job. I applied for six jobs and was shortlisted for four. There was no doubt that my doctoral experience was highly valued for the advanced knowledge and experience of working with different research techniques.

It was at the interview stage where I struggled. I had been successful in interviews for part-time teaching and research jobs at university because as a doctoral student you learn how to deal with academics asking you specific and technical questions about research methods and you feel comfortable in presenting a piece of your research or a lecture plan for a topic you know inside out.

The interviews I had in the outside world were very different. They were mainly competency based and involved a language and jargon that I was not used to. I found myself woefully unprepared for this. There were also, in several cases, unseen tasks. An academic research environment teaches you to be thorough, critical, empirically rigorous, to contextualise, and it gives you the time to achieve all of these things. Being thrown a hundred pages of research and given an hour to put together a presentation is not something you're taught in a social science department (but perhaps it should be!). I do question the usefulness of testing someone's ability to perform a task in an unrealistic timescale and unrealistic environment. Jobs which involve policy, lobbying and campaigning are fast-paced, but this pressure is impossible to simulate in a pre-interview assessment.

Beyond the issues of preparing to find non-academic work, I also found a psychological attachment to university. My emotions oscillated between the excitement of the new and stimulating experiences of my career ahead and the anxiety and depression of leaving behind the academic community that I had been a part of for such a long time.

Perhaps for some it is easy to transition from one life stage to another. For others it is harder. Doctoral study can produce a strong attachment both to the academic lifestyle, where you are immersed in an intellectually stimulating environment and the student way of life of being socially and culturally stimulated by your peers.

But I have quickly found that this experience is not exclusive to the university. The policy world is full of young, talented people who are still hungry for knowledge. The third sector in particular is developing an intellectual premium and there is a growing propensity for organisations to collaborate and share their knowledge and skills, creating a stimulating environment that mimics that of academia but with an added emphasis on practicality and impact (although this is also growing in universities as a result of the REF's impact element and the growing emphasis on knowledge exchange).

So the transition wasn't necessarily as bad as I had originally thought. If you like the academic lifestyle you can salvage the best parts of it by staying in an intellectually stimulating work environment on the outside.

Then there's the fact that I didn't really leave, at least not straight away. I started full-time work in my completion year rather than wait until after the PhD viva. I had a pretty good draft of my thesis, bar the introduction and conclusion, when I submitted for completion. I edited my final draft on the train while commuting into London for work – more stimulating than reading the *Evening Standard*!

Not everyone is in such a position, and even with what may seem to be a limited amount of work still to do, the last few months of revisions are like running up a downwards-moving escalator. However, I recommend taking the time both with the completion of a thesis and with finding work. The completion year is an excellent option. I could have finished in three years but I would never have found the time to apply for jobs and prepare for interviews and the transition would have been very difficult.

Most of my communication with my supervisor and the university was done via email. I booked time off occasionally to go and see my supervisor but this was more to remind myself I was still at university. This certainly helped to smooth over the transition into work as it provided an overlap. It was a carefully staged withdrawal from study until, post-viva, academic study became a purely voluntary activity. It became something I would do on the train or in the evening: reading a journal article, proofreading articles and theses for friends, running some statistics on Stata,[8] or writing a blog or an article about something I found interesting. It keeps me mentally stimulated so I stay sharp at work and more widely informed about politics and policy.

I did not actively prepare for the viva. I prepared myself mentally but figured I'd give better answers if they were spontaneous rather than rehearsed. I do the same when I'm called to give evidence on education

---

[8] A general-purpose statistical software package originally created in 1985 by StataCorp.

policy at committees or independent commissions which happens quite a lot in my work. I've seen people over-prepare for the viva and get stumped by a question they never expected which knocks them completely out of their rehearsed script. In the policy world being able to make informed answers to unexpected and unpredictable questions is an essential skill.

Everyone's transition is going to be different but I have learnt from my experiences both as a doctoral student and as a higher education policy advisor who talks regularly with doctoral students that the completion year is very important. Universities will push you to finish in three years because it is to their financial advantage; they may even charge you completion year fees as a deterrent and cut you off from vital student support structures. However, giving yourself time to find the right job for you, even if it is an academic job, requires time for you to prepare yourself, sharpen your skills and your approach to full-time work and construct a career pathway.

CONCLUSION

Universities are not doing enough to prepare their doctoral students for the realities beyond graduation. Fewer and fewer will find academic jobs and many of those who do will struggle for years to secure a permanent role.

Despite this, there are growing opportunities for social science graduates to make successful careers beyond the university. The skills and experience that a doctorate will generate are easily transferable to roles in policy research and campaigning. All that is required is a willingness to utilise these skills in a different environment, one which is more dynamic, at times volatile, and less insular, dealing with multiple audiences.

Gradually, some universities are beginning to address the lack of non-academic career preparation. Improved professional development courses are being offered and career opportunities in research and policy better publicised. There is even talk of creating a Higher Education Achievement Report,[9] now a common information source for graduate employers at doctoral level so that doctoral graduates can

---

[9] The Higher Education Achievement Report (HEAR) was launched in 2008 by the Higher Education Academy to allow institutions to provide their graduates with a comprehensive record of a learner's achievement, including academic work, extra-curricular activities, awards, volunteering experience and positions held in the students' union. The HEAR is currently being implemented at around 90 UK institutions. For more information, see www.hear.ac.uk/.

easily show to employers their skills and experience. It's a start, but there is still much to be done.

The government is also showing an interest with Her Majesty's Treasury keen to tap into the growth potential from increasing the number of highly skilled doctoral graduates in non-academic jobs. The then–Chancellor of the Exchequer, George Osborne, announced in the March 2015 Budget that additional support would be provided for postgraduate research with a 'focus on seizing new opportunities in postgraduate research and build on partnerships with industry, charities, academies and individual members of society' [9]. This included plans for a new income contingent loan scheme of up to £25,000 for PhD and research Master's students. The plans were re-stated in the 2016 Budget.

However, the expectation that institutions can rapidly expand their doctoral student numbers without harming the quality of provision reveals the government's lack of understanding of higher education, especially as there is no intention to increase much needed direct public funding for doctoral provision and the £25,000 PhD student loan scheme proposed by the government is unlikely to stimulate greater demand amongst graduates with existing student debt.

So, for the time being at least, it will remain up to doctoral students to enlighten themselves about the opportunities available to them and pick a suitable career pathway. I remain convinced that the path I chose was the right one. Perhaps one day I will return to higher education at a time when we have overcome the obsession with the market and all of its pernicious distortions. For now, I will continue to use my doctoral training to directly challenge the issues which face higher education, producing research-informed policy and campaigns to support students and academics in an uncertain future.

REFERENCES

1. Curtis, A. (2012) [interview] 'In Conversation with Adam Curtis, Part I', available at www.e-flux.com/journal/32/68236/in-conversation-with-adam-curtis-part-i/ (accessed 13 January 2017).
2. Higher Education Funding Council for England (2013) *Trends in transition from first degree to postgraduate study: Qualifiers between 2002–03 and 2010–11.* HEFCE, available at www.hefce.ac.uk/media/hefce/content/pubs/2013/201313/Trends%20in%20transition%20from%20first%20degree%20to%20postgraduate%20study.pdf (accessed 13 January 2017).
3. Vitae (2013b) *What do researchers do? Early career progression of doctoral graduates.* CRAC Limited, available at www.vitae.ac.uk/vitae-publications/reports/what-

do-researchers-do-early-career-progression-2013.pdf/view (accessed 13 January 2017).

4. Vitae (2013a) *Career Research Online Survey (CROS): 2013 UK aggregate results*, available at www.vitae.ac.uk/vitae-publications/reports/vitae-careers-in-research-online-survey-report-2015-for-cros.pdf/view (accessed 13 January 2017).

5. Research Councils UK (2015) *The impact of doctoral careers*. CFE Research, available at www.rcuk.ac.uk/innovation/impactdoctoral/ (accessed 13 January 2017).

6. Grove, J. (2015), 'TeachHigher 'disbanded' ahead of campus protest', *Times Higher Education*, 2 June 2015, available at www.timeshighereducation.com/content/teachhigher-disbanded-ahead-campus-protest (accessed 13 January 2017).

7. University and College Union (2014) *UCU Survey of work-related stress 2014: summary of findings*, UCU, available at www.ucu.org.uk/workload campaign (accessed 13 January 2017).

8. National Union of Students (2013) *Postgraduates who teach*, NUS UK, available at www.nus.org.uk/Global/1654-NUS_PostgradTeachingSurvey_v3.pdf (accessed 13 January 2017).

9. HM Treasury (2015) *Budget 2015*, HC1093. HM Treasury, available at www.gov.uk/government/uploads/system/uploads/attachment_data/file/416330/47881_Budget_2015_Web_Accessible.pdf (accessed 13 January 2017).

Part II   Industry and Related Occupations

5

Opportunities for Entrepreneurial Scientists and Engineers in the Post-Genomic Era

A GOLDEN AGE

We live in a golden age when scientists and engineers of all disciplines are coming together to solve major challenges of the world including:

- the composition, affordability and delivery of healthcare in light of an ageing population;
- the handling of extreme-scale, real-time data to address transport, logistics and security bottlenecks;
- the development of clean, renewable and sustainable energy to underpin future economic growth;
- and the securing, management and distribution of scarce resources within a growing global population.

Innovation that would previously be confined to an academic research laboratory is extending to industrial settings. Industry's access to significant capital combined with its commercial imperative to deliver multidisciplinary solutions to the complex questions posed by the modern world are drivers for this change. Academic-industry collaboration, open innovation and a horizontal view of how technology can best be deployed to feed, fuel and heal people is the new normal.

Because of this, the opportunity for research scientists to take career paths beyond the lab that have impact – while also delivering a fulfilling career path that yields commensurate financial return – has never been greater.

Successful Careers beyond the Lab, ed. David Bennett and Richard Jennings.
Published by Cambridge University Press. © Cambridge University Press 2017.

21ST-CENTURY HEALTHCARE

Life expectancy in most countries is increasing by one to five hours per day, and this rate of change, especially in the developing world, will fundamentally change the lives of us all. We need to prepare ourselves for the higher costs for social services, labour, pension and healthcare that result from our ageing population.

The biggest issue of the next 50 years will likely be the affordability of healthcare. The current economics of producing medicines designed for treating diseases of ageing such as Alzheimer's and cancer is not scalable due to high development costs and low patient efficacy. Fortunately over the past two decades there has been a convergence of technology – hardware, wetware and software – that is allowing both the elucidation of the fundamental genetic basis of disease and also the implementation of a personalised approach to medicine. This approach combines early diagnosis, targeted molecular therapeutics and companion diagnostic tests to match the right drug(s) to the right patient as well as the recent arrival of gene and cell therapies capable of curing an individual patient's disease.

In order for these personalized treatment regimes to be implemented and reimbursed effectively and efficiently, patient data must be linked into this post-genomic medicine cabinet. This data will now include real-time health and wellness telemetry along with predictive and prognostic diagnostic tools.

MULTIDISCIPLINARY R&D

The meeting of these future challenges requires the development of technology platforms that can only be built via a holistic research and development approach that links computer, natural and physical scientists with chemical, electrical and mechanical engineers in an environment that is conducive to multidisciplinary interaction under the pressure of delivery to commercial, economic and societal timelines.

A perfect example of this was the development of high-throughput DNA sequencing by the University of Cambridge spin-out, Solexa. In the mid-1990s, Cambridge scientists Dr Shankar Balasubramanian and Dr David Klenerman were using fluorescently labeled nucleotides to observe the motion of a polymerase at the single molecule level as it synthesized DNA immobilized to a surface. A series of discussions in the lab and at a local pub sparked ideas surrounding the use of clonal arrays and massively parallel sequencing using solid phase reversible terminators. This (subsequently referred to as sequencing by synthesis technology, or SBS) became the basis of a new DNA sequencing approach that would go on to change the very nature of life science research, as well as the economic model of the pharmaceutical industry and the life chances of those suffering with genetic-based diseases.

Balasubramanian and Klenerman approached the venture capital firm Abingworth Management and obtained initial seed funding to form Solexa in 1998. Early research and development work was conducted in the University of Cambridge Department of Chemistry. Corporate facilities were established at Chesterford Research Park near Cambridge in 2000 and in 2001 £12 million in Series A funding enabled it to build its management team. Solexa brought to bear significant multi-disciplinary innovation that combined biology (nucleic acid polymerization), chemistry (conjugated fluorophores), computer science (large-scale data handling), engineering (microfluidics, automation, instrumentation), physics (lasers, charge-coupled device (CCD) imaging) and radio astronomy (signal processing and analysis), which in 2007 resulted in their acquisition by Illumina (NASDAQ: ILMN[1]) for more than $650 million.

The cost of sequencing the first genome was $2.6 billion over a period of 10 years but this has now been reduced to about $1,000 in one afternoon using the Illumina HiSeq and MiSeq sequencers built on the Solexa platform. This platform enabled the global research community to identify minute variations in the human genetic code and their impact on disease predisposition, onset, progression and clinical outcomes of patients with genetically driven diseases such as cancer. This new field of translational genomics further powered by precision gene editing (see Figure 5.1) is ushering in this new 21st-century paradigm of healthcare.

My career as a scientist and entrepreneur preceded Solexa but has been significantly influenced by the company's evolution and success. Early in 2001 I led a consulting project for the company's new CEO, Nick McCook, looking into the scientific and engineering challenges of performing single molecule sequencing on a chip. Within months of this project I had co-founded a company, Adaptive Screening (Adaptive), that looked downstream of the genome to array a surrogate proteome on a chip. Later in 2007, I was introduced to Dr Chris Torrance with a view to raising funds and building Horizon Discovery (Horizon), which was using precision gene editing to create genetically defined cell line pairs

---

[1] National Association of Securities Dealers Automated Quotations System, the first electronic exchange where investors can buy and sell stock. ILMN refers to the company Illumina, Inc.

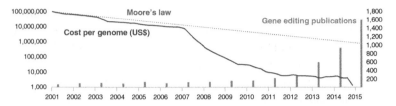

Figure 5.1. A comparison of the rapidly falling cost per genome and the growing number of publications on gene editing. *Sources: NIH, Published by PubMed, 2015.*

that harbored putative genetic variations – identified from DNA sequencing efforts – that were responsible for driving cancer. I discuss these companies and their pivotal role in my career beyond the lab later.

A LONG AND WINDING ROAD

My story is an improbable one. I was born into a poor family in the East End of London where my father was an ex-convict and builder and my mother a meals-on-wheels lady and cleaner. I was told at 13 that I was not good enough to study chemistry at O-Level and so went on to leave school at 16 with no formal qualifications in order to pursue first a career in professional football. Finding only moderate success with this, I went back for further education which eventually opened up a more rewarding career as a serial entrepreneur, angel investor educator and enterprise champion.

After balancing a three-year apprenticeship as a Science Laboratory Technician while also playing semi-professional football and studying for an Ordinary National Certificate (ONC) in Science at Paddington College of Further Education, an inspirational former school teacher named Brian Carline convinced me to apply to the University of Salford to study chemistry. Luck and coincidence then led to me arriving in Cambridge in 1991 to read for a PhD in Biotechnology under one of the United Kingdom's most entrepreneurial scientists, Professor Christopher R Lowe.

My journey of self-discovery started at Cambridge. Here I developed a new level of confidence that came from a realization that I could succeed in academia and hold my own on a social level with students that came from backgrounds that I had previously considered to be superior to my own. From a research perspective, I also identified that intellectual breadth rather than depth could be a strength instead of a weakness as it helped me to see how technology could be applied to deliver commercial and societal impact. This, along with an aptitude for bringing those smarter than me together to solve big problems, combined into a platform for building a career in the commercialisation of technology.

Following an extensive period of independent travel where I learned much about my character (both good and bad!), I was employed in 1998 by a leading Cambridge technology consulting group called The Technology Partnership (TTP) to manage the bioscience aspects of the new technology consortium, Acumen, that was being conceived in the area of high-content drug screening against human cells. I had no experience at all in the commercial arena and so was thrown in at the deep end working alongside members of senior management to both build plans and also pitch the consortium to top pharmaceutical company executives. I remember my shaking legs and profuse sweating during a particular pitch to the global drug discovery team of GlaxoSmithKline (GSK). We did get a commitment by AstraZeneca and Rhône Poulenc (formerly Sanofi-Aventis) to fund the consortium alongside TTP. This consortium was very successful and through it I led the launch in April 2000 of its first product, the Acumen Explorer, and subsequently the comPOUND random-access compound retrieval system and Mosquito nanolitre positive displacement liquid handling system developed in the consortium were launched. All of these are still on the market today.

This job gave me a strong grounding in how you develop complex technology solutions to industry problems. The Acumen Explorer combined confocal laser scanning with extreme-scale data signal processing, precision engineering and automation to enable multi-parametric, high-throughput analysis of human cell populations in microtiter plates of up to 1,536 wells. Working alongside talented engineers, data scientists, chemists, biologists and physicists from TTP and our pharmaceutical partners gave me a real understanding of how to manage multi-disciplinary teams to deliver both a scientific and a commercial outcome.

On the commercial side I learned what's often referred to as the lean start-up model: funding a company without equity dilution and building your product with your customers which then allows you to market it to a global customer base from a strong position. The consortium's success led to me being promoted rapidly and rewarded with more than 50% pay rises.

Unfortunately, the company had limited ambition for the biotech potential of the excellent instrumentation being built and was also unwilling at that time to set-up a spin-out company in order to properly motivate and reward founders. My frustration with this experience led me to look for new opportunities that could incentivize long-term participation and also give a level of enterprise control. To pursue this I moved to the United States on an O-1 Extraordinary Ability Visa endorsed by the NASDAQ-listed life science company Molecular Devices Corporation and supported by TTP. In the United States, I consulted for a number of other biotech companies learning what skills were needed to market and sell technology platforms, products and services. This gave me the drive to want to set up my own business when the next opportunity arose.

Returning to the United Kingdom in November 2000, I went to work at another Cambridge technology consultancy, Scientific Generics, in the Life Science practice where I worked on numerous consulting projects including the one with Solexa referred to earlier. Within nine months I had corralled the brightest scientists and engineers and spun out Adaptive, a company co-founded with Professor Tony Cass of Imperial College London and Professor Jon Cooper of the University of Glasgow to build technologies for reducing drug development timelines, attrition rates and costs. Adaptive's Surrogate Proteome and CytoFlux Biochip platforms were designed to challenge potential drug candidates 'in vitro' with the complex and non-linear biological questions they would be asked when undergoing animal and human trials.

In 2001, the first human genome had only just been sequenced and only 1,200 unique protein structures had been crystallized. So potential drug candidates were identified by screening millions of compounds against a very simple biochemical assay that had none of the genetic or proteomic context or complexity of the human body. Drug attrition rates at that time were more than 90% so the translation into effective clinical treatments was poor. To correct this, the Surrogate Proteome arrayed the known protein universe – including drugable functional motifs, transport, metabolism and excretion proteins – all on a chip. These were supplemented with proprietary protein sensors made by mutating the binding pocket of promiscuous odorant-binding proteins from the human nose to create sensing modules that had both tailored and diverse affinity. All combined, this recreated the 'affinity binding universe' of a proteome which was believed at the time to comprise somewhere between 150,000 and 1.5 million unique members.

By profiling compounds of known efficacy, mode-of-action, and toxicity over the arrays, patterns of binding could be identified and then referenced against the blind compounds which were the drug candidates. Bayesian statistics and neural nets were used to predict key properties of these candidates. Adaptive's CytoFlux arrayed up to 384 individual cells in a microfluidic chip. Each chamber of the chip could be electrically controlled to stimulate dynamic disease states within the function cell compartment. This allowed us to test drugs in a wide variety of high-content assays in conditions that closely mimic the disease state. With the addition of a strong bioinformatics over-layer, the Adaptive Screening Environment was created. The need to test a potential drug against biology that looks like real patients has been a constant theme in my entrepreneurial career, from Adaptive to Horizon.

At this stage of my career I still did not yet have the confidence to call myself a CEO despite being a co-founder, the first employee, the author of the original business plan, co-inventor on seven of its 15 patent applications and had led the raising of approximately $1 million in financing from venture capital sources. I built a multidisciplinary team of 14 people within the first 12 months and further managed the R&D programmes for the company's technology platforms. I went on to co-author the company's second business plan that would be used to secure Series A Funding and also played a key role in the investor presentation team while managing an extensive technical and commercial diligence process with multiple venture capital (VC) firms. Despite tough eco-nomic conditions we secured two term sheets from premier VC firms for private equity investment of $30 million and $3 million, respect-ively. The lead investors, however, insisted I recruit a CEO above me which destabilized both my personal confidence and that of the team I had built. Unfortunately the $30 million deal fell through following the post-9/11 market turmoil leading the CEO to move on and leaving me to work with Imperial College London, the University of Glasgow and Generics to complete a smaller fundraising. This didn't come to fruition so the company was wound up later in 2002.

This roller-coaster ride developed my know-how and steeled my resolve. It was more useful than any formal business school or entrepre-neurship training to prepare me for the realities of starting a company. I had never had any training in this so I compiled the first business plan using my own wits and raised the investment off my own bat. The entire process was difficult and stressful: the day after funding I had an office and a personal assistent, and thought, 'What on earth do I do now?' Everything I needed help with came at a cost and I relied too much on internal and external advisers, wasting cash on things that added little value. Eventu-ally after making many mistakes and kicking down a lot of doors I took enterprise control, hired my own team and pushed the business forward against a backdrop of meddling from those with vested interests.

Even with all the obstacles tipped in my path, it was the most exhilarating experience I'd had professionally until that point. I learned to manage people and investors, write a business plan, raise money, write legal documents, do management accounts, present to all sorts of investors and customers, deal with adversity and come through tough times under pressure. Even though I lost my investors' money, the end of the business afforded me the most valuable lesson of my career. In tough times you learn most about your own character and of those around you. The positive and constructive way I conducted affairs with all the stakeholders meant they all worked with me again. In fact, my first contract when I went out on my own was from one of the investor's portfolio companies, and Susan Searle, who founded Imperial Innovations Group plc, is a friend to this day and sits on the board of Horizon.

A NEW HORIZON

After the wind-up of Adaptive in 2002, I co-founded numerous businesses characterised by the simplicity of their business model. From these, DNA extraction devices and human growth factor research reagents were sold to good effect, generating revenue and profits. This created the 'space' so that when Horizon came along, I was still in a position to be able to participate fully in the upside of the business.

Horizon was founded in 2005 by Dr Chris Torrance and Professor Alberto Bardelli, who identified a novel gene-editing platform, Recombinant Adeno-Associated Virus or rAAV, which enabled one to generate tailor-made cell lines with virtually any genomic modification. Contrary to the usual flow of intellectual property, this technology was brought from the United States to Cambridge, UK. In the second half of 2007 Horizon had yet to gain commercial traction, and Dr Jonathan Milner (founder and former CEO of Abcam plc, and author of chapter 7 in this book) and I joined forces with the founders to grow the company.

The key founders and management agreed early on that we would use the vehicle to enjoy the journey of discovery together and demonstrate what can be achieved when like-minded people come together. We took it on trust that the destination (success) would take care of itself if we both told our story and also executed our plans well.

Our key motivation was to show that you can build a UK life science company that:

1. imported technology from the United States;
2. would grow via the export of products/services;
3. would maintain enterprise control for founders;
4. would provide financial returns to shareholders;
5. blended the best traits of academia and industry;
6. would make a difference to cancer patients;
7. and we would all be proud of and would survive our involvement.

The key to Horizon's success is a classic example of the lean start-up and patient capital at work.

When we started the cost of DNA sequencing was still more than $10 million per genome so there was almost no demand for our product – gene-edited cells – except for the very well-funded pharmaceutical companies. We started not by raising venture capital and taking on a shiny new building, but instead by running near-virtually and using a strong intellectual property (IP) position to provide a route for academic research groups around the world to commercialize their engineered cell lines. This enabled us to break even as a business in 2007 and 2008 on the back of growing product sales before we raised a Series B investment in 2009 from angel investors and the US biotech giant, Genentech.

As sequencing costs went down, demand for our products and associated contract research services grew, and the company created revenue momentum and a buzz within the investor community. Through good fortune, this coincided with the aftermath of the worst recession in a hundred years: since many other companies were struggling with the effects of this, it opened space for significant offers of investment when we didn't need any. This allowed us to raise significant capital in 2010–2012 on terms that were favourable, including a simple ordinary share structure and the return of more than $10 million to early investors, founders and management.

From there Horizon went from strength to strength, developing a commercial offering that addresses multiple adjacent markets totaling almost $45 billion in value. From its inception to the end of 2013, Horizon achieved revenue growth in excess of 120% on a compound annual basis which helped drive the company from IP to IPO in six years and a day and delivering 2–32 times their investment financial returns to its investors.

Since its initial public offering (IPO) on the London stock exchange's Alternative Investment Market (AIM) in March 2014 (raising $113 million in the largest ever float for a Cambridge life sciences company), Horizon has continued to grow rapidly. It continues to enter new markets and solve the critical challenges of its customers through a combination of organic development and acquisition of some of the most innovative technologies and companies from around the world.

BEYOND THE HORIZON

One of the many great opportunities becoming commercially successful as a scientific entrepreneur has conferred on me is working with so many brilliant and passionate young scientists and business students as they take their first steps beyond the lab or classroom and into the commercial world. I have been lucky enough to be able to fund a 10-year endowment of the Christopher R Lowe Carpe Diem Enterprise Fund, named in honor of the mentor who gave me a chance when no one else saw the entrepreneurial spirit that resided within a scientist of no apparent special ability. The Carpe Diem fund awards both needs-based and needs-blind bursaries and hardship grants, and also funds student entrepreneurship activities while providing early business support to emerging start-up companies.

Through my grassroots involvement with the activities of the fund and by committing myself to the success of the Cambridge scientific and entrepreneurial ecosystem I have been able to start, grow, invest and/or mentor more than 30 life science and technology businesses as well as several social enterprises. Many of these are the brain child's of research scientists and business students such as Axol Bioscience, Desktop Genetics, Footprint Cafes, GeneAdviser, GeoSpock, HealX and SimPrints. I feel deeply rewarded by their ongoing success and the fact they are starting to raise significant funding rounds and get national and international acclaim for their innovation, and the business success they deserve fills me with pride. It makes the 90-hour working weeks and financial sacrifices seem like a small price to pay to see the transformation of young scientists and engineers who often lack the confidence to step out of the lab take on leadership roles stamping their own skills, style, ethics and integrity on the cultures of their companies.

Whilst all the business success, industry awards and financial rewards are appreciated, the greatest achievement of my life was recently being conferred with a lifetime-held individual Queen's Award for Enterprise Promotion. This was given for the work I do helping others take those first steps outside of their core training and thus their comfort zone. Nothing means more and is more rewarding to me than seeing others fulfill their potential and go on to influence others by paying it forward.

FIRST STEPS BEYOND THE LAB

As scientists and engineers, you have skill sets that are highly transferrable into the business arena, including:

- posing clear and novel hypotheses, creating plans with defined tasks and performance indicators for measuring success;

- lateral thinking and problem solving;
- perseverance through difficult times in order to achieve a successful outcome; and
- the ability to forge a new direction when research orthodoxy dictates a more evolutionary path.

I have, however, seen researchers leave the lab for the wrong reasons. Your motivation should not simply be the need to manage others, or the desire to achieve peer recognition that mirrors that of colleagues who successfully set up a business, or simply concerns over financial reward. I would encourage each of you considering a career beyond the lab to produce a personal business plan that provides answers to the questions below *before you leave*:

1. What are your fundamental human needs?
   – those intrinsic motivations required to get you out of bed every day with a spring in your step
2. What are you long-term career goals?
   – those transient destinations that will define accomplishment and bring well-being if the journey to get there also satisfies your fundamental human needs
3. What are your strengths and weaknesses?
   – those traits you have to both maximize and minimize the achievement of your career goals
4. What development areas are necessary to maximize your potential?
   – the skills bridge you need to build between where you are now and the direction you want to travel
5. What does success look like for you and how will you measure it?
   – the key to feeling successful irrespective of how much wealth you have or awards you have received

You should find a career – whether in the lab or beyond – where you come into work knowing why you are there, why what you are doing is important, how you can move the agreed scientific or business plan forward and – most importantly – how you measure yourself against achievement of the agreed plan. The more days you leave your place of work knowing these things, the more successful you will feel, and the less time you will spend on a career path that is misaligned with your fundamental human needs. For those of you that feel that you might wish to take the path less travelled as an entrepreneur I next provide some thoughts for you to ponder.

SO WHAT MAKES AN ENTREPRENEUR?

After 18 years as an entrepreneur, angel investor and enterprise champion and having raised more than $300 million in financing and closed more than $450 million in sales, business development and merger and acquisition (M&A) deals for numerous businesses, I have identified many of the traits of what can make for a good entrepreneur:

1.   Hard working and goal driven
2.   Broad, not narrow
3.   Thinks out of the box
4.   Able to lead and inspire others
5.   Able to assess risk and reward
6.   Able to overcome fear of failure
7.   Able to make difficult decisions
8.   Does not take no for an answer
9.   Able to survive until opportunities present themselves

These are just traits, and you may exhibit some or all of them, but I think it is important to explore the mind-set of an entrepreneur before deciding if a career in commercially exploiting science and engineering is for you.

ENTREPRENEURIAL MIND-SETS AND MOTIVATIONS

There are two main human mind-sets exhibited by entrepreneurs. The fixed mind-set is typically adopted by people who believe their basic qualities, like their intelligence or talent, are simply fixed traits. They spend their time documenting their intelligence or talent instead of developing them. They also believe that talent alone creates success. In the growth mind-set, people believe that their most basic abilities can be developed through dedication and hard work: brains and talent are just the starting point. This view creates a love of learning and a resilience that bodes well for tough times.

Whilst the growth-based mind-set appears on paper to be the most attractive, on the surface both mind-sets are exhibited by highly successful entrepreneurs.

There are also many motivations that sit alongside these mind-sets, and each is capable of energizing behaviours and directing that energy towards a goal. These include:

1.   Need for connection
2.   Need for stimulation
3.   Need for independence

4. Need to improve self / prove self
5. Need to help others
6. Need to be recognised
7. Need to have monetary reward
8. Need to maximize pleasure and minimize pain

It should be noted that merely setting up a business does not alone constitute an act of entrepreneurship. The vast majority of small businesses remain today what they were when they started. So does this type of business owner demonstrate an entrepreneurial *mind-set* or is the business driven by a *motivation* to be independent?

My advice to you when you start your company is to approach it like you would if you were about to write a book. What would your book say? What would you, as the author of your book, wish to impart to your reader that would hopefully transform the way they think about their life, about their success, about their future?

As you go to work on your business, you must think beyond the day-to-day reality of what your business calls you to do. As an entrepreneur, you must rise above the task of doing it, doing it, doing it. You must ask meaningful questions about your role in the world, your community and how you can institutionalize your newfound perspective into the genes of your company so that it lives, speaks and demonstrates it in every action your company takes.

THE BUSINESS PLAN

There are many who have built careers out of advising others how to write a business plan. The reality is, it is not rocket science once you realize that the business plan is merely a primary sales tool designed to help your business to stand out from the crowd. It's the what, who, why, how and what's in it for the reader in 10–20 written pages, including diagrams.

The business plan lays the detailed technicalities of the business, giving a clear picture of the business and the investment opportunity. Its primary purpose is to encourage the reader to want to learn more about both you and your business. Do not expect for it to close the deal for you upon first read. This never happens.

The structure of the plan is pretty formulaic and can be taught by any business school programme in a variety of different ways, but the structure is typically:

1. Who we are and what we will become ('mission')
2. Key industry drivers ('market pull')

3. Technology solution ('science push')
4. Customers and markets ('align pull and push')
5. Unique selling propositions or USPs ('competitive positioning')
6. Business model ('monetization potential')
7. Financial summary ('monetization output')
8. Investment need ('how much money required')
9. Use of funds ('how will you deploy it')
10. Exit strategy ('what investors will get back on IPO or sale')
11. Management team ('who will deliver it')

My advice to you is quite simple: create a clear, concise, conversational and compelling document using language appropriate for reader. Start with a killer executive summary in the main body, sticking to the big picture. Don't dive into too much detail as this can be followed up later with due diligence. Make sure you define the unique selling point of your technology, product or service and what market there is for it. Stand out from the crowd but do not use hyperbole. Avoid overuse of generic adjectives like 'great' or 'extremely'. Be careful not to overestimate what can be achieved with the funds being asked for. Most importantly, show your passion for what you want the reader to buy into and give them an idea of what's in it for them.

THE AVOIDABLE MISTAKES

As an adviser to so many young entrepreneurs I am a keen observer of founder motivations, business models and corporate development strategies and so see a lot of the same problems repeating themselves despite the great wealth of knowledge that founders can draw from today. The main reasons for business failure I see are:

- misalignment of the interests between founder shareholders, technology transfer offices, management teams and investors;
- overly complex business models;
- misaligned scientific founder motivations;
- management limitations;
- and attempts by vested interests to subvert good corporate governance to gain control or bias the commercial outcomes.

My key advice (laid out below) to those of you thinking that your first step out of the lab might be starting your own business is heartfelt. I have seen failure to heed this advice lead to friendships breaking up, prolonged stressful experiences, ill-health, business failure, bankruptcy and personal ruin.

- 'Businesses are about creating alignments of interests between founders, investors, other shareholders, and most importantly your customers'
- 'There is no such thing as a lifestyle business'
- 'Don't blame others when things go wrong. Always look inside to understand what you contributed to every given situation before reacting'
- 'Never use the 'reply all' button, and learn to prioritize tasks: no e-mail has to be responded to immediately'
- 'Embrace your strengths, accept your weaknesses and don't take yourself too seriously'
- 'Delegate to those who have more specific skill sets'
- 'Not making a decision is not a decision and the timing of a decision can be as important – if not more so – as the decision itself'
- 'Building a business is difficult; if it wasn't, everybody would be doing it, so appreciate that it might not work first-time'
- 'Afford success and failure the same respect and learn from every experience – especially the failures'
- 'Know when to say 'STOP' and move on'
- 'Never compromise your integrity for any reason'
- 'Enjoy the journey – don't chase the destination'

SCALABLE AMBITION

I am on record as saying that new companies need to put global scale-up on their agendas from day one. There are still too many founders who are limited by ambition and an unwillingness to take the harder path to long-term, sustainable success. It is depressing but there are still too many founders who find it easier to align with investors and take early exits and early retirement. The scale-up model exemplified by Horizon and others can work but it means making tough decisions, holding firm and rolling the sleeves up for the battle, over a long period, with vested interests. Most founders find it easier to roll over but that has never been my mind-set.

YOU CAN DO IT

It may seem daunting to you taking your first steps beyond the lab. What I would say to you is that if someone who until the age of 32 did not achieve any outstanding scholastic, scientific or entrepreneurial achievement can make the change that I have, then so can you. There is nothing to lose, really: more than 99.9% of all people on the planet will be unlikely to know of our existence let alone that we failed in trying to achieve something. So why not try? In this golden age, it is a low-risk time to do high-risk things and, as a scientist, engineer or business major, you have the skill sets and the opportunity to make a difference.

I hope that some of the thoughts laid out in this chapter strike a chord with you and I wish you every success on the path you take.

6

From Monkeys to Medicines and Beyond
Navigating Careers in Industry and Academia

My parents told me that I had always wanted to be a scientist from a very early age although actually how and when I came to use the term was never made clear to me. I do know that I was very inquisitive and had an early deep and enduring love of all things biological (except spiders!). It was inevitable therefore that I would do science Advanced levels at school, but my choice of university subjects reflected my biological bent. I chose to read psychology and physiology at what was then Bedford College, University of London, partly also because as an asthmatic I have always been interested in the interplay between brain and body. After completing my degree I was offered a PhD position at the Wellcome Laboratories of Physiology at the Zoological Society of London. There I spent three happy years studying olfaction, aggression and sexual behaviour of the owl monkey, *Aotus trivirgatus* – a niche subject if ever there was one. I also played darts for the Zoo 'B' darts team and taught on some animal behaviour practical courses at Bedford College in my spare time, so I was certainly able to combine study and a social life.

I completed my PhD and obtained a Wellcome Trust Fellowship to work on the pharmacology of rodent sexual behaviour at St. Georges Hospital Medical School in London under Professor Cathy Wilson – a very talented scientist who was also an excellent artist. Although at the time I knew very little pharmacology, I was able to learn the techniques involved and began gaining a knowledge of drugs and neurotransmitters. During my time in the lab we published several papers and I also undertook some supervision of a junior technician since Cathy did not have enough time given her other commitments. This type of additional responsibility and experience is certainly something that I would urge others to seek early

Successful Careers beyond the Lab, ed. David Bennett and Richard Jennings.
Published by Cambridge University Press. © Cambridge University Press 2017.

in one's career since it increases your attractiveness to future employers whether they are in academia or elsewhere. After two years my Fellowship was drawing to a close and, to be honest, I wanted to do research that was more immediately applicable to human health than understanding rodent fertility so I applied to industry. The fact that I had spent two years on a pharmacology-based project allowed me to build up the knowledge and experience that enabled me to apply for positions in drug discovery in the pharmaceutical industry.

I was interviewed by a couple of London-based companies – Beecham Pharmaceuticals in Brentford for a position as a Clinical Research Associate and Glaxo at Greenford to work on Alzheimer's disease. I was offered the position at Beecham's but turned it down since they had told me at the interview that I would have to wear a skirt or dress to work – presumably as all the doctors I would be visiting would be male! Luckily Glaxo offered me the job and I went to work in their Pharmacology Laboratories on cholinergic approaches to the treatment of Alzheimer's disease. As is frequently the case with industry, shortly after joining there was a reorganisation and I was transferred from Greenford to Ware in Hertfordshire. This was before the days of a completed M25 motorway, and the round trip from Hanwell in West London, where I lived, to Ware took quite a while, especially in a rather decrepit 2CV (which led to a love of fast cars later in life – you only really appreciate speed when you don't have any!). At about the same time I began lecturing in the evenings for the then Department of Extra-Mural Studies of the University of London on animal behaviour and psychology. This was a great experience for future presentations and also taught me a lot about interacting with different people since people on the courses came from all sorts of backgrounds.

I spent four and a half years at Glaxo but for various reasons decided that I needed a new challenge and went to help Richard Green establish a new unit at the Institute of Neurology to work on Alzheimer's and other neurodegenerative diseases. It was interesting to be in at the start of something and also challenging when you have no big lab infrastructural support around you and you have to order everything from mice to micropipettes yourself! It was there that I became interested in stroke research and the potential of new drugs to treat ischaemic stroke as well as continuing to work on dementia. In addition, whilst the lab was being fitted out, I saw the need to set up a computer system for capturing data and storing compound information. I worked with a company, Adept Scientific, to help establish a system that at the time was unusual in that it allowed Apple and PCs to talk to one another and swap data easily.

After a couple of years at the Astra Neuroscience Research Unit of the Institute of Neurology I realised that the opportunities to progress in a small unit were limited and a chance meeting at a British Pharmacological Society dinner with Ray Hill alerted me to a vacant position he was recruiting for at what was then Smith, Kline & French in Welwyn Garden City. I had not seen the advertisement for the position but applied, was interviewed and was offered a job! About six months after I joined, Smith, Kline & French merged with Beecham's to become SmithKline Beecham (SKB) and it was then I that I got my first real management position as a programme manager with a department of approximately 30 people when Ray Hill left to join Merck Sharpe & Dohme. I didn't realise it at the time – indeed, not for well over a decade later – but one of the reasons I got the job was strong senior support from the head of Neuroscience at what had been Beecham's – Tony Ainsworth. One of the best things that my manager then did was to send me on an excellent week-long management course that brought people together from many different industries. I learnt some valuable lessons in terms of bringing people along with you, the importance of vision and harnessing the power of divergent views. I would always now recommend that people taking up a bigger management role for the first time engage in some form of appropriate management development.

During the next decade there were four major reorganisations in the company, and I headed up a number of different departments, had a daughter, got married and took several compounds to the stage of candidate drug selection. My team produced compounds that were taken into the clinic and even made it to market. At the same time, I was also active outside the company engaging with academia. I had a number of collaborations and jointly supervised a number of PhD students with academic collaborators through the Collaborative Awards in Science and Engineering (CASE) schemes of the UK Research Councils. Professor Peter Goodfellow joined SKB at the behest of the then head of Research and Development (R&D), George Poste. It was Peter who recommended that I should apply to be a member of the Biotechnology and Biological Sciences Research Council (BBSRC) Strategy Board. This was a senior-level advisory body to the Research Council which I would never have thought of applying for if he hadn't recommended that I do so. In turned out that the Research Councils are always looking for members from industry for committees and panels, and still are as a matter of fact! Anyway, I was successful and it was the beginning of a long association with the BBSRC as I chaired or sat on a number of panels and then joined BBSRC Council.

I also worked in various ways with the Medical Research Council (MRC) when not on BBSRC Boards or BBSRC Council – first with Professor Steve Brown and co-workers from the MRC unit at Harwell, as well as Professor Elisabeth Fisher and Professor Jo Martin from the Royal London Hospital on a large mouse mutagenesis project and then later as a member of the MRC Neuroscience and Mental Health Board. The then head of Neuroscience at SKB, Professor Frank Walsh, was very supportive of these external academic activities. Other managers in my career, both before and after Frank, were less supportive but I genuinely believe that you need to a have a broad perspective and experience from outside your own business, whether in academia or industry, to stay on top of leading-edge science. In addition, such activities also enhance your professional network which is good from both a company and a personal point of view.

In 2001 Glaxo and Smithkline Beecham merged and I became part of a new organisation headed by Frank, the Neurology Centre of Excellence for Drug Discovery (CEDD) for Neurology, one of seven such centres within GlaxoSmithKline (GSK). Initially I was Vice President of Biology and had to create a new organisation which also included building a gastroenterological disorders group from scratch. The first thing I did was to appoint department heads and then spend two days with them off-site to establish the vision for the new organisation and then the implementation plan, identifying the skills, technologies and programmes we would need to deliver on our goals. Of course we did something similar at the CEDD executive level and it was really interesting to be working in a new business model for the industry. The model was new because it broke down the traditional barriers between drug discovery and development, bringing bench scientists, pharmacokinetics and drug metabolism experts and clinicians together under a single organisation. CEDDs were not intended to be bigger than 350–400 individuals – a size that is considered by many organisational experts to be the maximum for an organisation to remain agile and nimble with a minimum of processes and operating procedures necessary for efficiency. The CEDDs were seen as being like small biotechnology companies within the larger GSK, the rest of the organisation being organised along platforms such as High Throughput Screening, Safety and Toxicology and later-phase Clinical Development. The CEDD portfolio spanned early drug discovery and target validation through medical chemistry, drug candidate selection and progression into early clinical studies (Phase I, IIa and even in some cases IIb).

About a year later Frank left to join Wyeth as Head of Research and I applied for his job as Head of the CEDD. There was an extensive search process – both internal and external to GSK – and I was up against some formidable external competition. In the end I was offered the job which of course I was very happy to accept! There were certainly some challenges along the way, as it is always harder to move up into an inherited team rather than one that is created from scratch, but over the next few years the CEDD (by now called the Neurology and Gastrointestinal (GI) CEDD) developed a strong clinical pipeline – eventually there were 21 compounds in Phase I or II clinical trials, that is, about the same as Amgen had at the time. It was a great organisation to work for with some fantastic members of staff, some of whom are still with GSK whilst others have gone on to progress within other organisations such as Mene Pangalos who is now Executive Vice President at AstraZeneca. The CEDD also showed that organisational changes can be a powerful driver of innovation since the budgetary control and accountability the CEDDs possessed allowed them to operate much more autonomously and to be more creative in, for example, the design of clinical trials in Phase II. We also did much at a local level to improve our efficiency and effectiveness, for example, adopting elements of Lean Six Sigma methodology[1] in the design of new buildings or decreasing our cycle times.

As this is a book dedicated to careers beyond the lab, now might be a good time to mention that drug discovery and development within the pharmaceutical industry and biotechnology companies have many careers for scientists that are not lab-based. Clinical research associates who work with doctors to deliver clinical trials, business development, patent attorneys, communication and policy, project leaders/ programme managers, data scientists, information scientists, regulatory officers – the list goes on. All these roles benefit from a scientific background but are office-based.

Of course, as a senior leader in GSK R&D, I was able to be involved in a range of activities across the company, and in the cross-CEDD leadership meetings, I was actively engaged in cross-disease area prioritisation and strategy discussions. I also represented GSK on the European Federation of Pharmaceutical Industry Associations (EFPIA), the industry body in Europe's R&D Group. At the time I joined the Group in 2003 there was a lot of concern in the European Commission that pharmaceutical companies were moving their R&D to Asia. The then head of the R&D group was Jonathan Knowles and he met with Octavi Quintana-Trias, Director of the European Commission's Directorate-General for Research

---

[1] A methodology of collaborative team effort to improve performance by systematically removing waste.

and Innovation, to discuss what might be done. I remember Jonathan coming back to the group at EFPIA in Brussels and a few of us sitting with him in a room discussing where the main bottlenecks were in the process of drug discovery and development and how we might work with the Commission to tackle them. Out of these early discussions a two billion euro public-private partnership called the Innovative Medicines Initiative (IMI) was born. It took several years to develop the IMI strategic research agenda and pass the required legislation but it was a success and shifted the boundaries of pre-competitive work in the pharmaceutical sector. One of the reasons for this was that the company's contributions were in kind – this meant that the problems worked on, such as novel clinical endpoints or better models of disease, were important and of long-term interest to companies and it also drove a more engaged form of collaboration. I was lucky enough to serve on the IMI Board as one of the EFPIA representatives and latterly to Chair the R&D group following Jonathan's departure. Since that time a follow-on project, IMI-2, has commenced as part of the European Commission's Horizon 2020 funding which has built on the success of the original IMI.

As well as being involved with the IMI I also worked on other projects with EFPIA, for example, leading EFPIA's priority action team on the proposals for a new laboratory animal welfare directive in 2006. Had the directive been implicated in its original form it would have had severe implications for biomedical research in Europe both in academia and industry. Because of this it was important for industry to have a strategic approach and work with others, including patient groups, to ensure that the legislation that was eventually passed would allow biomedical research to continue in a sensible way that benefitted patients as well as ensuring high standards of animal welfare. I also represented GSK on other important policy fora including the Institute of Medicine's Drug Forum in the United States. My job did involve a fair amount of travel on CEDD business, especially when we were preparing for GSK's investor R&D days. In these we showcased the R&D portfolio for important investors; the first one was held in London in 2003. It was here that I learned that 'less is more' in terms of the composition of PowerPoint slides. As scientists we can usually hide behind the experimental details on the slides but investors need clear strong messages with a confident delivery!

In 2007, for strategic reasons, GSK decided to set up a research centre in China and, since the person they recruited, Jong-Wu Zhang, was a neurologist who specialised in multiple sclerosis, a decision was made that the neurodegeneration research carried out within the Neurology and GI CEDD would transfer to China. Although people in the CEDD were disappointed, everyone behaved very professionally and the transfer of reagents and projects went as smoothly as possible. This did give me pause, however, to consider what I wanted to do next as the CEDD had delivered a large number of proofs of concept in the clinic which showed whether the drug works in a patient population and, more importantly, a number of these had been positive. Therefore, when Patrick Vallance, who was in charge of the CEDDs, suggested that I did something different and looked at establishing science parks on GSK sites and an external innovation strategy for GSK R&D, I decided to take up the challenge.

It turned out to be more of a challenge than I imagined as, shortly after I accepted the role – in 2008, the global financial crash happened. This made fund raising from investor developers for the building of the first science park at Stevenage impossible as a straightforward investment proposition. The reason for this is that the first building of a successful science park is almost always a bio-incubator to incubate the smaller companies that then grow and occupy much larger laboratories. These bio-incubator buildings are very expensive to build since they need to provide the facilities start-ups require to use but cannot afford to buy. So, although GSK was providing the land, none of the developers I spoke to such as Goodman's or Alexandria were prepared to invest the required funds which were on the order of £40 million. Indeed, one of the people working on the project from Jones Laing LaSalle (whom GSK had commissioned to help with the commercial aspects) said very early on that I would never get the money to fund it. This, of course, made it a challenge that it was impossible for me to resist!

As part of my research I visited a number of science parks in Europe and the United States to see what worked and how they were funded. One science park that really impressed me was the Innovation campus at Eindhoven in The Netherlands that Phillips had built. By the end of the 20th century Phillips was struggling in terms of the electrical side of the business with strong competition from Asia. The company made a bold move and decided to pursue an Open Innovation agenda, making intellectual property technologies available to collaborators, spinning technology out where it could be better developed outside the company and working with partners from other sectors as well as universities and other academic groups. Key to this was creating an innovation ecosystem on their key site at Eindhoven, where buildings were not allowed to have large catering facilities so everyone was motivated to come to the central restaurant area where central labs and prototyping facilities were opened up to companies on site and where projects were spun in and out of the company as part of the company's strategy. This allowed Phillips essentially to reinvent itself as a wellness and healthcare company.

I had always been interested in exploring the boundaries of collaborative research; first with the mouse mutagenesis project mentioned earlier and then when I was in charge of the CEDD, we initiated some novel external collaborations which allowed us to tap into financial incentives provided by funders as well as opportunities to work with excellent academic groups. For example, the Irish government was very supportive of investments in Irish research and the CEDD basically outsourced its work in inflammatory bowel disease to a collaboration with what was then called the Alimentary Pharmabiotic Centre in Cork (now known as the APC Microbiome Institute). Another venture, which also supported GSK corporate aims, was to establish a unit in the Biopolis in Singapore which was focussed on cognitive research. GSK had a significant manufacturing presence in Singapore but the Singaporean government wanted to see more investment in research in Singapore and were offering certain incentives to facilitate that. It was also an opportunity to establish a different way of working between chemists and biologists – placing the biological assays in the chemistry labs to see if this would facilitate a more rapid turnaround of results and more efficient medicinal chemistry. Many of these approaches were seen to fall under the banner of an Open Innovation strategy and it occurred to me that this could form the basis of a strategy for GSK. The science park at Stevenage was therefore positioned along the lines of the Phillip's campus at Eindhoven – except that here the open innovation agenda would be very much aligned towards developing new medicines.

This strategic positioning of Stevenage as the world's first open innovation campus for drug discovery and development enabled us to establish a dialogue with other types of funders. I talked to the Wellcome Trust as one potential source of funding. I also engaged with what was then the regional development agency (the East of England Development Agency, EEDA) and they were extremely helpful in terms of planning and accessing the right people in government. Ultimately it was the people in the UK government's Department of Business, Innovation and Skills (BIS) that we had to convince so that they would make a significant contribution to the building of the bio-incubator. Whilst waiting for the funding to fall into place GSK committed to getting outline planning permission and dealing with important things such as new access roads to the site – I learnt more about Section 106s, BREEAM (Building Research Establishment Environmental Assessment

Methodology), excellence certification and categories of building fit-out than I ever wanted to and it was certainly removed from behavioural pharmacology in the lab!

Eventually the £38 million funding to build the bio-incubator and a follow-on building was found through a partnership between GSK (£11 million), the Wellcome Trust (£6 million), UK government via BIS (£12 million), EEDA (£4 million) and the Technology Strategy Board (now known as Innovate UK, £5 million). I felt incredibly proud when the project was announced by Peter Mandelson at the annual Innovation conference in 2009. Completed in 2012, the science park is now known as the Stevenage Bioscience Catalyst and the bio-incubator is full. Subsequently it has grown with the announcement in 2013 of the move of the Medical Research Council's commercialisation arm, MRC-T, into the follow-on building and the building of the Cell Therapy Catapult's state-of-the-art £55 million manufacturing facility on the campus. There are plans to further expand the campus and I believe it is a real asset to the United Kingdom. However, after the announcement that it was funded I decided to leave GSK since the financial recession meant we were unlikely to be able to replicate the success at other GSK campuses. The closing of Neuroscience research at GSK, which had happened whilst I was working on the Open Innovation strategy and the science park, provided a potential opportunity to create biotech spin-outs and take neuroscience assets out of the company.

I left GSK after 21 years with the company in all its various previous forms but the fact that latterly I had been operating pretty much as an internal consultant across R&D with a small team, as opposed to the large line responsibility that I had previously, prepared me well for life outside the company. I formed two companies: OI Pharmapartners Ltd, an Open Innovation in Life Sciences consultancy company, and Neurosymptomatix (NSX), a spin-out vehicle. Little did I know just how hard it was to spin assets out of pharmaceutical companies which probably explains why so few companies have managed to do it!

When neuroscience research closed at GSK in Europe there were a number of groups that wanted to take assets out of the company. Of course this meant making pitches to GSK but also to the venture capital (VC) investors that would fund the subsequent development of these assets. For me and my partners in NSX it was a steep learning curve – one soon learnt that the beautiful technical slide deck of 70 PowerPoint slides needed to be whittled down to about 12 focussed much more on the financials and how the company was going to succeed, the quality of the management team and mitigation of risk. At this point I would like to thank all the VCs who saw our early drafts and gave us very valuable feedback. I myself got EU funding to go on an Astia entrepreneurs course in California (Astia is a non-for-profit company which is focussed on helping female entrepreneurs gain access to funding for their companies with offices in the United States and Europe).[2] This refined my pitching skills and enabled me to meet more potential investors. Unfortunately, when we did get interest from investors GSK decided to take their assets back but the VCs liked us and introduced us to another pharmaceutical company. We then spent the next 18 months doing due diligence on the assets, forming development plans and building a VC syndicate to raise the money which was for more than $25 million. However, in the summer of 2012 pretty much the same thing happened again and we were back to square one but with less money and enthusiasm than before. My one strong piece of advice from this period is that if you want to spin something out of a pharmaceutical company, move as quickly as you can before they change their mind!

Whilst all this was going on, I was still running my consulting company and we did some interesting things such as working with the Cyprus Presidency of the European Union on an Open Innovation in Healthcare Strategy, helping university institutions work better with industry and industry to work better with academia. I quite often worked in partnership with one associate in particular, Elizabeth Goodman, whom I had known at GSK. We had very complementary styles so worked together well and she was a fluent French speaker which was also useful when working in Europe. I had pretty much decided to concentrate on my consultancy when I was headhunted for the post of Chief Executive of the BBSRC. The last interview was to be a panel consisting of the Chair of the BBSRC Council, Professor Sir Tom Blundell who provides the Preface for this book, a couple of its Council members and representatives of the Department of Business, Innovation & Skills (BIS), the sponsoring UK government department. As I recall, I had to give a seven-minute-long speech and I made sure I rehearsed it to the second. I was also very frank about what I thought needed to be done going forward – I wasn't sure they would agree with me but I didn't see the point in taking the job unless I could do what I thought was needed. Before the interview I talked on the phone with several key stakeholders I know in various organisations – I have to say that one person on hearing I was being interviewed suggested that I was a token candidate and didn't stand a chance of getting the role!

---

[2] http://astia.org/

Luckily this didn't put me off and when I was offered the position I took great delight in letting him know I had got the job.

Admittedly I was an unusual candidate; at that point the only other woman who had led *any* UK research council was Dame Julia Goodfellow who led the BBSRC before my predecessor, Professor Doug Kell. It was also usually an academic who headed up a research council rather than someone with an industrial background. So it was all a big change and I headed to Swindon to meet my new team and organisation. The BBSRC is truly a wonderful organisation; the breadth of the research that it funds is huge and its remit is across sectors that are vital to the United Kingdom such as agriculture, nutrition, basic bioscience research, synthetic biology, bioenergy and industrial biotechnology. The actual organisation at Swindon comprised about 300 people who were split into several different areas covering people and development, science, grant and process delivery, finance, international policy and government affairs and communications. I knew some of the executive team from my previous time on the BBSRC Council which helped in terms of integration. BBSRC staff also prepared a series of briefing documents for me on a range of topics both scientific and non-scientific which was also extremely helpful. BBSRC still had responsibility at that time for nearly 1,500 staff who were still on BBSRC terms and conditions from the time of the BBSRC-sponsored institutes such as the John Innes Centre in Norwich and the Roslin Institute in Edinburgh. New staff in these institutions were recruited under institute terms and conditions which allowed the institute directors more flexibility in terms of employment contracts but some aspects of employment – for example, pensions – were less generous than under the older scheme.

One of the first things I did even before officially starting work at BBSRC was to give a talk to the staff at an All Hands meeting where I basically outlined the framework and vision I had given to the interview panel. On joining BBSRC formally in October 2013 I spent a couple of days off-site with my executive team exploring with them how we were going to work together, what they saw as the challenges and issues, and where our priorities lay for the year ahead. In 2014, we published a refreshed version of our strategic plan and also celebrated 20 years of BBSRC-funded bioscience. This celebration involved a range of activities, including a reception in London, a series of exhibits selected by a competitive process to inspire people about bioscience research and a Festival of Bioscience in Bethnal Green, London where all the exhibits came together in a large tent next to the Museum of Childhood. This latter event was absolutely superb, attracting adults and children from a wide range of backgrounds to participate in activities and learn about bioscience – there was also a giant inflatable colon which we all enjoyed walking down, prompting the immortal line from my head of communication to his team that 'the chief executive has left the colon'!

The reception highlighted the achievements of the past 25 years such as Dolly the Sheep (most people don't know Dolly was the result of BBSRC funding), the discovery of small interfering ribonucleic acid (siRNA) and sequencing of the first plant genome. Past chairs and chief executives were there, including the then current chair, Professor Sir Tom Blundell, who had the distinction of also being the first chief executive of the BBSRC. David Willetts who was then the UK government's Minister for Universities and Science paid a visit and talked to many of the BBSRC-funded scientists who were there about their work. I actually met with David quite a few times, both when he was minister and subsequently. He is generally recognised as being an excellent advocate for UK science in particular and research in general, and had a lot of interaction with all the Research Councils. In my role as Head of BBSRC I was invited to many functions in Westminster, whether House of Commons, House of Lords or Portcullis House. I also was fortunate enough to go to No 10 Downing Street a couple of times for meetings. At No 10 one has to hand in one's mobile phone on entry and, rather embarrassingly, I forgot to pick up my phone the first time I went. Sadly, I only realised this when I had left Downing Street and was on Whitehall; at least it gave the security patrol some amusement when I went back to pick it up.

As well as visiting Westminster I made it a priority at the beginning of my job to visit all the BBSRC strategically supported institutes. Along with the Roslin Institute and John Innes Centre, these included Babraham near Cambridge, two other Institutes at Norwich (the Institute for Food Research (IFR) and The Genome Analysis Centre (TGAC), Rothamstead Research near Harpenden, Pirbright Institute in Surrey and the Institute of Biological, Environmental and Rural Sciences (IBERS) at Aberytswyth. The BBSRC is the major funder of plant biology in the United Kingdom and much of the important long-term research in this is carried out in BBSRC strategically funded institutes. Shortly after I joined the new state-of-the-art virology centre was completed at Pirbright where much of the United Kingdom's high-containment work on viral diseases of cattle and other species is carried out. The investment in the facilities continues at Pirbright with further buildings for avian research and other work ongoing. Overall the investment on infrastructure there was over £200 million but this is essential to allow the United Kingdom to remain at the forefront of research into viral diseases of livestock. I also got to lay a foundation stone for the Innovation Centre at Rothamstead which is now completed – my first and only time doing so!

Of course, alongside the politics and administrative activities, leading the BBSRC allowed me to meet researchers both in the universities and in the institutes who were doing great bioscience. This was definitely one of the best bits of the job and I learnt a great deal especially about crop and livestock research where I was definitely out of my comfort zone initially. I also wrote a weekly blog and learnt how to tweet although I never got the hang of Instagram or Tumblr! One of the great things about such a role, though it is demanding: you can really make things happen. During my time at BBSRC, amongst other things, I was able to contribute personally to driving forward an animal and plant health strategy for the United Kingdom, push ahead with, and get the funding for, the new Quadram Centre for food and health at Norwich and ensure that the research councils as a whole, and BBSRC in particular, had a clear strategy for improving equality and inclusion.

Following the announcement of the Nurse Review findings[3] and the subsequent reorganisation of the research councils which would, in essence, see a decrease in the financial autonomy of each council, and the offer of a fantastic new opportunity, I regretfully decided to leave BBSRC. I am now back in industry leading a biotechnology company that is a hybrid of machine learning / artificial intelligence technologists and experienced drug discovery and development scientists. Hopefully we can have an impact on the drug discovery process and make a difference for patients.

I have certainly been away from the bench for a long time (I think the last time I held a lab rat was in 1990!) but have always been able to use my scientific expertise and build on it. The potential careers in biomedicine both in academia and in industry are extremely varied and people with scientific skills will always be in demand.

[3] Sir Paul Nurse, then President of the Royal Society, led a review of the UK Research Councils to explore how they could support research most effectively. www.gov.uk/government/collections/nurse-review-of-research-councils

7

Lessons from Evolution on How to Build a Business

'Nothing makes sense in biology except in the light of evolution.'[1]

My Advanced level biology teacher at Portsmouth Grammar School, Nick Knight, introduced me to evolution, and it has guided me from my career as a molecular biologist to an entrepreneur and businessman. I thought my fascination with evolution might just be a passing phase but the older I get the more extreme I have become and indeed have now reached the conclusion that nothing makes any sense anywhere except in the light of evolution. This is quite dangerous, as I sometimes fall into the trap of attributing my business successes to my understanding of evolutionary biology, but to do that makes me a victim of hubris and selective good data memory bias – I have also had a lot of failures. However, it is comforting (at least to me) that the evolutionary record is littered with failures. In fact, all of life today is built on evolutionary 'failure'. I find this consoling when one of my ventures fails and I like to believe it makes me more resilient.

You are probably wondering what my obsession with evolution has to do with building businesses and entrepreneurship. Well, to understand that I will tell my career story of bench to boardroom and weave in evolutionary anecdotes as I can recall them. Much in my career has been about serendipity, about drifting along with no particular outcome or goal, simply following what seems to be working.

Luckily for me, I had amazing liberal parents who didn't push me or pressure me into any particular path or career. I always knew they would love me whatever I wanted to do in life even if it was to simply

Successful Careers beyond the Lab, ed. David Bennett and Richard Jennings.
Published by Cambridge University Press. © Cambridge University Press 2017.

drift along and see where the current took me. After deciding that medicine wasn't for me (a trip to visit my brother in a hospital when I was doing my Advanced level courses made my mind up on that one) and armed with some mediocre grades in Biology, Physics and Chemistry (still can't do Maths to this day), I embarked on a four-year Applied Biology degree (a 'thin sandwich', as it was known then, being six months of study at the University of Bath followed by a six-month placement for four years). This ticked a lot of boxes, the main three being beer, girls and drifting along! Regarding the latter, Applied Biology was an especially good course because every six months we would get sent somewhere random to do a work placement and even get paid for it. My first placement involved a summer living in a caravan in a forest on the English-Welsh border with a beautiful rescue border collie/Alsatian cross named Shep. It coincidentally also involved working for the Forestry Commission on the biological control of bark beetles. Halcyon days! My second placement was at the University of Leicester Biocentre studying yeast genetics and it was there that I fell in love with molecular biology. I was astonished that you could actually get paid for doing experiments. The buzz and thrill of discovery was intoxicating and addictive. Messing about with a load of Eppendorf tubes and Gilson pipettes was my idea of heaven. Encouraged to pursue this by my tutor, in my final placement he sent me to the University of Michigan in Ann Arbor to work on more yeast genetics. This was 1987 and about the same time that a young maverick scientist called Paul Nurse was trying to convince the scientific world that yeast was really interesting and important. Paul and others discovered genes in yeast that control growth and cell division, and that subsequently enabled the discovery of similar genes in humans. This earned him a knighthood and a well-deserved Nobel prize, and Sir Paul remains one of my desert-island, all-time greatest heroes. Endless hours sitting at the computer and comparing gene sequences across species from yeast through monkeys to humans strengthened my fascination and belief in evolution; it was obvious to me that evolution is as real as the world is round and that gravity exists (incidentally, all three scientific discoveries were known as theories and sadly in some quarters evolution still is despite overwhelming evidence that it is a fact).

After returning to the United Kingdom and gaining a respectable 2.1, my career was now set. I would delay getting a 'real' job as long as possible and instead do a PhD in yeast molecular genetics with my supervisor at the Leicester Biocentre, Professor Mike Stark, who had by that time moved to Dundee. Sadly, my father became sick with lung cancer and, to be nearer to home, I opted instead for a PhD at the University of Leicester, finally graduating in 1994 with a dissertation entitled 'A molecular genetic analysis of the fireblight pathogen *Erwinia amylovora*'. Just before my father died I was accepted for my first post-doc position at the University of Bath to research antibody engineering. I hadn't quite realised how concerned my father was about my lack of career and direction until I told him the news and he broke down in tears of relief.

This is where serendipity comes into play. In my last few months at Leicester I met and fell in love with a Greek girl, called Rosy, who was studying for an MSc in Museums Studies. Rosy is now my wife and we have three teenage children and live blissfully happily in Cambridge – but, of course, I wasn't to know all this at that time. As we were both in the final months of our degrees, I asked Rosy if she wanted to join me in Bath as that was where I was heading next for my first post-doc. Surprisingly she said 'yes' and we spent three very happy years there with me happily performing experiments in the lab whilst being sponsored by Pfizer, the world's largest pharmaceutical company, to design drugs based on antibody interactions against a herpes simplex virus (HSV) enzyme drug target. Rosy's heart was set on working in a contemporary art gallery but jobs were few and far between. Eventually she found a job as a manager of Cambridge Contemporary Art on Trinity Street. Coincidentally I was finishing my post-doc in Bath so I decided to join Rosy and search for work in Cambridge. I didn't know Cambridge very well and after the beautiful rolling hills of the Cotswolds my first impressions of the surrounding countryside, of endless flat fields of cabbages, weren't inspiring. However, one Saturday, whilst walking around the centre of Cambridge and people-watching, I turned to Rosy and remarked, 'Cambridge has a very high nerd-coefficient', to which she replied, 'That's why you will fit in perfectly!' She was right, of course.

My scientific career up to then was neither stellar nor a disaster. I had a few publications under my belt but nothing like what I felt was good enough to win a research job at the University of Cambridge. Still, chancing it and with nothing to lose, I applied at one of the top labs in the country with Professor Tony Kouzarides at the Wellcome Trust Clinical Research Centre (CRC) Institute (now the Gurdon Institute). Tony must have seen something in me that neither I nor others had and to my delight and astonishment he offered me the position. I was in scientific heaven: the lab was well funded, full of super-bright and fun people, I could dweeb[1] about to my heart's content, and to top it all off, I was finally getting paid a decent salary. What's not to like? It was 1998, I was in my early thirties and, whilst not wishing to fully give up on drifting about, by the final year of my post-doc I started to worry about what I would do next. Rosy and I had bought a house together and also started to entertain thoughts of marriage and kids so I started to wonder if I should try to get a 'real job'. I didn't feel I was a good enough scientist to apply for a faculty position, plus the fun of just doing experiments for the thrill of it was beginning to wear off as the pressure to publish to further my scientific career intensified. Thankfully I was saved by what I would later realise was an 'entrepreneurial seizure'. Up to that point I certainly hadn't thought of myself as an entrepreneur despite, on recollection, always coming up with mad ideas for starting businesses.

In the final year of my post-doc, I was trying to work out the function of a protein involved with breast cancer but it was immensely frustrating due to the lack of quality antibody reagents. At the same time I discovered an obscure website called www.amazon.com that sold books online which was totally revolutionary and blew me away. Instead of having to go into bookshops in town to search though shelves of irrelevant books and then be told I had to order the one I was looking for, I could simply order it online and it would be delivered to my door within a couple of weeks! I had glimpsed the future. My entrepreneurial seizure was triggered one day in the lab when yet another of my experiments had failed due to a poor quality antibody from one of the largest suppliers at that time – wouldn't it be wonderful, I thought, if I could order an antibody online from a website with loads of accompanying honest data about its uses and limitations. I told my colleague working on the bench alongside me, Dr Luke Hughes Davies, who immediately said that he had entertained a similar idea and that I should start a company. The idea would probably have ended there with so many of my other half-baked ideas but serendipity and luck intervened. That same 'entrepreneurial seizure' day in January 1998 I had been invited by Rosy to a Christmas dinner (they couldn't find anywhere before Christmas) in one of the colleges with her work colleagues and partners from Cambridge Contemporary Art. I sat down next to a very interesting and lively person who was asking me what I wanted to do

---

[1] Oxford English Dictionary definition – North American informal: a boring, studious or socially inept person.

with my life so I told him about my frustrations in the lab and my idea of starting an antibody company. Gripped by entrepreneurial seizure, I was probably a bit manic and excited but instead of just being polite and not taking me seriously he said I should visit him in his offices to talk about it and he gave me his e-mail address.

So on a rainy Saturday morning I found myself sitting in David Cleevely's Analysys office on Castle Hill. I found David to be super intelligent, fun, dynamic and entrepreneurial; here was someone who seemed to think like me, and we agreed there and then to go into business together. Why did David and I 'click' so readily? My evolutionary and ecology lessons at university had taught me about how all of life is networked and interdependent and that species-to-species intra- and interactions fall along a spectrum of symbiosis (such as the lichen, which is a partnership of cyanobacteria supplying energy from photosynthesis and fungi supplying shelter and nutrients) through commensals (such as the numerous bacteria that inhabit our skin and gut) through parasites (such as tapeworms) to pathogens which can be deadly (such as the tuberculosis bacterium). I am quite introverted by nature so to help me overcome this I play a mind game when I interact with people, especially for the first time, by trying to guess which category they fit in (symbiont, commensal, parasite or pathogen). I concluded quickly that David was a 'super symbiont'!

First, however, there was the tricky question of money. 'Have you got any?' David asked. Trying to stop myself from laughing, I explained politely that, as a poor post-doc, I didn't have any. 'In that case', said David, 'go and see if you can find some and come back and see me if you do'. I mentioned that Rosy and I had just bought a house, and this turned out to be quite handy. In retrospect, this should have been a warning to the problems that would hit the world in 2008 but back then in 1998 banks would throw money at home owners. So I re-mortgaged the house and the following week skipped into David's office clutching a cheque for £11,000 from those kind and generous folk at Northern Rock Building Society. 'Great', said David. 'You'll get 60% of the company for that and I'll put in £40K for the remaining 40%'. 'Yeah, whatever, sounds fine', I thought and it would only be later that I would realise how important and generous David's offer was. My naivety meant I had no defence against parasites or pathogens but this super symbiont had just given me a great deal without ripping me off. As in any symbiotic relationship each party has to feel they are giving and receiving equal benefit otherwise it quickly turns into a dysfunctional pathogenic relationship that breaks down.

One of the lessons I quickly learned is that to start a business you need the support of a lot of symbiotic people. My post-doc supervisor Tony Kouzarides is one of those and when I told him what I wanted to do he immediately offered to help and joined David and me on the adventure. David also understands the power of networks of like-minded people (he has written a whole chapter about it in this book) and he plugged me into the Cambridge Network where soon we had convinced the likes of Hermann Hauser, Peter Dawe and Stephen Thomas, to name but a few 'Cambridge superheroes', to invest in our fledgling idea. Stephen, a highly successful, well-known entrepreneur, was particularly generous with both his time and money. I met him early on, even before the company had a name, at a Cambridge Network event, and in two minutes, over mouthfuls of *vol-au-vent* and wine, pitched the idea; two days later he sent me a cheque for £10K to invest in the business. I'm really not making this up; amazing, supportive, generous people like Stephen really do exist, although, sadly, he himself died tragically in an Antarctic expedition in 2005 [2]. I would turn to Stephen – another super symbiont – for advice when I needed it most. I remember one particular time Stephen turned up at a shareholders' garden party at our house on Roseford Road. I was struggling with how to juggle the pressures of building a business whilst keeping shareholders happy and giving them a return on their investment via an exit. 'Don't worry', he told me. 'Don't obsess about an exit, just concentrate on building the best business in the world, don't burn any bridges and the exit will take care of itself.' It was great advice that I found myself using over and over again in the years to come and something I am enormously indebted to Stephen for.

Back to the summer of 1998 when I was finishing the last few months of my post-doc whilst also working on the business. Tony was immensely supportive and, in August 1998 when I had left the comfort and security of the Gurdon Institute, he found me an old room just down the street in the University's Plant Biochemistry Annexe (which was formerly the morgue of the adjacent Addenbrooke's original hospital, now the Cambridge Judge Business School) in which to start building the business. By this point Tony had joined our fledgling board of directors alongside David and myself. David once again showed his enormous generosity and gave up virtually every one of his Saturday mornings for board and mentoring meetings in the first couple of years which were crucial to the early stages of growth. One Saturday morning I mentioned that we hadn't yet found a name for our company and Tony shot back with 'That's easy, look – Ab for antibody and Cam for Cambridge makes Abcam.' We all agreed on the spot and Abcam was born.

Unless independently wealthy any founder will have to persuade others to fund their fledgling start-up. This is critical in the early stages and one of the most important things to get right. Start-ups have value in their business model which is essentially an idea that competes with other money-making ideas in the world to realise future value. This means that instead of funding the building of the company with cold hard cash, if you could persuade a supplier to take equity on the promise of future returns beyond their wildest dreams, then this is a good thing for both symbiotic parties. I thought this would be a jolly good idea but in my enthusiasm forgot to look out for pathogens. Instead of paying for the website to be built I found a company that would offer to do it in exchange for equity to the value of £250,000 so I jumped at the chance. However, I was totally naïve, didn't read the small print and foolishly signed a contract which said that the supplier had the right to invoice fully for the amount in cash at any time (hidden in very, very small print of course). You might guess what happens next – an invoice for £250,000 was posted through my letterbox. It was devastating and I feel sick whilst writing this and recalling that moment despite it having happened 17 years ago. The company had only £50,000 in its bank account and this meant it would have to be wound up and the money transferred to the pathogenic supplier. That was the end of my dream and just as the company was beginning to gain traction. But, thankfully, David came to the rescue and accepted the equity in the business in return for paying off the supplier using his pension fund and we were saved. It was a hard lesson to learn: I had almost lost the business, our home and all the shareholders' money because I hadn't spotted the pathogen in symbiont's clothing. Of course the danger of being a pathogen is that if you are too successful at this role you will kill your host and then have nothing to feed on. I console myself today in the sweet knowledge that, had they kept their £250,000 of equity in the business rather than trying to wind it up, their stake would be worth somewhere in the region of £50–75 million!

What goes around comes around. I am now trying to pay back David's invaluable advice, generosity and mentoring. Indeed, over recent years I have had the pleasure of mentoring and supporting many young entrepreneurs and I am convinced the most valuable support comes from understanding the difficulties that are faced in building a company from scratch. These difficulties vary from founder to founder, as we are all unique just like the businesses we are building. My own particular problem arrived quite early in Abcam's history. Throughout the first part of 1999 I really struggled to transition from a bench scientist to a CEO / entrepreneur / founder of a fledgling life sciences company. As a bench scientist you only have one thing to do and that is to design and execute experiments in your research topic. This is enjoyable, relaxing and even energizing. Many times in the lab when I was on to something I would find myself 'in the zone', totally absorbed in my work, hours flying past in total bliss. One particular time I remember I was so absorbed I worked constantly for days breaking only to sleep (I even for a few days had a camp bed in the lab once so I could follow a time course of experiments) into the small hours of New Year's Day, intent on discovery and enjoying every moment.

However, starting a business, as I soon found out, is completely different, and the stress levels were astronomical, like nothing I had ever been through before. The stress was caused by the constant change in having to quickly move my brain from one subject to another with each one requiring immediate and urgent attention. One moment I would be interviewing someone for a job, then trying to do a tax return, next presenting a fund-raising presentation, followed by answering the phone for a customer enquiry, followed by setting up and negotiating an OEM (Original Equipment Manufacturer) agreement with a supplier, followed by bringing the accounts up to date (accounts – I had no idea what these were or how to handle them), followed by listening to an employee complaining about the state of the toilets or their commute into work and then finding no parking spaces. On top of this was the constant worry about running out of cash, the orders not coming in, the products having to be recalled, worrying that I was letting down my family and friends and other shareholders. The problems were endless, I felt at the end of my tether and on the verge of a nervous breakdown. I probably would have had one if it hadn't been for a wonderful golden retriever we bought as a puppy and named Boldrick (he always had a cunning plan as in the BBC TV series *Blackadder*), and that forced me to walk him every day and get away from it to be able think and wind down. Still, Boldrick aside, I painfully recall a particularly black time in early 1999 when I inadvertently sold a duff batch of antibodies to a lot of labs in Cambridge. I was devastated, embarrassed and humiliated and wanted to hide away in shame. I had let everybody down and people were laughing at me, or so I thought ('How on earth did he think he could start a company, he knows nothing about business', I heard them say in my head). I was a sham, a fraud, and my confidence was shattered. However, fighting every instinct in my body to run away from it all and give up, I decided to go and visit each of the research scientists that had received a faulty product and apologise and to listen to them. But instead of finding a lot of angry customers, most of the scientists I met were enormously sympathetic, supportive and very willing to tell me what their research needs were and how I could help them find the right products. Rather than being shamed and humiliated, I would come away from each interaction energised and determined to help and, each time I did, I learnt something new about how to offer the customer what they wanted.

I started to think about evolution, about how you can take an idea and vary it (by listening to your customers), then how you can select the ideas that are working and then how to embed them into the business to then start the cycle over again. Although it was still tough, with each supportive customer interaction my energy would rise again and, instead of problems, I would now start to see opportunities. With each therapeutic walk with Boldrick I started to gradually think differently about things. Instead of stressing about each unexpected problem, I would tell myself, 'Calm down take a deep breath, now lets fix the problem and then think of a way of solving the problem so it doesn't occur again in the future.' I was starting to use evolution to build and adapt my business. Suddenly the website crashing was no longer a problem, it was just one of those inevitable things that you cannot foresee, but now that we have this knowledge, how do we fix it and how can we improve the website so it doesn't happen in future? When there was the next angry customer on the phone, I could use this precious interaction as a gift – how could I turn this customer from Abcam detractor to advocate and then convert all the other angry customers stretching into Abcam's future? This became so important a way of thinking for me that I eventually started enjoying the endless problems that needed to be addressed and solved.

The freedom that this approach gave me was energizing and liberating. I had to admit to myself that I didn't have all the answers and that the design mode of building a company from the top down was not going to work. I was going to build it from the bottom up using an evolutionary approach, be flexible and allow the current to take it where it wanted. Another one of my all-time desert island heroes is Matt Ridley, the world's single most vocal advocate of this approach (he has recently published a book called The Evolution of Everything [3], a great read if you have time). Also, of course, what has now become a business classic and essential reading for any budding entrepreneur is

The Lean Startup, written long after I started Abcam but essentially outlining the same evolutionary process of continuous innovation [4].

However, in order to use this approach, I needed to critically examine my strengths and weaknesses. Whilst waiting for a plane at Heathrow Airport, I bought and read a book called *The E-myth Revisited: Why Most Small Businesses Don't Work and What to Do About It* by Michael Gerber and took away one simple idea [5]. Founders are a mixture of three different traits: entrepreneur, scientist and manager. I quickly concluded that I had ample entrepreneurship (leadership and persuasive skills so vital to getting the symbiosis from other like-minded people critical to the success of any venture), enough scientific acumen to create the products but precious little in the way of management skills. I really couldn't, and still can't, organise the proverbial 'piss-up in a brewery'. As a gross generalisation and by no means the rule, each time and only in my opinion, start-ups run by 'all entrepreneur' personalities can raise money and convince others initially but then quickly have no discipline so they run out of cash and spectacularly go bankrupt (think boo.com!). On the other hand, in general, companies run by 'all manager' personalities lack any soul or passion and get packed away very neatly and quietly and efficiently, go bankrupt and perhaps return any money that is left to shareholders. 'All scientist' companies tend to be very inward-looking and remain as cottage industries run within the comfort zone of the founders but this risks the founders working in the company rather than on it and they are in danger of burning out. Armed with this knowledge I quickly recruited an experienced finance director, Eddie Powell, who rapidly plugged the gaping management gap in the business.

Anyway, I digress; back to the lessons from evolution. Creationists and 'top downers' often quote the example of the human eye and ask 'What use is only 5% of an eye? It is so clearly designed by a creator as to be obvious'. Actually 5% of an eye is pretty useful in a world where every other living thing is blind. A great example of this is the search engine on Abcam's website – when we started the company search engines were clunky and primitive in comparison to today. By talking to customers I had seen their frustration in not being able to find the right antibody for their experiment so we put a basic search engine on the site to simply search the web for antibodies. It was real garage technology stuff but better than anything that existed at the time, and delighted scientists started to flock to the website. It became the '5%' foundation from which we could evolve the website to the sophisticated engine that it is today.

In the early days of Abcam I faced a lot of criticism about this evolutionary approach and was frequently faced with a legitimate question to take me out of the CEO role and replace me with someone more experienced who looked more comfortable in a suit and tie. This was painful but in hindsight one of the best things that happened to me because it continually made me examine my own skill sets to match what was needed by the business at each stage of its growth. I had to continually learn, adapt and evolve to re-invent myself in order to earn the right to stay at the helm. I never adapted to wearing a tie however!

As I write this in June 2016, Abcam has now become a company successful beyond my wildest dreams. It employs nearly 1,000 people worldwide across nine locations and is the world's leader in the supply of research antibodies and is happily still evolving new scientific tools of discovery in research, diagnostics and therapeutics. Of course this makes me immensely proud but I am not Abcam and Abcam is not me. Organizations are complex dynamic organisms like humans that evolve and adapt to an ever-changing world and all that we, as founder CEOs, can do is frame the conditions necessary for this evolution. In September 2014 after 16 years as CEO, I stepped down to make way for my successor and continue my own evolution into a mentor/entrepreneur who helps life scientists get started on their own evolutionary journeys.

My own personal journey from bench scientist to entrepreneur has been exhilarating and immensely rewarding. However, if you are considering evolving your career out of the lab and have any doubts, it's worth bearing in mind these beautiful words attributed to Johann Wolfgang Goethe: 'Whatever you can do, or dream you can do, begin it. Boldness has genius, power and magic in it.'

As you probably would have guessed if you have read this far, my all-time number-one desert island hero is, of course, Charles Darwin, the founder of modern biology. In 2009, around the world but especially in Cambridge, we celebrated the joint anniversary of Darwin's 200th birthday and 150th anniversary of the publication of *On the Origin of Species*. I was enormously privileged to be invited to Darwin's college (Christ's College, Cambridge) on the anniversary of Darwin's birthday, 12 February 2009, for a celebratory dinner in his honour. It was a magical evening with no wind but just a soft fall of fluffy snowflakes onto a pristine white glistening snow carpet. I had never seen Cambridge look so beautiful almost as if it was paying homage to the great man and the special day. Darwin would have felt immensely proud about what he had achieved with his remarkable insight and idea that has laid the foundation of modern biology and helped, more than any other discovery, to start to answer the question of 'Life, the Universe and Everything' in *The Hitchhiker's Guide to the Galaxy*.[2] Life evolves and we evolve, and so does Darwin's evolution idea. He would have found it highly amusing that a quote widely attributed to him is actually a paraphrase by Leon C. Megginson, Professor of Management and Marketing at Louisiana State University at Baton Rouge in 1963. However, as an evolutionary paraphrase, it is one of the greatest, and one, I am sure, Darwin would be happy to associate with:

> It is not the strongest of the species that survives, nor the most intelligent that survives. It is the one that is most adaptable to change.

REFERENCES

1. The Guardian. (2005). Explorer achieves dream then dies in crevasse fall. Retrieved from www.theguardian.com/environment/2005/jan/18/antarctica.climatechange (accessed 18 January 2017).
2. Dobzhansky, T. (1973). Nothing in biology makes any sense except in the light of evolution. *American Biology Teacher*, 35, 125–129.
3. Ridley, M. (2015). *The evolution of everything: How new ideas emerge*. London: The Fourth Estate.
4. Ries, E. (2011). *The lean startup*. London: Portfolio Penguin.
5. Gerber, M. (2001). *The e-myth revisited: Why most small businesses don't work and what to do about it* (3rd Rev. Ed.). New York: Harper Business.

[2] Number 42 is the answer according to The *Hitchhiker's Guide to the Galaxy* by Douglas Adams (Pan Books, 1979) calculated by a supercomputer called Deep Thought during a period of 7.5 million years. Unfortunately nobody knows what the question was.

8

Entrepreneurship, Management, Public Relations and Consulting

I am fortunate today to be working in a job that is exciting, interesting and very challenging in terms of what it seeks to deliver. Academic Health Science Networks (AHSNs) were set up following a report in 2012 into the poor pace of adoption of new technologies into the UK National Health Service (NHS),[1] and as Commercial Director of the Oxford AHSN, my role is to work with industry, academia and the NHS to provide a lit runway for new innovations to be adopted into clinical practice in the NHS. I never expected to be working in the NHS but looking back on a career of more than 25 years, the role combines all the different elements of experience gained in the life sciences industry: research and development (R&D), business and strategy development, finance and company creation, government policy and consultancy.

I would like to say that much of this was planned but in hindsight and reality I followed a sequence of steps which at the time appeared attractive, although in reality were not necessarily that logical. I did not sit down and map out a defined career pathway but rather strove to keep my options open for as long as possible and to build upon a diversity of experiences. Indeed, I suspect very few of us are able to map out a career progression that goes according to plan or is in any way related to what we thought we would do at the start. I had originally thought at university that I would become an academic but as this option became less attractive I was left with the question of "what's next?" and how to adapt to follow a very different career trajectory.

---

[1] Academic Health Service Networks, www.england.nhs.uk/ourwork/part-rel/ahsn/

Successful Careers beyond the Lab, ed. David Bennett and Richard Jennings.
Published by Cambridge University Press. © Cambridge University Press 2017.

Today the pressures on graduates seem to be much greater with the presumption that we should know our career path clearly. I have always found it something of an anathema to be asked, "Where do you see yourself in 5 or 10 years' time?" For me the challenge has been to avoid being pigeonholed and be flexible to new opportunities. I have never had a clearly defined path and for me the challenge has been to balance broader interests in writing and more spiritual pursuits with a traditional career in industry. This process has not been without its growing pains and various *cul-de-sacs* but I believe that if we pursue a process that provides an opportunity for expressing our interests and follow opportunities that make us excited and happy, then opportunities will open up in unexpected ways. The other important ingredient in this is hard work and effort, and a readiness to learn new skills and disciplines.

For me following the career pathway has been similar to walking down a corridor with a series of doors, some of which are open at different points in time. Much of our education system seeks to narrow down the scope of what we want to do as early as possible and requires us to make significant decisions at a young age when we lack the experience and judgement to do so. Doors become closed early on and it can be difficult to go back on decisions made. The path I chose was, first, to pursue an education in science because I knew that once that doorway was closed at school it would be virtually impossible to get back into it; the second step was to move away from academia and into industry. This necessitated broadening my options in a variety of different ways. Not all of it was plain sailing and there were experiments along the way that did not work out as anticipated.

My initial entry point into the system was at the University of Cambridge where I studied Natural Sciences. This for me was akin to being let into a sweet shop where I could broaden my academic interests and horizons. There were few courses at that time that allowed the scope and options to experiment, and although my focus was on biology, I studied geology and history and philosophy of science along the way. In my final year I specialised in zoology and in particular palaeontology, thinking at the time that I would become a palaeontologist. During the last term, however, I realised that this was not for me and after graduating applied to do an MPhil in the History and Philosophy of Science, again at Cambridge. This provided an opportunity for me to pursue varied lines of inquiry and throughout this time my goal was to study what interested me without any thought about a future career. I explored such diverse subjects as phenomenology and the philosophy of experience, evolutionary theory (always a passion) and continental philosophy spanning Kant through to Heidegger. At the end of the year I converted to a PhD, studying the underlying theoretical assumptions in evolutionary taxonomy and competing approaches to classification. This combined my interest in evolutionary theory with the philosophy of science and also provided an invaluable discipline in structuring and analysing large quantities of information and in understanding the constraints on hierarchical classification systems. While I retained a strong desire initially to become an academic, by the end of the PhD I realised that this path was not for me. Spending day after day with my head buried in books felt too isolating from the normal fabric of everyday life and I needed to get out into the real world as I saw it then.

I left Cambridge with little clue about what I should do, armed with the knowledge that my degrees came right at the bottom of the ranking system in terms of employability. Like all graduates I scoured the jobs market but little excited me. One possible fit was to become involved with the fledging biotechnology industry, as it was known then, and the United Kingdom was following in the footsteps of the pioneering United States in building a new industry sector. I had little idea of where to begin or what it would entail but was fortunate enough to have a friend whose father had set up a biotech company and was an entrepreneur. After several discussions he kindly took me on for a summer project searching the literature for fermentation processes for hyaluronic acid. I quickly became immersed in a whole new world, working in the centre of London and feeling my way into a possible career in industry. Whether it is a good or a bad thing, it is still as true today as back then: it is who you know, rather than what you know, that counts for a great deal.

My decision to move into industry was fuelled by a number of factors, not least a desire to be involved in building something. I still retained a passion for science and I saw this move as a way to enhance what I studied. I had no formal training in business and, with hindsight it would have been prudent to have done an MBA at some point, although at the time I had little appetite for further study. I also had little desire to start off in a sales or marketing position in the industry (not that the fledgling sector was really selling any products then). After I completed the summer project Swedish investors decided to buy out the management. My entrepreneurial sponsor invited me to stay on with another of his companies that specialised in chemical engineering and the construction of turnkey gas plants ready for immediate use. Over the next few months we discussed ideas for starting a new biotech company and teamed up with a retired professor of biochemistry to set up a business exploring opportunities for biotech contract research between the United Kingdom and the United States. As with most entrepreneurial activities this was a starting point and I became engrossed in how to build a business and learning some of the key facets required in generating income.

A fairly rich mix of blind ignorance and hard work, coupled with an emerging technology-driven sector, opened up opportunities and within a two-year period I was running a small biotech looking at vaccine development using insect cells. The contract research business dropped into the background and the collaboration for this new company centred around an academic team out of Oxford. We also developed links with a team out of Canada. The learning curve was very steep and I absorbed more through the mistakes that I made than anything else at the time. As with most biotech start-ups the challenge was cash to support the R&D and most of the time was spent knocking on doors looking for funding. One way or another we managed to raise £1 million but in the end my lack of experience contributed to the problems of raising sufficient capital and after an unsuccessful private placement I decided it was best to leave.

This was something of another step into the unknown and at the age of 29 I had no job lined up and little money – not quite what I had anticipated. On the plus side, I had contacts in the industry and after several months languishing I was offered a consultancy opportunity in Canada to set up a diagnostics company. At the same time I applied for a job in an emerging biotechnology company, British Biotech, as head of research administration. The job involved managing research contracts, running the intellectual property function for the company and supporting the director of research. I was fortunate enough to be offered the job and after some time weighing up the options between Canada and England, I decided to go for the position with British Biotech in Oxford, not least because I knew that there were big gaps in my experience and I could only learn this through working in a more structured, corporate environment.

British Biotech had been founded from the fallout of the acquisition of G. D. Searle by Monsanto so, although the company was young, there was a strong pharmaceutical ethos in the culture and an approach to drug development and corporate partnering that was more mature than at many start-ups. I was responsible for managing the company's patent portfolio and this built on the initial experience I had gained in intellectual property law in my previous role. I found this area stimulating and very quickly had exposure to all aspects of the international patenting process from filing through to examination and grant. I also spent time drafting research collaborations and licensing contracts with universities as well as absorbing the details of the drug discovery and development process. Initially the company focussed on four main areas – cardiovascular, inflammation, cancer and virology – and this provided a good basis for tracking the R&D process across both new chemical and biological entities. British Biotech grew rapidly in the 1990s, turning itself into an engine of R&D with ambitions to become a fully integrated pharmaceutical company.

New opportunities opened up and I moved into business development focussing on building collaborations with industry partners. I spent time working with companies in Europe, the United States and elsewhere, building up experience in pitching R&D opportunities and in licensing, in particular in cardiovascular drugs and in vaccines.

On paper this was a useful career progression but personally I felt increasingly frustrated and started to explore other ideas and areas outside the life sciences industry. In the background to the corporate world I had a long-standing interest in alternative systems of thought stemming from my days studying philosophy and I wanted to try something different. In my mid-thirties I started training in craniosacral therapy which was an off-shoot from osteopathy and about as far removed from the corporate world as you could get. It was all about learning to listen to the body combined with a detailed knowledge of anatomy that enabled one to track changes in the rhythm of the body and the cerebrospinal fluid like tides that flow back and forth. This also tapped into a long-standing interest in meditation and allowed me to explore various levels of experience and reality from a completely different perspective. The polarity of the corporate outer world was juxtaposed by this inner exploration and after two years of part-time training I became qualified to practice.

Around the same time as I was starting this alternative career pathway I was offered the opportunity at British Biotech to become involved with government affairs and the restructuring of the BioIndustry Association (BIA) which is the trade body in the UK responsible for representing the emerging biotechnology industry. The reorganisation was led by a handful of leading companies at the time and I played a supporting role in helping to implement the changes. I was also offered the opportunity to run two working groups, one for intellectual property and one for regulatory affairs. The passion for reorganising trade body representation in the industry then spread into Europe and a similar process was followed with EuropaBio (the trade body for European biotech small and medium enterprises (SMEs) as well as large companies) where I took on responsibility for intellectual property as well. Both of these roles gave me broad exposure to the workings of the Department of Trade & Industry (as it was named then) and the European Commission. In the United Kingdom there was also an informal group of companies that went under the name of the Senior Advisory Group on Biotechnology which had the remit of covering issues around the controlled and deliberate release of genetically modified organisms. I became a part of this group and was able to understand more about the interface between policy, regulation and legislation. The political and social issues surrounding the development of fit-for-purpose regulations and an intellectual property framework covering the patenting of human gene sequences took centre stage in the biotech industry's evolution at that time.

I rapidly found myself at the centre of supporting the industry response to the European Biotechnology Patents Directive as it went through the European Commission and the European Parliament. This was a very interesting experience which brought me into contact with a broad range of people from civil servants and members of the European Parliament (MEPs), to regulators, to a broad industry base and also to opponents of genetic modification (GM) and patenting. I worked very closely with the BIA, the Association of British Pharmaceutical Industry (ABPI) and EuropaBio for a number of years, putting forward industry's position on gene patenting to commissioners, MEPs and anyone else who would listen. The central question was around the patentability of a human gene sequence and whether or not it should be patentable once isolated from the human body. Opponents of the legislation argued that this was tantamount to owning a piece of the human body which was a wholly incorrect interpretation of the law. Consequently I was also exposed to the media debate, both in television and radio and having to quickly learn the ropes in interviews. Being grilled by Jeremy Paxman on BBC TV's Newsnight was one of the more sobering experiences!

All of this was extremely valuable experience and gave me the confidence to think about opportunities beyond British Biotech. I wanted to make time to pursue a practice in cranial-sacral therapy and transition through consultancy work to give me financial stability. After eight years at British Biotech I handed in my notice and, in retrospect, the timing could not have been more prescient since in the following year the company went into a terminal decline fuelled by a very public argument between the medical director and the chief executive.

During my time at British Biotech I had learnt a great deal about the drug development process, intellectual property, business development and strategy, and also government affairs. I had also built up a broad network of contacts both in the public and private sectors. Going it alone was still a leap into the unknown, and there were a couple of mornings when I woke up thinking "What have I done?" Fortunately, early on I was invited by my old boss at British Biotech who had left a year earlier to join his consultancy practice, Quercus Management, which I did with gratitude. After a short hiatus the work began to come in and due to the strong network of contacts I did not have to do much marketing. I focussed my services on intellectual property and strategy development while continuing to support the work in the United Kingdom and Europe on the biotechnology patents directive. I still spent a lot of time in Brussels and Strasbourg working closely with the European Commission and a handful of MEPs to guide the legislation through. The process was fairly surreal as anyone could draft and table amendments to the draft directive, which they did! Eventually, with the final vote in the European Parliament, the legislation was passed, significantly upholding the principle that gene sequences isolated from the human body could be patented provided they satisfied the key criteria of all patents of novelty and inventive step.

I continued to pursue a dual life, building a client base in consultancy and exploring the viability of running a practice in cranial-sacral therapy. After a year or so I realised that the latter was not a viable option and I began working on a part-time basis for two companies, Oxford BioMedica and PowderJect Pharmaceuticals. The work with Oxford BioMedica was exclusively on patents and freedom to operate issues in the complex field of gene therapy and retroviral vectors while at PowderJect I was involved with strategy development. I found the latter much more interesting, and although I split my time between the two companies for several years, I eventually joined PowderJect full time as Vice President Corporate Affairs, responsible for strategy development and government affairs. I worked a four-day week and spent the other day writing, eventually producing a book on meditation practice and spiritual development. Stephen Fry, English comedian, actor, writer, presenter and activist, once said that everyone has a book inside them and that is where it should stay, which always amused me.

My experience at PowderJect was rather like the law of opposites at work where the pendulum of corporate failure swung into the realms of corporate success. It was a novel but pleasing experience to be working in a company that generated significant revenues and which became profitable. In 2001 I was also awarded the MBE[2] for my work on the biotechnology patents directive. This was totally unanticipated but a source of unexpected pleasure.

I worked closely with the chief executive officer (CEO) at Powder-Ject running a strategy process that involved the senior management and was part of the team that looked at mergers and acquisitions (M&A) opportunities. One of the reasons I had originally been brought into PowderJect was to advise on the mistakes made at British Biotech and to ensure that these were not repeated. At the time I started to consult for PowderJect it was clear that the projected R&D timelines were very ambitious and sensibly the company changed into a fully integrated vaccines company, building the asset base through acquisition of vaccine businesses. This was the complete opposite of what happened at British Biotech where there was no strategy taken to reduce risk and generate revenues.

I also found the culture inside PowderJect more open and innovative, where good ideas could be pursued. I learned a great deal around the M&A process as well as overseeing more complex strategic analyses with a multi-disciplinary team. At the same time, the work in government affairs was challenging since it coincided with the threat of bioterrorism, the ongoing role of vaccines in public health and more specifically the question of individual donations to a political party since the CEO made a donation to one of the political parties. This latter challenge highlighted potential conflicts of interest for the company in vaccine procurement. We were supported by good advisors as the company sought to navigate a passage into calmer waters. Overall, PowderJect afforded me the opportunity to develop my skill sets across a broader platform and during my time there the company grew rapidly to more than 1,000 people.

While at PowderJect I still retained a desire to have a more flexible lifestyle and in 2003 the opportunity arose to rethink my career path. That year the United States biotechnology company Chiron which had a strong vaccines business made an offer for the acquisition of PowderJect and by the autumn I was in a position to strike out alone and pursue a diversity of interests, this time concentrating on writing. I took a redundancy package and moved to Wales to find time to write and pursue other interests. For two years I had little engagement with the corporate world, undertaking the odd piece of consultancy work but spending the majority of my time writing. I completed several books and, after

---

[2] Member of the Most Excellent Order of the British Empire

seeking a publisher with limited success, went down the self-publishing route. It rapidly became clear that a career in writing is not an easy option!

By 2007, I was ready to get back to a role in consultancy and started work with the BIA on the Pharmaceutical Pricing Regulatory Scheme (PPRS). This next phase of my career became much more focussed on pricing and reimbursement and financial modelling of businesses. Although I had done quite a lot of modelling work at PowderJect using Monte Carlo simulations, a technique used to understand the impact of risk and uncertainty in project management and other forecasting models, I became much more involved in issues around the National Institute for Health and Clinical Excellence (NICE) technology assessments and the health economics underpinning drug pricing. The National Audit Office had also published on the PPRS and put forward views on how a new approach to 'value-based pricing' could be more effective. I learnt a great deal from this work listening to company concerns, especially pharmaceutical, and understanding the policy drivers for the PPRS negotiations with the Department of Health. I also teamed up with a colleague from PowderJect and set up a consultancy practice aimed at strategy and financial development. My partner was a financial specialist so I became more involved in looking at valuations and financial modelling. This phase of my career was not without its challenges and it was evident that working out of Wales presented its own set of issues in terms of not being close enough to where the action was. During this period I also started to work more for public bodies, becoming involved in digital health solutions, as well as with a large spin-out company opportunity that in the end did not materialise. The digital health opportunity involved assessing the intellectual property and commercialisation of a capacity-planning tool in oncology healthcare delivery. I worked closely with the NHS and became interested in the delivery of healthcare as opposed to the conception and development of drugs.

This broadening of my experience was extremely valuable, although being back in the consultancy arena was very different from what it was a decade earlier. For a start my contact base was not nearly as up to date as it had been and the climate for small consultancy businesses had changed with client companies more interested in signing up the bigger names. Second, healthcare was constantly evolving and becoming more complex; whereas in the 1990s a company could launch a new medicine without too much trouble, the restructuring of the NHS and fragmentation of delivery bodies made the whole area of market access and uptake extremely complex and challenging. Although I gained valuable experience in working with the public sector and in understanding some of these different tensions, I felt increasingly that a more radical change was needed. At the same time the whole industry landscape had changed considerably and new emerging opportunities such as in personalised or precision medicine were beginning to emerge. I spent a considerable amount of time learning more about these areas as part of building up a solid background understanding. Perhaps most significantly from a personal point of view, I now felt much more comfortable in how to balance my different life interests and, having had several forays into an alternate career pathway, involving writing and the alternative health field, I now felt much more comfortable continuing to work in the health sector. I felt that I had integrated what I needed to during these excursions and did not feel the same polarity as when I was younger.

In the second half of 2013, I began actively to search for permanent job opportunities and knew that the best way forward would require a move back to Oxford. I looked up some old contacts who were still active in the industry there and also scoped out the type of activity that would interest me. This aspect of networking was essential and, having had discussions with a number of colleagues who I used to work with in the past, they have all conceded that this was more important than ever. With hindsight, although I did not know it at the time, much of the work I had done provided a good platform for my next step.

In planning the next phase I came across an opportunity at the Oxford Academic Health Science Network and pursued it actively through the interview process. As with all interview processes, careful planning and due diligence were crucial and I thought carefully about what I could bring to the job and in demonstrating how my background fitted all aspects of the role. I was offered the position which signified a transition from the life sciences industry into the healthcare service delivery sector. As an opportunity this made me very excited to be working back in Oxford and I quickly realised that things had moved on a great deal since I was last there. There was a sense of excitement and collaboration that was not present before. I found the NHS culture very different and was surprised to feel an underlying current of support and care for employees in a way that is not always evident in the commercial sector. I had to quickly learn a whole new language where acronyms and abbreviations conveyed a whole host of different and complex meanings. But what fascinated me the most was the complexity of healthcare delivery pathways and how innovations could be taken up. I saw for the first time the other side of the coin from the traditional industry push process of developing a new innovation and then expecting the NHS to automatically buy it and use it. This was too simplistic a model and it is the gap between the R&D push and real-world evaluation of a new technology in the NHS that has to be bridged meaningfully.

My current role also requires a great deal of networking and collaborative working, and this is something that has been very enjoyable and rewarding. I feel fortunate that at this stage in my career I have the most interesting and fulfilling job, being in a privileged position to see so many different types of innovations across the digital, medical technology, diagnostics and pharmaceutical industries, and to work with some incredibly bright people.

I certainly cannot claim that this was all planned although I have tried to follow my instincts and trust that things would work out. Building a career pathway that is satisfying and rewarding is a challenge and there are no easy formulae that can be followed. It is as much about getting to know oneself, where one's strengths and weaknesses lie, as it is about engaging with the external world and presenting oneself. I believe there are several things that are essential in developing a career. The first is networking. Speaking to people about their experiences in different jobs, finding out about prospective roles and what they entail, can be hugely helpful. Networking also means that people may come across opportunities that they can pass back to you. The second important aspect relates to due diligence and knowing your field. Even if you are starting out from a low level of understanding, building up a knowledge base is essential. It can also be very valuable to follow your intuition and to look at areas that interest you although there may be no particular reason for doing so at the time. Opportunities and experiences have a funny knack of coming back through when perhaps least expected. Another feature that I have experienced is that in making a career transition there are always risks but as one door closes, another will open. Even if things do not work out, the experience in and of itself is valuable. Building a career is as much about knowing what you don't want to do and steps that can be perceived as a failure are really the stepping-stones to success. All experience is valuable. Crucially, one should always be looking to broaden the skill base throughout one's career and be open to learning new skills.

In conclusion, while the career landscape is highly competitive, there are many more different opportunities within the life sciences and healthcare sectors that were not available in the past. For starters, there is a thriving SME life sciences sector and it is now feasible to plan a career in this which in the past would not have been so easy. Long-term careers in pharmaceuticals may not be as attractive as they once were as the industry undergoes profound changes and as more early-stage R&D is outsourced. The growing SME sector affords a range of opportunities from R&D through manufacturing, regulatory and market access and sales. New disciplines in bioinformatics, health economics and health service delivery also offer excellent opportunities for building up a career. At the same time, the health infrastructure that embraces the National Institute for Health Research (NIHR), NHS England, NHS Improvement, Innovate UK and the research councils offers a host of initiatives and new opportunities for career progression. The landscape is complex and varied but there are great opportunities across both the public and private sectors. Notwithstanding all of this, my advice is to do that which makes you happy and excited and, if at first this does not happen, it is best to keep on searching until it does!

9

From Science to Engineering and Business
The Converging Stories of Three Friends

This is mainly my story but I have asked two of my friends from the University of Cambridge to join in with theirs'. My friends are still at a relatively early stage in their careers and in one case from a very different part of the world. However, our varied experiences have led us to the same place at the same time and we all look forward to leveraging our current degree and establishing careers in technology-based ventures. Their stories add an interesting perspective to my own so I start with mine and go on to theirs' towards the end.

I have always enjoyed studying science and performed well in science-based subjects throughout my academic career. However, while I was always certain of my inclination towards science, I did not have a preference for any one subject within the sciences and never imagined myself pursuing a career in scientific research or academia. I graduated from high school in a small city in Pakistan. Like most developing countries, the best education offered in Pakistan is in the sciences, especially in medicine and engineering. When the time came to decide on an undergraduate degree, I considered the limited options available: a Bachelor's degree in pure sciences or a professional degree in medicine or engineering. The decision to select one degree over another was not straightforward, especially since I did not want to be a career scientist. In fact, my objective was always to leverage my scientific training to pursue a career outside of science. Although I did not know exactly how to articulate my career goals at the time, I realised eventually that I wanted to be an entrepreneur.

Successful Careers beyond the Lab, ed. David Bennett and Richard Jennings.
Published by Cambridge University Press. © Cambridge University Press 2017.

The path from science to entrepreneurship was not clear or straightforward and the easier option would have been to enrol in a business or management degree. I had done well academically in science so far so instead of pursuing an average education in business I decided instead to continue with a science-based field of study that would challenge me intellectually and help me to build skills that I could apply in other professional contexts. In a sense, versatility and intellectual rigour became the guiding principle for selecting a course of study. Once I had determined my objective I consulted many different people in various science-based careers from academics to researchers to practising doctors and engineers. Eventually, I opted for a Bachelor's degree in civil engineering. It was not immediately clear to me how civil engineering would lead to 'entrepreneurship' but at the time it seemed to be the most practical option considering my personal objectives and the limited options available to a science student in Pakistan. Engineering certainly appeared more practical compared to a degree in pure sciences and more versatile compared to medicine.

THE ENGINEERING YEARS

Fortunately, my expectations from the engineering degree turned out to be fairly accurate. Based on my personal experience, engineering is one of the most versatile forms of science education because it teaches the practical, real-world application of purely scientific concepts and strengthens quantitative abilities that can be used in careers outside engineering. Civil engineering, for instance, is the application of chemistry, geology, physics and mathematics to a real-world need for shelter, transportation, water and sanitation. In that sense, civil engineering applies pure science to create infrastructure that transforms and determines our quality of life. I acquired many important proficiencies through my engineering education: quantitative analysis, structural design, survey of physical spaces, mechanical and structural drawing and materials testing. However, the degree also taught me other skills that proved to be much more valuable to my career evolution. Engineering principles taught me the value of systems and applying system-wide thinking to identifying the easiest and least-cost solution to complex problems. I learnt to appreciate the importance of planning and project management. I understood the value of thinking through problems and considering multiple solutions before deciding on a course of action. Perhaps most importantly, I learnt how to work within the constraints imposed by time and resources or even the environment. The knowledge and skills I acquired through an engineering education have helped me in many different situations at every stage in my career regardless of the industry or role I worked in. In fact, these very skills made it possible to transition from an academic or research background to a business environment.

THE MBA EXPERIENCE

I initially planned to work as a field engineer for a few years but personal circumstances led me to pursue a Master's degree immediately after graduation from the Bachelor's program. The easiest option available to me was to follow the PhD track and pursue a career in research or academia. The university from which I had received my undergraduate degree provided generous scholarships to students who would commit to teaching at the university after completing a PhD at an institution of the students' choice anywhere in the world. The PhD option was very tempting but I realized it would set my career on a narrower course than I had envisioned and it would instead be more suitable to use the Master's education to broaden my professional skills. As a result I applied to a two-year Master of Business Administration (MBA) program in the United States.

Although I had no work experience, usually a pre-requisite for good MBA programs, I did exceptionally well on the Graduate Management Admission Test (GMAT) and was not only given admission but was offered a full-tuition scholarship at the George Washington University in Washington, DC. I attribute my success in the GMAT entirely to the engineering degree and the multi-year mathematics courses I took through my years as an engineering student. Even during my MBA studies I found my quantitative skills especially helpful in core business management courses such as accounting, statistics and finance. While several of the students in my cohort struggled with quantitative modules, I found most courses easy to manage and the workload much less intensive. As a result, I had more free time than I had anticipated and was able to take up internships with a World Bank project and a technology company in Washington, DC. One of these internships transitioned into a full-time job and after graduation from the MBA program I spent one additional year in Washington, DC as a product manager at the technology company.

PROFESSIONAL EXPERIENCES AND TRANSITIONING
ACROSS INDUSTRIES

After working in the United States I returned to Pakistan to explore professional opportunities closer to home. The experience of working in a technology company had been interesting and I initially explored opportunities at many different types of companies in various industries. Eventually I decided to join my family's construction business. The construction industry in Pakistan was performing well at the time and the company was looking to both leverage opportunities within the construction industry and diversify into other sectors. Working for family was not my first preference but the opportunity to be a part of the company's transition into new industries seemed an interesting challenge. There were also other advantages to working for family; the work environment was familiar and I had at least some flexibility in defining my exact role at the company. I opted for a business development function which required me to manage the acquisition of new projects through prequalification and tendering. I was also responsible for managing the development of marketing materials and business development collateral.

In addition to my full-time job at the construction company, I also consulted on construction industry–related projects for the World Bank in Pakistan. Again, I found that the combination of a civil engineering degree and an MBA placed me at an advantage when applying for consulting assignments. The construction company I worked at executed large infrastructure projects for the public sector. Through my experience at both the construction company and the World Bank, I was able to interact with professionals from many different areas but specifically with public-sector functionaries, including regulators, that I would otherwise not have had an opportunity to interact with. The exposure to the public sector in general, and the regulation process in particular, broadened my professional perspective in ways that would have a major impact on my career development.

I worked in the business development role for almost two years before shifting focus to the diversification efforts under way at the construction company. Our construction business had invested in several new areas including real-estate and financial services and was open to exploring other industries depending on the potential for growth and investment. The opportunity for me to contribute to the company's diversification came unexpectedly through a chance meeting with the regional head of a major European engine manufacturer. The engine manufacturer wanted to increase its market share in Pakistan and was actively looking to develop power projects in partnership with local Pakistani companies. Although my company did not have any prior experience in the power sector, this opportunity was a perfect fit because the equipment manufacturer was also offering to provide technical expertise throughout the project development process. Besides the technical assistance, the equipment manufacturer would also invest some equity in the project but their main interest was in selling their gas engines and providing operations and maintenance (O&M) services to the eventual power company. We signed a memorandum of understanding (MoU) with the European company and I established a special-purpose subsidiary to the construction business that would develop and implement the power project. I was designated Director, Project Development at the new subsidiary.

For the next several years I worked on the power project through various stages of the project development cycle from managing the feasibility study to supervising geological studies at the project site, negotiating agreements with equipment providers and power sector regulators, and arranging project finance. Although I had no specific knowledge of the power sector, my technical education and project management skills enabled me to navigate the new industry with relative ease. As always, experiencing a new industry in a different role enabled me to develop many new skills and acquire new interests that helped me to evolve both as a professional and as a person and enabled the next transition in my career. Through the power sector experience I developed a deep understanding of electricity generation systems and a lasting interest in the concept of renewable or sustainable energy.

The power project I was developing was to operate on gas or heavy fuel oil. Although the extraction and processing of fossil fuels is privatized in Pakistan, the sale and transmission is regulated by the government and fossil fuels such as natural gas and heavy fuel oil are traded through dedicated public-sector companies. Pakistan is dependent on natural gas to operate several key industries including energy and fertilizer production. Just as our power project reached financial close the country experienced a major shortage of natural gas and, although new gas fields were under development, the government tightened its gas allocation policy for power production despite a major shortage of electricity in the country. As a result of the change in government policy we were no longer certain of gas allocation to our power project. At almost the same time the Overseas Private Investment Corporation (OPIC), a bilateral financial organization based in the United States, expressed an interest in financing the project through a long-term loan. The terms of financing were extremely favourable; however, OPIC has very strict environmental guidelines for fossil fuel–based power projects and to qualify for the OPIC loan we were required to add a pollution control system to our original plant design. The addition of a pollution control system would mitigate the various environmental contaminants associated with burning fossil fuel such as heavy fuel oil for power production.

RENEWABLE ENERGY – NEW FOCUS AND A NEW CAREER

As I researched the requirements of pollution control systems based on OPIC's environmental guidelines I began to recognise the hazards of environmental pollution from industrial processes in general and power production in particular. Environmental pollution control and mitigation is a difficult and costly process. The addition of a pollution control system to our project would raise the total project cost by approximately 30%. What struck me particularly was that Pakistan had minimal regulations for controlling industrial pollution and under the local environmental laws we could set up a gas- and fuel oil–based power plant without any requirement for pollution abatement. The disparity in environmental policies in the United States and Pakistan was surprising!

The circumstances around fuel allocation for the power project and my newfound understanding of the scale of pollution from power production increased my interest in renewable energy as a cleaner and more sustainable source of energy compared to fossil fuel–based electricity. I initially looked into the possibility of setting up a second power project, this time based on either solar or wind technology, but realized quickly that there wasn't sufficient technical knowledge in Pakistan to develop the project without the help of expensive and difficult-to-manage foreign consultants. The lack of technical know-how was particularly problematic and seemed to be a concern for many other people within and outside the power sector. Although I was working in conventional energy I was constantly asked for advice or information on renewable power production which most of the time I was unable to provide.

As my interest in renewable technologies and environmental policies in Pakistan grew I realized that a more structured approach to learning might be more suitable and a better way to improve my knowledge of the renewables sector would be to enrol in an academic program. As a result, I applied for a fellowship in the United States and a degree program in the United Kingdom in 2014. By early 2015, I received the Hubert Humphrey Fellowship to pursue a one-year professional fellowship in renewable energy at the University of California, Davis. Simultaneously I was offered a Chevening Scholarship to study for an MPhil in Technology Policy at the University of Cambridge in the United Kingdom. I opted for the technology policy degree primarily because it offered a unique opportunity to combine courses in engineering, policy and business centred on any technology. In my case, the focus of my MPhil would be renewable energy. Although engineering and public policy is not a typical or usual combination, it is immensely relevant and has many different applications within the public and private sectors.

JORGE JARAMILLO ENCISO'S STORY

As of today, it is still not completely clear to me whether my academic and career choices are driven by internal compulsions or external pressure: was it an interest driven by curiosity or was it purely social pressure coming from a family of academics? Whatever it was, a career in the hard sciences always seemed like the right and, at some points, even the obvious decision to make.

When I was 17 and confident, I decided to pursue a Bachelor of Science degree in Electronic and Computer Engineering at one of the best universities in Latin America. Everyone around me approved of my decision to pursue engineering given my academic record and capabilities. I realized my potential, as perceived by those around me, and even went beyond what was expected of me by receiving a full scholarship for my undergraduate degree. My decisions seemed to be perfect in every way! The first four years of study confirmed this and were characterized by a form of 'scientific pride' – a strange but satisfying sensation of individually pushing the frontiers of knowledge. After that, things changed and they changed quite dramatically.

As engineers and scientists, we are continuously seeking evidence and facts on which to build our knowledge. The more I learnt as a scientist and an engineer, the more conscious I became of the limits of my own knowledge. For instance, I was not able to completely grasp the interactions between science and entrepreneurship or the practical applications of scientific concepts. I saw my inability to explain the practical applications of science as a weakness and a manifestation of my own lack of understanding. In an interesting twist, the same meticulousness and curiosity that helped me to develop an interest in science also inspired me to look outside the lab and find answers to problems through a broader view of the world.

I started my search for knowledge outside the lab by challenging myself to learn about businesses and innovation. This was essential because I always anticipated a future full of diverse experiences. As a next step, I started a Master's degree in information technology (IT) and focussed on opportunities in operational-excellence consulting. Although the transition from engineering to operational consulting was not easy because I firmly believed that it would enhance my understating of business and innovation, I did not give up. Eventually, I had the opportunity to consult for one of the largest international IT and strategy consulting firms.

My experience in consulting has been extremely rewarding. Currently, I am pursuing an MPhil in technology policy at the University of Cambridge which will allow me to gain a deeper understanding of the regulatory frameworks enforced around the world. The most useful lesson I have learnt in my career so far is the beautiful but sometimes undervalued exercise of paying attention and recognizing the difference between what we enjoy and what we are good at.

OMAIR KHALID'S STORY

Looking back, I would consider my career journey an unconventional one. It began in the second year of my undergraduate studies in electrical and electronic engineering at Imperial College London in the United Kingdom. This is when I met a senior utility professional from Pakistan who was starting a power sector consulting business and offered me an engineering internship position. The meeting coincided with my search for an area of specialization for my career and the possibility of moving back to Pakistan where there was an acute shortage of qualified professionals to deal with the country's electricity problems. I saw the offer as a good opportunity and accepted the position. When I formally joined the consulting firm as a full-time employee after graduating I was one of a handful of employees in the firm and the only one working directly on consulting projects with the founder.

Starting out, one of my biggest professional challenges in a sector in which most consultants were much more senior was establishing myself as a young professional and getting my voice heard. This required patience, resilience and commitment to my profession.

My engineering knowledge proved to be a key asset in this regard. Being able to solve tough technical challenges allowed me to 'get a seat at the table' during discussions both within the firm and outside it. By going beyond my initial technical expertise to developing a broader understanding of the issues in the power sector and of company management-related issues, I was able both to start leading teams and to interact with clients on my own. This accelerated my transition into managerial roles which I found both challenging and very interesting.

Over the next few years as we successfully completed our projects and our reputation grew, the diversity of projects that we took on also expanded. With this came increasing responsibility, leading larger teams and requiring the ability to contribute on issues such as the company's growth strategy. A key lesson I learnt in this regard was the importance of training junior team members and learning to delegate which in turn allowed me to focus on developing my own leadership skills. It also allowed me to take on different assignments and constantly continue to learn. I was also very keen about continuing to learn in a variety of ways including professional development courses. Watching me successfully apply this knowledge innovatively in my work also gave my company the confidence to put me in a senior leadership position.

Finally, in a start-up consulting environment the importance of having a mentor cannot be stressed enough especially through the early stages of the career. I was fortunate enough to find a great mentor in my company's CEO and from many senior professionals within the sector. The lessons that they taught me helped me to successfully navigate the power sector in Pakistan and develop my career.

CONCLUSION

My year in Cambridge is about to end, and as I look back on the path that led me here, I am certain that the route to this degree would not have been as clear and the degree not as easy to pursue without my education and experiences prior to this degree. My engineering degree was particularly relevant as without it I would have not considered taking the engineering modules offered at the University of Cambridge and would have therefore missed out on a major strength of the Technology Policy program. A year later, I have gained enough knowledge to feel confident to pursue a career as an energy entrepreneur and I look forward to establishing an independent renewable energy project in Pakistan. I will also explore opportunities to consult on energy policy–related issues for both the public and private sectors in Pakistan.

Although my eventual career path has turned out to be very different from the engineering education I received as an undergraduate, the engineering degree remains the foundation on which I have built my knowledge of several other disciplines including management and public policy. My professional experiences have been richer and more varied because of my science education and I was able to undertake several different degrees and streams of knowledge with a certain intellectual confidence that I derived in large part from the rigour of my scientific education. Scientists today have many more career options open to them than at any point in the past. The best academic institutions in the world offer degrees such as the technology policy program at the University of Cambridge that combine science with an unrelated field of study. These programs are particularly suited to scientists looking to transition from a laboratory-based career into new fields such as public policy and business management. A scientist today is only limited in career choices by her or his imagination!

10

From Lab Bench to Boardroom
The Patent Attorney's Tale

INTRODUCTION

When I was at school in the 1980s I filled in a questionnaire which was designed to tell me the job for which I was best suited. The output suggested that I should be a teacher but my mother was a teacher and I had no desire to do the same thing (too much marking). In any event, I distinctly remember that I wanted to be a deep-sea diver.

It's extremely hard to know how things will turn out. Things have, however, turned out well in that I do a job that I really enjoy, which stretches me intellectually and is hugely rewarding. It is also a career that I had never even heard about until I was at university.

In this chapter, I will give a personal perspective on life as a patent attorney. It is rare for someone to consider being a patent attorney before they go to university and everyone has a story about why they moved away from pure science. I'll give a brief reflection on why I made that same decision, then summarise the nature of the job, the training required and give examples of the experiences I have had in the last 20 years. Additionally, I'll offer my thoughts on ways to get into the profession.

HERE COMES 'THE SCIENCE BIT'

At school in Norwich I took the scientific route at Advanced level, doing biology, maths and chemistry. I had found the biochemistry

Successful Careers beyond the Lab, ed. David Bennett and Richard Jennings.
Published by Cambridge University Press. © Cambridge University Press 2017.

parts of my Ordinary levels fascinating, and during my Lower Sixth year realised that biochemistry was really what I wanted to do at university. I studied biochemistry on a four-year undergraduate course at the University of Oxford with Professor Eric Newsholme as a tutor whose particular interest was metabolism but Eric arranged tutorials with specialists in a wide range of subjects across the university and I particularly enjoyed genetics and molecular biology. I was fortunate enough to do an undergraduate research project in Professor, now Sir Paul Nurse's laboratory, looking at cell cycle regulation in yeast. It went well, and I was a named author for a paper in the journal *Cell* after the project and thought that a scientific career might well be the right thing for me. So I decided to do a PhD at the Institute of Molecular Medicine in Oxford but this time I found the further research to be much more challenging.

My experience over those three years was that 'effort in' did not for me equate to 'results out'. You never know with biological systems quite how research will turn out. The most interesting questions will inevitably provide the most risk in a research programme. Conversely, it may be possible to design a series of experiments that will provide certain results for a PhD although these may not necessarily always be the most interesting projects.

As I approached the end of my laboratory time I therefore made a decision not to carry on at the bench. I decided I wanted a job that gave me a more predictable output. However, it was very unclear to me what that job should be. I still wanted to use my science – you hear this from nearly all patent attorneys as an article in *Nature* confirms [1]. I didn't want to be a teacher. I didn't want to be a scientific journalist. I'd never heard of being a patent attorney until a fellow PhD student took a job in London with a patent and trademark attorney firm, where in fact he has remained to this day and now leads their life science team. It seemed worth exploring.

PATENT ATTORNEY STEREOTYPES

There are a number of jokes about patent attorneys. For example:

Q   What do you call an extrovert patent attorney?
A   Someone who looks at another person's sandals rather than their own.

Patent attorneys do have the unfair reputation of being slightly introverted.

My personal favourite is the one about the patent attorney, lawyer and a teacher walking in the countryside.

The teacher says,	"Look, there is a field over there with a sheep in it."
The lawyer says,	"Well, to be precise, there is a field over there with a *white* sheep in it."
"Well", says the patent attorney,	"That's still not true. There is a field over there with a sheep in it, *at least one half of which is white.*"

Likewise, patent attorneys do have a – more justified – reputation for being slightly pernickety.

THE NATURE OF THE JOB

What exactly is it that patent attorneys do?

First, I should clarify that in the United Kingdom, patent attorneys are not the same thing as lawyers. We do not usually have a law degree. In the United States, in contrast, all patent attorneys are qualified lawyers who then specialise in intellectual property.

A patent is a legal document which in effect is a contract between a government on behalf of the general public and an inventor which gives a monopoly to the patent owner over the use of the invention for a certain period of time in order to encourage invention and innovation. That is, the patent owner has the right to prevent a third party from practising the invention for a defined period of time, generally up to 20 years from the filing of the application. In return, once the patent expires the invention becomes available to the public for everyone to use.

PATENT APPLICATIONS – PRE-GRANT STEPS

To start from the beginning, the first role of the patent attorney is to sit down with the inventor, understand the invention and then write the patent application. This involves a degree of gentle interrogation of the inventor to make sure that all possible uses of the invention have been captured. Our science training comes into play both in understanding the science behind the invention and the thinking of the scientist to maintain good working relations.

It is important that, in preparing the draft, the patent attorney should describe the invention in a sufficient degree of detail such that it can be easily reproduced. The requirement for a sufficient disclosure of technical detail is a public policy point. The patent monopoly of 20 years is granted in return for public access to the patented technology once the patent expires. If the invention has not been described in sufficient detail to allow it to be used by the public upon patent expiry, then the patent will be considered invalid.

The scope of the monopoly position is defined at the end of the patent application by a 'claim'. This is a single sentence that captures the essential technical features of the invention. The shortest claim I remember working on was to 'Microfiltered coconut water' (see GB2318969.)[1] The invention was a method of treating coconut milk to prevent the milk from spoiling without losing any flavour. This was achieved by a microfiltration process. Thus the milk protected by the patent was different from naturally occurring coconut milk which is important as we shall see from the discussion that follows.

Once the patent application has been drafted it must be filed in those countries in which the applicant wants patent protection. The United States and Europe are very popular regions of choice with China increasingly so.

Once a patent application has been filed, searches are carried out by the patent offices to identify the so-called prior art – the body of public information available in the technical area of the invention before the filing date of the patent application. This is particularly important because a patent cannot be obtained if the alleged invention is not new.

As well as being new, an invention has to be 'non-obvious'. Patent office examiners will consider whether the invention that has been formulated in the claim is new and non-obvious in light of the prior art that they have identified and will usually raise objections about the scope of the monopoly that has been claimed. The prior art may be relevant for novelty of the invention, or obviousness, or both. The next step for the patent attorney is then to argue for the broadest possible monopoly position taking into account the prior art that has been identified. These arguments will generally have both a scientific and a legal component.

There may also be intellectual property which the inventor decides to keep as secret know-how, for example, because the advances may be hard to detect and police.

---

[1] www.google.com/patents/WO2015005790A1?cl=en

AFTER GRANT

After a patent is granted, patent attorneys are called upon to consider whether or not the monopoly position has been infringed by a third party. Taking my earlier example, what if a third party sells 'filtered' coconut water? Is 'filtered' coconut water the same as 'microfiltered' coconut water? If not, there is no infringement.

If the prior art discloses 'filtered' coconut water then a patent to microfiltered coconut water cannot prevent the sale of this filtered coconut water because a patent cannot protect what has been done before. To the extent that the patent was ever granted covering filtered coconut water then it would not be new over the prior art and therefore be invalid.

A number of patent offices (such as the European Patent Office (EPO) or Japanese Patent Office) also allow challenges to be made to the grant of patent by a third party, usually in a short window of time after grant of the patent. Patent attorneys are thus often called upon to attack the intellectual property position of their clients' competitors, or defend the patents of their clients, and this usually involves a mixture of written argument and advocacy in person before the patent offices. The European Patent Office hearings take place in Munich, Berlin or The Hague.

Patents may also be litigated in national courts, either by the patent owner to prevent patent infringement or by a potential infringer trying to invalidate the patent and clear a route to market. In the United Kingdom this action is usually the preserve of solicitors and barristers. The patent attorney will probably play a supporting role here. However, the future may see a more direct role for patent attorneys in patent litigation and I will describe this in a little more detail later.

A patent attorney must also be a trusted commercial adviser. All patent attorneys are expected to be able to do the day job – that is, drafting, patent prosecution to get to a granted patent and infringement analysis. The key to really helping your client is to understand their business and to advise them not only on obtaining patents and other intellectual property (IP) but also on the use of their intellectual property in obtaining a commercial advantage. Indeed, sometimes the 'non-use' of patents can also be a commercial strategy, such as a decision by some pharmaceutical companies not to enforce patents on certain medicines in particular countries, for reasons of corporate responsibility and from a public relations perspective.

QUALIFICATION AND EXAMS

The day job may thus involve meeting inventors, drafting patent applications, reading prior art scientific documents, amending patents and arguing with the patent office examiners to get allowable patent claims.

Drafting patent applications requires a degree of precision and care. It also requires imagination and a good scientific background. Prosecution of patent applications requires a good legal and scientific understanding and the ability to win an argument in writing or on the phone. These core skills of the patent attorney are thus tested during the qualification process. If you don't like exams, then the patent profession is probably not for you.

In order to become a UK patent attorney it is necessary to have a first degree in a scientific subject. You will then need to take a range of intermediate exams followed by four final examination papers. The intermediate exams are designed to give scientists an introduction to basic UK law and then over each of the areas of intellectual property, namely trademarks, copyright, design protection, competition law and patent law. The four finals examinations are a more practical test of the disciplines of drafting, amendment, UK patent law and finally an assessment of both infringement and validity of a patent.

For those working in Europe it is also necessary to qualify as a European Patent Attorney. Once again, there is a prequalifying exam after which there are four finals papers. These are designed to test European law, drafting, amendment and EPO opposition practice, the latter being the post-grant attack on a granted patent before the European Patent Office.

It generally takes at least four years to pass all of these examinations, not least because the EPO will only allow the finals exams to be taken after three years in the profession and the exams are held only once a year.

There are courses in intellectual property law that can provide an exemption from the intermediate UK examinations. Probably best known is the Master's course in intellectual property law run by Queen Mary University of London. This is a one-year course, but there are others.

It is not necessary to have taken any intellectual property courses before applying for a job in the profession. Many London-based employers will send their new recruits to a shorter, three-month Queen Mary 'certificate' in intellectual property course during the first year or so of their employment. However, taking a course in intellectual property can demonstrate a commitment to changing career.

GETTING INTO THE PROFESSION

Getting into the profession is not so easy. There are only around 1,500 patent attorneys in the United Kingdom and therefore not a huge number of potential employers. Patent attorneys are not often represented at the 'milk round' and recruitment often happens at random only when a vacancy arises.

Initially you will want to consider whether you would like to train in industry (also referred to as in-house) or private practice. The majority of the private practice firms are in London where there is a good training environment.

Industry and private practice offer different opportunities. I initially took a job in a patent attorney private practice in London and once qualified I moved to work in-house at GlaxoSmithKline (GSK). For the last 10 years I've been working back in private practice but within a patent attorney practice which is a part of a London law firm, Olswang LLP. I am therefore able to compare these three different options. Industry offers the chance to be completely integrated with the scientific and commercial strategy of the business. In private practice an attorney may not always have the opportunity to understand the client's business to quite the same degree although, as I have said earlier, that is what a good attorney should look to do. Private practice can, however, provide a greater degree of variety with a range of different clients who have different legal, technical and commercial needs. Private practice might have the edge in terms of providing a training environment because some in-house roles can place significant demands on attorney time for advice related to the running of the business that may not be always be helpful for training. This has to be balanced with the greater commercial training which an in-house role provides. Personally I decided that I wanted to see both in-house and private practice options.

Whichever route you take, there will no doubt be at least two interviews for any job. Interviews usually test some of the key skills needed for a patent attorney. Often this involves asking for a written description of a well-known object – for example, to see if the candidate has good written language skills and can identify the essential components of an invention without including the inessential features. For example, if one were asked at an interview to define the essential features of a table then having four legs would not be critical. Would legs *underneath* the table be critical? Not if you were to suspend the table from the ceiling ... always assuming that something suspended from the ceiling could be considered to be a 'table' (you can see where all of this is going).

There is no doubt that having a good academic track record is very important. There are a lot of exams to take and an employer will want to see that you are likely to be able to pass those exams.

As an employer it is sometimes difficult to identify individuals who will take to the change of profession from bench to office. I've worked with a number of individuals who, whilst extremely capable, have decided that the patent profession is not for them. It is sometimes hard to predict how well the transition from the laboratory bench to an office environment will work. An office environment is not for everyone.

Any employer will also need to be convinced that you really do have an interest in intellectual property. I have not yet seen a candidate who has themselves written and filed a patent application but I would probably be impressed if anyone had gone to the effort of trying to go through the patenting process themselves using the guidance on the patent office website, www.gov.uk/topic/intellectual-property/patents.

Before you apply make sure you do your research on the profession. Have something to say about intellectual property and why it interests you. Be sure in your own mind that you want to move away from laboratory science. Be aware that it is an office job. Also bear in mind that you will need to develop a good degree of legal understanding. Initially, your value will be as a scientific adviser to more senior patent attorneys who may not have the same technical experience that you have developed in the laboratory or university. Techniques and methodologies move on and it is extremely helpful to work with individuals who have actually carried out techniques or studied them in detail as a particular area of science has evolved. As you become more senior the importance of understanding the law increases as this is essential for effective written argumentation and advocacy before the various patent offices. Ultimately, a patent is a legal document providing a monopoly position. That patent can be used to prevent a third party from competing with your clients in the market so it needs to stand up to both legal and scientific scrutiny.

Some patent attorneys choose to focus their careers at the scientific end of the patenting process. Others move away from science almost completely and spend their time on licensing and commercial activities. There is a wide range of opportunity within the profession and, moreover, as a qualified European Patent Attorney you can work from within any European country.

REWARDS

We all want to do a job that is intellectually rewarding and stimulating. Each patent brings a new potential invention, new technology and different legal issues. The combination of new science, creative inventors and a commercial relevance to the work means that no day is ever dull.

In terms of salary, trainees in London currently start at approximately £25,000–30,000 a year, progressing to approximately £60,000–70,000 a year on dual qualification. Within private practice in London, the upper end of the non-partner band can be more than £100,000 a year with partner pay in excess of that.

COMMERCIAL CONTEXT

Many European patent attorney firms have a significant quantity of work that comes in from, for example, the United States, China and Japan. Patent attorneys in those countries need to use a qualified European attorney in order to obtain European patent protection and likewise attorneys in Europe need to use their counterparts abroad to obtain protection in non-European countries. Because the instructions into Europe therefore come from an overseas attorney firm, and not from the client directly, there is often no indication of what the client ultimately needs to achieve.

In my view, it is absolutely essential to understand your client's business and what they are trying to achieve with their intellectual property. There is no real point in having a pile of patents and patent applications, which are expensive things to prepare, file and maintain if you do not know what you are going to use them for.

Anyone entering the profession should do some reading and thinking about how IP is used commercially. Some interesting questions that any new applicant into the profession might want to consider include:

- Does the patent system gives enough protection for the investment needed to develop a new drug? Or too much?
- What is the business model of generic companies in the pharmaceutical space?
- Is there a difference between the IP strategy of a technology company and a drug company? If so, why?

- Has there been any change in IP strategy of technology companies since the Samsung and Apple smart phone wars?
- What is a patent 'troll' or 'non-practising entity' (NPE)? Is a university one of these?
- What impact will the new European unitary patent and unified patent court have on litigation behaviour in Europe?

These are all potentially quite complex questions but a headline understanding of the different types of strategic use of IP will certainly give a very favourable impression to any interviewer.

I was once told by the head of an in-house IP department that he regarded his team as a profit centre rather than a cost centre. This encapsulates the whole point of what attorneys are trying to achieve for our clients by using patents and other forms of intellectual property to generate value. For a start-up the patent applications and patents owned by the company may indeed be the main asset of the company.

SOME CASE STUDIES

I thought it would be helpful to give five examples of pieces of work that have been particularly interesting over my career and which illustrate the breadth of the job.

1. As mentioned earlier, I was involved in obtaining a patent for microfiltered coconut milk. The follow-on is that I was contacted by a London-based Caribbean radio station asking whether I would do an interview. They wanted to understand why it was acceptable to obtain a patent on coconut milk given that this has been known for hundreds of years. As mentioned earlier in the chapter, the point here was that the patent was not for coconut milk itself. That would not have been possible because coconut milk was known and not new. The patent was granted to a particular form of purified coconut milk which was new. Nevertheless, this highlights that patents have the potential to generate some public concern.

2. I opted not to do that particular interview although a few years ago I did do a television interview for BBC Worldwide providing a comment on a decision made by the Indian Supreme Court regarding the patentability of the Novartis drug Glivec® (and I should say now that I was not involved in the case or product in any way). The Supreme Court in India had decided that no

patent could be granted. I found out shortly before the live television interview that a representative from Médecins Sans Frontières had also been invited to join the interview. It became clear that this could turn into a discussion around whether the patent system is 'bad' and prevents access to medicines for needy patients. This is a very interesting topic in its own right and pharmaceutical companies may even employ specialists to advise on this 'access to medicines' area. Careful wording on the day was needed.

More recently I have had two European Patent Office (EPO) opposition cases to argue, both interesting for very different reasons.

3.   The first case concerned a patent granted on an improved method for identifying embryos for use in *in vitro* fertilisation (IVF) treatments. After grant the patent was opposed and the EPO – of its own motion – raised an objection that the patent they had granted earlier was invalid because it covered an immoral process, namely the industrial or commercial use of an embryo. If an invention is immoral it cannot be patented in Europe under the European Patent Convention. In the patent in question the technology involved observation of embryos using time-lapse microscopy and, based on certain observable parameters, embryos were selected for implantation. Ultimately the EPO Opposition Division decided that there was no lack of morality. However, it was necessary to provide detailed argumentation to explain exactly why this was the case. As scientists originally, we generally don't have a background or training in morality so this needed some special preparation.

4.   The second case concerned patents for the production of transgenic mice with partly human immune systems. My client in this case had been sued by an American pharmaceutical company that was also making and selling transgenic mice.

At the same time as the litigation was proceeding in the UK High Court we were trying to revoke the patent at the European Patent Office. Therefore there were parallel proceedings before the EPO and the UK court, both directed to the same patent. In the European Patent Office the only issue is whether or not the patent is valid. In the UK court the issue was not only whether the patent was valid but also whether it was infringed. Therefore a close degree of co-operation was required between patent attorneys, litigators and barristers.

Here is one of the claims that was granted in EP1360287[2] – a slight contrast from the coconut milk:

A method of modifying an endogenous immunoglobulin variable region gene locus in an isolated mouse embryonic stem (ES) cell by an in situ replacement of the endogenous locus with an orthologous human gene locus or by an in situ replacement of one or more V and J, or V, D, and J gene segments of the endogenous locus with orthologous human V and J, or V, D and J gene segments, said method comprising:

a) obtaining a large cloned genomic fragment greater than 20kb containing orthologous human V and J, or V, D, and J gene segments;

b) using bacterial homologous recombination to genetically modify the cloned genomic fragment of (a) to create a large targeting vector for use in a mouse ES cell (LTVEC);

c) introducing the LTVEC of (b) into a mouse ES cell to replace said endogenous immunoglobulin variable gene locus or said one or more V and J, or V, D, and J segments thereof in situ with the orthologous human gene locus or the orthologous human V and J, or V, D and J gene segments; and

d) using a quantitative assay to detect modification of allele (MOA) in the mouse ES cell of (c) to identify a mouse ES cell in which said endogenous immunoglobulin variable region gene locus or said one or more V and J, or V, D and J segments thereof have been replaced in situ with the orthologous human gene locus or the orthologous human V and J, or V, D and J gene segments.

This claim gives you a real-life example of a technology area that has seen recent litigation, and what such patent claims can look like.

5. Finally, whilst with GSK I worked on their cervical cancer vaccine Cervarix®. Cervical cancer can be caused by human papilloma virus (HPV) infection, and HPV infection can also cause genital warts in men and women. There are more than 100 types of the HPV virus, and two different companies were in competition to reach the market. GlaxoSmithKline was pursuing a vaccine with HPV types 16 and 18 specifically targeting cervical cancer. Merck's vaccine comprised not only HPV types 16 and 18 but also types 6 and 11 which provide protection against genital

---

[2] www.gov.uk/government/uploads/system/uploads/attachment_data/file/426648/ EP1360287_-_annex.pdf

warts. The two products also had different adjuvants, which are generic immune stimulants shared by other vaccines.

This product and project were particularly interesting for many reasons. First, the product was projected to be a big seller. Clinical trial results showed that there was a high likelihood of preventing a significant proportion of cervical cancer. The vaccine is now made available routinely as part of adolescent vaccination schedules. So we couldn't afford to get the IP strategy wrong – assuming all went to plan commercially.

Second, the two sides followed different strategies to promote their product to market. Was it commercially helpful for Merck to have the additional protection against genital warts provided by HPV 6 and 11? Would the different adjuvant components result in a difference in cervical cancer protection? Which strategy would succeed?

Third, did both parties have freedom to operate with respect to one another's patent estates? In other words, did Merck have intellectual property that would block the sale of GSK's product, or vice versa? Ultimately the two parties came to an agreement to cross-license their IP to ensure that both would be able to sell the vaccine.

Finally, there are probably many times when a patent attorney might become an inventor as our job is to make suggestions about applications of the technology for new uses and suggest avenues to explore. Patent attorneys get to know some technical areas in a lot of detail as we read the publications of all of the groups in the field. Inevitably ideas come to mind that feed into the drafting of the patent. And so within the GSK Cervarix® portfolio there is a patent with my name on it as an inventor – EP1758609![3]

CONCLUSION

These examples hopefully highlight that the profession allows us to be involved in, and advise on, an enormous range of different topics, such as considerations of morality, working with inventions that revolutionise global healthcare, dealing with the licensing and cross-licensing negotiations, contributing to scientific discussions to ensure maximum benefit for your client and ensuring joined-up patent office and High Court strategies.

Given my scientific background I have focused on the life science part of the patent profession but there are equally interesting challenges

---

[3] https://docs.google.com/viewer?url=patentimages.storage.googleapis.com/pdfs/74469c25d6c1e528d867/EP1758609B1.pdf

in the high-tech area. A mobile phone will have components that are protected by hundreds or even thousands of different patents. This is completely different from the situation with drugs which may be protected by one or only a few patents. Each technology area requires different thinking and has different issues, and each company will require a tailor-made strategy to help it succeed.

If you decide to go for it, then good luck! I don't think you will regret it.

REFERENCES

1. Patent law: Finding a balance – Scientists who decide to pursue a legal career can enjoy fresh challenges while staying connected to the research world, *Nature* 511, 621–623, (2014), www.nature.com/naturejobs/science/articles/ 10.1038/nj7511-621a

11
_____

From Molecular Biology to GMO Regulation and Policy

Already in high school it was clear to me that I would become a scientist as I thoroughly enjoyed all mathematics and science courses, be they biology, physics or chemistry. Another of my characteristics is that I like working with and for people. Hence, as a young adult, my career choice was straightforward and logical: I would become a medical doctor.

During my last year in high school when I was 18 years old, I had a sudden, and for my environment quite unexpected, change of mind. During the University of Leuven (Belgium) Open days, I visited – just out of curiosity – the faculty of bioscience engineering (former agricultural engineering) – and I was hooked. I loved the atmosphere and options this discipline provided. I learnt that with this degree one could become a scientist developing medicines, a conservationist protecting the Amazonian rainforest, an agricultural livestock advisor, a developer of plant protection products, a soil scientist working with African farmers – the list was endless. And best of all, the course would start with a more general education focussed on all science disciplines. This was good for me as I could never decide which scientific discipline I actually preferred.

The bioscience engineering program, including Bachelor's and Master's degrees, takes five years in total, and I must say it did not disappoint. Not once have I regretted my decision for this study. After two years of more general courses I started to develop a keen interest in genetics and biotechnology. I was fascinated by how the genetic code of organisms can be engineered to society's benefit and all the wide

Successful Careers beyond the Lab, ed. David Bennett and Richard Jennings.
Published by Cambridge University Press. © Cambridge University Press 2017.

applications it entailed. I was particularly interested in the use of the technology in agriculture as I could clearly see how it can help farmers in developing countries by developing crops with, for instance, increased drought tolerance or nutritional benefits. Hence I decided to major in agricultural biotechnology.

I spent the last year of my Master's degree studies at the Centre of Microbial and Plant Genetics working on my thesis characterizing the role of plant defensins in the model plant for genetic research, *Arabidopsis thaliana* (actually a weed). Defensins are small proteins, also called peptides, that play a role in plants' defense system against plant diseases. Upon graduation there was still plenty of research to be done and I managed to receive a scholarship to pursue a PhD and secure funding for four years of research at the same lab.

I spent four amazing years in the lab. Every day was different: transforming yeasts, bacteria or plants, doing plant disease assays, purifying proteins and so forth. In our lab, PhD students had to do all the experimental work themselves which allowed me to learn many practical skills, develop and adapt scientific protocols, define the research strategy and so on. I was supported by a wonderful group of colleagues with whom I could celebrate successes but who also offered support if experiments did not work out as planned. This was important because, let's be honest, scientific research is often trial and error, and such help was invaluable for keeping up my dedication and motivation to finish my PhD successfully.

I must say that in the last stretch towards finalizing my PhD manuscript, something started to 'itch'. I still had the image of the African farmer in my head and how agricultural biotechnology could help him or her. However, was I really contributing to this? I had no doubt the research our laboratory was conducting was extremely useful but I started to feel that I personally had to do something different, not behind the doors of a lab but closer to reality in order to be satisfied. And as much as I liked working with my wonderful colleagues, I increasingly felt I was missing contact with the outside world and not using and developing my social skills. When the question came if I wanted to pursue a post-doc, it was very clear to me. I had enjoyed the last years tremendously – I had learnt so much and there were still plenty of open research questions that I would love to find answers to – but I knew I had to do something different.

I had no clue about the next step in my career which was exciting and frightening at the same time. My husband and I both have an adventurous spirit and the fact that we both had no obligations at home prompted us to put all our (limited) possessions in storage, buy a four-wheel-drive car and drive through Africa. We spent almost one year in the bush – camping, meeting people, enjoying nature and exploring the most beautiful continent on earth. These months convinced me even more that returning to the academic world was not a good option for me.

Back in Brussels, the job hunt started. This was easier said than done. We came back at the time of the full economic recession and I had no idea what a PhD in biotechnology could do besides academic research. I talked to people with a similar background who were working in industry or teaching, but the majority of my contacts had stayed in and preferred the academic world and did not really understand my need do to something else.

I have sent tons of motivation letters and CVs and filled in dozens of application forms for a variety of positions. It was a frustrating process as I still had no clear idea what I could do and many of the applications seemed to get lost in cyberspace when submitted through an automated form on large companies' websites. I mainly applied for jobs in industry as I thought industry research would be more practically and commercially driven. Considering my background and interests, I of course preferred to work in the agricultural biotechnology sector. However, this industry has only six big players with research facilities mainly based overseas which made it even more challenging to secure such a position. Hence, I also applied for jobs in the pharmaceutical sector and I even considered the option of training myself to become an intellectual property lawyer for scientific inventions.

Coincidently, I stumbled across a vacancy for a position in regulatory affairs for the agricultural biotechnology sector at EuropaBio, the European trade association for bio-industries. I had to do some internet research to learn what this organization was doing and how trade associations work as these are aspects you don't learn at all in bioscience engineering training, and I grew more and more interested. I learnt this organization is mainly involved in promoting biotechnology innovations in Europe by informing stakeholders and creating awareness of the benefits the technology can offer. The association works in three pillars: industrial biotechnology, healthcare biotechnology and agricultural biotechnology. This particular vacancy in the agricultural biotechnology team entailed collaborating with the member companies to discuss mainly technical issues related to risk assessment of genetically modified organisms (GMOs) and, in particular, crops in the European Union (EU). At EuropaBio they were looking for someone who actually understands the science behind the technology. For me this job ticked all the boxes. I couldn't be closer to the commercial reality as it actually involved products pending authorization in the EU and I would have the chance to work with many different stakeholders, develop my social skills and learn something new. I was also excited to be able to contribute to the promotion of this exciting but unfortunately controversial technology in which, given my background, I firmly believed.

Having worked at EuropaBio for three and a half years now, I can indeed confirm that the job couldn't be more different than working in a lab and doing research. I spend most of my time coordinating technical working groups consisting of industry experts dealing with GMO risk assessment requirements. At the same time I am liaising with EU authorities such as the European Commission and the European Food Safety Authority or Member State experts. An interesting aspect of this job is that I also have the chance to work with different stakeholders who have an interest in the issue such as farmers, academics, traders, exporting countries and other industry associations. As you can imagine, every day on the job is different and it never gets boring. To me, the biggest advantage of this job is that it provided me with insight in the working of EU institutions and enabled me to see the bigger picture of how scientific innovation translates into products ready for the market.

On this note, I would like to highlight the importance of understanding this bigger picture and I regret that this aspect is often ignored in scientific faculties at universities. I do indeed understand that their main goal is to train scientists and develop scientific excellence but I am convinced it would be useful for all future graduates to get a better understanding of the political decision-making process and commercial reality of scientific and technological innovations. This would also help scientists to pursue careers related to their field but not in scientific research *per se*.

To conclude, when talking to young researchers who are unsure about the next step in their career and when they consider a career outside the lab, I can only advise to be open-minded. There are plenty of opportunities that you cannot even imagine. I would advise analyzing your own skills and defining your assets and possible added value, and just start applying for jobs that could fit your profile. Job interviews will help you in better understanding what different jobs actually entail and if a certain position would be suitable for you. In case, after reading my testimony, you feel a job in regulatory or public affairs would be something for you, it can be helpful to follow training or a course on EU policy making and to attend conferences and workshops related to the topic you are interested in for networking purposes and in order to identify the most important players in your domain.

No matter how you want to plan your career, I believe it is impossible to predict what your exact career path will look like. It is all about the opportunities and people that cross your path. I personally have no idea of what I will be doing in five years. And it is actually exactly this that I find the most exciting!

12

Rebel with a Cause?
From Physics to Activism

I have had what I think is an unusually varied career after leaving academia. Although, in writing this chapter, I saw some connections that I hadn't seen previously. I hope that some lessons which I draw from my experience will prove useful to others.

Over the years I have met many other people engaged happily in careers diverging dramatically from their starting point in science or physics in particular. I have tried to draw on this also in an effort hopefully to give the sort of advice that I might have benefitted from myself many years ago.

I have also tried to summarise my motivations, as knowing that what you want to do and like doing seems to be an essential starting point for developing a successful career. For a long time I didn't know what I wanted to do and I had no idea about how to develop a career. I also realise, looking back, that my skill set, abilities and motivations developed dramatically over the years either leading to or as a result of new work and life experiences. Nevertheless, I always found that having an expertise in physics was surprisingly useful in an unexpectedly wide range of areas.

MY CAREER MOVES IN BRIEF

My first career was as a research scientist in physics (my first degree) at Imperial College London (ICL). After completing my PhD (in the Chemistry Department, 1973–1976), I worked for a year as a programmer before securing a two-year contract in the Chemical Engineering

Successful Careers beyond the Lab, ed. David Bennett and Richard Jennings.
Published by Cambridge University Press. © Cambridge University Press 2017.

133

Department. Finally, in 1980 I was offered a tenured post as a research officer in the Physics Department. This post involved working with several other departments including Chemistry, Chemical Engineering and Physics as well as Metallurgy.

From this conventional, if multi-disciplinary, starting point, my subsequent career move doesn't appear to make any sense. My next job, in 1986, was a highly political one in local government. But the explanation lay in my scientific work outside the mainstream as an anti–nuclear weapon activist and author, and also with a growing dissatisfaction with the direction, funding and priorities of my paid scientific career. My next major career move, in 1990, as an environment coordinator in local government, was a completely new kind of role as an internal change agent. It had important political dimensions working with local and national groups. This opportunity was made possible by my previous career moves and brought together for the first time a new range of skills that I had acquired. This post then evolved, from around 2000, into heading some major environmental programmes.

Finally, as a result of the financial collapse of 2008, in 2011 I was offered early retirement from local government and, 25 years after leaving university life, I returned briefly to academia as an honorary professor (2012–2014). I also took on the role of director of a medium-sized energy company.

A constant, over all these years since my first involvement with the anti-nuclear peace movement of the 1980s, was my close voluntary involvement with Scientists Against Nuclear Arms which eventually merged into Scientists for Global Responsibility with broader aims of peace, social justice and environmental sustainability. I also continue to write a wide range of articles and books and undertake research in these areas.

BEGINNINGS

From a very early age I always wanted to know how the world worked. I recall observing small insects and birds very closely as a small child and having a keen interest in measuring and sorting things. I enjoyed reading and throughout my early life I read everything and anything.

Early schooling focussed on the three R's (reading, writing and arithmetic); I recall finding the little that was talked about science fascinating. Fortunately for me, my father, an electrical and mechanical engineer, was able to explain mathematics and answer most of my technical questions. At secondary school I found science and especially physics particularly interesting. I also spent a lot of time drawing and designing buildings.

Physics seemed to explain why the physical world was how it was. It included formulae which enabled one to predict how objects would fly through the air, how electrical motors worked and the mysteries of magnetism and gravity. Whereas most of my classmates thought our first physics teacher extremely boring, I was enthralled by the subject.

At this point I was decidedly science focussed. All the subjects I enjoyed had a scientific or discovery element. Geography, for example, told you how to get to places – many of which were unbelievably exotic. Geology explained how rocks and fossils formed and provided a deep understanding of the earth's structure and long life. Mathematics enabled the physics laws to turn into actual numbers such as speeds and distances. I studied technical drawing which built on my liking for drawing. I also had an aptitude for practical activities and enjoyed woodwork and metalwork. I did take some arts subjects at Ordinary level – English language and literature and French – but for me at this time the arts seemed frothy and unimportant. At Advanced level I took maths, physics and technical drawing. I also took a liberal studies course in philosophy which I found extremely interesting.

Being fascinated by science fiction and astronomy, I applied to take either astrophysics or straight physics and was offered places at six universities. Applying to go to university was not a considered decision. It was simply that I was probably good enough to do it, it sounded better than trying to get a job when I had no idea what to do and there were 100% grants to go. The career advice I received was laughably poor. One teacher thought that it would be a good idea for me to join the army as national service had been the making of him!

A professor at my chosen university, Queen Elizabeth College in Kensington, London, advised me that there were very few careers in astronomy and that the physics course would give me more options. So I chose physics and gained an honours degree. In retrospect this was both good and poor advice: good in that doing mainstream physics was a positive choice but poor in the sense that it put me off thinking of going into astronomy.

My first year at university had a major social impact on me. It was the early 1970s and London was swinging even more than it ever had done in the 1960s. I found the first year easy and achieved good results. I met people from many different walks of life and different parts of the United Kingdom. Many studied arts subjects that I knew nothing about. In my second year, I decided that I should educate myself about arts and literature. So, having both a good university library as a resource and the well-stocked Kensington library just down the road, I spent a large amount of time reading a wide range of English and translated foreign literature and philosophy. This opened my eyes to a whole new interesting world. I therefore scraped through my second-year exams and was advised that I was heading for a Third Class degree or, if I worked really hard, a Lower Second. I remember talking to friends and agreeing that a Third would not be a good outcome, so in my third year I applied myself to physics, but I now chose my topics carefully, favouring those which I was most interested in, and I also spent time going through past examination papers.

I don't remember getting any career advice. Expecting a Lower Second if I was lucky, I simply applied for jobs with firms that were recruiting. These were largely in the electronics and military sectors, for example with The General Electric Company (GEC) or Marconi. I did apply to Schlumberger, a somewhat notorious French oil exploration company, known for taking an unusual approach to recruitment and who paid enormous salaries, but was not successful. There must have been a much better range of jobs that I could have applied for but, in retrospect, I think that I really had no idea. I recall that some people applied to work for companies such as Mars but I had no idea what such a job would entail and I wanted to 'do' science of some kind.

I was not at all convinced about working for these companies. I remember being rather dubious about working on a bomb but thinking that an aircraft-based scanning radar might be OK. But the main impression I gained at the time was that I would be working in large anonymous buildings in boring parts of the United Kingdom (e.g. the London suburbs or Thames estuary) doing really boring things (e.g. fast Fourier real time processing of radar signals) and I didn't feel at all inspired by the jobs on offer. In some cases the secrecy surrounding the jobs was so extreme that interviewers would not show me the laboratory. I found this very off-putting. I also found that the organisational culture was to question having a pure science degree; often recruiters seemed to want either an engineer of some kind or were seeking people with the right range of personal attributes such as the ability to get on with people and communicate. I realised that if you wanted to do 'science' you would be seen as a backroom person and have a limited career but to be really successful you needed to have the teamwork and communication skills. One's degree – I was told – was almost irrelevant!

I was offered a couple of jobs pending my degree results. To my amazement, I secured an Upper Second (I had to read the letter several times). So the very day that the results arrived I decided to see if I could take a different path by studying for a PhD. The efforts of my final year had paid off! I phoned up several university departments choosing from a list of those who had FRSs[1] as heads of department!

I was offered places at Culham in Oxfordshire (in fusion power) and Imperial College London (in cosmic rays or surface science). These were important choices.

I wasn't convinced that anything would come of the fusion power research (laser-induced fusion) or research using a beam line. The cosmic ray research was based in Manchester (e.g. around Jodrell Bank radio-telescope). I plumped for surface science using a field ion microscope in the chemistry department at Imperial College. There were two main reasons: the microscopy with atomic resolution was interesting and understandable, and the location meant staying in London where I enjoyed living. It also amused me to do a PhD in a chemistry department when I didn't even have an Ordinary level in the subject.

In retrospect, perhaps I should have chosen the cosmic ray research. I say this now looking back as I realise that researching the wider universe was more in line with my primary interests than narrowing my focus. Also, the choice of surface science ultimately took me into the world of solid state physics and what I later felt was a dead end for me. At the time, of course, there was no way of knowing that this would be the case.

It will have become very apparent by now that I had no life plan – no sense of where I wanted to go or what I wanted to do. I recall being asked in one of my interviews where I saw myself in five years' time. I had no idea.

In fact, I still held the same views that I had as a child. I wanted to understand how the world worked and now by doing a PhD I thought that I might contribute to the sum of knowledge. I saw knowledge as something to be sought for its own sake. I fiercely believed in a concept of academic freedom – freedom to think what you thought was right and to do research without necessarily an end goal. Nevertheless, I was interested in applying my work to something useful if possible. My chosen PhD might contribute to the development of cheaper or better catalysts – for example, for food processing or for car exhaust purification.

In a similar way as in my degree, where I effectively took a year off, I cannot say that I concentrated 100% on the work I was supposed

---

[1] Fellows of The Royal Society

to do. I recall spending a lot of time continuing my pursuit of reading arts and philosophy, and a growing appreciation of the arts and theatre – particularly alternative or radical theatre and ballet. I also spent time exploring the many local museums in London such as the Victoria and Albert, Science, Natural History and Geology museums.

Mine was an experimental field and results were the end result of many days, sometimes weeks, of very precise steps which involved great care and often an extremely steady hand. I also learned much more about computing and ran some very large (by that day's standards) programs that needed to run overnight on the University of London's Cray computers.

I still recall days when I secured new results. One such was atoms behaving oddly by not moving as expected along atomic channels but rather across them. This led to a great deal of interest in my field, a whole new line of experiments and even an article in the *New Scientist*.

Key Learning Point from My PhD

I was good at research and I really enjoyed writing up my PhD thesis. It felt good to be communicating something fundamental in science. I also found moments of sheer happiness when the experiments simply worked and I intuitively knew what to do next and was free to creatively explore and observe phenomena at the atomic scale. Suddenly I felt as though I had learned how to communicate scientific concepts. I was more self-confident.

I still had no idea about a career but, having used and written some very complicated computer programs to simulate atoms interacting on a surface, I decided to try my hand at becoming a programmer. I found the recruitment process very irritating as the fact that I had a PhD didn't seem to count for anything. I did also have a job offer to teach in a private school for a few days a week or as part of a team of tutors based in central London. I was advised that having been the captain of the university badminton team and involved in many activities together with a PhD made me a good choice for working in a public school. In retrospect, this might have been a good career move but the idea did not appeal as I didn't agree with the existence of such institutions because of their elitist nature, so I didn't take it up. I did, however, take a job as a programmer writing programmes in Basic, COBOL and various other languages for a whole range of applications from banking to industrial processes, pricing and stock control. This job was quite varied and meant working in several customer locations all across London. I enjoyed this side of things but gradually realised that, whilst I was quite good at writing software, ultimately I found it quite boring and repetitive. It was definitely not the career for me. I did, however, enjoy collaborating with people and I saw the banking, computing and commerce industries from the inside (Olivetti, IBM, Exxon, several banks and manufacturers).

Thus, once I had my viva and was awarded my PhD, I decided to apply for a two-year post-doctoral post which had come up back at Imperial College which was in Chemical Engineering. It also paid better than being a programmer.

Finally, I felt as though I had found what I wanted to do. During these two years I coordinated the writing of a large multi-disciplinary funding application with the Physics, Chemical Engineering and Chemistry Departments. Securing this funding led to my securing the post of research officer in the Physics Department. This was a tenured post – one of the last few like this. The year was 1980.

Up till then I had been largely the master of my own fate in research terms but now things began to change. The major technical opportunities offered up by thin films came to the fore. These had applications with the military and for energy generation (e.g. solar cells).

As is still the case, the military or military applications were prioritised and had the best chance of being funded. I had a dislike of working with military funding. The Cold War was at its height and a UK task force set off to liberate the Falkland Islands. I disagreed strongly with some colleagues' 'gung-ho' support of these military adventures. Around the same time there was an incident when one of our PhD students funded by BAE Systems gave their security officer all the home addresses of all the researchers and students in our group. At the time we had a Russian visitor as well as a Chinese academic. My view was that publicly funded work at a university should be open to all and that BAE had no business running illicit security checks. My complaint caused tensions.

Perhaps more importantly, the direction and funding of the group with a new professor gradually moved away from my primary areas of research interest – multi-disciplinary surface science. It became much more focused on application-driven technology such as infra-red detectors, light-emitting diodes (LEDs), etc. utilising thin films such as gallium arsenide. I was seen as a useful resource to build a semiconductor and thin-film clean room. Unfortunately for me, this area of research was too much like technology and implementation for me. I wanted to do something more fundamental.

A key learning point for me at Imperial College was how much I enjoyed collaborations between different scientific disciplines. I enjoyed organising cross-departmental seminars. I was not interested in going deep into a highly technologically driven area. In retrospect, the university life was quite narrow. This probably was my unconscious motivation for getting to know people at the Royal School of Art – examples being rare earth jewellery and robotic mannequins.

SCIENTISTS AGAINST NUCLEAR ARMS

In 1981, responding to the overwhelming threat of nuclear annihilation, Scientists Against Nuclear Arms (SANA) was formed. Small groups of concerned scientists met to discuss issues such as civil defence, the transfer of civil to military nuclear material, the probabilities involved in various war-fighting strategies and new weapons such as cruise missiles and the 'tactical' Pershing-II Weapon System. It was the height of the Cold War. Over the next few years SANA motivated several scientists to switch careers.

I joined a SANA working group formed to study the effects of a nuclear attack. We took a recently leaked report of a civil defence exercise involving an attack on the United Kingdom and London and decided to take a look in more detail at London. The idea was to write perhaps a four-page leaflet to be handed out at Underground railway stations. At the time the Thatcher government insisted that many people would survive a nuclear attack (as described in the UK government's 'Protect and Survive' public information leaflet) and there were a widespread and active civil defence organisation, a network of underground command bunkers, observation posts and volunteers across the United Kingdom.

I will never forget sitting in a small room on a sunny day with five colleagues drawing some initial impact zones on a tourist map of London – circles of various blast distances around the point of impact. They were unbelievably huge! Most of London was covered by them. What did this mean?

This initial analysis led to much more than a four-page leaflet. After studying detailed US information about the effects of nuclear weapons we then embarked upon an enormous task. We studied the types of housing in London and its distribution as well as the location of services such as water, firefighting and hospitals. We calculated radiation fallout plumes using weapon test data and estimated the protective capabilities of undamaged and damaged housing. This work turned into a very detailed, borough-by-borough estimate of the deaths and casualties which would arise from a realistic nuclear attack. The findings were very shocking, and in the process we realised that government figures were based on underestimates of many important factors or outdated models and that many assumptions about the ability of people to construct heavy or underground shelters were deeply misleading. We also read confidential 'Restricted' documents – essentially nuclear war planning guidance that had been written for the police, fire, military, local authorities and government officials who were supposed to run Britain from secret and hidden bunkers under blocks of flats or under civic buildings. These documents revealed a world of summary justice, military rule, emergency feeding and distribution of reserves. It was a chilling insight into a possible future world that would be nasty, brutish and probably short. We thought about the longer term. How could a population survive in the longer term after such an attack after food reserves had run out and with the breakdown of basic vital services – all of which we take for granted?

So, to cut a long story short, the five of us wrote a book. Published in 1982 by Oxford University Press, it was entitled *London after the Bomb: What a Nuclear Attack Really Means*. One publisher, having read a draft, called it 'political dynamite'. It showed clearly and factually the reality that huge numbers of people would die or be horribly injured in a nuclear attack and that there would be little help for those that survived, and that government advice was unrealistic and existed to distract from this uncomfortable political reality.

Writing this book was an enormous effort over a year. I coordinated the joint effort and dealt with the publishers on contractual and editorial detail. A key learning point for me here was that I discovered how good it felt to work as part of a small team with a common goal. I discovered that I was good at facilitating this process.

The book's publication propelled us into a new world of TV and radio interviews, the front page of *Time Out*, the London activities' weekly guide, and coverage in most of the broadsheets. This was followed by the Greater London Council (GLC) sending copies to every library in the United Kingdom, well attended talks across London – many in bunkers opened for the purpose – and coverage in numerous local newspapers in the Greater London area. The book was on the Top Ten best seller lists for at least a week and sales topped out at around 28,000 copies.

I now know that this is an enormous number for any book. At the time we thought that this was the new normal. Our editor at Oxford University Press came under severe pressure as the Press reeled from the coverage. We collaborated with a wide range of other anti-nuclear organisations and engaged in many debates – when they would turn up – with government politicians or civil defence advisors. Around the same time the Greenham Common Women's Peace Camp started up and there was an enormous civil movement opposing the deployment of US nuclear-tipped cruise missiles at bases across the United Kingdom. We literally thought that there was a very real possibility of a nuclear disaster. Now, much later, we know that this feeling was correct. There were several near misses that could have resulted in a nuclear holocaust arising from exercises that became too realistic, faulty radar components etc.

It is fair to say that my motivation for my scientific career was affected. Frankly this seemed a much better use of my analytical skills at this time of international danger and crisis. Some of my colleagues did not see it this way whilst many others did and I received more support overall than criticism. I nevertheless did continue my academic work despite its drift towards military applications and military funders.

In retrospect, I was developing a new career, albeit one that did not provide a liveable income. At the time I regularly received invitations to arms fairs and military-sponsored seminars costing hundreds, even thousands of pounds. There was clearly a massive gravy train for those promoting arms. Despite ridiculous allegations of 'Moscow gold' funding the Campaign for Nuclear Disarmament (CND), anti-nuclear talks were free and, if you were lucky, expenses for travel were paid for. Book royalties even from such a best seller were not something that one could live on – the book was a relatively cheap paperback, and royalties were split five ways.

This publication led to consultancy work for the Greater London Council (GLC), which commissioned GLAWARS – the Greater London Area War Risk Study. Around this time the first suspicions came out about the possibility of a nuclear 'winter' caused by intense high-altitude smoke from the detonation of a few hundred thermonuclear weapons blocking the sun and contaminating rainfall resulting in darkness at noon, drought and famine for several years. I spent quite a bit of time at the GLC. Councillor Simon Turney and others became close allies and we worked together on securing legal opinions for the various activities that the GLC wanted to do opposing the government and where the legality wasn't clear. The GLC was in a bitter fight with the Conservative government which decided to abolish it later in 1986 in what I saw as an act of political vandalism. Over the next year (1983) three of us wrote *Crisis Over Cruise*, a Penguin special that sold 10,000 copies. It was also published in Spanish as *[La] Crisis de los Euromisiles*.

I also wrote a chapter in a book about the aftermath of Chernobyl[2] and the 'Star Wars' anti–nuclear missile defence system.

I felt as though I had been propelled into some kind of Z-list celebrity status. I met eminent scientists, including many Nobel prize winners, and I helped to organise the London Nuclear Warfare Tribunal in 1985 (with five Nobel prize–winning judges). This eventually led to the first international ruling of the illegality of the use of nuclear weapons. I met many well-known actors, many of whom, to my amazement, had read the first book, which eventually fed into a production by the Royal Shakespeare Company (RSC) of a post-holocaust play *Level With Us* at The Barbican; at one time we even started writing a screenplay adaptation of it for the cinema. I advised many film-makers and other authors. Some of this material emerged as TV plays (e.g. *Edge of Darkness* by Troy Kennedy-Martin). I was collaborating with people in Palomares in Spain where the United States had inadvertently dropped a nuclear bomb which spread plutonium over a large area. I met many senior Russian and US generals, including the Russian generals who had commanded Russian forces in Afghanistan. I also met with NATO advisors and military at the command bunker in Mons in Belgium. I remember having heated arguments with both the NATO and Russian military.

The GLC was finally abolished in 1986 after extremely close votes in the Houses of Commons and of Lords. At the same time, the government not only insisted that all local government authorities should write civil defence plans for nuclear attack but that they should set up civil defence planning teams to do this. They would pay originally 75% of the salaries and costs. After a short period this funding was increased to 100%!

By now I had learned a lot about military strategies and attitudes. I had also collaborated with international lawyers on the topic of the laws of war, for example the Geneva Convention and legal issues relating to the powers of local government.

SOUTH YORKSHIRE (1986–1990)

Some clever politicians saw an opportunity to embarrass the government using their own money. In South Yorkshire the four local authorities – led by Sheffield – got together and agreed to set up a civil defence

---

[2] A catastrophic nuclear accident on 26 April 1986 in the reactor at the Chernobyl Nuclear Power Plant near Pripyat, then part of the Ukrainian Soviet Socialist Republic of the Soviet Union (USSR).

planning team consisting of 12 people. The idea was to write realistic civil defence plans which, being based on realistic scenarios, would show that such planning was in fact largely impossible. A truly Kafka-esque situation! I applied for the post on the team with Simon Turney. He was offered the director post and I the deputy director.

So my choice was whether to stay in London and stay as a research officer with a tenured post or to move to South Yorkshire – an area I did not know and in what was probably a somewhat uncertain longer-term future. Other factors were that house prices were now rising alarm-ingly – beyond my reasonable reach now that I had a wife and there was a baby on the way.

I did have an alternative choice. This was to move into a new research area – solar cells at Imperial College. In retrospect, this might also have been a good choice but it would have radically changed – and narrowed – my subsequent career choices. I was also fairly terminally disillusioned about working as an academic. At the time solar cell research was very poorly funded; the main funder was Greenpeace as the regular funders weren't yet prepared to jump into the industry. Today, years later, this area has secure funding and an international reputation.

At the time it seemed like a simple decision. Colleagues remarked that I made a brave (or foolhardy) choice. I moved to South Yorkshire. My wife was from Manchester so that made it seem a bit more like home perhaps (I wasn't aware of the Yorkshire/Lancaster rivalry!). But it was a major culture shock after London to move to a post-industrial blighted landscape of closed pits, huge factory sites reduced to piles of bricks and weeds awaiting gentrification, and high unemployment.

These four years were a lightning introduction to local govern-ment, to strong council leaders who held enormous power, to govern-ment departments and more civil servants – particularly the Home Office (HO) but also the Ministry of Agriculture, Fisheries and Food (MAFF) and agencies such as the police and emergency services. I learned how to manipulate a budget. As it was 100% HO-funded, this meant that the main objective was to inflate the budget as far as possible in advance of any efforts to reduce it via imposed cuts.

My job was to coordinate the writing of emergency plans for a nuclear attack. We had to follow detailed guidance from the HO. We wrote plans for emergency feeding, communications, law and order and many others. We wrote realistic plans. We were clear that these plans would be completely useless and ineffective in a nuclear attack. Yet the more crazy we thought we made the plans, the more the HO liked them! For a joke we inserted menu choices in our emergency feeding plans.

The HO judged that this was a good idea! Looking back on this episode, it is clear to me now that the HO civil servants probably didn't really care *what* the plans said. As good civil servants, the key issue for them was that plans had been written.

During this time I was able to develop my thinking about a whole area of nuclear war planning that had never really been imagined or simulated: the aftermath of a nuclear attack. After the major casualties and immense destruction and the breakdown of all the normal vital services, how could a society try to function? Would it be possible to restart some kind of society or civilisation?

Through thinking about this issue, I became knowledgeable about the atmosphere and most pollutants, about water supplies, energy resources and types of energy generation, health and medical services, as well as the availability of crops and their distributions. In short I learned an enormous amount about the environment. I sometimes referred to this as 'learning about the environment by dropping an imaginary bomb on it'. A key personal insight was to realise just how amazing the natural world and environment is, how we have taken it largely for granted and how vulnerable it now is.

During this period I wrote another book, *New Defence Strategies for the 1990's*. This was a detailed analysis of the East-West conflict across Europe and suggested that there could be an enormous 'peace dividend' to be had if we could de-escalate this conflict. In 1989 I was in Warsaw discussing these very issues with Polish peace activists when we heard the exciting news that the Berlin Wall had been breached.

The period of employment in South Yorkshire taught me a lot about what being a manager entailed and about the various unfortunate events that impact people's lives (illness, sudden death etc.), but ultimately I did not find the work satisfying. The fundamentals were flawed. The work did, however, lead to the government abandoning ideas of civil defence. This was a real political victory, but this success would mean that ultimately I would make myself redundant.

WEST YORKSHIRE (1990–2011)

The environment, protecting it and dealing with climate change had now risen up the political agenda. Across the United Kingdom, local authorities started recruiting for a new kind of worker – an environmental coordinator. Kirklees, in West Yorkshire, advertised the first post of this kind in the United Kingdom. The job specification described a person with a scientific background, knowledge of the political environment and experience working with non-governmental organisations (NGOs). This sounded very much like me! The authority wanted someone to work closely with the Leader of the Council, John (now Sir John) Harman, and to act as a kind of green guerrilla working within the organisation to change it from within.

I got the job. Some of the other applicants secured similar posts elsewhere in the United Kingdom and became close allies.

There were now ten to twenty such posts across the United Kingdom and a group of us held the very first Environment Coordinators' Conference in Huddersfield in 1991 – later named Agenda 21 from the 1992 Rio 'Earth' Summit. Around 80 people came from all across the United Kingdom.

The next phase was working not only at a United Kingdom level but internationally. I secured 2 million ECUs (the forerunner of the euro and equivalent to about £1.5 million) for a large EU-funded project called ISIS[3] with partners in Berlin, Copenhagen and Madeira. This project developed new ways of looking at traffic impacts using new data techniques such as Geographical Information Systems.

I was lucky initially to have the support of both the Leader of the Labour Council and senior executives, although the latter were often less than convinced. As political fortunes changed, the originally Labour Council moved through various political parties and coalitions – first Labour-Green, then Liberal-Green, then Conservative. Each party in turn supported the agenda strongly. This was mainly because I was able to make a strong case for creating local jobs, for supporting community enterprises and often for self-funding projects. For example, I thought up the concept of an energy- and water-saving loan fund that would recoup the outlay at a rate of 50% of the savings so both parties benefitted. Ultimately the fund would become self-sustaining. This idea has been copied across the United Kingdom and in other countries. I also came up with the idea of giving away low-energy lightbulbs to reduce carbon emissions – a plan ridiculed in the Daily Mail newspaper which said: 'and the environment coordinator said "let there be light" and there was light'. This idea was later regarded as the norm and then, even later, seen as ineffective as the big six energy companies gave so many free lightbulbs away that many ended up in cupboards unused.

The final phase of this work in Kirklees was to truly embed environmental thinking into the working of the Council. This took place

---

[3] Integrated System for Implementing Sustainability

from around 2000 through influencing key decision-making committees – for example, building a new sports centre, a new Council building and housing developments incorporating various forms of renewable energy. I was now Head of the Environment Unit with a staff of 20 people. The pinnacle project was an enormous home insulation scheme, Kirklees Warm Zone, which insulated around 55,000 homes free of charge and cost £10 million over three years (2007–2010). I was also working with regional government offices and their successors, regional authorities of various kinds. I stayed in this job for 21 years and was very happy and fulfilled doing it. We won several awards at UK and EU levels.

It was the ideal job for me because it gave me a lot of freedom to act and be creative, and I liked working with and ultimately managing a small department. I was able to put into practice what I considered flexible and humane ways by working with people's strengths rather than a command-and-control approach. I worked with small and large NGOs, nationally and internationally, and there was a large and growing budget to do good works. My scientific training still proved very useful, for example in discussing the energy or carbon footprint of new buildings or developments. I was able to develop some new approaches in this area.

Another positive factor was that the job wasn't static. It kept evolving so each period of five years was quite different to the previous period. This meant that I kept learning.

After the financial crash of 2008, by 2010, things started changing for the worse. This was the case right across local governments and it continues to this day.

This experience highlights the difficulty of being funded by what is essentially a system of finance that doesn't care about or understand the importance of the environment for literally our survival. As the bank loans crashed governments bailed them out whilst making huge cuts to the financing of the rest of the public sector. In my view this was a huge mistake that is causing, and will continue to cause, immense problems downstream for many years to come.

For my part, by 2011 I was ready to retire being only one year from being able to leave at 60 and I saw two opportunities after my departure. The first was that I was now a well-known expert on practical energy saving on a large, city scale and also on implementing large-scale renewable installations. I offered to support a project at the University of Leeds on a part-time basis. I did this for a year in the role of professor working one day a week. We produced several academic and more general papers studying the impacts of the work that I had done previously – proving that there were real, visible energy savings years after the event. We also researched how future work could be funded and discovered that, now that conventional investments had crashed, pension funds were seeking investments such as large energy saving or renewable schemes. The difficulty was to make it actually happen as the pension funds were extremely traditional in their approaches and slow to take on new ways of working.

Whilst I enjoyed the return to academia, it reminded me of the somewhat narrow basis for actually making anything happen and the continual seeking of next year's funding. Funding in academia is now mostly even worse than it had started to be when I left in 1986.

The second opportunity was to continue my work as a non-executive director of a medium-sized energy company – Yorkshire Energy Services (now rebranded YES Energy Solutions). This work, which occupies me roughly one day a week, has given me new insights into how to keep a business profitable and in business at all as government funds, subsidies and structures dramatically change. I have found this area of work very interesting and motivating because the fundamental principle is to reduce energy consumption through insulation, greater efficiency or renewable generation whilst recycling any profits back into the community. So there is a close fit with my principles and beliefs.

But I have omitted what I now consider my ongoing third career. During my employment in West Yorkshire I continued to write articles and publications with Scientists for Global Responsibility (SGR). Once mostly retired, I found myself in demand to revisit calculations about the effects of nuclear weapons. A new international movement had sprung up – the International Campaign to Abolish Nuclear weapons (ICAN). After decades of no nuclear disarmament, they were working with diplomats from several United Nations (UN) to reframe the debate in terms of the unacceptable humanitarian consequences of the use of nuclear weapons. In 2013, I became an expert advisor to a series of international conferences (in Oslo, then Nayarit, Mexico and Vienna) culminating in action at the UN to form a new working group supported by over 120 nations to negotiate a ban treaty to confer on nuclear weapons the same pariah and illegal status as chemical and biological weapons of mass destruction. A new generation needed someone who could run the numbers. I did this with the organisation called Article 36 which had previously worked with other groups to bring about the banning of land mines and personnel cluster munitions.[4] We calculated the impacts of one 100,000 tonne nuclear warhead on Manchester – a typical warhead on a typical developed country-sized city. I think that this is a vital new initiative which I continue to support along with SGR.

GUIDANCE FOR OTHERS?

During my varied career I have met and know many people in varied roles who also started out in science – often in physics – but have ended up working in the environmental field or in political lobbying or campaigning. Whilst I cannot say that physics as such is the key skill, I think that the subject does teach you a key combination of a very high level of numeracy, the ability to manipulate data and equations and (hopefully!) to think systematically.

One key common thread between my experiences and these people is that we all decided to work on something that we really cared about and which we thought might make a difference of some kind. For example, a geologist may realise that his skills could help with detecting clandestine atomic bomb testing or a former quantum gravity specialist who now works on analysing carbon reduction pathways. Some had started their own businesses – for example, in solar energy and providing lighting to those off the electric grid in Africa or India.

Another common thread is that we all realised that 'pure' science wasn't coming up with the answers or actions that we thought really mattered. The real crucial world problems of today are ecological, not purely scientific. We understand enough about our world and we have known since the oil crisis in 1972 and the first Club of Rome report, 'Limits to Growth' that we are destroying our home, our planet [1].

Since the 1990s – perhaps even before – we have known what to do about it: reduce high-carbon energy emissions and overconsumption by moving swiftly to renewable energy sources and much better designed houses, vehicles and appliances. This requires a truly global-scale investment programme which makes sense in economic and ecological terms but which does not satisfy several very powerful vested interests. I have come to the view that this is because of the world leaders' fundamental misunderstanding about how the world really works in an ecological sense. Although many large corporations have asked for much stronger carbon emission restrictions, politicians have

---

[4] Article 36 – www.article36.org/

refused to give them! Again physics in my view does offer some key insights. The first is thermodynamics and entropy. You understand implicitly that the 'economy' doesn't describe reality, only a part of it. The data used every day to describe the economy once you look at it closely is very basic and fundamentally flawed. Classical economics omits vital so-called externalities yet is quoted as if it is reality. 'Externalities' is the jargon term for impacts that conventional economics does not take into account. Typically these are the costs (and impacts) of extracting materials (or growing crops) in the first place and of disposing them back to the environment after they are used – this means waste disposal and what happens to airborne pollutants in the atmosphere. Conventional economics assumes that the 'world' consists of three main things under a general heading of consumption: society (people), services and goods. If you take all these things together, extraction, consumption and disposal are deemed to make up our ecology or our environment. However, if the real costs of raw materials and waste disposal are ignored (the externalities), the remainder – consumption – is about three-fifths of what is really going on. In one sentence, first coined by Mike Nickerson in the 1990s, 'The economy is three-fifths of ecology' [2]. I also think that our obsessions with fighting wars and continuing cycles of violence, combined with the existing pressures caused by climate change–caused droughts, are a major part of the problem.

I now realise, as I would not have understood when I was, say, twenty, that a degree in history could equally well give you the analytical skills – and these probably to a greater degree in terms of human behaviour – but physics enables a person to understand numerical data and evidence in a mathematical way that many people are simply unable to. When I returned to university as a professor in the environmental field I found that I was able to analyse some key data in a way which experienced users of statistical packages could not. But having the analytical skills alone doesn't take you very far. These skills will enable you to be a backroom expert or a super-technician. The most useful skills in any job if you actually want to change anything are the ability to get on with people, work as a team and ultimately be able to 'manage' groups of people – humanely (I would hope) and aiming to get the best out of people. And it obviously helps your motivation if the task is something which you can identify with and which you think is worthwhile.

In terms of advice I can offer, I think the first thing is to 'know yourself' – try and work out what motivates and interests you. Then see how your knowledge and skills overlap with that area. If there isn't much overlap then you can choose a career that is closest to where you might want to be or which will help give you the skills that might be useful.

If you are not sure what to do, try something out and see. Try to keep an open mind.

There are some useful aptitude and interests tests that you can take; you answer a set of questions and are given suggested careers choices. For me the answers came out as scientific research, geologist, woodwork and a military officer! At least three of them were accurate.

You should think carefully about what you want to do several times during your life. Don't leave it all to chance. I now realise that I am something of an idealist but one who has been lucky enough to continue to be an idealist for the most part and to do a job that did not conflict with my principles of working with ecology and human, humanitarian and species rights.

In any age there seem to me to be two strategies to adopt. If you imagine the way the world is moving as a great river going in the wrong direction, there are nevertheless eddies moving against the stream – perhaps in a bend or a pool. You may be able to find a happy role in a job working in one of these areas – for example, in improving health. Or you may simply decide to avoid careers paths that you think are damaging or pointless: for example, by avoiding working with an arms manufacturer or with a major oil-extracting company or in one of many large food corporations.

The other more direct strategy is to take a job directly trying to oppose or block parts of the river: for example, developing renewable energy, saving energy, ways of extracting carbon from the atmosphere and storing it safely or reducing ocean acidity. You might choose to work with many of the various activist organisations and groups such as the New Economics Foundation or one of the set of major environmental charities such as the Sainsbury Trusts. There are now an enormous number of humanitarian organisations and very large charities.

Some of my career choices are still possible today. For example, there is always another book to be written! Opportunities in local government are now much more limited because of funding restrictions. But there are many opportunities in architecture and design – for example, on the low energy and low carbon side, and the renewable energy sector is growing very rapidly. Unfortunately, I think that universities have changed for the worse due to their much closer involvement with large private or business funders and a reduction in public financing. Perhaps the way forward is for those with a scientific background to establish their own small businesses using their expertise. But at the very least scientists need to be more politically aware and be willing to get involved in how their science is used or in the objectives of research. Whatever one's career choice, that at least is a worthwhile effort and – if my experience and that of many others is anything to go by – may lead to unexpected, interesting and fulfilling opportunities.

REFERENCES

1. Donella H. Meadows, Dennis L. Meadows, Jorgen Randers and William W. Behrens III (1972) *The Limits to Growth*, Universe Books – www.clubofrome.org/report/the-limits-to-growth/
2. Nickerson, Mike. (2009) *Life, Money and Illusion: Living on Earth as if we want to stay*. New Society Published, Revised Edition.

13

Science Public Relations – It Needs to Be in Your Genes

INTRODUCTION

Today science public relations (PR) is a burgeoning sector, spreading well beyond the original pioneering countries of the United States and United Kingdom. You will find science PR embedded at every level – from individual university departments and the smallest start-ups through patient groups and research centres to major international companies and organisations. Healthcare and life sciences are two particular areas that attract scientists.

As Andrew Ward, Health and Life Science Editor of the *Financial Times* (FT), revealed to me in a recent interview,

> Healthcare and life sciences are industries with big social responsibilities
> and sensitivities so public image and reputation are very important.
> They are also highly regulated and exposed to fraught political debates
> over issues such as drug pricing and industrial policy. All this makes
> communication with policymakers, the public and media very important.
> Having covered many industries over the years for the FT, I have found
> pharmaceuticals and healthcare to have some of the most intense lobbying
> and communications surrounding it.

Although the two are often grouped together, healthcare and life science PR are different. Healthcare PR tends to attract a wide range of people, often without science degrees, since most graduates think they can grasp and communicate the essentials of medicine. Life sciences, though, has maintained an aura of mystique, and, myself excepted, you will find few non-scientists willing to tackle the complexities of communicating issues such as gene editing. Therefore, I will

Successful Careers beyond the Lab, ed. David Bennett and Richard Jennings.
Published by Cambridge University Press. © Cambridge University Press 2017.   153

concentrate on life science careers in this chapter. Scientists looking to enter the field have the choice of working either in-house or within agencies. There are several courses now open in science communication which can be useful but are not a prerequisite. You are just as likely to be successful by directly applying for a position from the bench if you have an idea of what PR is and have practical experience – for example in helping charities or patient groups with communications activities.

RICHARD HAYHURST

First, however, perhaps a word on my own experience, which, in spite of me being originally a historian, not a scientist, the editors feel is relevant! After graduating, I took a job as an English-language teacher in Finland and gradually worked my way into the world of business-to-business (B2B) advertising. Finns being very logical, they accepted my suggestion that it was better for me to write advertisements directly in English rather than translating Finnish copy. This was a time of boom for the country which had an incredibly diverse economy providing the former Soviet Union and client states with everything from televisions to power stations. And so I became used to writing on a myriad of topics. Much of B2B advertising was also direct mail and in reality story-telling rather than a hard sell and so good preparation for transitioning into PR. Because there was no commercial TV at that time in Scandinavia the best talent worked in B2B and I had the privilege of working with and learning from multi-award-winning creative people. In the late 1980s, though, I made a major decision and applied for an in-house job with an exciting start-up company (Labsystems) that was producing the first HIV tests. Finnish and Swedish aid workers were among the first to contract the disease and were flown back to the Karolinska Institute, a medical university, and Helsinki where Labsystems worked on new diagnostics. The company was led by a charismatic physician/entrepreneur, Dr Osmo Suovaniemi, and we literally flew around the world setting up collaborations. The first HIV conference was then held in Stockholm, and to the surprise of the pharmaceutical and research community, a large group of HIV activists flew in from the United States and created an incredible buzz. Despite my lack of scientific knowledge, I felt I could contribute and help communication between the various groups. I must also say that at the same time I turned down a job with what was to become Finland's premier claim to fame after saunas and Sibelius, a rather dull conglomerate producing mainly toilet rolls, newsprint and Wellington boots, called Nokia! They had a sub-division with huge clunky cases that they claimed were mobile phones – and the future!

Labsystems was great, but I had always wondered what I would have done in the United Kingdom, and so with a couple of colleagues I decided to come back and set up an agency specialising in diagnostics and scientific equipment in general. Again with great Finnish logic, my employer Labsystems thought this was a perfect solution. I had left but I would now be based in London, one of the main media centres, and they could hire my new agency for their communications needs. However, it was also the time of the first big UK recession and overnight most of our potential business disappeared as US companies feasted on the carcass of the UK lab industry. Undeterred, we met up with and merged with our main competitor, De Facto, and to our delight and relief the biotechnology boom started. We had some great success, grew too quickly and burned! I had a nice franchise of clients in Scandinavia and then set up a new agency with my now ex-wife which was a highly successful combination since she was a former health editor for the UK national press. We were then acquired by a major US agency and helped to grow their UK business until I decided to start on my own again. So currently I have a joint venture in Sweden with a colleague where we look after Scandinavian biotechnology companies, a few UK clients and two NGO projects: Smart Villages on off-grid electricity in developing countries and Biosciences for Farming in Africa.

Lessons learnt are many. In PR, whether in-house or in an agency, you are in a difficult place – between clients and journalists. This can be a no-win situation. With clients, you should both listen and stand up to them. Problems will happen, and it is how you face up to them that matters most. But be realistic: clients are human and will change agencies through no fault of yours – don't take things personally! With journalists you need to understand their pressure points – and of course you are at the mercy of editors and what seems like an absolutely certain piece of coverage can be cancelled at the last moment. If you are thinking of setting up an agency, do it, but be prepared for highs and lows and also that staff and clients will come and go. If you can deal with all this, then yes, enter PR. Progress in science at the moment is incredible and you will get great satisfaction out of helping communicate this – much more, I guess, than I would ever have got out of pushing mobile phones!

SUE CHARLES

In the United Kingdom, the beginnings of modern life science PR can be traced back largely to one group of people led by Sue Charles whose agency De Facto handled the 'launch' of Dolly, the genetically modified sheep, in 1989. For this chapter I have interviewed Sue and other key figures in the growth of science PR along with a recent entrant to give readers an idea of the opportunities that might be open to them.

After a first-class degree in biochemistry at Oxford, Sue was naturally encouraged to do a PhD. She does not recall any other career option even being discussed at the time:

> At the end of my PhD I knew I would always love science, especially the cutting edge research in molecular biology, but I knew that I wasn't suited to bench science. I had learnt that I was a good communicator – I ran the department's journal club and was an invited speaker at a number of international conferences (quite impressive for a PhD student). So I decided to 'sell my soul to the devil' (in the words of my supervisor) and looked at commercial jobs away from the bench.
>
> I didn't know about PR – or even what it was – I knew I wanted to work in the scientific industry and in communications. I looked at journalism and marketing – and then saw a job advertisement in New Scientist for a technical writer with biotech knowledge to work for a Business Communications Agency – perfect – this was 1985 and was at the very start of the biotech era. I applied and got it.

This was typical of the time: B2B communications was literally big business. In the pre-Web era, communications actually meant journal advertising, direct mail and exhibitions. All of these areas were highly profitable and many agencies that were making lots of money in engineering, telecommunications and manufacturing saw similar profits in the world of science, especially assisting not only biotechnology but also scientific and medical equipment companies. The problem was the perceived complexity of the products. This lead to a belief that only scientists could communicate with other scientists, and thus came Sue's career break. However, the primary goal was to recruit copywriters; PR was still a very small part of the mix, consisting mainly of short product press releases being carried free by the journals to ensure there was something to read alongside all the glossy double-page adverts.

Having started as a technical writer, Sue moved into PR as her main focus and was quickly promoted through account executive up the ranks until after just four years, at the age of 29. she was appointed to the board of the company. The agency was the United Kingdom's first and leading science communications agency, employing some 50 people and operating globally. It was in at the start of the biotech boom.

To better understand client needs, Sue also wanted to widen her business skills and knowledge and in 1988 won PR Week's (the leading journal in the field) MBA scholarship to study for an Executive MBA at Cranfield Business School.

In 1991, Sue cofounded two companies: De Facto, a specialist biotech PR agency for which I was managing director, and Bang, a design agency for which she was part-time chairperson. They shared the location and clients. Over the next decade Sue and her colleagues expanded De Facto through organic growth and mergers and acquisitions (M&As). During this time, as regulations changed and money-losing biotechnology companies were allowed to list on the London Stock Exchange, she also co-founded the United Kingdom's first biotechnology specialist financial PR agency, Genus Communications, which was folded in alongside a merger with Hayhurst Conington Cripps to form HCC de Facto, a £5 million turnover consultancy headquartered in the City of London.

Nowadays there is a continuing flow of science graduates looking at PR as a profession. However, it was very different back in the late 1990s, as Sue recalls:

> Having found it hard to attract good staff into PR from science degrees, in 1997, with funding from the UK Department of Trade and Industry and sponsorship from *Nature* magazine, I launched an event to educate graduates and PhDs about career options away from bench science. Called Career Alternatives for Scientists, it grew from a one-day conference to a two-day conference plus exhibition. It was a great success and many organisations including *Nature* and *Science* now run their own events.

After 10 years and having become widely recognized as one of the leading practitioners in the field, Sue spent a year evaluating options for the next stage of her career:

> I became part-time Chief Executive Officer (CEO) of a University College London (UCL) spin-out biotechnology company, paid in equity, with a full-time role subject to us attracting finance – which, sadly, we didn't do! I also consulted to venture capital firms, writing business plans. But then many of the clients with whom I had built excellent relationships asked me to set up again – so I did! I set up Charles Consultants and won 16 clients in 6 months. To provide a ready set-up back office and design function, I merged Charles Consultants into a small science communications firm (STMP Marketing Solutions Ltd) owned by an ex-client, to form Northbank Communications. Northbank also opened an office in Munich as the German biotechnology scene was booming.
>
> I attracted a 10% equity holder into Northbank with a plan to grow it for 5 years and secure an exit for the investor and also for the founder of

Science and Technical Marketing Consultants (STMP). As CEO of Northbank between 2002 and 2007 we had grown it to a £2.25m revenue profitable agency with a very strong reputation in the life sciences industry. Having evaluated multiple options, the best option to deliver on the exit and at the same time secure expansion opportunities and investment for the future was to sell Northbank to College Hill, a boutique financial PR firm with ambitious growth plans.

So in late 2007, for the first time since founding my first agency in 1991, I was part of a bigger agency and no longer my own boss! In the years since, as global Managing Partner of College Hill's life sciences practice I have been given autonomy as well as the support to open offices in the USA and Australia. With a wider pool of senior colleagues and a wider breadth of experience, I have been able to continue learning and offer greater opportunities for the team. In 2014 College Hill rebranded as a single global entity – Instinctif Partners – now employing 450 people in 22 offices in 12 countries. The Life Sciences/Healthcare sectors represents about 10–12% of the consultancy's global revenues.'

In addition to her 'day job' Sue has taken on a number of not-for-profit roles including being an advisor for three years to Biotech YES (Young Entrepreneurs Scheme) and a trustee on the board of the Jane Goodall Institute, a global wildlife and environment conservation organization, for two years. Now, as she looks forward to her next decade, Sue expects to reduce her full-time executive responsibilities and increase her advisor roles and not-for-profit roles. All of that she believes will be in life sciences communications, using her routes in science.

You may choose to just work for an agency, but there is nothing like forming your own agency. Some idea of the rewards and risks can be gleaned from how Sue goes on to list the highlights and, with great honesty, the low points of her 30-plus-year career.

Highlights

- Being in the biotech industry at the start (1985) and ever since
- Pioneering life sciences PR in the United Kingdom
- Building companies and creating opportunities for a 'family' of bright talent
- Seeing bright individuals that have worked in my teams going on to have stellar careers of their own
- Working with clients in the area of ground-breaking technologies – GM, cloning, antibodies as drugs, gene therapy etc.
- Being known for my work on the launch of Dolly, the cloned sheep – a well-recognised great case study of well-managed science PR

- Winning a £10 million contract when we were a young agency of just 8 people!
- Never having a dull moment – still loving my job after three decades
- Having the opportunity to live and work part time in Australia (a wonderful country) whilst still being global managing partner (due to the trust of my employer and the superb support and skills of my team)

Low Points

- Seeing the first agency I worked for collapse after 21 years due to the 1990 recession, and having to sit on the liquidation committee and face creditors (with lots of life lessons learnt from this experience)
- Seeing my first agency implode after 10 years of growth and losing my job as a result (many, many lessons learnt about personal conflict management from this experience)

Equally useful are Sue's List of Lessons Learnt

- Find a job you love and put your heart and soul into doing it to the very best of your ability – but not to the exclusion of your personal life. Family, friends and outside interests keep you sane and make you human.
- People matter – my teams have become my family and it's important to work with people you like and respect in a mutually respectful environment.
- Client service excellence is the key driver of success in PR – but as a boss, always keep an eye on the numbers, as without profit and cash you don't have a business!
- Networks matter – in consultancy your 'little black book' of client, media and investor contacts is as valuable as your knowledge and expertise.
- Read a lot.
- Challenge yourself.
- Keep learning.
- Take risks.

Having earned a first class degree at Oxford, you might expect Sue to wonder what might have been, but to the question of any regrets that she gave up her scientific career, the answer is an emphatic 'No':

Although I do regret that I didn't write up my PhD – so my advice to anyone moving away from the bench after a PhD is to be sure that you have written up and don't have extra experiments to do before starting a new job.

I also slightly regret that during the first 15 years of my career I was so busy working that I didn't travel more sooner. At the point that I co-founded Northbank in 2001 at the age of 42 I hadn't taken a holiday longer than 10 days and my global travel map was very sparsely populated! I agreed with my co-founder that I could take two five week breaks within the first five years (with no contact!) and also that I would always take my 30 days annual leave. My travel map is now widely populated and I am lucky to have had some amazing experiences outside of work.

And of course, as you might expect, the answer to the final question of whether she would advise scientists to pursue a career in PR is an emphatic 'Yes':

Absolutely. Specialising in science PR is a great way of keeping up with science's advances (you have to read a lot, as discoveries move technologies on very fast!) and mixing with those still "at the bench".

MARK SWALLOW

Dr Mark Swallow, currently Director of the Healthcare and Life Sciences Team at Citigate Dewe Rogerson, also has much relevant experience and, interestingly, was someone Sue and I convinced to switch from journalism to PR, a route that many scientists might find themselves considering after perhaps working for a science publisher. Mark has also moved from trade PR into the corporate and financial PR sector. Mark earned a PhD in molecular biology from the University of London in 1995 following a BSc in biochemistry also from the University of London in 1991.

Mark decided to pursue a career in PR around the end of 2000:

I was an editor and journalist of a pharmaceutical and biotechnology business magazine at the time, and had been for a couple of years. This gave me exposure to how pharmaceutical companies and emerging biotechnology companies work via PR agencies to promote their science and business.

As time went on, I learnt more about the function and met various people involved. The opportunity became increasingly attractive as it would allow me to maintain my strong interest in biomedical science and combine that with learning more about the commercial application of that science on the international business stage.

I saw this as an opportunity to work closely with exciting science-based companies and be a valuable part of the team as they develop and grow.

Over time, I came to appreciate that communicating science is not just about getting coverage in the press; its reach is much greater and should be considered as crucial in every aspect of the way a company communicates with its stakeholders, be that in raising money from investors or attracting partners to develop the science and resulting products, among others.

Mark describes his career progress as 'logical', although there was some element of opportunism. He was a PhD research scientist working in molecular and structural biology.

My research was not entirely successful although I did enjoy it. What surprised me was how much I enjoyed researching and writing my thesis, and this led me to consider a career in scientific publishing.

His first job was as an assistant editor for *Trends in Biochemical Sciences* (*TiBS*) in Cambridge, which he looks back on as a fantastic introduction to the world of publishing:

It exposed me to high quality science and how it was communicated as well as writing, editing and production skills that have stood me in good stead ever since.

Mark spent just over two years at *TiBS* before joining a pharmaceutical business publishing and intelligence group in London, now owned by Informa. In this organisation he worked on and later managed international publications targeting pharmaceutical industry professionals where he analysed and reported industry news and provided longer features on new companies, trends in science/technology, therapeutic areas and investment, and focussed on some of the leading people driving the biotech sector.

Having made the switch from 'hack' to 'flack' (journalist to PR practitioner) in 2001 after about three years in journalism, he worked first at a small communications agency, HCC De Facto, that specialised in life sciences, and then at a larger and more diversified agency where healthcare and life sciences communications represent a major part of its business.

I have since worked with a large number of companies in the UK and Europe ranging from start-ups, private companies and public companies, all in the biotechnology and medical technology sector, and specialist investors (venture capital firms) who fund such companies.

Throughout my time in PR I have developed skills and experience to support the specific needs of companies at each stage of development, from messaging, corporate writing (for press releases, websites, annual reports), profile raising and media relations, investor-focused communications and deal communications (fundraising, partnerships, mergers & acquisitions).

I am currently a Director in the Healthcare and Life Sciences Team at Citigate Dewe Rogerson, having risen through the ranks from Account Manager and Associate Director. In my role I have responsibility for a portfolio of companies where I take a lead advisory role, and I act as a supporting advisor on several other companies.

'Science PR' is a small part of what I do. It is more about communicating how cutting-edge science is used in a commercial setting by companies to develop new therapies and technologies to address medical needs.

The audiences for this ranges from very technical people adept at assessing the potential of the science as a commercial proposition (such as venture capital investors, and business development professionals at pharmaceutical companies) to the general public who will view the science and its impact on a more humanitarian level.

We operate a team approach with each client and have a team with diverse but complementary skill sets that together cover the spectrum of needs a company might need throughout its life.

Looking at highlights and low points, Mark starts by revealing that, in his case, the most satisfying element of the job is seeing clients be successful, such as raising funds, or when they sign a major partnering deal with a pharmaceutical company, or when they have a product approved that will now have the opportunity to make a real difference in the lives of disease sufferers. The involvement of the communications team is an integral part of the process in concluding and communicating these defining events. He says he has been fortunate to have been involved in several such events for clients over the past decade.

However, the success of clients can be bittersweet as it can also lead to their acquisition by larger companies, at which point they cease being clients. A silver lining is that there is great demand for successful and experienced management in the biotechnology sector, so they invariably re-appear to lead other companies, and the strong relationships built over the years mean it is never long before there is an opportunity to get re-acquainted.

Turning to the question of lessons learnt, Mark replies in much the same vein as Sue that experience and relationships are everything in PR, from client and media management perspectives:

Many of the situations that a company may face, they will be facing for the first time. It is rarely the case for an experienced communications advisor, who will most likely have been through similar situations many times. This experience and the trust that is built provides reassurance to clients that they are in safe hands in times of good news and crisis.

Mark also strongly believes that understanding the needs and practices of the press and the individuals involved is valuable as this can have a big impact on the outcome of external communications around significant events, with consequent impact on the perception and reputation of client companies. Thus switching from journalist to spokesperson can often be a good idea:

> When starting out a career in communications it is therefore important to embrace every situation, good or bad, and to get to know your client and your audience well.

Mark has no regrets about leaving research science and is extremely grateful for the foundation it gave him to pursue his subsequent jobs.

> My current job allows me to keep in touch with cutting edge medical science, seeing how it can be successfully applied and, if done properly, seeing the difference it can make to people's lives through the products it generates.

As for entering the profession, Mark feels it is certainly something worth considering if you enjoy communicating about science and are interested in its commercial application. It can be a great introduction to the business of science and provide exposure to the great many players involved: from university researchers through to leading lights in the pharmaceutical industry, and from venture capital to corporate finance and investment management.

Both Mark and Sue entered PR with no formal training. Times have changed and there are several courses now open to students. One of the most successful is at the University of the West of England under the guidance of Dr Emma Weitkamp who actually worked with Sue and myself at De Facto. When I was looking to place a PR specialist with a client of mine, Emma recommended Emily Head. In less than two years Emily has already taken a few steps along what promises to be a highly successful career path. Since this chapter was originally written, Emily has become Press Officer for The Lancet.

EMILY HEAD

Emily decided to pursue a career in science communication when she was in the final year of her undergraduate degree in biological sciences:

> Within my degree I'd studied 'Biology in Society' and 'Science Communication' modules which showed how science fitted into the bigger picture and that really interested me. It also didn't help that I was terrible at lab work – I remember doing my dissertation in the lab and finding that I was terrible at 'doing science', but could happily talk about what I was studying for hours!

After finishing her undergraduate degree (biological sciences at the University of East Anglia) Emily went on to do a Master's degree in science communication at the University of the West of England. In the summer before starting her next degree she got her first taste of science communication in the real world by interning in the press office of *Bloodwise* (then *Leukaemia & Lymphoma Research*) writing press releases to explain their newly funded science. For her Master's degree she studied Writing Science and Hands-on Science Communications modules as well as learning about the science communication field as a whole. Building on her experience at *Bloodwise*, she did her dissertation on how cancer charities communicated information about the disease online.

At the same time as studying she kept building her experience and got another internship working in a multiple sclerosis (MS) charity to help them to develop their communications to supporters.

> I remember that stage of my life being the most busy so far as I was also working a part-time shop job to get some money in.

> Once lectures finished and I was only working on my dissertation from home I got a part-time role at the British Society of Rheumatology as their Press and Marketing Officer. Once the whole degree was done I was offered another part-time role with Imanova Limited as their Communications Officer.

> Being split across two organisations, I was able to get a lot of experience including the press work which I realised I enjoyed most of all. During that time I promoted the newest research from journals and conferences, as well as organising a photo call with the Mayor of London. Ultimately these experiences were what inspired me to look for press officer roles and led me to my current position as Science Press Officer at Cancer Research UK.

> Having studied the charity's work in my Masters degree, Cancer Research UK was an organisation I'd always wanted to work for as I was impressed

by how well they communicated science. I'd ear-marked the role of Science Press Officer as my dream job, and when it came up never thought I'd be offered the role in a million years.

Looking at the highlights of her, granted, relatively short career, Emily cites getting the job she'd always wanted as a science press officer at Cancer Research UK and working in an inspiring organisation with dedicated colleagues. Conversely, she found attempting to transition from a more general communications career to one specifically in science press difficult:

I interviewed for a number of jobs and faced a lot of rejections before I got the role as Science Press Officer at Cancer Research UK.

As for advice, Emily considers it to be hard to specialise from more general communications roles into one specific one:

If you know what you want to do don't settle for anything else. Alternatively, make the most of the opportunities in your area of interest so you can really sell them in interview and consider some extra-curricular work – meeting up with people in the job you want for advice, or approaching them for a day of shadowing them in the office – to show your dedication to getting into that area.

With no regrets about giving up her scientific career, Emily would also advise scientists to consider PR:

My career has opened my eyes to many areas of new research, while also giving me the chance to focus on specific areas when working on particular projects. It's insightful and variable and uses my science brain every day. It's also given me the chance to show the world what exciting science is happening and share my passion for science.

CONCLUSION

So whether in-house or in an agency, a career in science PR can often prove a rewarding choice for scientists based on the experience of both those interviewed for this chapter and numerous others I have met over the years. The three interviewees also nicely illustrate the main ways of entering the market. First, as in Sue's case, by joining an agency. Positions are still being advertised in scientific journals, and some specialised recruitment agencies can help. However, it is easy enough to identify the key agencies in the United Kingdom with life science interests – Instinctif, Citigate, Zyme, Alto, Scott Partnership – and approach them directly, perhaps starting as an intern. Second, you could follow Mark's example and start in trade journalism where you will soon get to know the various agencies and the chances to switch. Last but not least, there is the possibility of adding a communications module to your degree. However, as you can see from Emily's case, it was probably the fact that she had also done relevant charity work that gave her an edge.

I would only add that it is not easy – communication is an art, not a science – and requires tact, diplomacy, clarity, tailoring for different audiences, courtesy and confidence. It can't be done solely by e-mail; much of your work will involve picking up the phone and pitching your story to stressed, cynical journalists. You have to get out and meet people and impress them with not just your scientific knowledge but also your ability to understand and meet their needs. This is very different from being in the lab alone with your experiments. In short, don't expect automatic entry; science PR remains a field to which many are attracted, but few are chosen.

Part III   The Public Sector

14

From Rock Pools to Whitehall

To start at the end, so to speak, I retired in 2012 from the UK government's Department for the Environment Food and Rural Affairs (Defra), where I had been its Director for Science and Deputy Chief Scientific Adviser (dCSA) since 2001. I'll say more later about this post, but suffice it to say here, that was not at all how I had intended to finish my career when I started out. But I'm pleased I did, and this chapter tells how I got there.

My childhood seaside holidays in Cornwall and Connemara on the west coast of Ireland, in both of which rock-pools are rich in life, led me to an early goal of becoming a marine biologist. My obvious interest led my parents to give me C.M. Yonge's marvelous *The Sea Shore*[1] to read when I was nine, and I was hooked. In my teens, reading Alistair Hardy's equally wonderful *The Open Sea*[2] introduced me both to the amazing diversity of plankton but also to the world of fisheries. At Trinity College Dublin I took a degree in zoology with a special topic in marine ecology with the goal of becoming a professor of marine biology. However, I began to realise that a lot of the ecological research I was interested in had been done already, much of it as long ago as the mid-nineteenth century![3]

As a student, I earned money in my summers working for the science team at the Irish Sea Fisheries Board[4] collecting statistics on crab fisheries for population analysis (and a bit more on the side

[1] Collins New Naturalist series, 1949.
[2] Collins New Naturalist series, 1956 and 1959.
[3] For example, Philip Henry Gosse, *A Year at the Sea Shore* (1859).
[4] An Bord Iascaigh Mhara (BIM).

Successful Careers beyond the Lab, ed. David Bennett and Richard Jennings.
Published by Cambridge University Press. © Cambridge University Press 2017.

in my free time by crewing for the fishermen which led to some enjoyable adventures). I also once, accidentally, found myself managing a crabmeat-processing plant in Connemara for a week when its nice Norwegian manager went temporally missing after a serious Nordic alcoholic bender. It was an interesting introduction to management!

As an undergraduate, my thoughts became focused on aquaculture, then emerging in Northwestern Europe as a real commercial proposition and seen as a potential contributor to world food supply. This led me to a PhD at the Salmon Research Trust of Ireland, focussed initially on the potential for using a type of native shrimp for feed in salmon rearing. The immediate disappearance of my study population (one of those inexplicable ecological mysteries) led me to extend my research to the physics and chemistry of the tidal lake system on which I was working, and this proved very useful in the longer run.

Jobs in aquaculture research were scarce when I completed my PhD so I applied reluctantly for a post with the Department of Agriculture and Fisheries in Dublin to work on marine pollution, and, rather to my surprise, got it. This proved to be a bit of luck (a key component in any career).

I was joined by an excellent chemical analyst and a small team of lab staff. The field of marine pollution was new to us; I thought it was all about oil spills, the 1967 *Torrey Canyon* disaster still being a vivid memory.[5] Since we were new to the business, very young and inexperienced, we learned rapidly from equivalent organisations in Britain, Europe and the United States.

The work involved lab and field science, mostly in testing wastes and monitoring marine waste disposal sites; in the 1970s, dumping of industrial and sewage wastes from ships at sea was still considered a sensible option; 'the solution to pollution is dilution', as my engineering colleagues were fond of saying. This made use of my ecological training but, in practice, most of my time went to providing scientific advice on waste disposal licenses and to helping to develop national and international regulations. Both brought me into contact with industry and with other national pollution control and environmental management agencies. This provided a crash course not only in the technicalities of pollution control but also in its policies and politics.

After the United Nation's (UN) seminal 1972 Stockholm Conference on the Human Environment, many countries, including Ireland, developed environmental legislation. I was particularly involved in the

---

[5] One of the world's most serious oil spills off the south-west coast of England in 1967.

1981 Dumping at Sea Act but also advised on other Irish environmental planning and pollution controls. This gave me a good grounding in how legislation is put together and how the political and policy processes work, as well as introducing me to both the interest and the difficulties of working with multiple stakeholders.

Working in a small country was also a bit of luck. In small countries you take on a much wider range of duties and are given responsibilities for which in larger countries you would only get opportunities in mid-career. Marine pollution being, by nature, an international issue, I found myself from an early stage as an Irish government delegate working with scientists of other countries in two contexts.

The International Council for the Exploration of the Sea (ICES) had been established in 1902 to solve the overfishing problems of the North Atlantic and its regional seas (the North, Irish and Baltic). Overfishing problems, alas, are still with us a 100-plus years on, despite ICES's successes in developing the scientific tools of fish population dynamics that enable it to advise European and North American governments on Total Allowable Catches (the maximum amount of fish that could be taken sustainably from a fish population). ICES's members are the national fisheries departments and agencies; ICES convenes working groups of their scientists to address particular issues. In the late 1970s, ICES began developing the science around marine pollution and its control because of its impact on fisheries. I joined its Working Group on Marine Pollution in the North Atlantic and shortly afterwards, inexperienced as I was, became its chairman. This was another useful lesson in practical politics; I was chosen because our working language was English but I wasn't seen as British being the Irish delegate (I actually have dual nationality but that was overlooked). Britain, as often, was taking a somewhat distinctive line on pollution control policy and had a rather dominating voice in discussions so an Irish chair was seen as a neutral option. I later joined other working groups on issues such as the development of indicators of environmental health using sea floor animals or fish diseases. I also joined ICES's top-level Advisory Committee on Marine Pollution, responsible for formulating advice to governments and international regulatory bodies, particularly to the commissions of two post-Stockholm regional conventions, the Oslo Convention on the control of waste dumping at sea and the Paris Convention on control of the pollution of the sea from land-based sources.[6]

---

[6] Known collectively as OSPAR, and subsequently becoming a single Convention for the Protection of the Marine Environment of the North-East Atlantic (the 'OSPAR Convention') in 1992.

These commissions, given the technical issues involved, were also supported by working groups of scientists and engineers to draw up control standards and monitoring protocols. As the Irish delegate negotiating agreements on these issues, I had an epiphany about how 'objective' scientists could nonetheless quite reasonably come to different 'scientific' conclusions based on different political philosophies and legal approaches.

By the early 1980s I became concerned with 'red tides', coastal micro-algal blooms sufficiently intense to cause visible discolouration of the sea, and sometimes to cause fish kills, or, of even more concern, to require closure of shellfisheries because of human health risks. These problems emerged at a time when Ireland's aquaculture industry was getting off the ground and shellfish in particular were an important, valuable export, so potential toxicity was a major commercial risk. Researching what led to these blooms and providing a toxicity testing service to the aquaculture industry became important priorities and gave me a greater understanding of the commercial challenges of this industry and how its markets operated.

By this time, I was seriously weighing up the direction of my career. I was enjoying my small amount of fieldwork and research but also getting more involved in science for policy making. A family need took me to London where I spent a happy sabbatical year at the Natural History Museum (NHM) analysing a collection of marine worms that I had taken from waste disposal sites off the Irish coast. Taking the time to get deeply into the taxonomy of these fascinating and beautiful animals[7] was a privilege; my collections yielded a remarkable addition to the European fauna, a worm previously found only in the southern hemisphere and, even more excitingly, a species new to science. Nonetheless (perhaps because of the preserving-alcohol-fume-laden gloom of the NHM's old Spirit Store, now replaced by the beautiful Darwin Centre), I realised that I couldn't see this as a life-long career.

Luck, in the form of perfect timing, presented me with an opportunity to successfully apply for a Principal Scientific Officer post at the British Ministry of Agriculture Fisheries and Food (MAFF). My English colleagues on the ICES and Oslo/Paris Commissions' committees were mostly drawn from MAFF's Directorate of Fisheries

---

[7] A social tip: don't start conversations at parties about the beauties of deep-sea worms. You'll be right (they are aesthetically extraordinary), but eyes will glaze over!

Research (DFR) which at that time (1983) had a marine pollution lab at Burnham-on-Crouch in Essex on the south east coast of England.

My Burnham team was a good deal larger than my small Dublin team. A lab and seagoing team undertook dumping site monitoring, and there was a four-strong Licensing and Inspection team. Neighbouring teams on marine chemistry (widely recognized as one of the best in Europe) and toxicology provided our chemical analysis, lab testing and eco-toxicity services. This gave me a serious management role, both of my team and as part of the lab's top management, as well as a voice in the wider organisation where I led work streams on red tides and fish diseases. As in Dublin, a large part of my time went to advising the policy team in MAFF headquarters (HQ) and in international work; I continued my work with ICES and the Oslo Commission in particular, adding engagement with the global London Dumping Convention, managed by the UN's Inter-governmental Maritime Organization.[8] This raised my understanding of the wider political context of marine pollution control and of the international bodies supporting it, particularly the United Nations Educational, Scientific and Cultural Organization's (UNESCO) Intergovernmental Oceanographic Commission.

In ICES, I had the excellent experience of organising a major international conference on the 'Red Tides' issue and editing its proceedings. A further spell of chairmanship, this time of the scientific advisory committee of the Oslo Commission, and consequent attendance at Commission meetings themselves, extended my negotiating skills. However, after four fulfilling years in the role, I began to feel that I had 'done' dumping at sea and looked for ways to move on. In particular, I reconsidered the balance in my life between science as science and my ever-growing interest in science for policy making.

Since the 1968 Fulton Commission deliberations on the effectiveness of the UK civil service [1], there had been much concern about the capabilities of the civil service in the modern world, and in particular its ability to deal with the scientific and technical issues, then including emerging environmental and pollution concerns as well as more traditional problems in energy, health, transport and food production. One specific concern was that scientists were neither given sufficient responsibilities and opportunities nor were induced to apply for

---

[8] Now the International Maritime Organization.

'administration'[9] (i.e. policy making and management) roles, then dominated by humanities graduates. Fulton's solution was to introduce a training programme for senior professionals (not only scientists and engineers but also economists and social scientists, accountants and lawyers). The intention was that specialists would get extensive training in the methods and legalities of 'administration' and then be given a two-year policy 'experience' posting; it was expected that most would return to senior management in their own organisations but that some might transfer to 'administration'.

Access to the programme was highly competitive, including a challenging series of interviews, and required the support of one's senior managers. The latter was not instantly forthcoming; my director had lost my predecessor to this programme and was unwilling to give up another senior staff member. While this was flattering, I felt it was worth persevering, and I received support from the senior policy maker with whom I worked in MAFF HQ. At a major career change such a mentor is essential and I was blessed with a good one. I eventually got permission and, to my own surprise, passed the application interviews and spent what now seems to be a ludicrously extravagant three months at the Civil Service Training College with other specialists learning about administrative law (and lore – BBC TV's *Yes, Minister* played a part in our programme) and policy processes. There followed a frustrating period of *not* getting the promised policy posting; for some unaccountable reason policy assistant secretaries were strangely reluctant to appoint wet-behind-the-ears scientists to run important policy work. I was eventually offered a boring, backwater post on food contamination policy, seen as politically low profile and rather 'techy', suitable for a policy neophyte. The height of excitement was that this branch managed the post-Chernobyl[10] controls on all those radioactive sheep on the Cumbrian Fells, but that was a just a licensing issue and pretty dull.

Er . . . that was then. Within weeks of meeting my small team, the Chernobyl story became the focus of a sustained campaign by the Labour Shadow Agriculture Minister convinced (at least partially rightly) that the Conservative government had got it all wrong. There

---

[9] This was the period of maximum nationalisation when government really was responsible for administering not just public services but also many nationalised industries.

[10] A catastrophic nuclear accident on 26 April 1986 in the reactor at the Chernobyl Nuclear Power Plant near Pripyat, then part of the Ukrainian Soviet Socialist Republic of the Soviet Union (USSR).

followed some 300 Parliamentary Questions and four Parliamentary debates. This was also a period in which the great British public started taking holidays abroad seriously and came back with the notion that it was not necessary to boil your food to death; raw or lightly cooked foods could be delicious. Inevitably, a food poisoning epidemic ensued, enlivened by a junior Health Minister, Edwina Curry, announcing that British flocks of egg-laying hens were all infected with *Salmonella*; this led to something of a collapse of egg and chicken sales and industry uproar. Food additives (not my responsibility) had been a policy issue in the immediately preceding years but now the public began to realise that there were many more sources of contamination from agri-chemicals, storage / preserving chemicals and packaging, among others. The newspapers whipped up a storm on food safety. To cap it all, genetically modified organisms (GMOs) crept into the national consciousness, initially seen simply as a good news story but then turning to one of 'Frankenstein foods'. The lobby groups for farmers, industry and consumers, as well as some purely politically motivated, got active.

All in all, 'bliss it was in that dawn to be alive, and to be young [at least in policy-making terms] was very heaven!', to quote Wordsworth.[11] I packed in an amazing amount of experience in the two years I was in the post, including joining the team working on what eventually became the Food Safety Act of 1990. By the time I left it my little branch had grown into two divisions; my last role in it covered the GMO issues and other novel foods and, as an afterthought, the very early stages of the BSE (Bovine spongiform encephalopathy) problem – Mad Cow Disease.

So great was the excitement that I wouldn't have moved, had not a higher-grade role been advertised in the MAFF Chief Scientists Group, to manage agri-environmental research commissioning. I noted that it was only offered to food scientists, which struck me as odd, so I wrote to the Chief Scientist to ask why. This was taken as a formal appeal; I was called to interview and offered the job before I really understood what it entailed. My predecessor (who was in fact a food scientist) was happy to leave to take up a senior post on food safety and radiation, but even happier because he had seen, as I had not, that a major period of upheaval was due.

Back in 1971, Lord (Victor) Rothschild introduced to government the idea that its R&D commissioning should be done on a customer-

---

[11] Wordsworth, W. (1809). *The French Revolution as It Appeared to Enthusiasts at Its Commencement.* First published in The Friend, 26 October 1809; see B. E. Rook (ed), The Friend (Princeton, 1969), ii, pp. 147–148.

contractor basis. Causing uproar at the time [2], this reform had been introduced in a gentlemanly way in which Ministry Chief Scientists and their staffs discussed future research programmes with Research Institute Directors almost independently of the real customers and users of research output, the departmental policy makers. Come the 1980s, Mrs. Thatcher's government determined to put a bit more muscle into the relationship as well as deciding that government should stop funding 'near market research' (NMR; research on issues already ripe for take-up by industry). I took over a role in which, on the one hand, budgets were going up as the environment was a growing area of agricultural policy and, on the other, coming down, as we shed NMR, at the same time as processes were being tightened and made more contractual. Coupled with this, as with previous jobs, I had instantly to learn about a new field, agriculture and its environmental implications.

I was inherently in sympathy with the idea of identifying the scientific needs of policy makers and then finding ways to turn those into exciting research opportunities, and to find the research teams to commission to do the work. I became familiar with the work of the Agriculture and Food Research Council,[12] whose institutes were our main external contractors, and of the enormous Agricultural Development and Advisory Service, the Ministry's in-house provider of research and advice to policy makers and farmers. Reorganising the budgets also brought me for the first time into close contact with departmental economists and started me on a campaign that lasted the rest of my career to get scientists and economists working closer together on evidence provision; later, I added to this a campaign to get the department to take the potential contribution of the social sciences to policy making seriously (a matter made more difficult by the tendency of social scientists to talk in impenetrable and often ideological jargon).

Apart from a brief spell in the Cabinet Office Science Secretariat,[13] supporting the government's Chief Scientific Adviser (GCSA), I spent eight years in the MAFF Chief Scientist's group, being promoted halfway to become Deputy Chief Scientist for Agriculture and later taking on my old interest in Fisheries. This gave me oversight of the whole of the agriculture and fisheries R&D budget (then measured in hundreds of £ millions per year) and an opportunity to develop my ideas both on a policy-needs-led investment strategy and on the organisation of

---

[12] Now the Biological Sciences and Biotechnology Research Council (BBSRC).

[13] Now the Government Office for Science and housed in the Department of Business, Energy and Industrial Strategy.

specialist staff to support policy making. We were a central Group whereas our colleagues in the Department for the Environment (DoE) embedded their scientists within policy teams, a much more effective model (and one that provided more interesting jobs for scientists). Being at arm's length from policy customers made us less effective at engaging with their needs. We were rather better at engaging with the science community and one of the pleasures of the job was to see an enormously wide range of science during visits and meetings at institutes and field stations.

Towards the end of this period I took an opportunity to become an interim director at a MAFF scientific agency, the Central Science Laboratory (CSL).[14] I took over its Food Science Division at a critical moment when it was closing a lab and moving over 100 staff from Norwich to its main site in York which gave me new experiences of really difficult personnel management issues. CSL was also having to radically review its strategy for the future in the face of government budget pressures. Scientifically, the 200-strong team, including a major group on pesticide safety, was handling analytical and ecological issues of great interest so, while this was quite a stressful time, it was never less than interesting, in management, scientific and policy terms.

The experience of managing part of an agency led naturally to taking on responsibility for the Ministry's overall policy and management approach to its delivery agencies. Since the Thatcher's government's decision to privatise government services where possible and, where not, to form them into quasi-contractor 'agencies', MAFF had found itself with a range of mostly scientific agencies delivering services, for example, to conservation, animal health, and fisheries management. The constitutional and legal issues were complex and the role was both intrinsically interesting and greatly widened my understanding of both law and policy relating to government bodies.

My previous stay in the Cabinet Office Science Secretariat had been very brief; though the interview process was swift (Government Chief Scientific Adviser [GCSA] Professor Bill Stewart: 'Do you want the job?'; Parker [surprised]: 'Yes'; end of interview), the vetting and other processes for working in Cabinet Office were not, so I was only in the post three months before MAFF promoted me and took me back. So when a post was advertised in its successor, the Office for Science and Technology (OST), working for GCSAs Sir Bob May and later Sir David

---

[14] Now Fera Science Ltd, a private-sector company; before privatization, CSL had become the Food and Environment Research Agency.

King, I leapt at it. I was particularly interested because the role was that of International Director.

As MAFF Deputy Chief Scientist, I had become involved with the negotiation of the agriculture, fisheries and food components of the European Commission's (EC) Framework Programmes 4 and 5, and much enjoyed getting back into international work. Negotiating in the European Union (EU) was very different to working in ICES and OSPAR but the challenge was exciting and I rapidly realised that it needed a lot of effort away from the negotiating table, ranging from bilateral meetings to informal get-togethers with other delegations, if one was to succeed in getting anything across at the extremely formal meetings chaired by the European Commission. It was equally important at home to liaise with other government departments, given the overweening strength of the then Department for Trade and Industry[15] as both policy lead and major budget holder. I formed a 'Gang of Four' with colleagues in Environment, Transport and Health to make sure that our voices were heard in the development of the UK position. Away from the EU, I also contributed for MAFF to the annual 'Tetrapartite' meetings of the US, Canadian, French and UK heads of agricultural research.

The OST post gave me responsibility for leading and coordinating the official side of the cross-government negotiations on the EC's Framework Programme 6 and supporting Science Ministers at EU Council discussions. This brought me into contact with a much wider range of departments than before and a wide range of external lobbyists. I repeated the lessons learned in MAFF by organising informal meetings of national delegates in Brussels before each Commission meeting, combining some hard work with good socialising (business in national research offices; fun in the lovely Art Nouveau restaurant *Le Falstaff* afterwards). I also managed to develop an excellent working relationship with the Deputy *Chef de Cabinet* of the Research Commissioner. All of this helped to develop new ideas from several sources, notably some of the early thinking that lead into the European Research Area concept.

The other half of this post involved engagement with several other countries outside the EU on science and technology (S&T) issues including India, South Korea and South Africa with which we had research and development (R&D) agreements, and supporting Ministers and GCSAs on visits to others like the United States, Canada and Japan

---

[15] Subsequently the Department for Business, Innovation and Skills and now Department for Business, Energy and Industrial Strategy (BEIS).

including the G8 Carnegie Conferences of science ministers. These provided an excellent opportunity to observe how other countries were handling the same problems that we faced and how the institutions and processes could be adapted.

I had made the choices to go to CSL, the Agency Policy role and the OST partly out of interest in the specific functions but also to broaden my experience away from the MAFF Chief Scientist's Group (CSG) with a long-term aim of applying for the Chief Scientist (CS) role when the time came for the then CS to retire. I was acutely aware that the path I had been pursuing at the intersection of science and policy was rather narrow and that opportunities for further promotion were few. Given that I might remain at the same level (Civil Service Grade 5), I looked at other outlets at this level elsewhere, in academia, in the Science and Innovation Network of the Foreign Office, and in other government departments. But in the event timing suited me though politics meant that the opportunity changed shape when I reached it.

After the huge problems posed by BSE in the 1980s–1990s and the great outbreak of Foot and Mouth Disease in 1999–2000, MAFF's reputation was low and the then Prime Minister Blair decided on a change of 'government machinery'. A new Food Standards Agency was set up to take MAFF's interest in food safety away from its concerns for the agriculture, fisheries and food industries, and these interests, along with those on rural development and conservation, were backed into the Department for the Environment to become the Department of Environment, Food and Rural Affairs (Defra). The other outcome of Lord Phillips's BSE enquiry was a great deal of advice to government departments about how they should use and manage scientific evidence when making policies, subsequently codified in the government's Chief Scientific Adviser's Guidelines.[16] Among many recommendations was one that Chief Scientist posts (usually at Civil Service Grade 3) should be replaced by Departmental Chief Scientific Advisors at Director General level, with a place on departmental boards and greater access to Ministers; DCSAs should be eminent scientists appointed from outside the department. The new Defra took up this recommendation and, to be sure that the new DCSA could operate effectively, decided to make a director-level (Grade 3) appointment to head the Chief Scientist's Group and become Deputy CSA (dCSA). Professor (later Sir) Howard Dalton FRS

[16] www.gov.uk/government/uploads/system/uploads/attachment_data/file/293037/
10–669-gcsa-guidelines-scientific-engineering-advice-policy-making.pdf

of Warwick University, an eminent microbiologist, got the CSA role, and I became his Deputy.

We faced two challenges: restoring a reputation for good science that had been lost by MAFF and bringing together two very different approaches to organising science and evidence-based policy making. For me, this was a culminating opportunity to put to work ideas that I had developed in all my previous roles. Working with Howard Dalton, and later with Professor (later Sir) Bob Watson FRS, his successor, we

- instituted a planning process for Defra's investment in science and other evidence (the Evidence and Innovation Strategies);
- established the routine publication of all Defra's 'evidence' in easily accessible form;
- worked with the Chief Economist to bring the economic analysts and scientists closer, and to appoint a senior social scientist;
- set up professional development processes for scientists, including improving their policy skills; and
- embedded scientists, economists and social scientists in policy teams.

All this took place in a context of shrinking government finance, reduction in the size of government and through a series of 'events' with high political implications such as animal and plant disease outbreaks, floods and droughts, the volcanic explosion in Iceland in 2010, and many more (Defra is known as the department for biblical plagues). The challenge was great and greatly enjoyable. Given that we reduced in size and decentralised, my 'director' role called for a lot of people management; it also needed a lot of internal stakeholder management with policy colleagues and heads of other professions as well as continuing diplomacy with colleagues in other government departments, the EU and elsewhere.

Despite all of this, the Deputy CSA role continued to bring me into contact with serious and challenging science issues such as the long-standing problem of how to control bovine tuberculosis and to understand the relationship between the disease in cattle and in badgers. The underlying challenge was always how to link policy makers to the best available science and to translate it for them in a political economic and social contexts; the corresponding challenge was how to explain policy problems to busy and eminent scientists in ways which would capture their imagination and get them engaged with finding solutions to important or urgent national policy problems. What more could you ask for?

Having retired (when I got on to my third DCSA), I have brought some of my thinking to Cambridge University's Centre for Science and Policy and am, in particular, trying to help a new generation of science graduates in Cambridge and other universities to consider science for policy making as a satisfying and exciting career option.

If I have to draw conclusions from my career, I would advise trying, especially in your early career, to widen your experience and skills development, and to work as far out of your comfort zone as possible. Don't be despondent when the jobs you want don't emerge; do grab opportunities and run with them even if they aren't your first choice. Always have a goal in mind but be aware that plans will go off-course; always think about the widest range of opportunities that your current experience has opened up. Especially in early and mid-career, look for a good mentor, ideally one with a wider view over the prospects. Finally, looking at your current experience, consider what additional skills, experience or depth would open up further possibilities. Good luck!

REFERENCES

1. The Civil Service Vol. 1 Report of the Committee 1966–68. Cmnd. 3638. London, HMSO.
2. Parker, M 2016 *The Rothschild Report (1971) and the purpose of Government-funded R&D - a personal account.* Palgrave Communications DOI: 10.1057/palcomms 2016.53

15

Science for Global Good – A Polymath's Approach

I have always been interested in nature and understanding how things work.[1] Living in a small rural village in northern India, I was lucky enough to have a natural playground that constantly challenged me and I was always encouraged to question and explore the environment I lived in. This early interest in nature provided a foundation for my future interest in science. As I entered formal education, I became increasingly interested in biology and I went on to study biomedical sciences and pharmacology at university.

In my second year, I undertook a research placement with the Psychopharmacology Research Group at King's College London. This was my first introduction to the world of research. My research focused on better understanding the biochemical mechanisms underlying anxiety and depression. Working closely with excellent post-doctoral researchers, I was able to apply my academic knowledge to practically addressing a real-world problem. I designed experiments, conducted the research, learnt new skills and techniques, analysed data sets and interpreted the results in the context of the global body of research in my research field.

This early opportunity also exposed me to some of the challenges of a career in research. Senior colleagues would regularly discuss the difficulties of gaining continuous funding, especially the independent funding important for more 'blue-skies' research essential for

---

[1] This text reflects Jasdeep's personal perspective and does not represent the official view of the UK government.

Successful Careers beyond the Lab, ed. David Bennett and Richard Jennings.
Published by Cambridge University Press. © Cambridge University Press 2017.

understanding the underlying mechanisms of diseases. In the absence of such funding, the team would have to conduct more applied and directed research funded by the private sector. This continuous juggling of funding risked basic science (which had impact several years down the line) being compromised for more applied, industry-driven research deliverable in a shorter time frame.

However, these early challenges did not deter me. As I progressed to my final year, I developed a strong interest in the brain, the fundamental organ in which mind and body converge as home to self-awareness. My curiosity about how the brain works was further driven by the eminent neuroscientist, Professor Keith Webster. His theatrical lectures and tutorials were game changers for me, and I became certain that neuroscience was my research calling. Professor Webster was a great mentor to me. He challenged me to think through my motivations for pursuing a science career that looked beyond research. That approach to my career would stand me in good stead in later years.

Following several conversations with academic tutors, I decided to pursue a Master's degree in neuroscience at the Institute of Psychiatry of King's College London, a world-leading research organisation in both basic and clinical neuroscience.

My Master's degree built upon my strong biomedical science foundation and introduced me to the complexity of neuroscience as a discipline and a research field. I came to the realisation that I was motivated by trying to solve a problem, by taking a boarder contextual approach to better understanding the problem and then exploring the options and solutions available. This meant working outside my research expertise and learning about new areas of science that would be essential to helping to address the problem. I was learning that I liked multi-disciplinary research. This interest was encouraged during my six-month research placement in a multi-disciplinary neuroscience research team investigating novel stroke and Huntington's disease models for assessing the effectiveness of new therapeutics.

My work involved working with leading stem cell experts in a new SME (small and medium-sized enterprise) that had spun out of the core research team at the University. This was an exciting working arrangement which allowed me to better understand research environments both within academia and within an innovative SME. Early results from my work were very promising and highlighted the need for more translational research. I approached the lead principle investigator (PI) to discuss possible future research in the field. I was encouraged to write a proposal outlining the new research needed and core interdisciplinary experiments required. Having already understood the value of undertaking impartial problem-driven science through my Wellcome Trust, King's Fund and Medical Research Council (MRC) studentships, I decided to apply again for independent funding for a PhD. I was successful in winning a MRC-funded scholarship and I began my PhD investigating the potential of new therapeutic stem cell lines for brain repair and recovering lost function using novel behavioural, cellular and neuroimaging techniques.

My PhD consolidated my knowledge and expanded my experience and understanding of pre-clinical and clinical research. I enjoyed the research process and the increased intellectual autonomy, and I developed core skills in data presentation, science communication, robust critical appraisal and research leadership and management that were to transcend my career in the lab. As an early-career scientist, I liked the challenge of working in a cutting-edge multi-disciplinary area of science where there was a new and growing global science community. I enjoyed the challenge of learning new skills, new disciplines critical for my research such as medical imaging and working with experts from different scientific backgrounds from physicists and engineers to geneticists and behavioural scientists, all working on providing solutions for the same problem. This period of multidisciplinary working allowed me to mature as a scientist and begin recognising the importance of looking at a problem through multiple lenses in order both to understand better the core research problem and to offer solutions to the problem which could then be tested.

WHAT CAUSED ME TO RECONSIDER

Several factors influenced me to consider careers wider than academia. The most significant factor was my interest in exploring further what role science plays in tackling real-world problems that affect society today. In order to do this, I realised I had to explore beyond my formal technical expertise and research fields.

During my PhD I had already began to expand my interests beyond my core research expertise. I became increasingly interested in better understanding the fundamental global challenges we face today, especially the challenges faced by the world's poorest. In 2013, the year of the latest comprehensive data on global poverty, 767 million people were estimated to have been living below the international poverty line of US $1.90 per person per day.[2] These people are the most vulnerable with little access to the basics of life such as food, water, shelter, sanitation, health care and

---

[2] www.worldbank.org/en/publication/poverty-and-shared-prosperity

education. Science, technology, innovation and education play a key role in helping to reduce poverty by providing solutions to these challenges. Driven by this agenda, I began to educate myself about how these sectors could address some of the most critical global challenges such as responding to international emergencies, reducing poverty and building resilience to climate change. I also became increasingly interested in how science drives, shapes and informs big decisions in national and international policy, such as engagement with the Global Sustainable Development Goals agenda.[3] I began to attend cross-sectoral networking meetings and discussion forums run by think tanks, NGO's and charities. These discussions allowed me the opportunity to better understand the opportunities and challenges around scientific and technological engagement with global organisations such as governments, multilateral actors such as the United Nations (UN) and European Union (EU) bodies and other international players.

However, following conversations with a range of colleagues and peers, it became increasingly clear that in order to fully realise any of these broader interests beyond the lab I would have to take the decision to leave basic research. No formal mechanisms existed to allow early career scientists to explore or navigate these complimentary but traditionally considered divergent career paths. I was particularly concerned about the limited guidance available through established university career offices on how broader career investigation would be undertaken. In my experience these offices often did not have access to the relevant cross-sectoral networks and often alumni who had moved across sectors were not used for guidance. In addition to this challenge there were three particular factors within the traditional academic career pathway which I felt limited the more innovative, polymath approach that I wished to pursue.

First, a constant message throughout my early career was the unpredictability of research funding for basic science. Having worked in several research teams, I was fully aware of the pressures on early-career PIs to focus increasingly on winning new funds. As a core member of research teams, I had already contributed to a number of funding bids and was responsible for addressing the recommendations put forward through the internal and external peer-review processes. The processes were often several months long with no guaranteed results in terms of whether the bid would receive final funding approvals. This process was harder for early career scientists trying to break into established or new research areas. As a result, a new PI had to plan carefully how continuous funding could be delivered in the medium-to-longer term. Having spoken

---

[3] www.un.org/millenniumgoals/

with both new and highly experienced PIs, I was made aware of the increasing pressures on early researchers to bid for independent funds in order to remain competitive in the research market. However, the core research management skills required to improve the chances of successful bids were often not formally taught during PhD training. Early researchers often felt unprepared and unsupported for the challenges presented by the bidding process. My experience highlighted the realities of building a long-term career in research and the fact that as my career progressed I would need to focus increasingly on winning further funding rather than pursuing and conducting the core research in the lab.

Second, throughout my PhD studies I was exposed to the world of 'publish or perish'. This mantra was often repeated by new PIs who were at the sharp end of research funding bidding. For them publishing was critical to building the evidence for bids and establishing them as scientists within a field. In my experience this primary objective and consistent push to publish risked the quality of science being conducted. As an early scientist, I had already experienced the challenge of experiments not providing sufficient quality data for publication or simply delivering negative results. At the time, I argued that such information in itself was valuable for publication and would help to provide important evidence on the design of similar experiments, the robustness of experimental models and the general challenges of multi-disciplinary research. However, more senior researchers advised me that publishing negative results could be career limiting. I found this thinking at odds with my interest in independent, impartial research and my view that whether the results are positive or negative, the data should be made publicly available for other researchers to review and use. In the years after I left basic research, and in my government posts, I continued to champion the need for open data in research and I am very pleased to see significant changes and incentives now in place for early career scientists to share data both through peer-reviewed papers as well as live online dataset repositories. A more recent move towards real-time data release is particularity game-changing. A great example of this is the recent work by preclinical researchers at the University of Wisconsin–Madison in developing a Zika Open Research Portal which is helping the world to tackle the ongoing (in 2016) global outbreak of the Zika virus by better understanding how the virus behaves in vivo and providing this data in a timely way for anyone to access.[4] During my work in delivering the UK Governments response to Zika Outbreak, I

---

[4] https://zika.labkey.com/project/home/begin.view?

used this real-time repository (as a part of a boarder science response) to help ensure the most cutting research was being used to inform the Governments approach.

Third, I become increasingly aware of the lack of women maintaining their research careers as they had children. Several of my colleagues (me included) had been informed by senior male colleagues (who sincerely thought they were being helpful) that women typically dropped out of research careers once they started a family. The perception amongst some senior male PIs was that women may not return to a full-time career in academic research and that a reduction in publication during maternity and child care leave could result in women being less competitive than men in securing future funding. Although there are laws which provide formal protection for women at work, these more subtle influences can significantly affect female career trajectories. Even with these rather depressing perceptions by some colleagues, I was able to seek out female research mentors who provided powerful examples of how to make a career in science. These women typically grew a thick skin through years of pushing back on traditional views whilst still focussing on finding the right approach for them between an active research career and family life. This background resistance to the status quo has now received a significant helping hand through universities adopting initiatives such as the United Kingdom's Equality Challenge Unit's Athena Swan Charter.[5] The Charter was established in 2005 to encourage and recognise commitment to advancing the careers of women in science, technology, engineering, maths and medicine (STEMM) higher education and research. The result has been institutional-level push and clear incentives to develop female scientific leaders of the future. These positive steps forward are enabling female early-career scientists today to take a stronger position on their future careers without compromising their personal lives.

HOW I WENT ABOUT FINDING OTHER OPPORTUNITIES
AND WHAT HAPPENED

I initially spoke to my research colleagues about the options of moving beyond academia and a career outside research. Although these conversations were insightful, they did not provide me with new networks or opportunities that I needed. Much of this was due to the fact that many researchers had not themselves explored other possible careers and so

[5] www.ecu.ac.uk/equality-charters/athena-swan/

they did not have this broader experience. However, these conversations did prompt me to take a more detailed look at my skills set and consider how these could be applied to other careers. I mapped my skills, experience, expertise and, most importantly, future career interests, and used this as a framework to explore new opportunities. I began investigating online careers options for research scientists and this helped me to develop a broader career perspective. I took time to consider which sectors I would like to investigate further and undertook some research on key organisations in these areas, investigating them further if I had an interest. These processes lead me to consider a wide range of possible sectors of interest from government and the private sector to the charity and NGO community. I also thought about the core values I wanted to see in any future employer. This helpful step allowed me to focus down on potential areas of interests. In order to better understand possible sectors of interest I attended various networking events and open days. This allowed me to meet people and provided the opportunity to hear first-hand the kinds of careers paths and progression routes different organisations offered.

I developed an interest in how government worked to deliver policies that could help to improve society. I began investigating in more detail the types of posts and careers offered by the UK Civil Service. I spoke to friends who had previously held positions within government to get a broader understanding of the career structures. I also undertook my own research and identified key departments that I was interested in exploring further. I followed this up with introductory e-mails asking for advice and guidance on how I could look for future post opportunities. I received several helpful responses which informed my decision-making and these included more details about the huge variety of different careers offered by government and invitations to open days. These helpfully allowed me the opportunity to engage with several civil servants from different analytical disciplines working on diverse policy areas.

I asked for feedback from civil servants on whether my skills would fit the Civil Service. The most helpful feedback I received was that my background would be of value in a broad range of government policy and operational areas but that I needed to broaden my competencies and gain new experience within government programme delivery. I also asked for guidance on how to translate my skills from research into this different working environment. This was essential information as the language used in different sectors often varied and it is important to understand how to communicate your expertise, experience and career ambition when moving between sectors. My proactive approach led to my first Civil Service post within the Government Office for Science working with the Government's Chief Scientific Adviser on improving the way the central government departments used science and evidence in strategic and operational decision-making.

Reflecting on this transition, it would have been helpful to have taken more time to understand the cultural differences between sectors. Both academia and government have clearly defined cultural norms and ways of working. Transitioning between these two significant sectors presented new opportunities such as greater career development and progression in government than in academia. There were also new challenges such as the requirement to remain impartial and neutral as a civil servant versus taking a clear scientific position in research where public recognition of your work was encouraged. A significant reward of moving across sectors is developing new skills that enable you to take a wider perspective on how lessons could be shared and applied across sectors.

I have now held several other posts within the UK government which have all helped refine and often broaden my interests. In recent years I have taken on posts within the Department for International Development (DFID) which have allowed me to more fully exploit and use my skills in science and research, and apply these to address some on the most pressing development challenges in the poorest countries. During this time, I have delivered a diverse range of initiatives that have strengthened the use of evidence-based decision-making in the department. Examples have included building new cross-government systems that allow the sciences to be used to better predict, plan and respond to international humanitarian emergencies and disasters. These systems allow rapid access to operationally relevant scientific information and multi-hazard risk assessments when responding to global natural disasters. I have worked on the government response to the 2015 West African Ebola crisis, the 2015 Nepal earthquake and the ongoing 2016 Zika outbreak. I have also led innovative programmes which are building new global South-South-North research partnerships. These partnerships are building new African scientific capacity and leadership across the continent in critical areas of research required to address the development challenges of the continent.

My experiences in new sectors outside academia have expanded my horizons, allowing me to continue to challenge myself and become more creative in thinking about future career posts. In summary, there is life beyond a traditional academic career!

I have had helpful mentoring relationships both within my peer network and with more senior colleagues (both within government and outside of it) which have allowed me to consider and reflect upon new areas of interest. These relationships have allowed frank and constructive conversations and have provided new networks to investigate. Mentoring relationships are an enabling tool when considering new career paths allowing you the space to reflect and receive impartial feedback. These relationships also allow a neutral forum for discussion of the opportunities and challenges that you encounter and the opportunities to lesson learn from previous experiences. This process with more formal coaching will help to define better your career goals.

WHERE IT LED ME AND, CRUCIALLY, HOW OTHERS MAY FOLLOW

A career, like many things in life, is about the journey. By keeping your mind open to new possibilities you can develop a portfolio approach to a career that spans many interests and sectors and is tailored to your motivations rather than taking a linear trajectory. It is important to be proactive in exploring possible career options in which you have an interest and in building networks that allow you to engage and investigate options by talking to people already in posts. Spending time to identify your skills experience, and expertise is a good exercise, allowing you to explore gaps in knowledge, experience or expertise and plan for how these could be filled. Continuing to learn, develop new skills and develop new interests is critical to ensuring you are in demand and have the opportunity to apply yourself in different career paths. It is also valuable to develop mentoring and coaching relationships that allow you the opportunity to explore new options, learn from the experience of others and develop new professional networks. Both mentoring and coaching have different but complimentary objectives and, used together, can help you to progress further.

My experience has highlighted that there is no single perfect career path but that careers are made up of different jobs that are connected by your interests. Dispelling the myth of a linear, life-long career in one field is important. With the future of work changing dramatically in the coming decades, graduates today must become ever more comfortable in changing roles, sectors and ways of working. This means that more focus is placed on exploring posts that allow professional development and learning new skills that will help to open other doors for future careers and posts. Above all, it is essential to remain curious and explore new possibilities driven by your own passions.

16

Skills, Networks and Luck

One of my earliest memories is of a scientific investigation. I must have been just three years old when I repeatedly bit a worm in two to see what was on the inside. I can still remember the feeling of curiosity as I tried to see if different bits were different on the inside.

As I got older my tastes changed somewhat. I built Meccano robots that could walk but never quite got them to climb stairs. I developed an interest in rockets which culminated with one over 2 metres long made from a cardboard carpet-roll tube. It got off the ground, but only just. It was just as well that my friends and I hadn't quite understood how to optimise the design otherwise my career might have ended rather differently.

I had liked biology but the rote learning put me off. I messed up my Biology Ordinary level (General Certificate of Education) and couldn't imagine where being in a lab would lead me so I took a rather different tack involving business and engineering. I persuaded my school to let me keep bees and sold the honey to pay for the hives. For a school biology field trip I built a kite with a camera suspended from it to take photos of the field rather than counting species on my hands and knees.

So I suppose it was inevitable that I should do maths, physics and chemistry at Advanced level even though I couldn't see where they were going to lead. I was a very disorganised secretary of the 6th Form Science Society but managed to get a professor from Surrey University to visit with his travelling exhibition that ended by bringing the school to a halt when it was discovered what I had arranged.

Successful Careers beyond the Lab, ed. David Bennett and Richard Jennings.
Published by Cambridge University Press. © Cambridge University Press 2017.

I had thought of becoming a doctor but (unlike my medic daughter) I couldn't cope with blood, vomit and other body products. I'd thought of doing psychology but it turned out that on the form we had to fill out I misspelled the word and – after an interview with the headmaster – never recovered my enthusiasm.

It was about then that I was walking down the school corridor during a free period when the Deputy Head was looking for victims to be an audience for someone from Post Office Telecommunications (which ended up as BT – British Telecommunications plc). They were offering sponsored places at university provided that you followed a STEM (science, technology, engineering and maths) subject, preferably engineering. So despite thinking engineering was a bit boring – based entirely on some misunderstood ideas about what engineering actually was – I began to think seriously about it. I was a fan of Dr Who and the Cybermen,[1] so that, together with my walking robots and a book by Norbert Wiener called *Cybernetics*,[2] I convinced myself that I should do one of the two courses on cybernetics in the United Kingdom at the time.

So it was that I found myself at the end of a series of chance events one September at the age of 18 sitting in Horwood House near Bletchley Park, then the General Post Office's College of Engineering Studies, with 17 other sponsored Post Office students beginning a pre-university year which covered electronics, relativity, Boolean algebra, building an analog computer, mending cables in filthy junction boxes, climbing telegraph poles, building a steam engine and badly bruising myself when I forgot to remove the chuck key from a lathe.

That year opened my eyes to engineering. I began to get fascinated by telecoms and computing in particular. I never lost my misgivings about getting pigeonholed in a narrow discipline but here was something where the pace of change and the possibilities seemed endless.

A year later, arriving on my course at the University of Reading where I was doing Cybernetics with Instrument Physics and Mathematics, I was in for a bit of a shock. For a start, I was a year older than everyone else but, more importantly, we started to go over ground that I had already covered. I even contemplated dropping out for a year and applying to the University of Cambridge but thought I couldn't afford another year's delay. I took an economics option but resisted their

---

[1] www.thedoctorwhosite.co.uk/cybermen/cybermen-episode-guide/

[2] Wiener, N. (1961) Cybernetics or Control and Communication in the Animal and Machine. MIT Press; 2nd Revised edition.

attempts to get me to change course. I got involved in politics and ended up with a paid trip to Berlin one cold and snowy January. That could have been another life-changing moment: one of my companions had a map of the minefields and machine gun emplacements, and was stopped by the East German border guards. It's just as well they didn't find it.

One of the many great things about being a Post Office student was that they gave you a job during the summer vacations. I opted for the Long Range Studies Division, part of Post Office Telecoms which looked ahead 20–30 years. I spent that first summer investigating video-conferencing and building a model to choose the best locations for video-conferencing studios.

It was then that I began to realise that the maths and engineering I was learning had practical consequences and that a rigorous approach was crucial. We were trying to work out how many meetings people had, where they travelled for the meeting and how big the meetings were; the idea was to use this information to work out how big the market for video-conferencing might be. Then one of my colleagues pointed out that the survey was biased: there was a bigger chance of picking up a large meeting in a survey than a small meeting, and that the observed frequency of meeting sizes in the survey should be divided by the number of people at the meeting. Obvious really, but it had a profound effect on me as I realised I could have produced results which were meaningless. I think about 5 or 6 of the 30-plus locations I recommended were built – and well used for the few years before further changes in technology began to make them largely irrelevant.

Research shows that if you spend at least a year living in a foreign country you are more innovative than your home-bound counterparts – with the most likely explanation being that it shows you how things can be done completely differently. I've been lucky enough to have clocked up well over a year working outside the United Kingdom and the first part of that experience was four weeks in France as the guest of what became France Telecom. With their own private wine cellars, holiday homes and building new telephone exchanges in less than 18 months (we took years in the United Kingdom), the French had quite a different approach to both employment policy and engineering. It was 1975, and France was in the middle of a series of five-year plans to increase six-fold the number of telephones from a woeful 7 per 100 population. Paris was a maze of road works and the plans on the walls in their laboratories covered 20 years and many generations of technology yet to be realised.

Returning to the United Kingdom, I decided that when I finished my degree the following year I would not go to Martlesham Heath – the home of BT's Research Labs – but would instead re-join the Long Range Studies Division which was just relocating to Cambridge. I'd seen enough to realise that I didn't want to work on the technology – I wanted to see what the future was going to hold. So, armed with a shiny new degree, I turned up and did research for what was probably the most formative 18 months of my life.

The world of technology in 1976 was utterly different from that of 2016. No desktop computers, hardly any mobile phones (and those had to use an operator to make calls) and communications was almost all analogue, not digital. Yet, if you looked carefully, you could see the straws in the wind and I was lucky enough to work on some amazing projects which set out how technology was going to change the world.

I worked on what might happen if computers became small and cheap enough so they could be used for word processing and messaging (the Apple 1 had just been released). I looked at trends in mobile telephony and concluded that there was a huge potential market (and found my report was then 'rebadged' and claimed by a senior person in marketing in London as his own work). I helped to develop a model of the telecom market in the United Kingdom to explore what would happen if competition were introduced (telecoms was a monopoly, and there was almost no talk of changing that then).

But two things really stand out. First, I was asked to participate in a Delphi Panel – a group of experts who were forecasting the prices of integrated circuits and computer memory. This was needed to work out the best architecture for the planned digitalisation of the United Kingdom's telecoms network. I read Gordon Moore's book with his now famous law that the price performance of chips doubles every 18 months or so.[3] I looked at the fundamentals of the physics of materials used in integrated circuits and memories. I remembered seeing the red LEDs in the lab in Brittany in France and discussing how these might be the future of lighting. It dawned on me that – apart from some technological dead ends which were obvious – there was effectively no limit to the fall in price of the technology. I bought some five-cycle log graph paper and drew lines to show how the different technologies would fall in price by 30–60% per year, year on year. I submitted my work and waited.

The answer came, but not quite as expected. I had a visitor from London who, after he had overcome the shock of seeing how young

---

[3] www.cs.utexas.edu/~fussell/courses/cs352h/papers/moore.pdf

I was, patiently explained that all the other experts had forecast price falls of 3–8% per year. Did I realise, he asked, that I was forecasting that a whole page of A4 text (roughly 10 kilobytes) would be stored for less than 0.1 pence (in 2016, memory is less than 1/100,000 of that price). This was incredible. I had to revise my forecasts. I refused. I was asked to leave the panel.

The second event was when I was taken down to London with Jim Cowie, my Head of Division, to see a crazy presentation on this new technology called packet-switching. The US Department of Defense had funded a project called ARPANET[4] which had first gone live in 1968, and which was now courting funds to help extend the London node which had been built in 1973. As the presentation drew to a close, Jim asked me if we should provide the £100,000 University College London (UCL) were asking for their part in the project. I said 'yes, because someday all communication will be by packets'. Whilst I cannot pretend that I understood at the time the full implications of what I said, I thought the outcome was pretty clear. Moore's law and the simplicity and scalability of this new approach meant that the old, special-purpose dedicated networks were never going to win in the long run.

But all this had brought home to me that I needed to improve my skills. I knew enough engineering and economics to get by but I felt I needed more – especially in maths and statistics. So I decided to go for a PhD.

The choice was between 'optimal control of the UK economy' and 'telecoms and economic development'. I chose the latter. My supervisor, Geoff Walsham, had experience in Kenya and I had already been working on projects with a consultancy, Communications Studies and Planning (CS&P), which had a strong interest in developing countries. Through them I met Bob Saunders and Bjorn Wellenius from the World Bank who amazingly arranged for me to be the economist on a three-person team to look at funding Kenya's new telecoms project following the break-up of the East African Community. The World Bank went on to fund my field work in Kenya and used my thesis and a published paper in their book, *Telecommunications and Economic Development*.[5]

At the time telecommunications was thought to be mostly irrelevant for economic development. There was a handful of people, mostly

---

[4] The Advanced Research Projects Agency Network was an early packet switching network which, with the TCP/IP (Transmission Control Protocol/Internet Protocol), became the foundation of the Internet.

[5] http://documents.worldbank.org/curated/en/244111468763783754/pdf/multi-page.pdf

in the United States, who believed that improving telecommunications could have a disproportionate effect on economic growth. Looking back, it seems almost incredible that, for the most part, telecommunications was treated as a luxury, not a major underpinning for all economic activity and growth.

The four years of my PhD enabled me to learn about many more things than the immediate topic. I attended economics and statistics lectures and supervised students in operational research – and that forced me to stay on top of things. Most importantly, I found that being challenged by a professor of geography ('no one has ever succeeded in doing that') was just what I needed to break through the mire that threatened to engulf my work.

As my PhD came to an end, I drew on the network of contacts I had built up and found a job with the Economist Intelligence Unit in London alongside some of the people from CS&P who had left to form a new Informatics Unit. I found myself in at the deep end – running consulting projects for BT, the European Commission and Mercury, the newly established competitor in the UK market. Looking back, it is amazing how I survived – but the PhD had taught me how to deliver the goods whilst keeping a strong logical framework.

After two years or so and with a growing family, I began to find that commuting from Cambridge was getting too much. So I began to think about starting my own consultancy. Once again the network of people I had built up played a crucial role. Roland Hüber at the European Commission gave me some important breaks, as did contacts at BT. By the end of 1985 I had managed to get Analysys Ltd up and running and making its first faltering steps to becoming a real business.

For the next five years Analysys was more like a think-tank or research organisation than a consultancy, mostly because of the research-based work we did for clients like the European Commission and because that's where we built up our expertise and our track record. But then we got a major contract to model the future of tele-communications investment in Europe from 1990 to 2010. We had the economics, maths and computing skills for the job but crucially we lacked the project management. The contract nearly broke the company but in doing the work we attracted attention from telecoms operators throughout Europe and many more commercially oriented projects followed (almost all of them better managed).

My background in information and communications technology made me an enthusiast. By the mid-1990s Analysys had built Web systems which enabled us to share information and projects well in advance of anything that was commercially available (or even being used elsewhere). Looking back, I can see opportunities missed: we had built the precursors to Salesforce and LinkedIn years before these were launched. But one opportunity did not slip. In January 1998 a chance conversation with Jonathan Milner led me to provide the main funding for starting Abcam and using the technology developed at Analysys to build the Web site and back office systems for what is now a £1.75 billion company which Jonathan describes in his chapter. The irony is that my most successful venture was a return to the biology that had bored me as a 16-year-old.

Since then I've sold Analysys and started and sold a number of other companies, almost all of them in communications technology. My experience of the value of networking has lead me to co-found the Cambridge Network, Cambridge Wireless, Cambridge Angels and the Centre for Science and Policy at the University of Cambridge. I've served on one of the Boards of the Ministry of Defence, and at the communications regulator Ofcom. I've become Chairman of Raspberry Pi, a series of credit card–sized computers[6] – a role that draws on pretty well everything I have ever learnt.

But in the end a lot of this comes down to luck.

There's an interesting experiment which shows that some people really are lucky. The subjects are asked to fill out a questionnaire which asks them whether they perceive themselves to be lucky or not. They are then asked to count the number of photos in a newspaper and then run up a flight of stairs to report the result to an office. The ones who say they are unlucky diligently count the photos and run to report how many they have found. The one's who say they are lucky are the ones who spot the half page notice in the paper which says 'there are 49 photos in this newspaper' and, on the way up to the office, spot the £10 note left lying on the stairs.

So the 'lab' – a rigorous, evidence-based approach where you hone your skills – can lead to a good career. But there are three things you need if you decide to pursue a career elsewhere. First, never lose the rigour of the logical approach to addressing problems. Second, build your network – the people you meet will be those who will be hugely valuable to you in your career. And finally be lucky – look out for the chance events and don't blindly follow instructions.

[6] www.raspberrypi.org/

17

Politics and Policy

Most scientists I know have opinions on what is happening in the rest of the world; the stereotype of the white-coated eccentric up in an ivory tower unaware of the rest of the world isn't accurate.

However, what does seem to be accurate is that a lot of scientists have their strong opinions – and do nothing about them. Somehow, getting involved in public issues – the messiness of politics, the agonies of trying to change public policy – feel like things a proper scientist shouldn't do.

That, of course, is nonsense, and dangerous, and needs to change. As Aaron Sorkin says, 'Decisions are made by those who show up'.[1] If we as scientists, as engineers, as STEM[2] graduates don't show up, other people, with other ideas, perhaps with less grasp of evidence and facts, will do so to our detriment and the detriment of our values and principles.

In this chapter I want to encourage you to get involved in policy, and maybe even politics. I'll try to persuade you that it's worth doing and, while there's no single route to it, I'll tell you my own route into politics and policy-making, and some of the impressions I formed there. Then I'll suggest some other options you might want to look at.

---

[1] www.slate.com/blogs/browbeat/2012/05/16/aaron_sorkin_s_syracuse_recycled_commencement_speech_also_had_lines_from_the_west_wing_and_sports_night.html (accessed 18 January 2017).

[2] Science, technology, engineering and maths.

Successful Careers beyond the Lab, ed. David Bennett and Richard Jennings.
Published by Cambridge University Press. © Cambridge University Press 2017.

WHY CARE ABOUT POLICY

All our lives are affected by decisions made by governments. Our legal system, our financial model, how education works, how healthcare is provided, how transport is operated, how much support we give to those in need, nationally and internationally, what efforts we make to tackle climate change and save our environment – the list goes on. Any and all of these decisions can be made in different ways, and most of them are being reconsidered at any time.

Changes at the policy level have the huge benefit of operating at large scale. An excellent teacher will transform the lives of a thousand pupils, perhaps. An excellent Education Secretary can help millions – and a poor one can cause harm to millions. Policy is more nebulous, less direct – but the prizes at stake are much more substantial.

Let me give you an example. After the 2010 UK General Election came a Comprehensive Spending Review (CSR) – a plan for how much each year would be spent on all government departments. Many people lobbied on lots of areas, and one key topic was how much would be spent on science and research. Lots of effort went in from many directions: learned societies put in economic analyses showing the benefits of investing in science; Science is Vital organised a huge public rally outside the Treasury; and the Campaign for Science and Engineering secured media coverage.

As a newly elected MP, I took advantage of the access that allowed me to speak directly to all the members of the so-called Quad – the four key ministers who would decide the outcome. These were the Prime Minister and Deputy Prime Minister, the Chancellor of Exchequer, and the Chief Secretary to the Treasury. On the Sunday evening before the CSR, the plan was for the science budget to be cut by £200 million a year. Those four were having dinner at Chequers, the Prime Minister's residence in the country, and a phone call came through from the Treasury, saying that they had rerun the figures, there was £200 million surplus and what should they do with it. Nick Clegg, the Deputy Prime Minister, said, 'Let's put it into science'; the others agreed and they moved on.

In the space of 30 minutes, the science research budget leapt up by £200 million a year – with huge consequences for many scientists across the country. (I should confess that although I have multiple sources to confirm the sudden increase, my only source to say it was Nick's decision was Nick himself). It's a powerful case for the benefits of being inside, being able to influence – but it also shows one of the frustrations of policy involvement; you can rarely be sure that it was your work that made the crucial difference. If I had done nothing, would this have happened anyway? Or was my focus the pressure that achieved the tipping point? Who knows? Unlike an academic paper, where it is normally clear who did crucial experiments, the policy arena is far more muddled – and, as John F. Kennedy used to say, success has many fathers.

So policy engagement is frustrating – but it is completely worth it.

MY STORY

My training was very much as a traditional scientist: double maths, physics and chemistry at school for A-levels, and then natural sciences at Cambridge, followed by a PhD in biological chemistry.

I tell the story now of how much I enjoyed the research, and some of it I did – but like many people, my PhD went through some rather tougher times as well. Nothing from the first two years of my work made it into my thesis and I got to the stage of discussing dropping down to an MPhil. In the end, I discovered that by giving up on most of the experimental work I was doing and moving to computational biology, I could address some really interesting questions about unusual DNA structures.

Part of the challenge in doing my work was that just before I started my PhD, I was elected County Councillor, a Liberal Democrat representing East Chesterton – the North Eastern corner of Cambridge and a fascinating demographic mix ranging from wealthy housing through to struggling council estates. In his Preface to this book Professor Sir Tom Blundell tells how he became similarly involved in local issues in Oxford and a member of its City Council working on local planning.

Local government plays a crucial role in our system but it is little discussed – it lacks the glamour and media fascination of Westminster. However, it is in many ways far more important for people's actual life experiences with responsibilities for such day-to-day issues as transport, housing, social services and education.

It's also very much a part-time activity which means it is possible to combine it with having a non-political career as well. There's also the interest in representing people and so getting to see the realities of the lives of a wide cross-section of society. It pays (not much, usually) and offers the real chance to make a tangible difference. The time commitment started off at around a half-day to a day a week; I then took on extra responsibilities, such as becoming Chair of the Cambridge Traffic Management Committee – as anyone who knows Cambridge will tell you, an almost impossible job! More than a decade later, there are still road schemes that I designed (or, rather, set parameters for and approved; actual engineers did the detailed design, fortunately).

I also served as Leader of the Opposition – an important job, and one I learned a lot from, but one which was ultimately frustrating. The role of the Leader of the Opposition is to challenge, hold to account and make suggestions that will be defeated. I remember once working carefully on a budget speech, crafting it immaculately (I hoped) and suddenly realising that if it was an excellent speech, then the Liberal Democrat Councillors would vote for my proposals, the Tories would vote against, and the handful of Labour Councillors would abstain. If it was a rubbish speech, the same would happen.

But there are longer-term benefits even then; many of the proposals that we made would be adopted a year or two later by the administration although somehow they would always forget to acknowledge where they came from. By following Harry Truman's advice, it was possible to get a lot done – he's said to have remarked that 'It is amazing what you can accomplish if you do not care who gets the credit.' For example, I remember advocating for a particular environmental scheme to be told by the Conservative Cabinet that they were utterly opposed to it and would not fund it – only to be told by an officer that it was alright, it was in the budget, but in such a way that the Tories would never find it.

This experience and many like it stood me in good stead when I then became an MP. I'd never really intended it to happen – unlike the stereotype of the Oxford PPE[3] graduate who wanted to be Prime Minister from their first breath, it was not a deliberate plan. I'd got involved in politics through an interest in international human rights and the United Nations (UN) – and a programme called Model UN in particular.[4] Having grown up under Margaret Thatcher, I knew I was left of centre, and then when I discovered liberalism as an idea, I realised that was me. I was a Liberal and hence a Liberal Democrat. I was driven by the philosophy, and how it could be used to improve people's lives and empower them – not by any desire for power in and of itself.

---

[3] Philosophy, politics and economics. There are about as many MPs who studied PPE at Oxford (200 graduates a year) as STEM (90,000 graduates a year) across the United Kingdom.

[4] In which students learn about diplomacy, international relations and the United Nations.

Indeed, in 2007 I decided that juggling politics and science was too much for me to do at the level I wanted to do and I decided to retire from politics; I stood down from my Leadership, secured an academic position (strangely, in physics) and left the Council in 2009.

However, later that year, just as I was feeling the odd sensation of being free – I missed my first party conference in years – I discovered that the Liberal Democrat MP for Cambridge, someone I had helped get elected five years previously, was going to stand down, unexpectedly. I decided I couldn't pass up the chance to represent my home town and stood – successfully. Had it not been for that fortune, I would have continued, hopefully quite happily, as an academic.

THE HOUSE OF COMMONS

Parliament is an odd place. It's incredibly archaic in how it operates, and feels very much like a village – everyone knows everyone. I had spent very little time there before being elected, unlike many others who were old hands. However, I thought that if I could cope with the more than 800-year-old University of Cambridge and the College system, I'd be fine. Far from it; Parliament is far odder!

I was one of the few scientists in the House of Commons in 2010. The exact number depends on exactly how you measure it – there were two of us out of 650 with science PhDs but others had had involvement in science or a STEM[5] degree.

It was fascinating to see the attitudes of MPs to science. There was a decent cohort – maybe around 75 – who got it. Some had studied sciences, some hadn't, but they understood how it worked and what it could do. However, we were definitely a minority.

Most MPs were positive about science – but didn't get it. They were the sort of people we see quite often who may have dropped sciences at 16 and think of it as a really hard thing to understand. They know it's really powerful and can do some amazing things but they don't really get it. They're, frankly, a bit scared of it.

This sometimes leads them to place a huge amount of faith in science and scientists; when we were debating mitochondrial replacement therapy (known in the tabloid newspapers as 'three-parent embryos', although 2.00001 parents would be more accurate), there was a free vote so I acted as a whip to encourage people to vote the

---

[5] Science, Technology, Engineering and Mathematics

right way (right is here defined as being the way I wanted.) Several MPs rushed up to ask 'Which way for science?' when the vote happened. Science is, of course, not capable of answering the moral and ethical question as to what we should do with an embryo; it tells us what we can do.

Then there are also a few people I would have to characterise as anti-science. There were not many of them but they were capable of causing a lot of harm and damage. In the US Congress where there are more like this, they have caused huge harm by denying the realities of climate change against all the evidence. Here in the United Kingdom, the quintessential example is David Tredinnick, MP for Bosworth in Leicestershire in the centre of England. He advocates all sorts of 'alternative medicine', astrology and much more. To give you a flavour, here's a direct quote from him in 2009 when he was arguing for more funding for astrology research.

> In 2001 I raised in the House the influence of the moon, on the basis of the evidence then that at certain phases of the moon there are more accidents. Surgeons will not operate because blood clotting is not effective and the police have to put more people on the street. (HC Deb, 14 October 2009, c414)

This is of course a testable hypothesis – do feel free to ask any friendly surgeon if they stop operating during a full moon, or indeed, if you know anyone who cut themselves during a full moon and survived to tell the tale. Fortunately, most MPs are not as bad as Tredinnick.

The scientific method is, above all, about being able to reject a hypothesis. We pride ourselves on being neutral about our ideas, prepared, even eager to abandon them if the evidence so demands. Politics is not like that, and this was a huge shock to me.

One of the worst things a politician can do is a U-turn. People are attacked for it and the press will count up how many U-turns have been performed (e.g. the *Daily Mirror* in May 2016: '24 screeching U-turns David Cameron has been forced to make'). We would never criticise a scientist for proposing and rejecting lots of hypotheses, but we do for politicians.

As a result, politicians feel forced to continue to argue things, even when the evidence has turned against them. Time and again, the pressure is on to look for some new way of justifying a statement that had been made previously, some new way of analyzing reality, rather than admitting that an idea was a bad one. We, the public, also have some responsibility here – rather than attacking politicians who change their minds, we should congratulate them for rethinking and listening to facts and experience.

This phenomenon also means that if you want to truly change a policy, whether as a politician or from the outside, the best time is to change it before it is said. Once a minister has said something, it is hard to amend it, even a little bit. It's not impossible – there are many examples of it happening – but it is far, far easier to stop things before they start. However, that means having a very acute insight into what is being considered and thought about.

One specific example of many was an amendment to the Infrastructure Bill. I wanted to see a legal commitment for the government to have a Cycling and Walking Investment Strategy – I spent a lot of time promoting those forms of active transport. I made the case in various ways and, although we almost got there, I got a letter from the minister saying that it would not happen for a range of reasons – the government just didn't back it.

I could have publicised that letter but instead I kept fighting quietly and got Deputy Prime Minister Nick Clegg to intervene. In the end, the government accepted my case and proposed an amendment to do exactly what I wanted. I then had to listen to the minister wax lyrical about how this was always the intention. Had I let anyone know about the letter, they would have been locked into having to oppose it, and we would never have secured the much-needed strategy.

YOUR ROUTES IN

I hope that has given you a flavour of my own route into politics and policy. But everyone's route is unique. How can you create one for yourself?

If you want a political role, then party allegiances are important – but they also give you a structure to work within. Is there a party you feel aligned with? It's not important that you agree with everything they say – that would be extremely unusual indeed. But it is important that you feel they do broadly align with your own values. The story is told of Charles Kennedy that when he was campaigning in 2005, he spoke to some voters with TV crews recording. Discovering one was very supportive, he asked her, rather bravely, if she would join the Liberal Democrats. She said 'No', as she only agreed with about two-thirds of their policies. He replied, 'That's slightly more than I do, so welcome aboard!'

Most parties have internal organisations for scientists, and they can have a real influence – the Association of Liberal Democrat

Engineers and Scientists[6] has been very effective, and I believe Scientists for Labour[7] are also. They can be a very useful point of contact to discuss how your skills, knowledge and expertise can be used to change what happens at the national level.

I'd also encourage you to think about standing for election, locally or nationally. I found it an incredibly rewarding experience, even though it also gave me some of the toughest moments of my life. One frustration found in research was the slow pace of progress but, on the other hand, when you help a constituent who is homeless to have somewhere to live, there is an instant sense of achievement. Contact the local branch of whatever party feels closest and offer to help out; they will be delighted! And if you are reading this, serious about getting involved further and can't get any response from your party, do contact me directly, no matter your political beliefs. We need more good people in politics!

If you don't want to go for the political route – or at least not yet – there are lots of other options. They partly depend on whether you want to use your expertise to deliver policies set by others or whether you prefer to become an advocate of policy change. It also depends on whether you want to do this full time or as a sideline to another career. One of the pleasures of working in policy is that it is possible to transition over.

Parliament has a number of places for scientists who want to feed expertise into the political process, including some short-term placements. The Parliamentary Office of Science and Technology (POST) provides impartial advice for Parliamentarians, in particular through POSTnotes – four-page summaries of the state-of-play in a particular field. They offer funded three-month fellowships for a range of PhD students and post-docs – an excellent chance to get a flavour of the work and Westminster.[8]

It's also worth engaging with MPs, no matter their politics. In my experience, very few people go to see an MP to discuss a policy issue and those that do normally want something. Befriend your local MP and offer them advice in your field, especially if there is something coming up that you know about. I benefitted hugely from detailed advice from a veterinary researcher when discussing the regulations for animal experimentation. The Royal Society organises an annual pairing

---

[6] www.aldes.org.uk/   [7] www.scientistsforlabour.org.uk/en/
[8] www.parliament.uk/postfellowships

scheme, bringing scientists to Westminster for a week to spend time shadowing an MP.[9]

Select Committees are another useful place to feed in advice. These are relatively small cross-party committees which focus on particular areas of government. Their hearings are public, streamed live, and they always have calls for evidence when they start an inquiry. Writing a response, with your experience in and evidence about the subject, almost certainly guarantees that they will publish it, and the staff will definitely read it – and you may well get quoted in the final report. As I write, the Science and Technology Select Committee, just one of many, is looking into everything from science communication through to satellites and space.[10]

The Civil Service also recruits a number of scientists, especially in departments such as the Department of Environment Food & Rural Affairs (Defra). There is a specialist science and engineering fast stream specifically designed to ensure that people with these crucial skills can get into the parts of government where they are most needed.

If you're more senior, every government department now has a Chief Scientific Advisor and they generally have a team in place to provide scientific advice.[11] Centrally, there is the Government Office for Science that looks ahead to ensure the best scientific evidence is used to inform long-term policy-making.

There are also many groups outside government, seeking to have an influence on what decisions are made. These tend to be organisations with a particular interest so it's quite important to make sure you are interested in what they work on. These include organisations that work on science itself, such as the Campaign for Science and Engineering (CaSE),[12] which is well worth joining in any event, or the Royal Society.[13] Most learned societies also have a policy wing, particularly the bigger ones.

Many NGOs and charities also play important roles in pressing for policy change in areas such as health (e.g. the British Heart

[9] https://royalsociety.org/grants-schemes-awards/pairing-scheme/

[10] www.parliament.uk/business/committees/committees-a-z/commons-select/ science-and-technology-committee/

[11] Dr Jasdeep Sandhu, author of Chapter 15, is Head of the Chief Scientific Adviser's Cabinet, Research and Evidence Division, Department for International Development.

[12] www.sciencecampaign.org.uk/   [13] https://royalsociety.org/

Foundation,[14] Cancer Research UK[15] or the Wellcome Trust[16]), environmental issues (Royal Society for the Protection of Birds (RSPB),[17] Greenpeace[18] or Friends of the Earth[19]) or almost any other area. One challenge is that there are often not that many jobs available in any particular organisation and so it can take a while to identify the right role in an area you know about and are interested in; sadly, it's very common for people to have to do fairly long internships before they can go for a permanent job.

There are now increasing numbers of think tanks in the United Kingdom which aim to produce new ideas. Originally, they prided themselves on thinking more outside the box but as the Civil Service reduces in size they are increasingly playing a more central role in helping to design and develop current ideas. Consultancies are also increasingly asked to do detailed policy work.

A good place to look, whether you want a temporary or permanent position, is the excellent w4mp website.[20] It's moved on from its original aim of helping people find a job working for an MP to be a clearing house for all manner of political and policy roles.

If you feel you need additional training to enter a career in policy-making or just fancy an extra year in a university out of the lab, a few universities now offer Master's degrees in public policy (MPP). The MPP course at the University of Cambridge, in which I teach, is an intensive one-year programme designed to be both academic and vocational, and to ensure you develop the skills needed to be able to develop ideas and work critically with experts; students do enough economics, statistics, philosophy, media training and so forth to be able to understand and challenge the advice they may be given.[21]

Everyone has a different route into policy and I would recommend you explore as many of the options suggested here – as well as others you might discover – as you can. See if you can find a mentor, someone who has already made it into the policy space and can easily advise you and expose you to the options that are available. A glimpse of the realities of policy-making will either thrill you for a lifetime or make you realise it's not for you. But I hope it is your thing. Achieving large-scale change for the good is a truly worthwhile thing to aim for.

---

[14] www.bhf.org.uk/   [15] www.cancerresearchuk.org/home

[16] wellcome.ac.uk/   [17] www.rspb.org.uk/

[18] www.greenpeace.org/international/en/ and www.greenpeace.org.uk/

[19] www.foei.org/ and www.foe.co.uk/   [20] www.w4mpjobs.org

[21] www.polis.cam.ac.uk/study-at-polis/graduates/MPhilPP

Part IV Journalism and the Media

18

The Wonderful World of Reporting, or the Marsupial Mole Revisited

I can name the day I first realised that science was a marvellous generator of stories that might gain in the telling: stories that no-one had ever told before, stories that invoked almost operatic emotions, stories that played to the theatre of the mind.

I opened my *New Scientist* dated 1 January 1976 and read the Monitor column, which picked up the best of other journals, and found the magazine's own take on a study of the male marsupial mole.[1] There, in deadpan narrative, was a story of first love, of last love, of sex and death and indescribable poignancy, and not only did I instantly feel the drive to share it with somebody else – always the first test of a good story – but a less than laudable desire to embellish it with tiny mundane details that further offset its integral beauty. And – I realised this very quickly – that it illuminated something vital about Darwinian evolution that I had never quite grasped. I told this story, perhaps animatedly, at the Valpolicella- and Soave-fuelled parties that characterised the suburban 1970s and watched people's eyes widen.

Then – 15 or more years later – when asked to talk to scientists about the science that makes the media interested in science, I repeatedly used this one as my example. I had long lost that copy of the *New Scientist*, so I repeated what I could remember, including the unsupported embellishments. And I apologised for any misremembering but, since nobody else seemed to remember it at all, nobody ever told

---

[1] https://tinyurl.com/m4qnaus

Successful Careers beyond the Lab, ed. David Bennett and Richard Jennings.
Published by Cambridge University Press. © Cambridge University Press 2017. 211

me I had got it wrong. And in any case, I had remembered the nub of the story correctly.

It was a chronicle of the enormous, self-sacrificing love of the Australian marsupial mole, a creature that potters about for most of his life without knowing the meaning of the word 'love'. Then, suddenly, during the all-too-brief mating season, he bumps into a female marsupial mole. Their lives are transformed. Courtship proceeds rapidly to lovemaking. And as the Romeo of the partnership declares his ardour in the most unambiguous way possible, the excitement is too much for him. As he engenders the next generation of little baby moles to fill his new love's tiny pouch, he also releases a sudden rush of corticosteroids within himself, trips his aching heart, has a coronary and dies. It isn't bad luck: he is programmed to pop his clogs as soon as he has fulfilled his biological function. That way, Mrs Marsupial Mole, widowed within minutes of her marriage, has a better chance of making it on the slender resources hitherto available to both. Love is supposed to be a matter of making sacrifices; it is also supposed to be undying, which makes it all the sadder. At the time I called it the most poignant case of post-coital *tristesse* I have ever read. The *New Scientist* was not nearly so sentimental. The headline read: 'When a mole's had it, he's had it.'

I called the story unforgettable. In fact, I had swiftly forgotten the species (*Antichinus stuarti*) the authors (physiologists from Monash University) and the source (*The Journal of Endocrinology*). But I had remembered not just the outline but the headline. It was a revelation: a realisation that science told stories that appealed to a sense of life's comedy, or poignancy, or wonder. (The phrase 'sensational journalism' was always a lazy one. We read what we read because it appeals to some sense or other.) But there was something even better. That story told me something about how the world worked that had never occurred to me before: that sex and death are part of the same inexorable bargain. And there was something better still: clearly, science was a source of stories that had never been told before. And best of all, it was a source of unforgettable headlines. It was not the start of a career reporting science. I spent many years doing other things. But it was the beginning of an interest in science as the source of what journalists want most: good stories.

First, an admission: there was never a lab. It's not that I had never been in one. My secondary school had pipettes, retorts, Bunsen burners, two kinds of litmus paper and a row of jars that contained magnesium, sodium, phosphorus, sulphuric acid and so on, and I probably watched demonstrations with some measure of pleasure. But scholastic or formal science education was embraced lightly. Mathematics at the time was largely algebra and geometry; chemistry involved understanding chemical notation and sorting elements from compounds; physics seemed to be only electricity and magnetism in one aspect, heat, light and sound in the other. I preferred Latin – that's how dull school science was in New Zealand in the early 1950s.

But there was the other lure: from the age of 11, I delivered morning newspapers and was already and perhaps separately fascinated by the daily miracle of the morning newspaper. In addition I read the Superman comics and was more interested in, and more curious about, the personae of Clark Kent, Lois Lane and Perry White, the editor of the *Daily Planet*, than in the Man of Steel himself. I developed a taste for books written by former newsmen – Charles Dickens, Rudyard Kipling and Damon Runyon among them – and B-movies in which hard-faced but humane men in trench coats and trilby hats exposed corruption and confronted criminals before calling the city desk.

Most of all, I liked the magic of a printed news page, this black-and-white thing that somebody had made happen, every night; had written, taken the photographs, thought of the headlines, composed all the text in hot metal and scratched the photograph onto a metal plate with acid and a needle, had assembled all the reports, results, advertisements and imagery to fit neatly into a standard-sized frame, converted this broadsheet artefact into a curved plate that could be fitted onto a roller; did the same with 15, or 23, or 31 other pages all at the same time, smeared them all with ink, threaded great rolls of paper through the rotary presses and then printed this one achievement ten thousand or a hundred thousand times, and did it all at a pace dictated by the railway timetables.

So, admission number two: there was no academia, no college, no degree or diploma. At 16, not long after the start of my second sixth-form year and just before the Easter weekend, I walked into the *New Zealand Herald* office and applied for a job as a cadet reporter. It was a world of full employment, a world in which you could leave school at 15, a world in which you went into higher education only if you wanted to be something that needed a degree: a doctor, lawyer or, of course, a scientist. It wasn't a very long conversation: the chief reporter asked me if I thought I was good at English, and then said, 'Can you start on Tuesday?' And so, on 23 April 1957, my life changed. I had become, like many of my friends, an earner, with a brown envelope that contained £5 14s 6d at the end of each week. Even more enjoyably, the notion that I had to be home by dark or in bed by 10 PM also ended forever.

Auckland had its own evening newspaper that reported all the news that happened in the morning, so the early shift for daily newsmen began at 2 PM and ended at 11 PM with the first edition. A skeleton staff stayed on until 2 AM to complete what everybody called the graveyard shift. Within a few days, I had been given my own responsibility: the shipping news. This was before the jet age. It was before the coming of the container traffic. And it was before the age of the public relations department. Those who flew to New Zealand were most likely to land in Auckland harbour from Sydney or Suva in Fiji by Solent flying boat run by Tasman Empire Airways Limited, but the vast majority of humans still travelled by sea, and so did almost everything that humans then grew, packed, made or sold. It was lowered into, or taken from, the holds of freighters, liners and tramp steamers and stowed or unloaded by stevedores and dockers – known also as water-siders or 'wharfies' – who carried cargo hooks, handled by fork-lift truck drivers who took the goods in or out of warehouses and then piled them onto delivery lorries, or railway wagons. The ships arrived daily with bills of lading from anywhere in the Pacific or Indian Oceans, from Vancouver or Seattle, from Yokohama or Zamboanga or Trinco-malee and with passengers mostly from the United Kingdom, California or Australia.

Part of the job was to walk around all the docks, every day, talking to the harbourmaster's office, the shipping agents, the companies, the unions, the managers and the police, to assemble a daily register of things that had happened or were expected to happen. That included the stories of cargo workers who fell down holds to be saved, seemingly miraculously, by landing on bales of wool, or of first mates who con-tracted malaria or yellow fever while in the South China Seas, and arrived on ships flying the Yellow Jack, the flag that said 'infectious illness on board'. It also meant getting up long before dawn to join the pilot boat and hitch a ride to meet a visiting cruise liner out in the Hauraki Gulf, long before it turned to enter the Rangitoto Channel and then into Auckland Harbour, to jump from a pitching cutter onto a suspended stairway or rope ladder, climb on board and ride with the ship through the dawn to tie up, take on fresh food and water, and give the passengers a day in the city. We'd knock on the purser's cabin door and ask politely if there were famous people on board. 'We've got Robert Mitchum in the suite on A-deck,' the man might say, and journalists would troop to his stateroom in the hope of a photograph and an interview. So within a week, a schoolboy had stepped into the world of John Masefield, Joseph Conrad and the Marlon Brando who starred in *On the Waterfront*: a world of romance and adventure at second hand, but delivered freshly and unpredictably every day. And I was being paid for it.

In the course of the next 50-odd years, I confronted politicians, chased fire engines, reported on natural disaster and human tragedy, flew over the forests of Chernobyl in a former Russian military helicopter, whitewater-rafted down some Himalayan rapids, rode an elephant through the Nepali wetlands, lay awake all night on the roof of a village house on the banks of the Zambezi listening to the lions across the river, travelled with a port chaplain out into the North Sea to deliver a turkey and read a service on a lightship, slept overnight in the monasteries of Mt Athos in Greece, visited Soviet Russia and the Central Asian states and then the Russian Federation, toured research laboratories that most of us had never known existed in Siberian cities we had once been forbidden to visit and of course – but we will come to that – been witness to a series of quite astounding revolutions in the worlds of science and technology.

As a conference party trick, I often compare journalists and scientists: both are fully paid-up members of the human subspecies *Homo sapiens inquisitivus,* and both regard the statement 'I don't know' not as a statement of surrender but as an invitation: What is it I do not know? How would I find out? And of course, both rely on six simple all-purpose tools: the questions who, what, where, when, how and why. Nor is a morning newspaper reporters' room so very different from a laboratory. Both are within institutions dedicated to research and packed with eager young researchers who have learned to identify something that is simultaneously not known but worth knowing; have learned to begin with a search of the literature, to frame a question or a hypothesis and then start looking for data.

Having gathered the evidence, these researchers then write a paper, submit it for peer review and then publish. The trivial difference is that in a laboratory, the process takes months, or even years; in an old-fashioned daily newspaper, everything described above happened between about 11 AM in the morning and 9 PM or 10 PM at night. The really big difference is that scientific papers are read by a very small number of people and the research lives on – if it lives – in other people's citations and the author remains a scientist. But reporters, above all, must be read: of course, they should be right, but if they are not read, then they cease to be journalists and the journals that employ them don't last long either. The difference is that scientists publish research and journalists write stories.

So my other piece of debating imagery is Queen Scheherazade, the voice of the *Thousand and One Nights*. The caliph had the nasty habit of marrying, ravishing and then beheading his bride of the day the following morning so she could never be unfaithful. Scheherazade understood the power of the story, and told wonderful stories – so wonderful, we tell them still – literally to save her life: each paused with a cliff-hanger, and to hear how it ended the caliph kept her alive for another night. Printed newspapers, too, were once addictive and the people who worked for them thought themselves – mostly – the luckiest people in the world. Each day delivered a new story and a different adventure. A day just ended could be a triumph, or a humiliation, but what mattered most was the next day: nobody remembered for long the good things you did and your failures became the wrapping around the fish and chips.

I made a comparison between science and journalism, and it is true that journalists, like scientists are interested in how the world works, and why, but for journalists the reward comes in the form not of an established set of facts, or a convincing hypothesis, but in the fleeting shape of a good story.

And science provided these, although for the first 20 or so years of my working life, I wasn't (I thought) interested in science. You couldn't be a reporter and not be conscious of science. I had been on the *New Zealand Herald* for about six months when the Soviet Union launched Sputnik 1 in October 1957; New Zealand scientists were partners in the International Geophysical Year and in the formal exploration of Antarctica and, besides, we lived on the North Island of New Zealand, home to four active volcanoes and potentially vulnerable to earthquake.

As a child, I learned to identify scoria and its plutonic partner pumice, and knew that they were not the same as sandstone or clay; as a teenage reporter, one responsibility was to pick up the weather map from the meteorological office every night and to check the supply of paper and ink for the office seismometer.

As an ordinary functioning suburb-dweller, I had seen science change our lives: my face is not pitted by smallpox, my limbs are not withered by polio and my lungs not scarred by tuberculosis because mass vaccination arrived in the 1950s. Households discarded the old iceboxes – in which meat was kept cool by a great block of ice delivered weekly – and installed refrigerators and, then gradually, telephones, vacuum cleaners and even motor cars.

It was a world of Cold War, of implacable confrontation between the Soviet Union and Red China on the one hand and the treaty powers of the North Atlantic Alliance on the other. Within a few years we were to live in the shadow of intercontinental ballistic missiles armed with thermonuclear warheads that could notionally obliterate London or any European city, an event that would be preceded by a warning that we had just four minutes of remaining life. The doctrine of Mutually Assured Destruction (MAD) did indeed seem like madness, so the Cold War was fought by proxy, most notably in Korea and then Vietnam, increasingly with the advanced chemistry of napalm and the defoliant Agent Orange. Simultaneously, we marvelled at the Soviet and US space programmes, and the race to the moon.

So we were all aware of science. If I didn't pay much attention, it was perhaps because there were so many other things to think about, one of which would now be described as economic migration. At 20, at the beginning of 1961, I boarded a passenger ship, sailed to Southampton for a total of £92 and started working in British newspapers. Until 1963, passports issued in the Commonwealth and the last bits of the Empire were British passports and New Zealand operated in the sterling currency zone. In those days, one could simply move to a new address 12,000 miles away. So I did.

I became a sub-editor on the weekly *Fishing News*, and the less frequent titles *Fish Selling*, *Fishing News International* and *Self Service Times*; I became a reporter for the Hull *Daily Mail*, covering – of course – the waterfront and the fish docks; I joined the Dover *Express* and learned the challenges of newspaper production in exquisite and unpredictable detail. ('You know all those monotype headings on page five?' the head printer once shouted through the hatch. 'Can you rewrite them? We have run out of the letter E.')

And for a few years, I became a Whitehall information officer, an unestablished civil servant employed by the Central Office of Information, writing and editing what we called 'white propaganda' to promote the interests of the British government through its embassies and commissions. White propaganda – as opposed to black propaganda then supposedly disseminated from some sinister department of the Foreign Office – could be defined as undeniably true, but selective.

And this organisation had a science correspondent: a man called Roy Herbert who had been a founder member of the staff of the *New Scientist* and who also wrote the magazine's Ariadne column.

Because of chronic illness – his, not mine – I found myself covering the occasional Atomic Energy Authority press conference, attending a British Association for the Advancement of Science conference and even (because these were the years of anxiety about acid rain and organochlorine pesticides) making a pilgrimage to the Natural Environment Research Council's Monk's Wood research station in Cambridgeshire to learn more about research into environmental pollution. But I imagined no career as a science writer. How could I? I knew nothing about science.

And anyway, I soon joined *The Guardian*, within a few years to edit the arts pages, a job that still seems to me to have been the best in the world: a job that required me to absorb film, music and theatre on a scale that I could never have been able to afford as a mere audience member and to see amazing things performed by actors then in their first shining maturity: Alan Howard, Judy Dench, Patrick Stewart, Helen Mirren, Ian McKellen and many others.

But I continued to read the *New Scientist* along with the *New Statesman* and *New Society*. I cannot now tell you why except that it seemed to me to be a brilliant source of stories about really interesting things that I had never thought about before. And it was during this period that I began to understand that some profound change had begun to happen: that, at around the time my children had been born, physicists and astronomers had confected an entirely rational story of Creation from a Big Bang beginning; that biologists seemed to be on the track of life's most intricate biochemical machinery; that earthquakes and volcanoes – and mountains and floodplains and seams of minerals and all other geological phenomena – were not random presences but the consequence of imperceptible but explicable movement of a living planet. And of course, after the Apollo programme, that humans began the systematic exploration of the solar system and the faltering expansion of computer technology.

And most of this wasn't – it seemed to me even then – being reported as it should have been: in-depth and with enthusiasm. Science correspondents for the most part occupied an unenvied and mostly undisturbed niche in the journalism's ecology. It was not considered something as important as crime, day-to-day politics, City scandals, aristocratic divorce, Royal visits or the state of the economy. It was considered probably important but certainly boring, mostly incomprehensible and – above all – not a reason for buying a newspaper. So, even before I had been plucked, unwillingly, from the arts pages and given the bigger job of helping to run a whole features department, I had started thinking of ways to make the stories that science could tell as exciting and as compelling as any narrative of sex and death.

As it happened, science at the time turned out to be terrific on the themes of sex and death and animal behaviour research, and delivered examples by the bucketful. Never mind marsupial moles; who could forget the paddle-footed worm that turned up in another issue of the *New Scientist*? At full moon and high tide in the tropics, the little creatures stomachs' shrivel, their sexual organs swell and almost their entire bodies become containers for sperm and eggs. Then they all scramble madly to the surface for an orgy. As soon as the bristly paddles of the male worm touch the skin of the female, they both explode in a frenzy of lust, expelling showers of eggs and milt, and then all that is left is just two empty bags, tumbling slowly back to the sea floor.

That, as the phrase goes, was sex to die for. And who could resist the tropical reef-dwelling palolo worm? The palolo worm doesn't lose his head when it falls in love. As its little heart beats faster and it gets that funny feeling in the pit of the stomach, something very odd happens. The lower half of the worm breaks off from the head and lurches towards the surface for the mating dance, leaving the brains and the teeth behind in the reef to carry on eating. This may be the only known case of a creature sending forth its own loins to be fruitful and multiply while the rest of it settles down to a good dinner. And – I thought at the time – it seemed to add new resonance to the coarse expression 'having it away'.

And I had already made a discovery: the science behind a major news event could enrich the story. That's a commonplace now. The mechanics of a tsunami – the physical forces that mean that it can race across an ocean at jet speed yet create no more than a ripple on the surface and then slow down and build up to a wall of water capable of mass murder when it reaches the shallows of the coast – register as my first bit of self-driven scientific investigation.

In 1976, what we then called a tidal wave hit the coast of the southern Philippines, and I spent my lunchtime in the British Library's science section, then near Chancery Lane. The mechanics of reporting, communication and public information at the time, the timetables of newspaper production, and the sheer difficulty of getting information from a disaster zone meant that it made sense to have, at least for the first edition, a piece describing what might have happened, how it must have happened and what the consequences may have been.

The principle is that if you can't write about what the earthquake did because you can't get there in time to report something for the first edition, at least write about what earthquakes do and why, and who is most vulnerable. When you ask questions like that, the very first thing you learn is that natural disaster isn't random or even very natural. The people most likely to lose everything, including their lives, are over-whelmingly the poorest, the dispossessed, the people who have almost nothing in the first place.

But knowledge is power: if scientists and engineers could explain calamity after it had happened, then maybe the same scientists and engineers could inform and help people to be ready for the next shock. In which case, there was an obvious role for the newsman. I was, in 1976, still editing *The Guardian*'s letters page; I was already acting as the newspaper's deputy film critic, I was soon to take over the arts page and experience the sustained delirium of great music, theatre and the visual arts both at first and second hand. And there I was, fretting about all the geophysics I didn't know that I needed to know for an 800-word piece.

It seems now, with the perfect perspective of hindsight, that I had already begun to change direction. It is important to stress that at the time I knew that I knew nothing about science but I could not under-stand why my colleagues weren't interested. In 1980, I changed jobs, and – while fretting about work shifts, copy deadlines, edition times, page design, picture choice and all the other things that make a news-paper work – I took over a once-a-week page, rang up a scientist and asked him to write something for me.

I very quickly learned that the older the scientist, the more poten-tially impenetrable the text. Post-docs on a meagre grant income, how-ever, responded with enthusiasm to the challenge to write something a human being would wish to read, especially if they were to be paid Fleet Street rates for it. Within a few years, the page had turned into a multi-page supplement, supported by advertising, and a number of scientists I had first encouraged had made themselves not just professional jour-nalists but direct competitors on other papers and I had to keep on recruiting new writers. Other scientists stayed on in the universities but carried on as contributors and managed to win the annual science writing prizes awarded by the Association of British Science Writers.

I was already, effectively, a science editor. And so it didn't seem unusual to me or to my colleagues when, after three years editing *The Guardian*'s literary pages (I had, separately, been reviewing non-fiction for various newspapers and journals since 1959), I followed in the footsteps of J.G. Crowther who claimed to be the first science corres-pondent of any newspaper, John Maddox (later Sir John, and later editor of *Nature*) and the unforgettable Anthony Tucker, known as Phil, a former Spitfire pilot who first entered *The Guardian* to paint a mural on the canteen wall.

I became science editor in 1992 and held the by-line until I retired in 2005. Science coverage was, at the time, fairly low on any news desk's list of priorities and there were days when I felt I had entered into a new personal competition: How many stories could I write that would be rejected in any one day? Attitudes, however, had, imperceptibly, begun to change. I had already become involved in Copus, the Royal Society initiative called the Committee for the Public Understanding of Science that John Durant writes about in his chapter 23, and separately, perhaps because I had talked to so many earthquake scientists and engineers, I had been drafted onto the UK Committee for the International Decade for Natural Disaster Reduction.

Climate change seemed to have begun to announce itself in the shape of more calamitous floods, tropical storms and landslides. Space research became ever more ambitious and so did its promotion by scientists and space agencies. Biologists had already started to do bewildering things with DNA, among them identifying potential criminal suspects, cloning sheep and tracing human evolution. America abandoned its superconducting supercollider – the machine that was supposed to identify the agency that made the universe possible – and CERN[2] took up the challenge in Geneva. The Internet happened, and then the communications revolution.

A few years later, I found myself playing another game: How many by-lines could I score in a single day? I had begun to think myself one of the luckiest journalists on the paper: I had ventured into a playground that took me in a few days from subjects such as chemical weapons research to discovery of the tomb of the sons of King Ramses II in Egypt's Valley of Kings, from the devastation of the 1998 El Niño to an encounter with the man who thought up Inflation Theory and then a meeting with the man who published the first accounts of Cosmic Microwave Background Radiation and told the press conference, 'If you're religious, it's like seeing God.' I was lucky enough to share public platforms with Stephen Hawking, Martin Rees, Miroslav Holub, Richard Dawkins, Richard Fortey, Stephen Pinker, James Lovelock, Paul Davies, Douglas Adams and many others, and the fun didn't stop when I retired.

I cannot stress this enough – I never felt I knew much about science, and when I got something wrong it was because, idiotically,

---

[2] The European Organization for Nuclear Research.

I thought I did know something about the science. I thought of myself always as a reporter, open-mouthed, delighted by the things I heard, thrilled to have the opportunity to shape them into stories that other people might want to read. Science delivered these, over and over again, stories beyond fiction: stories you couldn't make up, stories that had never been told before. It has been wonderful. But I wouldn't have missed all the other fun, too, on the waterfronts of Auckland and Hull, or the magic of the Royal Shakespeare Company under Trevor Nunn, or the long-running near-farce of Westminster politics, or encounters with policemen at the scene of a crime, or the mechanics of newspaper hot-metal production, a vast train set you could play with every day. To which I can simply add the additional thrill of being able to fashion a poignant fable about a marsupial mole.

19

Reflections of a Thinking Pinball

The Surprises, Challenges and Rewards of a Career in Radio

More than 50 years ago, a young University of Oxford graduate stood poised for a future in academia. Specifically, he was intent on pursuing his passion for the complex imagery of late 19th-century French poetry and had duly embarked on a higher degree at another prestigious centre of research excellence. At the time, no other path seemed remotely interesting.

Now, decades later, that same individual finds himself writing this chapter on a long career as a broadcaster and writer specialising in science, technology and medicine with a huge output behind him in radio (and television) production, articles and books on science, teaching, editing, consultancy and even experience of running a small communications business. This account attempts to trace the serendipitous path from a putative research career to quite another, unexpected corner of the professional universe, and to describe some of the skills and aptitudes needed to reach that end.

The format adopted is a combination of first-person narrative, sometimes with a confessional flavour, which is set in italics, and third-person commentary and analysis whereby the experiences of one individual are viewed within the broader context of the radio business at large.

EARLY RADIO DAYS: AM I REALLY HERE?

This feels quite surreal. I'm sitting behind a microphone in a windowless basement radio studio in the BBC's Broadcasting House, in central London. I've just

Successful Careers beyond the Lab, ed. David Bennett and Richard Jennings.
Published by Cambridge University Press. © Cambridge University Press 2017.

said thank you and goodbye to an American condensed matter physicist who has given me an excellent interview on a line from Arizona. I'm now waiting for my next interviewees for a face-to-face interaction. One is a palaeobotanist (a discipline I only heard of for the first time yesterday) and the other an inorganic chemist who is an expert on molecular modelling. We'll be discussing science funding in the context of economic cutbacks. After that, I'm due to scurry across town to a press conference at The Royal Society on genetically modified food. In the few minutes before my guests arrive I'm reflecting on the unlikely situation I'm in.

It seems only yesterday – actually more than ten years ago – that I began my post-Oxford career. After deciding, on a gut feeling really, to turn my back on academia, I was lucky enough in those heady days of full graduate employment to secure a job at a major educational publishers – Macmillan – as a commissioning editor responsible for secondary- and tertiary-level books on modern languages, my degree subject. That was followed by two other editorial jobs in book publishing, broadening out from languages into general books. Then, out of the blue, came an invitation to devise and edit a new weekly magazine on psychology,[1] in which I had an interest but no particular depth of knowledge.

The events that lead to that invitation were typically fortuitous. The magazine group that published the New Scientist *and the* New Society *decided that, with the booming popular and academic interest in the behavioural sciences at the time, it might be a good idea to launch a psychology title in the same stable. As it happened, when casting around for someone to develop the idea, my name entered the head of the then editor of the* New Scientist, *Dr Bernard Dixon,[2] whom I'd met during my general book publishing days. Five years later, and here I was, getting involved in the new project.*

When the magazine's brief life came to an end (that happens quite a lot in this advertising-driven business), it seemed an appropriate juncture to try to go it alone as a freelance writer using the experience with behavioural sciences as my calling card. It was tricky at first to get commissions but eventually I did manage to find a niche producing feature articles for a newspaper designed for general practitioners, having met the editor – indeed, having commissioned an article or two from him while editing the magazine.

Writing medically-based articles for trained physicians was a bit difficult at first. Let me rephrase that: it was extraordinarily taxing for someone with a wholly humanities-based background. But economic necessity kept me at it until

---

[1] *New Behaviour* (IPC Magazines, April–October, 1975).

[2] Bernard Dixon's doctorate was in microbiology but he too abandoned a research career in favour of science journalism of which he is unquestionably one of the United Kingdom's most distinguished practitioners.

I learned the ropes: how to get one's head around complex technical matters and make them palatable for a weekly newspaper reader. Not long afterwards I met with a publisher who commissioned me to write a popular medical book[3] – on migraine – where the challenge was not just to understand biomedicine but to make it accessible to a broad audience that may or may not have had any scientific training at all.

Some years later I'm doing the same thing really, this time by means of radio: talking to people with a profound knowledge of their subject matter, some even Nobel Prize winners, and encouraging them to make their sharp-end science accessible to my listeners on BBC Radio 4,[4] in all their variety of backgrounds, interests and tastes. Looking back I can – sort of – see an intricate logic to the events that have brought me here. But that is just a post hoc rationalisation. In truth, it's all been by accidental twists and turns. And I'm not alone in that.

THE RANDOM CAREER PATHS OF JOURNALISTS

Not everyone now working as a radio presenter or reporter seems to have started out with that end in mind. To some extent that is changing with the growth of journalism and media studies courses in higher education that, rightly or wrongly, appear to offer students the prospect of direct, specialist career training.[5] Generally, however, most radio broadcasters – and many other sorts of journalists – appear to have arrived at where they are now by a variety of circuitous routes.

An image that comes to mind here – hence the title of this chapter – is that of the passage of a pinball down the table, batted from one obstacle to the next in an unpredictable manner, finally arriving at the single end point. In the real world of journalism, those obstacles – let us call them springboards – can take many forms and send the recipient in all sorts of directions before the final stop is reached.

Let us look at some of those direction-switching influences in practice.

---

[3] *Mastering your Migraine* (Granada Publishing, 1978).

[4] *Science Now*, a weekly magazine-format science news programme that began in 1974. The author was the main presenter for more than 20 years, until the initiation of the *Frontiers* strand.

[5] The number of higher education establishments offering courses in media/journalism and related disciplines has rapidly expanded. Clearly it could be useful for would-be radio journalists, be they aspiring presenters, reporters or producers, to look in detail at what is on offer. In the United Kingdom, one post-graduate course that has enjoyed conspicuous success in placing its students in media jobs is the MSc in Science Communication at Imperial College London.

- One well-known broadcaster, after having studied biology at university, undertook training as a studio technician and sound engineer because it seemed an interesting line of work. After years sitting in studio control rooms, he was asked if he'd like to reposition himself on the other side of the microphone and 'have a go at interviewing'. He managed to combine his biological background with his inherent interest in radio to become a distinguished practitioner.

- Another individual was called up, quite out of the blue, by a radio producer he'd known (but had not seen for a few years) when they had both been colleagues in a previous editorial job in publishing. The producer was short of someone to 'do a bit of interviewing'; her friend was under-employed as a freelance writer. Again the hook-up worked out long term.

- A third example is that of a PhD with a research background in biomedicine who, having found his job prospects limited, started to do some freelance medical writing that caught the eye of a producer who, again, needed some help researching a programme. From researcher he progressed to interviewer and eventually to presenting his own long-running programme.

In none of these cases did the people who would go on to become skilled radio presenters have any idea or intention of ending up where they did. It all just happened by chance. What this suggests – and this is something that many may find unsatisfactory – is that there is no reliable, predictive algorithm one can devise for getting into the business.

This is not to say that one cannot work towards that end. Indeed, much of the remainder of this chapter is given over to analysing the experience, techniques and attitudes that can lead to a broadcasting career.

PROBLEMS, PROBLEMS

With very little time left, I'm putting the finishing touches to a script before the producer and I go into the studio to record this week's programme. As usual, there are some writing problems to resolve as I try to find the right words to introduce – 'set up' in trade-speak – the interviews we will be running.

One of these concerns the mechanism of cancer, so it's all about cells and cell signalling, genes and proteins and mutations. Does my audience know any (or all) of the basic biology here? Can I use the acronym 'DNA' without expanding it? What about 'RNA'? Will 'protein' suggest to them steak or fish instead of the notion of a tiny cellular operative?

The second interview is on particle physics. Here I need to introduce 'nucleus', 'electron', 'proton' and 'quark'. Have my listeners some familiarity with these terms, remembering them from their school days? Actually, we ran a similar interview in the programme a fortnight ago, so perhaps they remember the meanings of the terms from then? Or maybe not all of tonight's listeners were actually listening to that programme! It's all a bit tricky.

Another interview concerns astronomy, so 'galaxies',' light years' and 'red shift' need to drop into the mix. Again I'm not totally sure about which of these terms are in my audience's comfort zone of comprehension. Then we are on to an earth sciences piece where 'tectonic plates' and 'geomagnetism' come into the picture.

In short, I'm worried about giving my listeners too many new words with which to wrestle, especially some of the many acronyms that seem to bedevil modern science. I want this to be an entertaining programme for them, not sound like a lecture or course module. If it does, they'll do what I would do in their place and simply switch off!

MAKING ASSUMPTIONS – THE UNSEEN AUDIENCE

All effective science writing on radio, by reporters or presenters, depends, like any other kind of good writing, on a clear understanding of one's audience – a generalisation that is easier to state than to execute in practice. Radio people, producers as well as presenters, are constantly asking themselves basic questions about their listeners:

- Who exactly are they?
- What are their demographic characteristics: how old are they; do they have higher education or a professional occupation? And so on.
- For science programmes in particular, what assumptions can I make about their specific knowledge of the subject matter in hand?

Of course, broadcasting organisations, like the print media, do a certain amount of research on these vital topics. The BBC's Audience Research unit can, for example, say some important general things about BBC Radio 4, its main speech channel (outside the dedicated news channel BBC Radio 5 Live), such as the fact that the average listener is well educated with an average age of around 50 years. From that one might make deductions about the degree to which these listeners might follow the thread of a particular interview.

But this only takes the broadcaster so far. Suppose, for example, a presenter is writing a script to precede an interview on a medical topic such as heart disease. As he or she begins to fill out this introduction, a number of terms, some quite commonplace, spring to mind: artery, ventricle, red blood cells and so on. Or the topic may be climate change, for which stratosphere, greenhouse gases and convection currents are relevant.

How confident can the writer be that those 'well-educated' listeners have the right kind of education to cope with any or all of these terms? And even if, in theory, they do, they may have received it more than 30 years ago. When lecturers address an unfamiliar audience, they can at least infer from their facial expressions whether they are following the plot or not. Radio journalists get no such instant feedback. They need to use a certain amount of guesswork and hope that their listening figures the following week bear out their judgment!

That is one of the challenges of writing for radio. Another is that of 'writing for the ear', not for the printed page. There are, when you think about it, some profound differences between the two, the most obvious being that radio is for the most part a one-off, real-time medium where the listener does not, usually, go back and listen again, and again, as a newspaper reader can revisit the text if it is a bit difficult to take in. In other words, whatever words are coming out of the radio's speaker have to be instantly comprehensible.

The broadcast journalist also has to take account of the limitations of listeners in terms of narrative style. Radio and television programmes (with the exception of those expressly designed to be 'educational' for a note-taking student audience) are not really suitable media for cataloguing long accumulations of facts in the manner of a textbook. Indeed, they rely rather on personal anecdote and experiences wrapped around factual information quite thinly spread. If key pieces of information are necessary to drive the narrative, the writer has to make sure that they are emphasised pointedly, often using a certain amount of repetition.

Another important stylistic lesson for the would-be script writer is that radio (and TV) should embody the natural features of the spoken word. Colloquialisms, elisions ('can't' not 'cannot' etc) and many of the other features of everyday speech lift the text from the page. Take, for example, this extract from the presenter's script for a radio science documentary on human evolution: 'We don't, for all our culture and civilisation, appear to have moved on genetically from our Stone Age ancestors. And we've used our big brains, tool making abilities, language and social skills to shape an environment that – on the face of it – makes it unnecessary to evolve further. Or have we?'[6]

Elision, first-person 'we', interjection and rhetorical questions: these are the stuff of everyday speech that 'humanises' the presenter's links between interviews. That is what writing for the ear is all about: making an inert script leap off the page as if it were alive and spoken.

LEARNING TO REMAIN IGNORANT

I'll never forget the first interviews I conducted. In truth, I feel slightly embarrassed when I think back to them – and here's why.

The interviewer is an intermediary – the link between the listener and the interviewee. His or her job is to ask the sort of questions a listener might ask in order to move the interview along and to clarify any words or concepts emerging from the interaction. Questions such as 'What does that mean, exactly?' are very common.

When I started out, I was, however, conflicted. On the one hand, I knew I needed to ask questions to get a scientist to elucidate a technical matter or a piece of terminology that my audience would probably find unfamiliar. On the other hand, I was not quite sure how 'ignorant' I should be. There was no problem if a term such as 'ionisation' or 'homozygous' cropped up: one could safely assume that these would cause a substantial fraction of my listeners a bit of difficulty. But I can remember making rapid internal assessments about terms such 'hominid' or 'neurone' and coming to quite confused conclusions, often because I myself was a bit unclear as to their meanings but thought that 'they' – the audience – could or should understand them.

For a while things got even worse. After many hours interviewing scientists from every imaginable discipline, I began to become far more familiar myself with their strange languages. So much so that, if 'DNA' or 'proton' popped up, I would – because now I knew what they meant – tend to assume that everyone else would too. That was a very dangerous assumption that I quickly learned to set aside.

---

[6] This and other illustrative examples are taken from the BBC's *Frontiers* documentary strand broadcast on Radio 4. Specifically, this extract comes from a human evolution programme aired on 4 May 2005 between 9 and 9:30 in the evening. This is one of more than 100 programmes that was presented by the author until 2008.

My golden rule has to be: If I think there is any chance, however remote, of my interviewee's words going over my listeners' heads, I ask for clarification. I don't worry about looking ill-informed or foolish; better that than have listeners struggling to follow what they're hearing. My job is to make it easy for them.

WHAT MAKES A GOOD INTERVIEWER?

Good interviewers should, for the most part, remain fairly unobtrusive. Their job is simply to act as a conduit between audience and interviewee, teasing out information in comprehensible language and suppressing any inclination they may have to show off their own knowledge.

Of course, some high-profile political or celebrity interviewers adopt a different posture, becoming themselves part of the centre of attention. Hard-hitting verbal battles with politicians, for example, are often designed not just to elicit information but to create discomfort and unease as the interviewer challenges ideas, policies and attitudes.

That arm-wrestling paradigm is hardly ever appropriate for the science broadcaster. Indeed, it can be extremely unproductive, for two reasons:

- First, if interviewees think that they are going to be on the receiving end of unfriendliness or downright hostility, they will probably become uptight and anxious. Such feelings are a very poor foundation for performing well: finding the right words, being warm and sympathetic, obviously enjoying the interaction – all these are important ingredients for a successful outcome.

- Second, an interview is not really an activity between two people on different sides but on the same side. They are putting on a little performance for the benefit of a third party – their audience. The interviewee wants to come across as well informed and fluent, and that is exactly what the interviewer wants as well. They are, in short, both in it together.

This means that the interviewer needs to develop some important interpersonal skills in order to put his or her guests at ease, making them relaxed and able to perform optimally. More often than not, researchers are perfectly able to explain their science clearly and entertainingly. But sometimes they are anxious, unsure of how to bring their messages to the level required by the media. Occasionally, they are quite worried and intimidated by being thrust into a strangely unfamiliar milieu. Here, some thoughtful coaxing and confidence building is needed on the part of the journalist.

Basically, these kinds of interactive skills, coupled with being a good listener and staying alert to what is going on in real time, are more important than specific academic qualifications. If you are a specialist presenter in the mold of the zoologist David Attenborough, concentrating on one area of science, then a background in the relevant discipline is certainly a huge advantage.

However, if you are a general-purpose interviewer ranging over the whole of science, then a qualification in one discipline often has little value when interviewing a researcher in a totally different field, speaking what amounts to a different language. A degree (or two) in quantum physics does not, *ipso facto*, equip you to cope with research on proteomics or cognitive neuroscience. Indeed, some knowledge may even be confusing. As a mathematician you would have one idea about the meaning of 'differentiation', while an embryologist has quite another!

So, lack of specialist knowledge is relatively unimportant. So too is how one speaks, especially regional accents. The days are, mercifully, long gone when radio folk were expected to have those upper-middle-class voices that used to be associated, in the United Kingdom at least, with affluence and a public school education (which is anything but public since it costs a lot to attend such schools and obtain it). Today, anything goes, provided one speaks clearly and at a measured pace. The most important qualities in the voice of the broadcaster are commitment and enthusiasm.

A PRIVILEGED JOB

Over the past year or so, I've logged a substantial total of air, rail and road miles – and revelled in some mind-expanding experiences – as I visited different locations to carry out interviews.

Few sights, if any, can surpass that of the blue whale diving off Monterey Bay accompanied by a battalion of leaping dolphins. Then there was the nerve-wracking drive up a mountain in the Canary Islands for the opening of a major new optical telescope, after which it was a trip to Sweden where, deep below ground level, I heard all about the merits of geological repositories for nuclear waste.

Of course, it's not always so glamorous. A trip to Yellowstone Park to survey the supervolcano that lurks beneath the spectacular landscape was interspersed with plenty of more mundane locations: a dusty museum basement to

look at fossils; a shabby physics laboratory to talk materials science; and count-
less face-to-face interviews in cramped offices, frustratingly interrupted by the
sound of a vacuum cleaner in the hallway or the tinkle of a coffee trolley.

Whatever the environment, though, one thing remains universal: the
willingness of scientists to do their best to help me to convey their research to a
lay audience, sometimes at considerable inconvenience to themselves. Scientists go
out of their way to be obliging: using up their lunch breaks; travelling after work
to find a remote studio linked by a line to my London base; coming out of a key
conference session for an impromptu five-minute face-to-face; even interrupting a
beach session on a family holiday for a telephone interview.

Not only that, they also make tremendous efforts to speak clearly and
comprehensibly to someone who knows virtually nothing about what they do
and how they do it. I used to think – probably as a result of the arts/sciences
separation in the traditional English educational system – that we humanities-
trained folk were the great communicators, good with words and comfortable
with finding ways to explain. And that scientists were, well, let's say considerably
lacking in those attributes.

How wrong I was. Not a week goes by without my being lost in admiration
at a well-chosen analogy or graphic metaphor conjured up on the spot by my
interviewees. It's as if they were giving me my own rapid little seminar on the very
front end of their discipline.

REWARDS OF CONTINUAL STIMULATION

Arguably the most attractive feature of working as a radio presenter in
science is the continual, daily surge of intellectual stimulus from direct
contact with those who pursue a profession of which the currency is
novelty. The job is to capture what is new and try to make it relevant
to one's listeners even if it is esoteric, theoretical or, at first glance,
downright impenetrable.

Fifteen years ago, for example, few people in the street (or
listening to the radio) would have had much idea about the meaning
of 'genome', that is until the Human Genome Project came along and
captured their attention. The job of the radio interviewer at the time
was to find, and interact with, those who could build up a picture for
the lay audience of what this novel term was all about. Here's one
successful attempt by Jeremy Nicholson of Imperial College, London.

> My analogy is that if we have, for instance, the blueprint of an atomic
> power station so that we could build it exactly if we had all the parts, that
> would be fine. But it wouldn't tell us how atomic physics, nuclear fission

or nuclear fusion worked or anything about quantum mechanics. And so, in some respects, the human genome is a bit like that: it's a beautiful blueprint but it doesn't say how the bits work together.[7]

Here is another example of a researcher – paeleobiologist Simon Braddy from the University of Bristol – bringing to life events taking place long before, and far beyond, human experience, in a programme on the first land animals.

> Five hundred million years ago there really was no vegetation on land and the rocks were bathed by lethal ultraviolet radiation. It would have been windswept. It would have been a very, very inhospitable place. So you would have had low oxygen, strong sunlight, a lot of erosion – obviously there were no soils or vegetation ... binding the land surface together. So you'd have lots of rivers running off across the land: a very, very inhospitable place.[8]

The other major reward for the broadcaster and other media reporters is that of helping ordinary people to understand better what scientists do and how they are constantly contributing, directly and indirectly, to the betterment of society at large.

Indeed, one could argue that the media is the primary means by which research is communicated to the public. Making intelligible and engaging the science that bears on climate change, world hunger, the spread of neurodegenerative diseases, energy generation, pandemic infections and so on brings enormous satisfaction.

MANAGING A MIXED PORTFOLIO

My schedule for the coming week looks pretty horrendous. It begins with an early-morning appointment to do a voice-over for a short film on reinforced concrete, followed by a quick taxi ride to Broadcasting House to record a line interview with a French cardiologist. Then it's back home to finish an article for the Daily Telegraph, *promised for today.*

Tomorrow is even more crowded, not least because I need to be on an early train to Birmingham to collect material for a newsletter I compile for the Medical School, followed by a visit to some friends in the University Press Office who tell me that they have a good story for my programme. Thankfully, Wednesday is an at-home day, even though it's taken up with talking to my accountant about upcoming tax returns, fixing up interview times with my BBC producer, and

[7] *Frontiers*, 23 October 2002.   [8] *Frontiers*, 16 October 2002.

assembling material for a new book I'm contracted to write over the next nine months or so. And then there's that phone call from someone asking me to deliver media training to a group of chemists in Aberdeen the week after next.

The visibility (and audibility) generated by being a radio presenter can open many doors. Having become a 'science expert' – I'm being a bit ironical here – I've found myself invited to give lectures, chair meetings, write articles and books,[9] deliver training, do voice-overs, interview candidates for media-related jobs and, indeed, present other radio programmes, all with a science, technology or medicine slant. It has also lead to television work both for the Open University[10] and in more mainstream TV as presenter, writer and associate producer.[11]

Managing this mixed array of commissions means being really well organised, for one supremely important reason: deadlines. The media depends on its workforce – writers, presenters, producers, directors, contributors etc. – making sure that they do what they say they will do on time. Newspaper editors want the correct number of words of copy when they say they want it, and television producers want to see the individual voicing their script promptly at the studio at the appointed hour.

As all freelance employees, in any field, quickly learn, no-one's particularly interested in your personal scheduling problems; it's your work they're paying for.

PASSPORT TO OTHER OPPORTUNITIES

Radio science broadcasters tend to be freelancers, whereas their producers, for the most part, are full-time staff members. Sometimes staff producers also double as presenters, especially on BBC World Service with its relatively restricted programme budgets. This means that they tend to do a variety of work beyond their main broadcasting job, such as:

- *Contributing to radio programmes* on other channels including book reviews, commenting on current research findings, talking about science-based exhibitions or films etc. As well as broadcasting,

---

[9] At the time of writing, eleven books have been published and another is being planned.

[10] The Open University connection was long and fruitful resulting in presenting (or voicing-over) literally hundreds of radio and TV programmes and, eventually, the award of an honorary degree from the Open University 'for services to science communication'.

[11] Thames Television's *How to Last a Lifetime* – a six-part psychology series on stress. There were also writing, production and voice-over commissions from Channel 4's *Equinox* strand.

there is also the possibility of 'narrowcasting' via podcasts and other Web-based vehicles.

- *Voice-overs* for films and videos for a wide range of clients, some commercial, others organisations such as charities or government departments.
- *Lecturing*, usually but not invariably about the nature of science media and the experience of being a journalist in that context. This can take the broadcaster outside the United Kingdom as can most of the other activities that follow here.
- *Chairing conferences* with a science/technology theme where experience in interacting with speakers (and keeping them to their allotted time!) is invaluable. This could range from a lively discussion on the pros and cons of animal research to a session at the British Science Association's annual meeting on science in the media.
- *Consultancy* and other work for industrial clients. Usually this takes the form of communications and/or media training to help researchers in commercial organisations to encapsulate their messages for an internal audience (sales, marketing etc) or for an external audience such as the media.
- *A huge variety of writing* commissions can also flow from broadcasting: books, book chapters, newspaper and magazine articles, Web pages, newsletters, speeches, even leaflets, brochures and prospectuses.
- *Television* writing, presenting and sometimes production. Many television programme makers, being generalists with little scientific experience, welcome the input of someone familiar with the language and concepts of science. A related area is the corporate video – a short film made by an organisation to promote a product, service, initiative or campaign.

GETTING INTO THE RADIO BUSINESS

The media is overcrowded: far more people would like to work in it than there are jobs available. Nowhere is this more true than in the presenting world where only a handful of opportunities seem to exist. A radio strand, for example, can continue for many years using the services of a single presenter (with occasional back-up for sickness or other absences).

On the other hand, the media, like science, thrives on novelty, with new ideas for programmes constantly being considered and aired.

So what may seem like a closed shop is more open than would appear. Producers are always looking out for new talent.

How then can a scientist who aspires to become a broadcaster break in? Here are a few ideas.

- *Try to get some relevant experience*

    In trying to break into any new occupation, it helps to be able to claim some experience, however limited. Many university student bodies run local radio franchises where one can glean insights into the technical set-up, production and presenting skills required by the medium.

    Local hospitals also offer internal broadcasts and usually welcome unpaid help. Local radio stations might be another way of gaining experience which might, in the first instance, be confined to coffee-making!

    A good first step is to talk to your institutional media and communications folk – the university press office, for example. They will probably have some useful contacts in the local media.

- *Think about taking one or perhaps two or three intermediate steps towards a media career*

    It may be overly optimistic to expect to jump straight into radio work from your present position: you may need to edge towards it. One biomedical researcher, for example, left the lab bench and started out working in the press office of a large charity then progressed to helping out with the podcasts on its website. She now combines podcasting with quite a lot of media work for radio and television channels while remaining in her job with the charity.

    Another researcher worked in a research institute's press office writing media releases and answering enquiries from journalists before applying for a full-time job as an assistant radio producer.

- *Learn two basic journalistic skills*

    Wherever you work in the media as a reporter/presenter, you will need to acquire two essential skills. The first is the ability to identify a 'story' – that is, in the case of science, a novel and intriguing piece of research that you can make relevant to your audience, written or spoken. This is important. However theoretical or esoteric a journal article, say, might appear, and however important it may be to science, it simply has to be put across in ways that resonate with ordinary consumers.

This takes us to the other vital skill: writing clearly and succinctly in language that anyone can follow, and structuring your writing to give it maximum impact.[12]

- *Listen critically to the radio*

  How, in detail, do radio reporters and presenters go about their business? How do they grab and maintain our attention? What makes a good, as opposed to a dull, broadcaster? As a researcher, you have proven intellect and sharp analytical skills. Use these to deconstruct radio broadcasts in a critical manner.

- *Acquire the ability to compromise and to meet deadlines*

  In some ways, radio (and other media) work is radically different from research. The latter tends to be quite slow and reflective, the former often operates in an atmosphere of speed and frenzy. Where a scientist will be reluctant to go public with research findings until he or she has checked, double-checked and then had yet another run through, journalists often simply have to settle with the 'least worst' product they can achieve within their constraints of time and space. Compromise, then, is necessary in the pursuit of a deadline.

- *Prepare to be flexible in your lifestyle and build up your stamina*

  The trouble with reporting on research, especially in a fast-moving newsroom, is that the journalist has to get the story – an interview, say – as and when this is possible. This often means working unsociable hours (missed children's sports days, birthday celebrations etc) and moving around a lot to get to where the action is. No-one in radio can afford to have a 9 to 5 mentality.

---

[12] There are innumerable sources of information, in print and on the Web, to help you to write journalistically. A good starting point (cited by many websites) is George Orwell's classic, *Politics and the English Language*, which, although first published more than 50 years ago, still contains the essential wisdom for all would-be writers. Note in particular Orwell's basic Six Rules which are:

1. Never use a metaphor, simile, or other figure of speech which you are used to seeing in print.
2. Never use a long word where a short one will do.
3. If it is possible to cut a word out, always cut it out.
4. Never use the passive where you can use the active.
5. Never use a foreign phrase, a scientific word, or a jargon word if you can think of an everyday English equivalent.
6. Break any of these rules sooner than say anything outright barbarous.

CONCLUSION

A second career in radio can deliver immense satisfaction and researchers have many of the attributes needed to make such a step work: intelligence, tenacity, imagination and drive. Couple this with a realistic attitude towards the constraints and demands of the media as outlined earlier here and there is no reason why a radio career should not take you well into your old age. The journey down the occupational pin table can deliver an excellent result.

20
_____

From Science to Storytelling

At the very end of a winding corridor on the 19th floor of Beth Israel Hospital in downtown Manhattan is a nondescript door. The dull gold plaque on the wall next to it says in bold typeface: Donna Mildvan, MD, Chief of Infectious Diseases. As I nervously knocked on the door as a 23-year-old student journalist, I was greeted by a perfectly coiffed, petite 70-year-old lady with a big handshake and an unexpected belly laugh.

From her first patient in July 1980, a 33-year-old gay German chef who went blind before he died of raging diarrhea, to the hundreds who swiftly followed him, Dr Mildvan's 40-year career was shaped by a single disease. She had been witness to the birth of a terrifying new plague called AIDS that hit New York City in the summer of 1980.

At first, she had identified clusters of gay patients with similar symptoms and labelled this a new disease, and then tirelessly tested novel life-saving treatments for her patients. She figured out that unexplained swollen lymph glands were early stages of fatal AIDS and described these findings in one of the first Center for Disease Control reports of the new disease.

When I went in to see her, she was still running clinical drug trials at her clinic in Beth Israel Hospital, 30 years after she collaborated on connecting AIDS to the HIV microbe. 'I have watched this apocalypse coming and growing,' she told me, 'It's entire evolution from beginning to now ... it's been an extraordinary trip.'

HIV was particularly special to me because I had studied it as an immunology graduate student at the University of Oxford. For my

Successful Careers beyond the Lab, ed. David Bennett and Richard Jennings.
Published by Cambridge University Press. © Cambridge University Press 2017.

research project, which I had only submitted a few months before I met Dr Mildvan, I chose an HIV lab at the Weatherall Institute of Molecular Medicine at Oxford led by a passionate young principal investigator (PI) called Dr Nilu Goonetilleke. The Institute was part of an international collaboration, the Centre for HIV/AIDS Vaccine Immunology, which was running human clinical trials for an elusive HIV vaccine. My project, a drop in the ocean, was trying to analyse the human T-cell (part of the human immune system) response to viruses such as HIV in order to replicate it in a vaccine form.

The overarching idea of the project was thrilling – inventing an entirely new cure to a deadly disease. It wasn't just the clinical manifestation of HIV that was fascinating to me – it was the basic biology of the virus itself. It had been outwitting the human immune system for decades, employing evolutionary wiles that the world's best immunologists were struggling to predict and foil.

But the reality of the lab work was in stark contrast to the excitement of the hypothesis: I spent weeks failing at step one of a multi-step process only to realise the machine I had been measuring my RNA on had been calibrated incorrectly and I had been throwing perfectly good RNA down the sink everyday.

This is hardly a rare story in science: failure is part of the process, and there are far more downs than ups. It's like spending years of your life banging your fists on a locked door. What makes it worth it for experimental scientists is the rare 'Aha!' moments, the tiniest shaft of light from under the door that confirms something you had only theorised or proves something you had imagined or hoped for.

When I compare that period in my research career to my husband's – he is currently completing a PhD in quantum computing – I realise that the biggest difference between us isn't necessarily just raw ability (although that is certainly one of them!), but mainly one of perspective: his single-minded focus on an achievable goal means failures seem surmountable whereas I constantly had my eye on the dramatic big picture – developing a vaccine to cure HIV – and felt every setback in the lab keenly because it seemed impossible to achieve everything in a short time.

My favourite part of that year spent in the lab was writing the thesis after the experiments were all wrapped up. While all the other Master's degree candidates complained about the length of the write-up, I spent a week structuring, polishing, providing context and analysis and slotting in my methods and results section with ease. Writing about science was a lot more fun than doing it, I realised.

Eight months later, here I was in New York, asking Dr Mildvan what it was like to have to treat droves of dying patients without any available treatments. In her clinic, I spoke to HIV patients and AIDS activists from the 1980s about their personal struggles with the disease – most survivors had lost many loved ones in the early years before anti-retrovirals.

The biggest national newspaper at the time, *The New York Times*, was reporting virtually nothing about AIDS even though thousands had died by 1985. In fact, the *Times* published its first headline about the disease – 'Rare Cancer Seen in 41 homosexuals' – three months after it had first been covered in a gay weekly newspaper called *The New York Native*.

The story of HIV wasn't just a scientific one, I found – it was a social and cultural narrative with dozens of courageous and brilliant scientists, doctors and patients who had helped to transform it from the swift killer they were confronted with to the chronic, manageable condition that we know today.

When I sat down to write about Mildvan's work for a class assignment, I knew I had made the right choice to leave science. I didn't have the temperament to be a laboratory researcher but I believe strongly that cutting-edge research is too important to be confined to the academic world of conferences and peer-reviewed papers. What I did have was the ability to put a human face to science and to explain why the average person should care. That's how I ended up in Manhattan studying for a second Master's degree in journalism at New York University's Science, Health and Environmental Reporting Program (SHERP), surrounded by like-minded science graduates whose paths, like mine, had converged onto writing.

One of my all-time favourite fictional characters is Roald Dahl's whimsical Matilda, the little girl genius ignored by her parents but nurtured by a school teacher. Matilda's favourite pastime – like mine – was reading books that transported her into worlds far away from her own. 'Oh. I was flying past the stars on silver wings,' Matilda says. 'It was wonderful.'

To me, science and stories both ignite this same feeling of wonder and escape: inhabiting invisible, impossible worlds far removed from the humdrum of everyday existence. The microscopic underworld of microbes, the mysterious power of DNA, our inscrutable brain – they all hold the same fascination for me as fiction did.

The love of science, particularly biology, persisted through my young adulthood and I felt it was an obvious choice for my undergraduate degree. I briefly considered studying English, but discarded the idea, unprepared to give up biology this early in my academic life. Having South Asian parents means the decision to study a solid scientific subject was gleefully encouraged and my mother reassured me that I didn't have to give up writing; I could just continue it as an extracurricular hobby.

As an undergraduate at Queen's College of the University of Oxford, I soaked up the lectures on evolution, animal behavior, genetics and neuroscience but I was never drawn to the lab as many scientists are. Experimental biology seemed to me a necessary evil – a place with tools that could help me to explore further but one I was never able to master. I was more interested in writing opinionated essays on the hygiene hypothesis behind allergies than pipetting samples for hours on the bench.

In my three years as an undergraduate I did spend one term writing for the *Oxford Student* newspaper where I reported news and did a bit of editing. But unlike the other students who had thrown themselves into its production and considered the 'OxStu' a stepping-stone to their future career, I just dabbled. I also wrote some freelance pieces for a Singapore-based magazine called *India Se* about the cultural quirks of being an Indian student abroad and became part of the University's Yearbook committee which involved writing a few vignettes. When the magazines with my by-line in them came to me in the post I squirreled them away carefully but I never seriously considered journalism as a career.

Instead, when I graduated with a BA in Biological Sciences, I didn't want to look for alternatives to the scientific life; there was so much left to learn and discover. So I applied and got a place on the MSc Integrated Immunology course also at the University of Oxford which promised to educate graduate students in both basic, laboratory science as well as the clinical side of immunology that explores how immuno-logical diseases manifest in real patients. The idea of human patients was compelling so I took my place on the program.

The MSc gave me a solid grounding in laboratory research: I was trained by some of the best post-docs and PhD students at the Weath-erall Institute and I had my first brush with practical genetics: extracting RNA, building cDNA and actually sequencing every A-C-T-G of a gene. I found the laboratory too limiting and my bench skills were far from dexterous so I considered graduate medicine as an option. It would be a sensible and obvious choice with my background in human immunology and the thought of spending another five years studying didn't put me off at all. It was a lifetime commitment, I knew, so this would close any doors that I had left diffidently open for myself.

One of these doors led to the idea of being a writer. The delicious possibilities of a blank page have always attracted me. As a child, I spent hours making up stories either lining pages of writers' notebooks with character dialogues or creating my own books from sheaves of white paper that I would bind together with bits of stray ribbon.

Meanwhile, biology, the human body in particular, was a far more enigmatic universe: What makes it tick, why does it sometimes go wrong, how does the brain control our thoughts and actions, what makes us human? So I grew up exploring and experimenting with biology at school, feeling sure that it would be my career but coming home to bury my nose in a book.

But years later, one afternoon during studying for my immunology degree when I should have been working on my thesis, the thought struck me: what if I could write as a job? I didn't want to leave science behind completely because I knew it could bring something unique to my writing: it is far easier to explain complex concepts to a lay audience if one has some real grasp of scientific process. I decided to idly browse the Web for publications that scientists write for.

Of course, I knew both *Nature* and *Science* had news and features sections for writers, but there were a host of popular science publications too: *New Scientist*, *Scientific American*, *Popular Science*. There were radio shows and TV programs devoted to science and technology, and newspaper editors who specialised in these areas. They all must have trained somewhere, I thought. What were their paths?

A quick search for 'science journalism' brought up Imperial College London's science communication program but I felt it was too safe. I didn't want to stay tied to a primarily scientific institution; that would be my comfort zone. I wanted to supplant myself from the familiar and infiltrate a new world – the mainstream media.

As I idly clicked around I came to the SHERP website advertising a journalism Master's degree for those with a scientific background and experience but who wanted to learn the business of journalism.[1]

The courses were all completely new to me – reporting and interviewing techniques, how to formulate a book proposal, analysing data to write investigative pieces. The professors were all prize-winning

---

[1] The Science, Health and Environmental Reporting Program (SHERP) – http://journalism.nyu.edu/graduate/programs/science-health-and-environmental-reporting/

writers in their own right and the alumni were dotted across American media from National Public Radio to *The New York Times*, *WIRED* and *Slate*. The only catch was that it was in New York.

Looking back, I never once worried about having to move countries – all I had to do was secure a place. For the first time, I was applying for a degree that I had nothing much to show for; a handful of freelance pieces and some work on a student newspaper were my only evidence of any ability. But the program's director, Dan Fagin, decided to a take a chance on me – we chatted over Skype one afternoon, and the next thing I knew, I was packing my bags for New York City.

What was comforting about the SHERP program was that all its alumni had started off in science. Like me, many had felt like misfits in the lab and had dabbled in writing or science communication in some form during their student years. But at our core we had all spent time in labs and had immense respect and some understanding of how science functions as an industry. We were committed to producing entertaining, awe-inspiring and, above all, accurate stories about a sometimes impregnable world whose inhabitants often feel misunderstood by the media and general public. We were idealists who wanted to do science journalism 'right.'

There are several paths into media: some have known it's what they want their whole lives and train in the traditional ways via graduate jobs on national and local media schemes. Others start out as interns, fact-checkers or freelancers.

Of course, you don't have to do a graduate degree to break in but for me the biggest advantage as an outsider was the powerful network of faculty and alumni that eased my route into this dynamic and somewhat wobbly world. Through that alumni network I've found amazing mentors who continue to point me in the right direction at each step of my still-nascent journey as a journalist.

An editor in New York called John Abell gave me that first break after we had a chat at a college networking event. I hadn't even heard of *WIRED* magazine back then but when I explained to him that I loved the human angle of science and technology stories he invited me to apply for a spring internship at *WIRED*.[2] I remember being absolutely terrified because it was my first 'job' outside a laboratory. My first proper by-line there was on a story titled 'DARPA's[3] five radical plans for military medicine', outlining the most futuristic science and

---

[2] WIRED – www.wired.com/   [3] Defense Advanced Research Projects Agency

technology projects by the US military's blue-sky research arm. The thrill I felt that first day has stayed with me ever since.

During my 18 months at New York University, I interned at three different publications – *WIRED*, *Popular Science* and *Nature Medicine* – and pitched to editors at several others. Being thrown into the deep end in this way meant I had to quickly grasp the nuts and bolts of the job – how editors like to be pitched and what makes a good story – but it also made me realise that good pitches and reliable writers are in demand.

Interning and pitching (albeit often unsuccessfully) meant the New York media world began to seem less daunting and opaque. There is no secret formula, I found. If my curiosity led me to a genuinely good story, I just had to find a platform to tell it on. If my pitch wasn't quite right but the editor's interest was piqued they would write back when they had a different idea or encourage me to keep pitching.

Often it's easier to pitch to a publication when you've spoken to the editor face to face. Most editors will be happy to sit down for a quick coffee or chat as it's often flattering to be asked. I found that once I'd had a conversation with an editor about what they were looking for I could tailor my pitches far better. The trick is to just get started by reaching out to publications you admire and your first story will become the stepping-stone to all the others.

As I approached the end of my MA studies I began to cast about for jobs both in New York and London. The one that made my ears prick up was an opening as an editorial assistant at *WIRED* magazine's UK edition.[4] It was a publication I knew and loved, and the idea of producing a print magazine was exciting.

Again, as my luck would have it, I had stumbled across someone who was willing to take a chance on me. This time it was the editor of *WIRED UK*. I was still a student in New York and had no plans to fly to London in the coming weeks but he was happy to Skype with me. On the day of my interview *WIRED*'s Skype connection failed so we had to resort to an old-fashioned telephone chat.

Three months later I was back in London and starting my first full-time job in journalism at *WIRED UK*.

The bulk of my career so far has been spent at *WIRED UK* where I worked for three and a half years. There I wrote about science, technology and innovative businesses covering everything from futuristic architecture to vaccines for drug addictions and brain-controlled

---

[4] WIRED UK – www.wired.co.uk/

prosthetics. In my last year there, I edited the opening section of the magazine, called Start, which covered science, technology, start-ups and data. Because real estate was precious and limited and the section included a diverse set of story types from infographics to character profiles, I learnt to dig beyond a cool idea: I learnt how to evaluate the success of a business and discovered that the most fascinating stories aren't just about people; they can be about data too.

The sensibilities of the editors, designers and writers at WIRED shaped the kind of journalist and editor I am today. Just as I had had the values of evidence-above-all and pursuit of an absolute truth drilled into me as a scientist, my colleagues at WIRED taught me to rely on reporting rather than conjecture, the importance of visuals in enhancing words, and journalistic integrity. As a scientist, it helps to write for a publication whose values dovetail with your own ideologies.

After WIRED, I moved on to write for The Daily Telegraph where I was Head of Technology and worked with a team of talented writers who covered technology and innovation. Here, too, I had been brought into my role with a healthy dose of trust by my editor who had taken a chance and believed that he could train me to keep up with the frenetic pace of a national newspaper.

Today I work as European Technology Correspondent for the Financial Times (known as the FT) in London. Although my specialism has morphed from science into the business of technology and innovation my remit is wide-ranging and I continue to write about scientific breakthroughs in various forms: I have written about universities spinning out scientific research into commercial enterprises, opinion pieces about life-saving genomic techniques and features about artificial intelligence and empathetic robots.

To keep up I have had to fast-forward my mental schedule from that of a monthly publication to a daily website; I have had to learn about the business of digital journalism and the value of multimedia in storytelling – things I'd never considered before.

As a freelance writer I have endeavoured to stick with science: I turned a classroom assignment about pediatric HIV nurses into a piece for the BBC and interviewed scientists, including an epidemiologist solving gang crimes in Chicago and a whale biologist in Sri Lanka for the New Scientist.

Currently I'm working on a magazine piece for the FT about the transformation of our smartphones into doctors allowing our mobiles to easily diagnose everything from chlamydia to Ebola and diabetes, and even sequence our own DNA within minutes. It will already have been published when you read this.

I have found that my perspective is most considered and thoughtful when I'm writing about subjects I've worked on or learned about because that's what I'm most passionate about.

There's no easy how-to guide out there about moving from science to journalism especially because so much of it is about luck and how you jump on it: in my case I was extremely lucky to have met several fantastic editors whose advice and training took me from step to step in my journey.

But I live by two mantras. The first is to meet with as many writers and editors as I can because each person comes with their own origin story, advice and career path, and you never know what or who might spark an idea or an opportunity that resonates with you.

The other is to just start writing. If I ever I have an idea percolating in my head I try and follow it up by reading and talking to scientists in that area just to see if the seed can germinate into a story. Has anyone else written about this? If yes, why is now a good time to follow up? What could I bring to it? If the idea does have potential I start writing up a pitch straightaway because putting a notion into words often helps to crystallize the story for me.

Recently I met one of the scientists I had interviewed extensively for one of my longer feature pieces – a neuroscientist at Brown University who works on mind-controlled prosthetic devices for paralysed patients. I had won an award for science journalists under 30 for that piece, and I shared the news with him.

He was absolutely delighted to hear about it and took immense pride in the part he had played in the piece. It is hard for scientists to convey complexity in a way that gets an average person excited, he told me. 'I'm so glad you are able to share our story with the world.' His research, like so many other scientists, engineers, coders and entrepreneurs inventing world-first solutions, is one of the many stories I've been privileged to hear, and tell, so far, and is the reason I wake up and look forward to going into work every day.

Part V A Life on Camera

21

Propelled by Science

Science is often sold a bit like a plate of broccoli: 'It's good for you, eat it up.' Actually, to me, it has always been more like a box of delights. And as one door opens, dozens more seem to open in front of it.

For an eternally curious child, science was an inexhaustible treasure. My favourite book as a seven-year-old was *Tiny Toilers and Their Works*, a folksy American book about ants. For a while the natural world captured me, not just animals but wild flowers, fungi and, since I grew up on the coast, sea creatures of every sort. Indeed, I wanted to be a marine biologist just like Jacques Cousteau. But two things changed all that. First, Miss Bevan, my inspirational science teacher. She announced on Day One of our Advanced level work that by the end we would realise that we knew nothing compared to what remained to be discovered. Wow! Second, she introduced us to DNA. And that was it – it had to be the human body and medicine for me.

But life does not always go to plan. I was set for Oxbridge examinations and medical school but my father became very seriously ill during my Advanced level years and then died. He was a larger-than-life character who owned a tattoo parlour outside the dockyard gates in Portsmouth and had a slot machine empire. He only dealt in cash and not notes, you understand – mountains of coins. Even though my mother was a businesswoman in her own right, his death at just 40 years old meant I couldn't stay on at the fancy private school that the tattoos had provided me with. And the trauma inevitably affected my exam results and a career as a doctor seemed impossible.

Successful Careers beyond the Lab, ed. David Bennett and Richard Jennings.
Published by Cambridge University Press. © Cambridge University Press 2017.

I had a boyfriend whose sister had a London flat and the attractions of boyfriend and London were compelling. So I stuck a pin in the *Universities and Colleges Admissions Service* (UCAS) handbook in the London section and it came up with an intercalated degree (that's one where you can do different modules at different institutions) based at Bedford College, then in Regent's Park London, and oh joy, I could do genetics and immunology at University College London (UCL) as well as freshwater and marine biology.

At University I discovered that I was the world's worst bench scientist. Truly appalling. I had to work with shore crabs and my lab notebooks are a litany of: No 27 'Lost', No 49 'Escaped' and even No 72 'Fell off bench'. Worse, I broke every single piece of equipment I touched. UCL told me firmly after the smashing of a particularly precious ground glass chromatogram tank lid that I had to stop doing practicals as they could no longer afford to teach me. But I continued to be entranced by the science and particularly by the elegance and beauty of DNA.

After university I took a shorthand and typing course and cast about for a job. It had to be something to do with medicine or science and I applied for a job that I wasn't remotely qualified to do editing a science journal at the Royal College of Obstetricians and Gynaecologists. 'We think you'd be bored with that job' they said kindly to me at interview 'but we've got this job coming up with our research charity'. 'You have to run the research programme (it was on women's health) and, by the way, there's a royal charity film premiere coming up in six weeks' time, the Queen is coming, there are 2000 tickets to sell, get on with it'. Clearly I wasn't qualified to do that either but here comes the first learning point: be brave, say yes. You never know where it's going to lead.

So I then spent the next 15 years running the research programme, going out talking about research to Women's Institutes all over Britain and organising major fundraising events. A couple of years in, Diana, the Princess of Wales, became the charity's Patron. She was a rookie princess and I the rookie charity organiser. We got on famously and it was the beginning of a working relationship that lasted 12 years and had a major influence on my life. The charity became hugely fashionable and I organised everything from balls at the Royal Albert Hall to film premieres and concerts at Buckingham Palace. During this period I also had my two sons.

But I was becoming restless. The events were fabulously successful, I was mixing with celebrities and royalty, but I began to hanker after something different. And it had to involve science. Television appealed to me enormously. Partly this had to do with what happened at all those women's meetings I tramped to all over the country. When I explained something about how the body worked and people said, 'Ah, now I understand', I got this terrific buzz. The other side of it, it has to be said, is that if the fridge door opens and the light goes on, I'm the one instantly tap dancing. I have show-off genes in spades, thanks to my father's side of the family who are all artists and actors.

I had already begun to branch out at work, cutting my days down to four a week in order to concentrate on writing for magazines on the other day. I'd got into this because a magazine editor told me that she was fed up with sending journalists my way to explain things, why didn't I just write it myself. So I did, and my health and science journalism began to blossom.

But I longed to get into television. I wrote TV treatments for health shows, I badgered people, but nothing happened, although I did get myself an agent who believed in me. Meanwhile I felt like a bee in a box, desperately buzzing about waiting for someone to open the door and let me fly. If I told my friends about my aspirations, they were brutal. 'Vivienne, you are a 39-year-old Muswell Hill north London housewife with two children who is the breadwinner. On no account give up the day job'. So that's exactly what I did because I had finally realised a truth which ought to be universally acknowledged: you are the one with the key to your future, the one who can unlock that box. So I resigned my safe job without actually telling my husband. Looking back, it was the bravest thing I've ever done in my life.

I got myself a stopgap job: organising the Centenary Motor Show. Meanwhile I had applied for a job which appeared in *The Guardian* newspaper. 'TV presenters wanted, must have evidence of science communication skills'. The BBC had placed the ad and I wrote a ridiculous cheeky letter saying that on any night of the week I was to be found in twilight homes for the elderly talking about nuclear magnetic resonance. Intrigued, the BBC asked for a showreel – a compilation of TV footage featuring yours truly – but of course I didn't have any so I fibbed a bit and said that the broadcasters couldn't make it available in time. Not an outright lie but certainly bending the truth. Reluctantly they agreed to see me without.

I can't tell you the thrill of walking into the BBC. I was astonished to even be interviewed and didn't for one minute think I would get the job which I had now discovered was presenting the iconic science show, Tomorrow's World. Several thousand people had applied including many big-name TV stars. Half-way through the interview came the question I had been dreading. Exactly how much TV experience do you have, Vivienne? 'On a scale of not very much to bugger all, it veers towards the bugger all actually', I replied, thinking I had now blown it. 'Well, we'd better send you off to make a film' came the reply.

And thus it was that the very first film I made – a film, ironically, on the genetics of breast cancer – was my TV debut. From charity organiser to prime-time TV. It was a leap-and-a-half. My presenting, which was dire at first, improved. My journalism was incredibly useful because I could spot stories and those years tramping round women's clubs meant I could explain complex science simply. I was a pig in muck. Often people ask me how to get into TV. As I always say, have a passion and an enthusiasm for a particular subject because it is this that will get you noticed, not brains or beauty of which both were certainly in short supply in my case. In fact, I was so anxious on the beauty front that very early in my career at the charity, I had turned down an invitation from the Chief Executive of Thames Television to present a new series because I didn't think I had the looks for it. A dozen or so years on, it was science that gave me confidence and a bedrock.

Some fantastic years followed. I travelled all over the world, I met fascinating people. I covered some extraordinary stories – a mouse with a human ear attached, for instance, the beginning of the then new science of tissue engineering, a man with a tooth in his eye and many new advances in medicine. I did Panorama and also a series of my own called Morning Surgery. But then came a new editor to Tomorrow's World and the first thing he did was clear out all the presenters. It's not personal. It's just life in TV which is brutal. On no account must you ever believe that it will go on forever, especially if you are a woman. Just love it while it lasts.

I started doing more radio, and I continued to develop, write and present many programmes and series for Radio 4 including eight series of 'Am I normal', four series of 'Inside the Ethics Committee' and my favourite, 'Just So Science', two series based on the science behind the Just So stories. I use my science knowledge in every single programme I do. I also continue making films for a wide variety of organisations and corporates. I still do TV but mostly as an armchair pundit and the skills I learned in TV have all been transferable because a further career that has developed as I have got older is that of a conference host and moderator. This too takes me all over the world. I have facilitated the G8 Dementia Summit, a global UN climate change congress, the launch of many events for the European Commission in science and innovation and a host of others. Knowledge of science has been essential to them all.

In 1997, the Princess of Wales died in that dreadful car crash. I knew her very well and was trusted by her family. I briefly became a Trustee of the Diana Memorial Fund. This was not a happy experience and I was in the eye of a media maelstrom. It taught me resilience and I made some great friends – there's always something good that comes out of tough times.

By this time I had been a columnist for *The Guardian* newspaper, and one day was having breakfast after doing the Frost Programme (a Sunday morning paper review hosted by Sir David Frost) with the editor of the *News of the World*. 'I've been looking for a woman columnist for ages', he said. 'I'll do that', I found myself saying. And, blow me down, but I suddenly found myself writing the main column for a tabloid Sunday newspaper. It made me possibly the only journalist to have simultaneously written for the Screws, as it was called, and the *Journal of Molecular Biology*. I subsequently became the columnist of *The Times*, writing weekly on medical science, and was also briefly an agony aunt for *Good Housekeeping* and continue to be its science editor. Once again, say 'yes' to everything and you never know where it will lead.

I have always had a strong public service ethos and I applied to be a member of one of the 250 or so science advisory committees advising the UK government as a lay member. I joined the Joint Committee on Vaccination and Immunisation. I always advise early-career scientists of the importance of these sort of appointments because they begin to lay down the track record that will eventually decide whether you will become a member of one of the influential and important grant-awarding bodies. I should say that I had no plan of this sort – I was really interested in public health and always have been. Don't ever do something that you are not interested in. But it was probably this experience that led me to then be accepted as a member of Council of the Medical Research Council and also of UCL – yes, the very same university college that begged me not to do practicals. I eventually became Vice Chair of Council. Both these appointments were intensely rewarding and stimulating and I served the maximum term for both.

My life turned full circle in 2013 with the 100,000 Genomes Project. DNA had filled me with wonder as a 16-year-old and, in 2001 as a journalist, I found myself reporting on the first draft of the human genome. We hacks felt able to predict confidently that it would usher in a new era of medicine by, ooh, Tuesday teatime at the latest. In fact, it was to be 15 years before genomic medicine became possible, not because of advances in genetics, but because the introduction of next-generation sequencing meant the cost of sequencing a human genome dropped from $3billion (the cost of the first genome sequence) to less than $1,000.

The 100,000 Genomes Project is an audacious one, bringing together the genome, health and medical record data of some 70,000 people with rare disease and cancer. Comparing this data allows patterns to be spotted enabling new insight and discovery. It is a National Health Service transformation project, a clinical service and a major research project in one, that also has profound implications for society. I was asked to head up engagement, listening to the public and patients about their hopes and fears and weaving their wishes into the future direction of the project. It brings together my communication skills, my science and my love of people.

I made a major career switch in my 30s; I will almost certainly do so again. And although life sciences are my forte, I take great pleasure in actively accepting jobs in subject areas that I know nothing about just for the thrill of learning something totally different.

In the course of my career I've met Nobel prize winners and royalty, celebrities and extraordinary human beings, I've seen technology in its infancy turn into paradigm-shifting disruption, I've nurtured the careers of young researchers and trained them, and I've explained game-changing discoveries to millions through television, film, print and radio. I've been awarded an OBE[1] and been part of setting the direction for the future. None of this would have been possible without science.

To summarise, be bold, take some risks and don't be afraid of failure which is a part of every successful person's career. Say 'yes' to every opportunity because you never know where it's going to lead or what doors it may open. Remember that you are the one with the key to your future. Don't wait for others to open doors for you. Make it happen for yourself. And, finally continue to challenge yourself with new fields – it will enrich you.

---

[1] Officer of the Most Excellent Order of the British Empire.

22
_____

A Career in Science Radio and Podcasting

CHRIS: Hello and welcome to the Naked Scientists. I'm Chris Smith.

KAT: And I'm Kat Arney, and over the next chapter we're going to take you through the history of the show, how we got involved and what we've learned along the way.

CHRIS: Plus, we'll share our top tips on how to get involved in science radio, so stay tuned. First, let's go right back to where it all started.

I've always been passionate about talking about science. The reason I got interested in science myself was that, when I was little, there were people like Johnny Ball on television who was incredibly entertaining for young minds.[1] Although it wasn't very high-level science, it was interesting science. But by the time I went to the University of Cambridge to study medicine, all that had disappeared and I felt that there was very little to capture the imagination of young people, like the 'future me'.

To compensate, I started doing things for the Cambridge Science Festival. In the first year, 1998, I made a nerve stimulator demonstration to measure how fast impulses went down nerves. Then, in 1999, to coincide with the genetically modified food scandal, I came up with a protocol so that people could make DNA out of fruit using ingredients in their kitchens such as pineapple juice to break up the proteins and aftershave to precipitate the DNA. That led to an invitation to appear

---

[1] Johnny Ball presented several series of popular science and technology UK television programmes for children in the late 1970s and throughout the 1980s.

Successful Careers beyond the Lab, ed. David Bennett and Richard Jennings.
Published by Cambridge University Press. © Cambridge University Press 2017.

on a local commercial radio station called Cambridge Red on a show hosted by Pete Cousins. It really opened my eyes – and my ears – to the power of radio. And I also met this person called Kat Arney who turned up to that first show. Funny enough, I didn't see Kat again until four years later when we launched the programme on the BBC radio and she was first person I hired to help me present it.

KAT: I'd always wanted to be a writer, and while I was studying natural sciences at the University of Cambridge I started writing a science column for the University newspaper, *Varsity*. As a result of that, my editor, Harriet, and I were invited to go on that radio show with Chris. I remember talking about genetically modified foods in a very squeaky voice, and there's still a recording in existence somewhere that Chris threatens me with from time to time!

CHRIS: The idea of the show was to mix up science with music, which seemed to work OK, so a month later we went back. Eventually we were turning up every week and I started pulling in PhD students from every part of the University because I thought it was quite fun and it was a good way to teach people some communication skills. But after six months of this I realised that the music was getting in the way of the science so I negotiated with the station to buy some airtime every Sunday evening so that we could set up our own show and, crucially, get more editorial control over the content and format.

That show was called *Science World*. It ran for a year from 2000 before we rebranded it as *The Naked Scientists*. We also launched the Naked Scientists website which I made in the summer holidays before I became a junior doctor so we could put all the back catalogue from the previous shows up and make it available for free to download and subscribe. So we were actually one of the very first podcasts before podcasting even really existed.

The next step was to move to our regular Sunday night slot on the BBC Eastern Region radio broadcasting from Cambridge. We had managed to persuade every local BBC Radio Station in the East of England to take the show live so we were broadcasting across the entire region which gave us a potentially massive audience.

Today we've got 80,000 active pages on the website which attracts more than a million unique visitors every month. We've grown a stable of more than ten different podcast strands over the past 15 years with more than a thousand hours of downloadable content available entirely for free. We now have about a million podcast downloads from the site every month including thousands of downloads of episodes we made ten years ago which I think is incredible. More than 55 million programme episodes have been downloaded in total since we started. We've also published four books including the best seller *Crisp Packet Fireworks* which I wrote with Dave Ansell [1]. It's packed full of around 50 experiments that anyone can do at home and we've recently re-released it in a refreshed format for 2016 under the name *Boom!* [2]

KAT: After my initial appearance on Cambridge Red I didn't work properly with the Naked Scientists until around 2003 after it had moved to the BBC. A friend mentioned to me that this new science show had started up and that it was the kind of thing I'd be interested in. And it turned out to be Chris running it! I got in touch and volunteered to get involved but on my very first evening in the studio I made a massive mistake. I left my mobile phone switched on inside a plastic carrier bag on the other side of the studio. So as soon as a friend heard me live on air they tried to call me, so I ended up rustling around trying to switch it off while the show was still going on. I'm amazed I was ever let back in the studio for another go!

I can also remember my first reporting assignment back in 2004, which was to interview Colin Pillinger on the day they announced the Beagle Mars lander had been lost. I had no idea what I was doing and was so worried about my technical equipment that I couldn't focus on a word he was saying. Needless to say, it wasn't the greatest interview I've ever done and I still cringe when I think about it, but practice makes perfect and I've done hundreds over the past decade or so.

Chris had also realised that the Naked Scientists needed to be more than just a radio show and podcast archive so he started commissioning people to write short articles for the website about interesting science topics. One of them was me and I found it a welcome break from my PhD in the lab and it taught me a huge amount about how to write clearly and engagingly for the public. The website was really the IFLScience of its day and packed with fascinating articles; there are now hundreds of pieces and they get thousands of page views.[2]

CHRIS: Although we started small the novelty of the concept meant that we were able to raise significant funds from organisations like the Wellcome Trust and several other research councils. That

___

[2] www.iflscience.com/

meant we got a lot bigger very quickly. At one point there were more than ten people working on the project. Now we have three full-time producers – Georgia Mills, Graihagh Jackson and Connie Orbach – as well as a number of freelancers like Kat and a rotating cast of interns funded by the Engineering and Physical Sciences Research Council (EPSRC), the Science and Technology Facilities Council (STFC), the University of Cambridge and the Genetics Society. Over the years we've had something like a hundred people pass through the project and use the opportunity as a springboard into other professional media. I'd like to think we've created a fantastic incubator for talent giving people the opportunity to learn on the job and try things out.

I want to emphasise that this is really important to me because I struggled so hard to get anywhere in the media space to start with. Thinking about the hurdles I'd had to get over to start the show and get it on the radio in the first place made me want to make it easier for people to get into radio and podcasting. I always say don't worry if you don't know the first thing about radio broadcasting because I can teach you that but what we want is your enthusiasm, your knowledge and your ability to bring a story to life. It's very easy to make science boring. It's much harder to make science intelligible and fun but we do it by getting great people to work with us.

KAT: My trick is that I always like to try to make a guest smile or laugh – that's how I know an interview has gone well. Usually I just try and crack terrible jokes until it happens and I always smile and laugh myself.

CHRIS: The other thing I try to do is expand our range of offerings by encouraging people to play to their strengths. We've created an umbrella organisation so we can all work on the same stage, everyone is pulling in the same direction, everyone can benefit and learn from everyone else, and it creates some long-term stability which is often lacking in a media world dominated by short-term freelance contracts. For example, we recruited Dave Ansell who was good at physics and coming up with experiments so he put enormous energy into developing a big library of 'kitchen science' experiments that we then put up on the site and turned into the *Crisp Packet Fireworks* book. Thousands of people look at them every month and do them at home with their kids so I hope we're nurturing the next generation of scientists.

Then there's someone like Sarah Castor-Perry who was interested in making videos for us and also very good at art so she developed our

Naked Science Scrapbook series.[3] Overall, I've been very proud to have been able to support and develop people's interests and passions, and we've had a lot of organisations coming to us asking us to work with them such as the *BBC Bitesize* revision guides.[4] But it's also important to maintain high standards; one of the things you have to be careful of when you diversify is that you don't spread yourself too thin and compromise on quality.

KAT: My background is in genetics and I still follow the field as much as I can, so making the monthly Naked Genetics podcast in association with the Genetics Society has felt like a nice fit. More broadly, the skills, opportunities and experience I've gained through the Naked Scientists have been invaluable. I left the lab in 2004 to work as a science communicator for the charity Cancer Research UK and was quickly trained up as a media spokesperson thanks to my experience behind the microphone. I've also continued to work as a writer and broadcaster on the side, finally going fully freelance in March 2016.

Over the years I've made science documentaries for BBC Radio 4, written for outlets including *New Scientist*, *WIRED* and *The Guardian*, and recently published my first book with Bloomsbury Sigma – a pop-science guide to genetics called *Herding Hemingway's Cats* [3]. All of that's really come about by just plugging away at it, making connections with people and taking up opportunities as and when they arise, and honing my skills and building my knowledge. There's no magic trick to growing a career in science communication – it's about giving it a go, network-ing as much as you can and a lot of hard work. At the same time it's a huge privilege to do this job. We get to talk to some of the best scientists in the world, which is just fantastic.

CHRIS: I worked out the other day that I've probably done more than 5,000 interviews with scientists over the years. So when people ask me how I know so much stuff, I say, 'Well, if you'd talked to 5,000 of the world's brightest people and hadn't learned anything along the way there'd be something wrong!' I think what is telling is that these people hardly ever turn us down for an interview. In fact we often find that they've heard the programme and enjoyed it, which is hugely rewarding and they're more than willing to come on the show.

---

[3] www.thenakedscientists.com/scrapbook

[4] www.bbc.co.uk/education

KAT: It's amazing what happens if you just ask to talk to people and show a chatty interest in their work. There's a mistaken perception that scientists won't talk to the media or shy away from interviews but I often find that they're keen to share their work and enthusiasm for their subject. Even the dullest-sounding topics (or guests!) will have great stories waiting to be unearthed and shared with the listeners, although sometimes it takes a bit of digging to get them out.

The other thing that's important to know is that unlike the early days of the Naked Scientists, you don't have to have a radio studio or a lot of funding to get started on podcasting. I still make my monthly Naked Genetics podcasts in my bedroom and record all my links under my duvet – it gives a great sound and also means I can work in my pyjamas if I'm feeling lazy. With today's smartphones you don't need an expensive microphone or recording kit. There's free audio editing software such as Audacity,[5] simple templates to build your own website and audio hosting sites like SoundCloud.[6] Anyone can do it!

CHRIS: Because it's now so simple and low-cost to get started, and it's easy to practise and get that all-important experience without actually having to spend a fortune. However, with a lower barrier to entry a huge number of podcasts have started up. So now the competition isn't a financial one but a fight for attention. It's a crowded market and it's also harder than ever to make money.

When I first started the Naked Scientists, I always said, 'I'm not giving up my day job' and I still work half the week as a medical doctor. My advice to anybody would be if you try to live hand-to-mouth as a freelancer is that it's very hard work and you'll probably fail. Some people won't but many will. Much better is to have a job that pays the mortgage and covers your living expenses but, in the background, also allows you to slowly build up your communication activities on the side. Gradually you then transition into it full or part time. It's a long-term game to play – a marathon, not a sprint! I like to throw my full passion into everything I do and I think I'm quite good at broadcasting and I like doing it but I don't do so much that I get bored with it or have to rely on it exclusively to make a living.

KAT: Passion and enthusiasm are really important in broadcasting as well as a great eye – and ear – for a story. Because the technology is so

---

[5] www.audacityteam.org/   [6] https://soundcloud.com/

accessible nowadays, having great content is vitally important. I also think it's essential to listen to great radio and podcasts for inspiration and there's a wealth of fantastic shows out there which I listen to while walking or running. I don't want to steal or copy their ideas but I like to hear what the competition is up to and how they tell stories using the material they have. Ultimately, I want to make great audio that people will love, enjoy and learn from.

CHRIS: What's the best bit of my day? When I get e-mails from kids saying that we helped them to get an 'A' in their science GCSEs or that they've now gone to university to study a science subject because they grew up listening to us and we switched them on to science. That lights up my morning, and it happens quite often. At the last count we've had something like 10,000 e-mails from people telling us that they are loyal listeners and that our infectious passion for our subject has rubbed off on them too. They're a very loyal bunch of listeners and their ranks keep swelling so we must be doing something right! It's a huge privilege to have so many people give us their time each week to tune into our programmes and we're really grateful. Did I ever see myself doing this when I first went to medical school? Not in a million years!

REFERENCES

1. Smith, C. and Ansell, D. (2008) *Crisp Packet Fireworks: Maverick Science to Try at Home (Naked Scientists)*. New Holland Publishers Ltd.
2. Smith, C. and Ansell, D. (2016) *Boom! Fantastic Science Experiments to Try at Home*. IMM Lifestyle.
3. Arney, K. (2016) *Herding Hemingway's Cats: Understanding how are genes work*. Bloomsbury Sigma.

Part VI   Science Communication,
          Teaching, Ethics and
          Environmentalism

23

What to Do When You Don't Know What You're Doing; Or, My First Twenty-Five Years in Science Communication

During my first freshman term at the University of Cambridge in the autumn of 1969 classes were punctuated by passion and protest. Students demonstrated almost weekly: about Conservative Member of Parliament Enoch Powell who had recently given his notorious 'Rivers of Blood' speech and who was billed to speak at the Cambridge Union Society; about the Vietnam War, of course; and about much else. During my second term, the Greek Tourist Board organized a 'Greek Week' in Cambridge with special events at the Garden House Hotel on the banks of the River Cam. On 13 February 1970, student protests about the Greek Colonels' Regime culminated in what came to be known at the Garden House Riot. Sitting in my room at Queens' College, I listened with mixed horror and delight to reports of what was happening through the evening just a few hundred yards away. One of my own professors, University Pro-Proctor Dr Charles Goodhart, was hit by a flying brick that night and taken to hospital.

Getting an education in the 1960s was about much more than merely obtaining a degree. It was about discovering the meaning of life, and putting the world to rights. *Hair* was running in the West End, *Sergeant Pepper* was playing on our turntables and Don McCullin, Bobby Seale and Aleksandr Solzhenitsyn were on our bookshelves. Enlightenment of various kinds – personal, political, religious – was on the agenda and somehow the very processes of learning – yes, even learning in the natural sciences which I had gone up to Cambridge to read – were all part and parcel of the *Zeitgeist*. In this heady atmosphere no one worth talking to was thinking about anything quite so boring or

Successful Careers beyond the Lab, ed. David Bennett and Richard Jennings.
Published by Cambridge University Press. © Cambridge University Press 2017.

so quintessentially bourgeois as a career; after all, in the world of our dreams wasn't everyone going to be famous for 15 minutes? I still remember our wizened Senior Tutor Max Bull telling a group of us that all of this silliness would stop just as soon as the economy went into recession.

Give him his due, Max was right. The 1960s didn't end with the advent of the 1970s; rather, they ended almost overnight in October 1973 when the Organization of Arab Petroleum Exporting Countries imposed an oil embargo on the West. In less than a year the price of oil went up four-fold. This put the brakes on most Western economies and in the United Kingdom it wasn't long before a new Conservative government was instituting a three-day working week. There's nothing quite like regular power cuts to put a chiller on things and the national mood changed very rapidly. By this time I was still at Queens' but now as a graduate student reading for a doctorate in the history of science. Then as now, the custom was for graduate students to supervise undergraduates and I was utterly dismayed to discover that many – most? – of my supervisees now appeared to be far more interested in grades and career prospects than they were in either discovering themselves or changing the world.

It was during this spell of partial disillusionment that I received the letter that helped to determine the course of my professional life. The letter hadn't been sent to me personally; instead, it was addressed to the History and Philosophy of Science Department of which I was a very junior member. Would the department be willing to provide a lecturer to teach a 10-week evening class in the village of Willingham just a few miles outside Cambridge? There, the local branch of an august organization called the Workers' Educational Association (WEA) had decided – wonderfully – to take on three great thinkers one after the other: Darwin, Marx and Freud. The reason the letter had come to me was very simple: nobody higher up in my department wanted to sacrifice 10 Wednesday evenings to talk about Darwin to a WEA class in the middle of the Fens. If I didn't say yes, the invitation would be politely declined.

Going out to Willingham for the first time was a thrilling, if slightly unnerving, experience. Assembled in the Village Hall were around 25 people who had decided to give up one evening a week for several months, not for the sake of a qualification (none was offered), nor yet for the promise of a new career (none was available, at least from me), but simply in order to learn about all things evolutionary. Many of these people were, as the WEA's name implied, workers; village workers for the most part, at least some of them doing various kinds of agricultural labour. In my vast inexperience, I went out that first evening prepared to start my account of Darwin's work at the beginning – namely, with Copernicus (!). I'd borrowed an orrery (a mechanical model of the solar system) from the University's Whipple Museum of the History of Science; equipped with this, I tried my best to explain Copernicus' great idea that it was the sun rather than the earth that stood at the centre of the universe.

I have no idea how well or badly I performed in this task but after I'd finished a middle-aged man came up to thank me for helping to resolve a mystery that had long puzzled him: Why did the moon change shape over the course of a lunar cycle? As I'd demonstrated the orrery, this man had come to realize that the moon was not, as he'd always assumed, a source of light; rather, it reflected the light of the sun. And so, depending on the angles between the sun, the earth and the moon, different amounts of the moon's sunlit surface were apparent in the night sky. Here was someone who'd looked up at the moon all his life and never really understood what he was seeing; and here was I, less than half his age, being thanked for helping him to appreciate the nature of the solar system in which we both lived. I was hooked. Talking about science with people like this who really wanted to know was much more rewarding to me than teaching far better-trained undergraduates, many of whom appeared to want nothing more than a passport to prosperity.

I had no sense of embarking on a particular kind of career but when it came time to look for a first job I decided not to focus on conventional academic lectureships (which was what most of my graduate student friends were after). Instead, I took an interest in the wider world of continuing education. At that time, many British universities had departments of 'Extra-Mural Studies', which, as the name implies, offered courses of part-time instruction outside the walls of the university; and in 1976 I was appointed Staff Tutor in Biological Sciences in the Department of Extra-Mural Studies at the (then) University College of Swansea. Now, my main responsibility was to organize and teach evening classes of roughly the type that I'd taught in Willingham but this time over a fairly wide area of South Wales. I still had a doctorate to complete and I was still set on a research career in the history of science; but as far as teaching was concerned my task was first to arouse and then to cultivate the scientific interests of adult students whose main reason to learn was the joy of learning itself.

I loved my time in Swansea. The people were warm-hearted and kind and my colleagues – especially Dr Geoffrey Thomas, the far more experienced Staff Tutor in Physical Sciences who took me under his wing – were generous-minded and good-humoured. (Among many gifts, my colleagues in Swansea gave me the art of seeing the funny side of – well, almost everything.) From the beginning, I had a sense that my students were teaching me more than I was teaching them. They indulged me, to be sure, dressing in their 'Sunday best' for evening class even when their feckless lecturer turned up in blue jeans; but they also managed me, letting me know in the nicest possible way when I'd misjudged an issue or a situation. On one memorable occasion, I remember an audience in Maesteg, Mid-Glamorgan coming to the rescue of a hopelessly inexperienced guest speaker, whom I'd been incautious enough to invite along, by bursting into applause when he finally paused for breath in the midst of some interminable technical explanation. He stopped, looked around slightly surprised, and then – to the eternal relief of all concerned – sat down. Such dexterity!

For me, trying to teach science to adult students was a revelation. My department was unusual in many ways, not the least of which was that every academic staff member specialized in a different subject. What became clear very quickly was that Geoffrey Thomas and I laboured under special difficulties by virtue of our scientific responsibilities. Where the tutors in English literature, Welsh literature, history and so on taught students who were self-confident (sometimes, perhaps, to a fault), we seemed to attract people who were plagued with self-doubt. Time and again, I would turn up to a new class, teach an introductory 'taster' session and then have someone come up to me at the end of the evening asking for permission to drop out. Thankfully, this seemed hardly ever to be because of anything I'd said or done; rather, it was because the person was utterly convinced that they weren't 'up to' taking the class: 'You see, I'm not particularly gifted and I've not had much of an education; I just don't think I'll be able to handle it.' Part of my job was persuading would-be students to stay in the class they really wanted to take against their better judgment.

Geoffrey and I talked about this a great deal. What was it about our subjects that made so many otherwise interested and motivated people think that they couldn't possibly handle them? We sensed that, uniquely among the academic disciplines, the sciences might occupy a problematic place in the public domain. Almost universally regarded as important, and often seen as compellingly interesting, it seemed that the sciences were widely viewed as remote and inaccessible. It was as if the sciences and the people who produced them were up on some high mountaintop, hidden from public view by clouds of impenetrable fog. Of course, these were just impressions but out of such musings there slowly emerged what seemed to be a pretty compelling question: How could we get a clearer picture of the place that the sciences occupy in that most elusive of things – 'the public mind'? In this way, the experience of trying to teach science to non-scientists began gradually to influence my research interests.

In the late-1970s I became involved with a group of other adult educators who were interested in 'public participation in science and technology'. We were asking questions about how non-scientists might more effectively contribute to public policy- and decision-making in areas that were substantially scientific or science-related. There was a small literature on this subject in the 1970s and at least one Cabinet-level political figure in Britain (the Labour Party's Tony Benn) had contributed to it. In May 1979, we convened a two-day workshop in Coleg Harlech, a residential adult education college for mature students in North Wales. There was genuine excitement about new ways of engaging the public in scientific decision-making and this was further heightened by the fact that, as luck would have it, our workshop coincided with a General Election (as I recall, several workshop participants went home midway through the proceedings to vote in their constituencies). Before the end of the meeting, however, the upbeat mood was broken when the election was declared in favour of Margaret Thatcher's Conservative Party. We all went home much more subdued, thinking – correctly, as it turned out – that ideas about public participation in science might have to wait a while.

In 1982, I followed Geoffrey Thomas to the University of Oxford where by this time he had become Deputy Director in the Department for External Studies (later, the Department for Continuing Education).[1] By now we were in touch with Professor Jon Miller at the University of Northern Illinois who was responsible for conducting the National Science Foundation's regular 'Science Indicators' surveys of American public perceptions of science and technology. Nothing like this, to our knowledge, had ever been attempted in the United Kingdom. And this is

---

[1] Geoffrey Thomas went on to become Director of the Department of Continuing Education, and also Founding President of Kellogg College, the first fully fledged College at the Universities of Oxford and Cambridge to specialize in continuing education. Now *there's* an unconventional career in science that's worth the telling.

how things would very probably have stayed were it not for the fact that in the early 1980s the monetarist policies of the new Thatcher government threw the United Kingdom into a severe economic recession. In spite of the fact that she was the first prime minister for many generations to have a scientific background (she had read chemistry at the University of Oxford), Prime Minister Thatcher did not spare the scientific community from the general belt-tightening; and so it was that, for the first time since World War II, British science faced financial cutbacks. In a community that had grown accustomed to steady growth in everything – numbers of scientists, research funding, numbers of doctoral students, etc. – these cutbacks provoked anxiety and a considerable amount of soul-searching. What had gone wrong? Why was science being defunded? And above all, what could be done to secure greater public support for science?

These concerns were arguably the second factor after that fateful letter from the Willingham branch of the WEA to decisively shape my career. Spurred by the funding crisis gripping the British scientific community, the President of the Royal Society, gifted chemist and science communicator Sir George (later, Lord) Porter, established a Committee on the Public Understanding of Science (COPUS)[2] under the Chairmanship of the distinguished geneticist Sir Walter Bodmer, who contributes the Advance Review to this book. Shortly after that a number of other leading scientists created a lobbying organization with the memorable title: *Save British Science*.[3] Through the mid-1980s, therefore, the place of science in the public domain moved centre stage. COPUS set up all kinds of initiatives designed to improve the relationship between science and the public – media fellowships for working scientists, lobbying efforts with newspaper editors, a science book prize and so on – and it called for social scientific research designed to throw new light on the dynamics of the relationship between science and the public. Responding to this call in 1987, the UK Economic and Social

---

[2] COPUS was established in 1985, and it played a central part in the 'public understanding of science movement' in the United Kingdom until 2000, when its main work – to put the public on the scientific community's agenda - was widely seen to have been done. See: Parliamentary Select Committee on Science and Technology, 3rd Report, House of Lords, 2000,chapter 3: 'Public Understanding of Science', at: www.publications.parliament.uk/pa/ld199900/ldselect/ldsctech/38/3805.htm

[3] Set up in 1986, Save British Science still exists. See: www.sciencecampaign.org.uk/about/history/advert.htm

Research Council set up a first research programme on 'public understanding of science'; included in their request for research proposals was a call for a national random sample social survey. Here was our chance!

There is a lot to be said about the process of moving from one branch of research to another. In retrospect, my particular transition from the history of science to quantitative social science feels multiply hazardous. Quite apart from purely technical considerations (of which there were many), one thing I completely failed to recognize at first, but quickly came to learn the hard way, was that the discipline of sociology was riven by ideological disputes about the proper ways in which the subject should be pursued. If I'd known more about these disputes at the outset I might not have ventured quite so confidently onto the terrain of the quantitative social sciences. Once there, however, I soon found that significant numbers of my new colleagues – especially in the sociology of science – were deeply suspicious of the whole enterprise of applying 'scientific' methods to the study of social phenomena. Apply them we did, however, and in 1989 I joined with Geoffrey Thomas and our talented research assistant Geoffrey Evans (now Professor in the Sociology of Politics in the University of Oxford and Official Fellow in Politics at its Nuffield College) in publishing in *Nature* a summary of the findings from the first national survey of public perceptions of science and technology in the United Kingdom [1].

Through the course of the 1980s the 'public understanding of science movement' (as it came to be called) steadily gathered pace in the United Kingdom and I had the strange feeling that the wider scientific community was finally catching up with my long-standing interest in communicating science to non-scientists. In fact, I clearly recall a conversation at about this time with the Chief Executive of the British Association for the Advancement of Science (now the British Science Association), the excellent Dr Peter Briggs, in the course of which one of us – honestly, I forget which – said: 'Who knows, perhaps there are careers to be made in this business of public understanding of science, after all!' From being what had felt like a personal idiosyncrasy, my professional interests were becoming more widely recognized; before long – amazingly – they would feel positively mainstream. This was exhilarating but also, I confess, a little disconcerting. Sometimes it's more exciting to be in the vanguard than to be in the mainstream.

Towards the end of 1988 I accepted a new twin-track position in London: Assistant Director of the Science Museum and Professor of the Public Understanding of Science at Imperial College. The very fact that this novel position had been created reflected the influence of the burgeoning field of public understanding of science: Science Museum Director Dr (later, Sir) Neil Cossons was a member of COPUS and he was keen to position his Museum within the nascent movement. By the time I took this job I'd been in continuing education for more than 12 years. It was a wrench to leave the intimate world of adult learning that I felt I knew so well but the compensations were tremendous: for one thing I was working in a place that attracted not just a few dozen but a few million people through its doors every year; and for another, I was charged with putting in place an initiative that would harness the nation's best-known and best-loved museum of science with one of its leading scientific and technological universities to make a meaningful contribution to this newly emerging field of public understanding of science.

Being appointed to what was widely touted as the first Professorship of the Public Understanding of Science in the world (Was it? How would one know?) was a humbling experience. For one thing it taught me a lot about the social construction of expertise. One day I was a Lecturer at the University of Oxford trying his hand at implementing a national survey of public perceptions of science; the next, I was a leading authority on anything and everything to do with the public face of science and technology. Suddenly, journalists called to ask, not just about our survey, but also about all kinds of other topical issues. What did I think about the supposedly parlous state of science education in the nation's schools? And what were my opinions about 'cold fusion', genetically modified (GM) foods and bovine spongiform encephalopathy (BSE or 'mad cow disease'), all of which were in the headlines at the time? I quickly adjusted to the need to think twice before answering unexpected questions on the phone. All the same, I probably deserved what happened in the summer of 1991 when I told my friend, the science correspondent of *The Guardian* Tim Radford who contributes chapter 18 to this volume, that in setting out to attend the British Association for the Advancement of Science annual meeting in Plymouth I had inadvertently driven to Portsmouth some 170 miles to the east. (Needless to say, I arrived at the meeting horribly late.) The next day Radford published a short *The Guardian* piece entitled (from memory): 'Professor of the Public Understanding of Geography?'

The early 1990s were heady times for me. With few formal responsibilities in the Science Museum (that would change later on), I was able to focus on building an academic programme around the public understanding of science. In collaboration with science communication specialist Jane Gregory (who, unlike me, actually knew what she was doing in the world of publishing) I launched a new quarterly peer review journal named (inevitably) *Public Understanding of Science*; and, with the active support of the Rector of Imperial College Sir Eric Ash, and a helpful grant from the Leverhulme Trust, I launched a one-year (full-time), two-year (part-time) Master's programme in science communication. Of necessity, my models for the Master's programme were taken from the United States (there were no Master's programmes of this sort in the United Kingdom at the time) but my aim was really very simple. I knew that many freshly minted science graduates didn't want to be bench researchers but still wanted careers in science. Those who were able communicators often aspired to become science writers, or broadcasters, or exhibitors; but without any practical experience, it was often difficult for them to get a foot in the proverbial door. Our Master's programme offered a formal training that included building a personal portfolio of real-world communication. And it worked: students enrolled and our graduates got jobs! In 2012, I was delighted to attend a 20th-anniversary reunion of staff and alumni from the Master's programme which is still going strong today under the excellent leadership of Dr Stephen Webster.

Research opportunities abounded in all directions. Soon after moving to London I was able to appoint Martin Bauer, a freshly minted post-doc from the London School of Economics (LSE), as a Research Fellow in the Science Museum. With Dr George Gaskell at the LSE and a number of other European colleagues, Martin (who is now Professor of Social Psychology and Research Methodology at LSE) and I designed a battery of questions about biotechnology for inclusion in the regular 'Eurobarometer' public opinion surveys that were conducted in a number of European Union (EU) member states through the 1990s. Also at this time, I accepted an invitation from one of the co-editors of this volume (David Bennett) to chair a European Federation of Biotechnology Task Group on Public Perceptions of Biotechnology. In these ways I slowly came to appreciate the comparative cultural dimensions of the relationship between science and the public.[4]

In the midst of these efforts, in the mid-1990s, I vividly recall being visited by two representatives from the Monsanto Corporation in the United States. Monsanto was best known for its GM, so-called

---

[4] For accounts of some of these dimensions in the particular field of biotechnology in Western Europe in the 1990s, see: John Durant, Martin Bauer & George Gaskell, *Biotechnology in the Public Sphere: A European Sourcebook*, Science Museum, London 1998; and Martin Bauer & George Gaskell (Eds.), *Biotechnology: The Making of a Global Controversy*, Cambridge University Press, in association with the Science Museum, London, 2002.

'Round-Up Ready', soybeans which rapidly achieved high market pene-tration in North America because they made it easier for farmers to control weeds in their crop fields. The first cargo ships containing an unsegregated mix of GM and non-GM soybean were on their way to Europe and there was intensifying public debate about this in many EU member states. The Monsanto representatives earnestly explained to me how uncontroversial their biotechnology product was in North America and how illusory were the concerns of their company's European critics. Flatteringly – but absurdly – they appeared to be under the impression that if only they could persuade me of the truth of what they were saying all would be well so far as GM soybeans in Europe were concerned!

Based on our research I did my best to explain to my visitors from the United States: first, that judging from the comparative survey evi-dence (as well as the daily press), Europeans appeared to view these matters rather differently from Americans; second, that genetically modified soybeans offered no obvious benefits to European consumers (as contrasted with American farmers); and third, that their company might want to reconsider its stated position that it was 'impractical' to segregate GM from non-GM soybeans at source so as to enable European consumers to have a choice in the supermarket. I'm not sure that my visitors really understood much of what I was saying (which, in retro-spect, constitutes some sort of historic failure on my part as a science communicator). At any rate, no policy change from Monsanto on this issue was forthcoming and over the following months and years I looked on rather forlornly as the attempt to impose 'Round-Up Ready' soybeans on European food markets helped to swing European attitudes firmly against the entire field of agricultural biotechnology – to the obvious benefit of absolutely nobody.

A number of graduate students came to work with me on the public dimensions of science and technology in the 1990s. One, Simon Joss (now Professor and Director of The Graduate School at The Univer-sity of Westminster), was interested in the 'consensus conference', a new model of public participation in science – or what Simon preferred to call 'participatory technology assessment' – that had been pioneered for some years in Denmark. In the mid-1990s, almost a generation after my initial interest in this subject, the political wheel in the United Kingdom had come full circle: a series of Conservative administrations led first by Margaret Thatcher and then by John Major had got themselves into hot water on sensitive policy issues involving science and technology – everything from radionuclide contamination post-Chernobyl, through climate change (already an issue then, as now), to sundry food science and technology scares (yes, GM foods again; but also salmonella contamination in eggs and listeria contamination in foods made from raw milk).

Again and again, media coverage of these issues threw the spotlight on narrowly technocratic policy processes that paid scant regard to wider public attitudes and interests, and hence failed to produce socially sustainable policy recommendations. British policy-making traditions based on the supposed value of closed deliberation among a small group of experts seemed to have few answers to this problem. But the Scandinavian democracies had long favoured decision-making based on open consensus-building; and in the 1980s the Danish Board of Technology had pioneered a new form of deliberation in which panels of citizens were convened well ahead of scheduled Parliamentary debates to conduct their own investigations of the relevant policy issues. Calling their own witnesses and publishing their own reports for Parliament to consider along with other evidence, these consensus conferences seemed to be helping the Danes, at any rate, to do their science and technology policy-making more effectively.

With Simon keen to study consensus conferences and the mood in the country favouring a more inclusive approach to policy-making, I saw an opportunity to combine research and practice in science communication in a rather unusual way. We applied to the UK Biotechnology and Biological Sciences Research Council for funding to organize a first national consensus conference on agricultural biotechnology which Professor Sir Tom Blundell refers to in his Preface to this volume; and with grant in hand, we focused intently for almost a year on learning about consensus conferences, recruiting a citizen panel (we used newspaper advertisements) and then supporting this panel through its own investigation of the issues, all under Simon's watchful graduate student gaze. Our efforts culminated in a two-day public consensus conference in Central London in 1994. Here, we staged that rarest of rare spectacles (in the United Kingdom, at least, and at that time): a group of ordinary citizens inviting their chosen expert witnesses to the stage one after another in order to cross-examine them – intelligently, and sensitively – in public. As I stood in the audience that day I felt as if we were making a tiny piece of history. Simon wrote up his findings as a successful thesis and we published an essay collection about consensus conferences together [2]. Though I claim no credit for it, I can at least say that I was not at all surprised when, shortly after this, 'New Labour' made the convening of 'People's Panels' part of its successful campaign in the 1997 General Election. 'People Power' of a sort was suddenly fashionable in the United Kingdom, at least for a season.

Through this period my responsibilities with the Science Museum steadily increased and eventually I was put in charge of the project to construct a major extension devoted to contemporary science and technology, the Wellcome Wing at the Science Museum. At the same time, though, my involvement in larger debates about the place of science in public continued. Along with my colleague Professor Brian Wynne at the University of Lancaster, I was invited to act as an expert advisor to the UK House of Lords Select Committee on Science and Technology. Under the amiable but canny chairmanship of Lord Patrick Jenkin this Committee had decided to undertake a review of the relationship between science and society. (The initial idea had been to call the subject of the inquiry 'the public understanding of science', but by now this phrase was coming to be regarded as problematic.) For several months I biked over from South Kensington to the Houses of Parliament to sit in one of its many oak-lined committee rooms while a group of unelected – and therefore, by definition, unrepresentative – members of the House of Lords debated in private about how to make the conduct of scientific affairs in the public domain more democratic and open.

This experience was truly extraordinary. With the support of the Chairman, Brian and I gently nudged the House of Lords Committee towards emerging ideas of dialogue and inclusion suggesting that top-down communication was rarely as effective as two-way and multi-way exchange and pointing to the poor track record of purely elite processes of deliberation and decision-making. And then we watched as the committee members played with and occasionally seemed to lose these ideas, reverting regularly to older, more familiar and generally more paternalistic patterns of thought. On one memorable occasion, Lord Jenkin proffered the view that 'We can't go back to decision-making in smoke-filled rooms', whereupon an older Scottish member of the Committee could clearly be heard to growl 'I've always been a great believer in smoke-filled rooms myself'. However, when the House of Lords Select Committee on Science and Technology published its 3rd Report on Science and Society in February 2000, it began with these words:

> Society's relationship with science is in a critical phase. Science today
> is exciting, and full of opportunities. Yet public confidence in scientific
> advice to Government has been rocked by BSE; and many people are

uneasy about the rapid advance of areas such as biotechnology and IT – even though for everyday purposes they take science and technology for granted. This crisis of confidence is of great importance both to British society and to British science.'[5]

Of course, my career didn't stop in 2000. Later that year I became Chief Executive of At-Bristol, a new science and natural history centre in the West of England; and five years after that I moved to the Massachusetts Institute of Technology where I currently direct the MIT Museum and teach in the Science, Technology and Society Program. I could say much more about these more recent chapters in my career: about the multiple new challenges and opportunities that have continued to keep me on my toes; about what I've learnt about the dynamics of science in public from a move to the United States; and about the way in which taking up a teaching position at a world-class research institute at the age of 55 finally got me past my 'post-Sixties' disillusionment with undergraduate teaching.

But the turn of the Millennium is perhaps as good a place as any to bring to an end this narrative of my own very particular unconventional career in science. It was in the mid-1970s that I first discovered in myself a passion for talking about science with non-scientists. In the 25 years between that discovery and the publication of the House of Lords report the situation for science communication and science communicators in the United Kingdom had been utterly transformed. Then, science communication had been a backwater. Now, a Select Committee of the House of Lords had given its imprimatur to the need for greater openness and greater dialogue between science and the public at all levels of society, not least so that the trust on which science depended for its license to operate might be maintained.

What lessons do I draw from this truncated autobiographical sketch? First, follow your passions, and don't be put off when you can't always see clearly where they may lead. Second, be willing to take the road less travelled – even, dare I say, a road to a small place with people waiting for you in the village hall – if it promises to get you somewhere interesting. Third, when unexpected opportunities arise – and they will – seize them with both hands. Only a few of the careers that exist or might exist in this world, and not even all of the more interesting or rewarding ones, are clearly marked out in advance. Many, many more are there to be made if you stay true to

---

[5] See: www.publications.parliament.uk/pa/ld199900/ldselect/ldsctech/38/3802.htm

your values, work at things, and remain light on your feet. For all I know, this is true in all areas of human endeavour; certainly, I've found it to be true of a life in science!

REFERENCES

1. J. Durant, G. Evans & G. P. Thomas, 'The Public Understanding of Science', *Nature* 340 (6 July 1989), pp. 11–14.
2. Simon Joss and John Durant (Eds.), *Public Participation in Science: The Role of Consensus Conferences in Europe*, Science Museum, London, with the support of the European Commission Directorate General XII, London, 1995.

24

A Butterfly Career in Science and Beyond to Public Engagement

I've had a very interesting and rewarding time with jobs that have involved science communication, public engagement with research and now the interface between science, research and policy. It took me until my third degree to come to study scientific subjects that I was really interested in and I think my career story so far bears out my conception of myself as being a bit of a butterfly flitting from one interest to another. I hope that my story might help others who have lots of interests and varied skills and experience to consider what they may like to do too.

BEGINNINGS

Many of the interests that I have that relate to science have arisen since I left school but I do remember some of the ways in which I didn't develop much enthusiasm for scientific subjects at school. I remember the transition from primary school where subjects seemed to blend into one another and that included some learning about nature to the secondary system where we went into different types of classrooms to learn separate subjects for defined periods. The laboratory for science seemed quite dark and even gloomy, and I didn't get a sense of how what we were studying would add up to us being able to tackle issues in the world one day.

I remember at this time of moving into secondary school being interested in renewable energy, the destruction of rainforests and cutting out pages from magazines about these subjects for the

Successful Careers beyond the Lab, ed. David Bennett and Richard Jennings.
Published by Cambridge University Press. © Cambridge University Press 2017.

occasional project for secondary science but I couldn't relate these interests to the scientific fundamentals I knew we needed to learn. I could learn the facts and methods and pass the exams but during secondary school I didn't have the sense of science as a creative and experimental enterprise. The practical classes that we did do seemed more like following 'recipe book' instructions to gain expected results rather than genuine explorations.

When the UK secondary science curriculum was reformed in the 2000s the '21st-century science' approach brought in many of the aspects I might have found more rewarding. At the time some science teachers and commentators objected to the changes and even called the greater inclusion of ethical and social questions 'pub science' – akin to just talking about scientific issues down the pub without the right kind of factual input. I still disagree with that point of view and I think that the 21st-century science approach puts science in the personal and social contexts that I as a teenager would have related to more.

TRANSITIONS

My first degree was in history at the University of Cambridge. I had been very inspired about the subject by excellent teachers at school and I liked the way it was possible to study such a wide variety of topics and time periods within such a broad subject. I think I always had a sense of wanting to know 'how we got here' with 'here' being the societies we live in today. I found history to be a good subject for considering questions of truth and the reliability of evidence – it's a subject where debates about what we reliably know about the past are always ongoing. Evidence from more distant periods is limited and for more recent times may be overwhelming so the choices that historians take in weighing up evidence and presenting narratives are interesting to me.

I found it difficult to know what I wanted to do after leaving university but I was drawn to investigating jobs in the public and voluntary sectors. I initially volunteered for a charity called Addaction which runs services to help people to overcome drug and alcohol misuse and this led to an interesting and challenging job there in fundraising management for the next four years. My first exposure to the potential of science communication as part of a career came in my second job in the voluntary sector in London. I was working for a charity called Fight for Sight at the Institute of Ophthalmology as a fundraising and marketing manager. From time to time I would meet with scientists in the institute who received some funding from the charity and

I would seek to understand from them how the research they were doing could make a contribution to tackling blinding eye disease. This then led to me writing articles for the charity's newsletter and website, and prior to publishing I would check my drafts back with the scientists to see if the understanding I was communicating was correct in scientific terms. Something I am always conscious of in the field I work in is 'knowing my limits' – I have been able to make a career from being a non-specialist in the scientific and academic fields, and this has been built upon wanting to check whether my communication which explains some scientific and technical terms is seen as correct by the academics involved.

While living in London, I also remember seeing someone reading the book *The Language Instinct* by Stephen Pinker [1] on the Underground, and something about the title seemed really interesting, and that was probably the first popular science book that I then read. I was really inspired by his talent for communication and by the way in which he presented arguments from Noam Chomsky and others about whether human brains had evolved with particular propensities for language development leading to some commonalities about human languages across all their diversity. I enjoyed learning about science and arguments and evidence for and against particular scientific hypotheses, in a more narrative way than I had encountered in science at school and I went on to read other popular science books by authors such as Matt Ridley who I found skilled at communicating their topics for general readers.

I read a lot of non-fiction in those days but it was a TV programme (and its accompanying book) that really inspired me to come back to Cambridge: 'The Day the World Took Off'.[1] I was excited by the way in which a key academic involved in that project, Professor Alan Macfarlane, brought in historians of science, anthropologists and others to look at how and why the Industrial Revolution happened where it did, when it did. The time frame for the programme looked back 200 years, then 500 years, then 1,000 years and more to look at how science and technology developed in Europe as compared with China and the Middle East. I was really stimulated to see the way in which Alan involved academics from different disciplines in tackling the relevant questions and it really set me thinking about disciplines I hadn't really thought about in detail before, particularly history of science and social anthropology. Another influential book I went on to read as a result of that programme was 'Guns, Germs and Steel' by Jared Diamond [2].

---

[1] www.repository.cam.ac.uk/handle/1810/270

The author is a real polymath and draws on varied sources in his investigation of how human societies have developed in the way they have across the world.

I decided that the gap in my knowledge and experience I was most keen to address would be met best through applying to study for a Master's degree in social anthropology back at the University of Cambridge. I had not travelled beyond Europe and the United States by this stage, and I saw social anthropology as a way of understanding the society I lived in by way of contrast with many others. Before starting the Master's degree I had an amazing three months taking the Trans-Mongolian highway from Moscow to Beijing. Social anthropology proved to be a fascinating subject and I enjoyed its breadth across the study of politics, religion, kinship and economics.

CAMBRIDGE SCIENCE FESTIVAL

After a really stimulating and eye-opening year studying for a Master's degree it was difficult to know what to do next. I was very attracted by the academic environment and stimulation in Cambridge but I think I always felt that I had what I think of as a 'butterfly brain', flitting from one subject to another rather than having the focus to proceed to a PhD. I was looking on the University of Cambridge website for jobs, thinking that I might go back down the fundraising and development route, when I saw that there was a part-time seven-month contract advertised for a Science Festival coordinator. I had not known there was a Science Festival in Cambridge but something about the idea was very interesting to me and I followed the web link.

I presumed that the job would require perhaps a first degree in a scientific subject, but on clicking for further details, I could see that what was needed was a 'Jack or Jill of all trades'. The job was based in the University's communications office and called for a mix of experience in event organisation, raising sponsorship, some ability in the field of science communication and a mix of all sorts of other things including managing health and safety. I had had some experience organising events during the roles I had held at three different charities, as well as the science communication experience at Fight for Sight in particular.

When I went to the interview, the test was to come up with some launch event and content ideas for the Cambridge Science Festival[2] with

---

[2] www.sciencefestival.cam.ac.uk/

the suggested theme being 'Chaos and Spontaneity'. I remembered the kinds of popular science I had encountered through books about chaos theory with the main idea I remembered from that being 'if a butterfly flaps its wings in Brazil, could it set off a tornado in Texas?' I suggested we could ask a TV weather presenter (like Michael Fish, famous in the 1980s for playing down the forecast of a hurricane just before it hit the United Kingdom) to come to the Festival and talk on aspects of the subject alongside scientists. My interviewers were keen to know that I could meet with academics at all levels in the University of Cambridge and partner organisations and liaise appropriately with them about their involvement in the Cambridge Science Festival. They wanted to know that I would have the ability to grasp key aspects of their research and enter into dialogue with them about how their subjects could be presented for a general audience. I found that this discussion took me back to my experience of science communication at Fight for Sight, little realising at the time that this experience would be particularly useful for me in future.

I was delighted to be offered the job as Cambridge Science Festival coordinator in September 2004 and this began a fascinating and rewarding stage in my career so far. On starting the job I was told that I did in fact have the chance to choose the theme for the Science Festival in March 2005 and I quickly decided that there was no chance we would pick a theme incorporating 'chaos' as that seemed like a bad omen for the first Festival I was coordinating! That was notwithstanding the excellent contribution that the student society, Cambridge Hands-On Science (CHaOS)[3], made to the Science Festival each year – but I found that they had over time developed many risk assessment documents for the practical experiments they shared with visitors, and these were reassuringly available for checking by me and my Health and Safety colleagues at the University.

It also became apparent to me straightaway that this kind of job was all about networks of people and that was one of the attractive and rewarding aspects of the job. Within a few weeks I got to meet a great set of people working around the University and other organisations involved in the Science Festival at a group meeting planning the Science Festival. In those days in the early to mid-2000s it was most common for those who had a role in coordinating their department or organisation's participation in the Science Festival to be doing so in a way that

---

[3] www.chaosscience.org.uk/

was a bit 'off-job description'. Their line manager or head of department would usually be keen for them to spend a bit of time organising events for the Science Festival but often people had volunteered to take on that role. Over the years this made for a network motivated by enthusiasm and commitment to the idea that sharing scientific research with public visitors of all ages was something that should happen. Downsides could exist where time and effort weren't recognised but in general my time spent working in this field coincided with greater policy emphasis on public engagement with science from research funders. This in time led to the creation of more jobs around the University and beyond where public engagement and science communication were part of the explicit focus of the jobs.

As well as working with the creative set of people coming up with event ideas and content across departments and beyond I had valuable meetings with a number of heads of department and University leaders including Pro-Vice-Chancellors. These meetings helped me understand the benefits and challenges they saw in the University organising events such as the Science Festival. I was keen to learn from these meetings and work out how operationally I could respond to strategic points they shared with me. A head of department that I met during my first week, Professor Jeremy Sanders in the Department of Chemistry, was an important figure in my career over the next ten years particularly when he took on a Pro-Vice-Chancellor role and supported public engagement.

The first Science Festival I co-ordinated took place in March 2005. It was 'Einstein Year' marking 100 years since the extraordinary year when Albert Einstein published four articles which changed views on space, time and energy and contributed substantially to the foundation of modern physics. We chose 'Time Travel' as the theme for the Cambridge Science Festival that year and a key supporter of the Science Festival in Cambridge, Professor Malcolm Longair, gave a great demonstration lecture where he recreated some of Einstein's famous experiments. I also looked for other communicators and figures who could transmit their enthusiasm for physics in particular. Helen Czerski, now a respected scientist and BBC presenter, was then a PhD student at Cambridge and she was recommended to me as a speaker on physics and her research. I also found out that the BBC TV Blue Peter programme presenter, Konnie Huq, was a science enthusiast, having studied science Advanced levels before an economics degree at the University of Cambridge and she agreed to come back and launch the Science Festival.

I came up with the theme 'Time Travel' in consultation with the network of Science Festival event coordinators in Cambridge and it was sufficiently broad to allow event contributors working in fields from astronomy to zoology to apply the theme to the events they organised. In subsequent years we went for similarly broad themes, choosing ideas like 'Planet and People' to give a very loose framework to suggest to event contributors and to provide a focus for our communications with the media.

The first Science Festival I worked on was of course a major organisational challenge. At that stage there were three part-time staff working on it and we had more than 100 events in the programme during the week. The main planning hurdle was in fact the production of the print programme and website to be ready two months before the Festival to give us time to market the Festival. This meant that all events for the programme had to be submitted by mid-December and for a busy time between Christmas and early January finalising design.

Putting the programme together made me reflect on how I had grown up with festivals having had the good fortune to live in Edinburgh, a famous festival city. I realised that in Cambridge I was in some ways coordinating a smaller version of something akin to the Fringe in Edinburgh. This is the renowned counterpart to the official Festival in Edinburgh in August each year and sees thousands of theatre groups, comedians, musicians and more find venues in Edinburgh and submit their event listings to the Fringe programme. I find this to be an inclusive if sometimes organisationally challenging idea. A major event can be created by providing a framework and asking for event contributions which are mostly not funded centrally but are resourced by event organisers and setting a deadline for event contributions to go into a programme.

For Science Festivals there is often no financial transfer between event contributors and a core organising team, and balancing the good-will transactions with the necessary generation and management of financial resources was a major element of managing the Science Festival and other public engagement projects over the years. When I took on the Science Festival job the central University of Cambridge funded half of the organisational costs and we worked with local sponsors including the TTP Group of technology development companies, the American Association for the Advancement of Science and Cambridge University Press to raise the rest.

DEVELOPMENTS IN PUBLIC ENGAGEMENT WITH RESEARCH

Despite the long days and the press-ganging of colleagues, friends and family into helping me run the first of the Cambridge Science Festivals that I coordinated, I had to say I thoroughly enjoyed the experience. I liked the way in which it opened up the University of Cambridge to the public and allowed visitors of all ages into laboratories and lecture theatres to find out more about so many areas of science and its relevance to people's lives, interests and concerns. Immediately afterwards I thought it would be great if we could organise a parallel festival which would open up the arts, humanities and social sciences at Cambridge for the public. I thought of the humanities subjects I had studied at Cambridge and thought how good it could be if we had open days in those subjects which allowed visitors to interact with researchers and students in a similar way to the Science Festival. A name for this vision had come into my mind when a great contributor to the Science Festival, the then *The Guardian* newspaper science editor Tim Radford who contributes chapter 18 to this book, told me one day that he was off to speak at the Adelaide Festival of Ideas. I thought we should develop a Cambridge Festival of Ideas (and indeed later I found out that there was a well-established Festival of Ideas in Bristol). It was when I mentioned the potential of a new festival to the Pro-Vice-Chancellor for Research, Professor Ian Leslie, about a year later that he said he thought it was a great idea and that he would allocate some Higher Education Innovation Funding (HEIF) funding for an additional member of the team and some print and production costs to get it going. The small team I worked within recruited some excellent staff over the years and we launched the first Festival of Ideas in 2008. It has continued annually since then and now rivals the Cambridge Science Festival in scale. Both festivals offer more than 250 events each year and record in the region of 20,000 to 35,000 visits, with most events being offered free of charge to visitors.

The context at the time of developing the Festival of Ideas in the mid-2000s was that the idea of public engagement with science was being increasingly adopted as an important policy area by research and higher education funders as well as other organisations including learned societies and businesses. I thought that the idea of public engagement with science would probably increasingly extend to public engagement with research in general and so there would be an argument for the University of Cambridge to find ways to encourage public engagement with researchers in the arts, humanities and social sciences as well as the sciences and technology.

I had found my introduction into the field of public engagement with science to be a fascinating one, learning how controversies in the 1990s over bovine spongiform encephalopathy (BSE), the measles, mumps and rubella (MMR) vaccine and genetically modified (GM) food had led scientists and policy-makers to seek to understand more about public responses to major issues with science at the centre. In the United Kingdom encouragement for scientists to spend time promoting 'public understanding of science' had grown since the Bodmer report of that name in 1985 for the Royal Society chaired by Sir Walter Bodmer who contributes the Advance Review to this book. By 2000 the House of Lords Science and Technology committee recognised the need to develop this idea into 'public engagement with science and technology' as John Durant describes in Chapter 23 of this book. This marked a transition from a one-way communication model: encouraging scientists to transmit knowledge to the general public to a two-way communication model involving dialogue between scientists and non-specialists about topics of importance in society. I found it fascinating that experts needed to understand more about the public reception of scientific developments and to understand more about the political and economic questions asked about subjects like GM food as well as to understand the safety questions raised by individuals and groups in society.

ORGANISATIONAL DEVELOPMENT AND SOME AREAS OF FOCUS

While the Science Festival co-ordinator position was still part time I spent some months filling in part time as a press officer with colleagues in the University of Cambridge's communications department. I worked on some stories about the collections in the famous tower of the Cambridge University Library and responded to press inquiries but I lacked a real journalist's sense of what makes news. I always found too many areas of research emerging from Cambridge academics to be interesting so it was a pleasure working on event coordination to be able to be bring researchers and audiences together on issues that weren't necessarily on the news agenda for a particular week. With confirmation of funding for the Festival of Ideas and the formation of a new team working on both community affairs and public engagement, by the mid-2000s a small staff team was put together and colleagues and I were able to develop planning and activity from there.

I spent some time focusing on evaluation of the Science Festival in the context of public engagement with research. I thought that we were in a fortunate position with the Cambridge Science Festival in that it was supported by many stakeholders and funders including the University and private sector sponsors, and this gave us a chance to set out our own aims for evaluation. I was interested to find out how a social scientist might help to provide more objectivity in evaluation than was possible with our own internal evaluation exercises. I had found the e-mail distribution list PSCI-Com[4] to be a useful informal network in the UK public engagement scene and I used that to ask if anyone with evaluation experience might be interested in providing us with a modest quote for evaluating some aspects of visitors' responses to the next Science Festival. I was pleased when Dr Eric Jensen responded. He had done his PhD at the University of Cambridge looking at aspects of how therapeutic cloning had been dealt with in media coverage and was now a lecturer at Anglia Ruskin University in Cambridge. He and I met up to talk about what might be desirable and feasible to do in evaluation for the next Science Festival. We decided to make use of short evaluation postcards that were widely distributed at the festival and take the section of those that asked for general comments at the festival and work with a research assistant to see which themes emerged out of those 'free text' comments. I learned that this was an approach that accorded with 'grounded theory', a process of seeking categories that might emerge from data rather than beginning with categories and coming to the data that way. We eventually co-authored a paper on Science Festival evaluation which was published in the journal *Public Understanding of Science* in 2012 [3]. I found it helpful in my career development to spend some time focusing on evaluation issues as it helped me to consider the evidence base for the potential value, or not, of what we were doing with the festivals. Spending time on evaluation helped to inform our planning too as we could look at which audiences were more regularly engaged with the festivals and which sections of the communities within travelling distance of Cambridge we could direct more outreach efforts towards, for instance through scientists visiting schools.

At this time, I had also decided to pursue an MSc in Science and Society with the Open University.[5] I wanted to find a course that would enable me to explore contemporary issues in science that were important in society to inform how I did my job. I found this to be an excellent course and one that I valued being able to study through distance learning while having a full-time job. The module on 'Science and the Public' went through a fascinating set of case studies of controversies from the last few decades involving science from vaccine scares to public consultations about stem cell science and much more. I valued

---

[4] www.jiscmail.ac.uk/cgi-bin/webadmin?A0=PSCI-COM

[5] www.open.ac.uk/science/main/studying-science/msc-science

finding out about the academic study of science in society, for example, what empirical findings there were about public perceptions of risk.

I have been fortunate to have had a number of professional development opportunities through working at the University of Cambridge. I did a diploma in event management at Edinburgh Napier University,[6] where I did a week-long course at a centre for festivals and event management. I found it valuable to do that course as I wanted to know that I was basing my event management experience on the most up-to-date health and safety planning guidance as well as seeing what project management advice I could gain from experienced event managers and a limited number of books written on the subject. I have always learned a lot from attending other large-scale events and it has been a pleasure since 2009 to be involved with organising an annual series of Cambridge academics speaking at the Hay Festival.

In 2009 I also had the chance to do a six-week secondment in the Science and Society team at the Department for Business, Innovation and Skills in London. This was during the run-up to the preparation of the new Research Excellence Framework (REF), the exercise in the United Kingdom that reviews research at all universities and allocates quality-related research funding. The 'impact' element[7] was being introduced for the REF in 2014 during this time and I became aware of the issues but also the opportunities with that. It meant that academics were increasingly incentivised to spend time considering how their research might be taken up by non-academic 'users of research'. Public engagement activities were not straightforward to use in impact case studies in the 2014 REF but the impact agenda has meant that many academics do increasingly plan and budget for public engagement, and seek evaluation data on public engagement too.

CAREER DEVELOPMENT

In 2010 my predecessor left her role as Head of Community Affairs and I took on the role as maternity cover initially. In 2011 we renamed the team as Public Engagement and when the position of Head of Public Engagement was advertised I was successful in applying for it. More of my time from that point was spent on developing strategies that aimed to focus on which activities we were able to coordinate in fulfilment

---

[6] www.napier.ac.uk/courses/msc-international-event-and-festival-management-postgraduate-fulltime

[7] www.hefce.ac.uk/rsrch/REFimpact/

of University of Cambridge public engagement goals. I had to keep attending to financial issues too. My colleagues and I had developed a fairly complex mix of income sources to underpin the University public engagement projects. The University provided core funding for the festivals and community relations activities but this was supplemented by one-third of our income coming from other sources including projects delivered for European Commission grants, the Wellcome Trust and private sector sponsorship for the festivals among other sources. The European projects I worked on were great learning experiences. I worked with Living Knowledge,[8] a network of universities and non-governmental organisations (NGOs) that linked civil society organisations' research questions with student dissertation opportunities and we facilitated a number of those types of projects in Cambridge.

Throughout my career in Cambridge I took up some Trustee roles relevant to my job at Cambridge Student Community Action and at STEM Team East.[9] STEM Team East is one of the regional organisations receiving funding from the national charity STEMNET which in turn receives government and other funding for programmes including STEM ambassadors.[10] I was also asked to join the board of trustees for the Cambridge Junction[11] in 2014. This is an arts organisation with a mission to be a place where 'art meets life', and it had been a rewarding organisation to be involved with through the festivals as well as an important part of my free time in Cambridge over the years. I became the chair of Trustees of the Junction in 2015.

By the end of 2015, I was interested in looking for other opportunities and I became aware that the Centre for Science and Policy in Cambridge[12] was looking for an Associate Director. The Associate Director manages the Policy Fellowships programme in particular. This programme seeks government policy officials who apply to become Fellows for two years, bringing with them policy questions that would benefit from scientific and academic input.[13] I take the challenging questions that about twelve Policy Fellows per term come forward with and invite academics at the University who could provide relevant input to meet them. It is another stimulating and interdisciplinary role to work in and I find it very interesting to see the questions raised by civil servants and

---

[8] www.livingknowledge.org/   [9] www.stemteameast.org.uk/about/

[10] www.stem.org.uk/stem-ambassadors/ambassadors/

[11] www.junction.co.uk/   [12] www.csap.cam.ac.uk/

[13] Dr Jasdeep Sandhu who contributes Chapter 15 of this book is a Fellow of the Centre.

those with policy roles in industry and NGOs, and to broker connections with Cambridge academics and more. So far I have worked on programmes for Policy Fellows on topics from counter-terrorism to antimicrobial resistance, and it is great to have a job where I continue to learn so much and find out more about academics' work at Cambridge which can have public policy relevance.

SUMMING UP, SO FAR

I have never really felt at a disadvantage in pursuing a career that has involved so much work on public engagement with science in not having an initial foundation in a scientific degree. I think I have always had respect for scientists and people who work in technological fields and a sense that my own strengths lie more with the humanities. I have been able to pursue interests in science through the MSc I did with the Open University and have combined those in my working life with organisational and management questions about how to implement public engagement projects. I have spent time recruiting, managing and working alongside colleagues who have made great inputs into the projects I have worked on and to whom I am very grateful. I have had to manage financial resources, both raising and spending money in pursuit of public engagement goals. I feel fortunate to have found my way through a career which has been meaningful and continued to open doors for me.

If you feel like a 'butterfly' in your interests too and if you can tie that to some organisational and management abilities, my sense is that there are a number of interesting careers beyond the lab that you might find work for you. I was anxious when I first left University about not knowing what I wanted to do but I have found that it is impossible to predict the opportunities that turn up. Looking back, I see that I have been able to pursue interesting opportunities that have come my way and that I have had a good sense overall of where effort would result in meaningful outcomes. The job titles I have had over the last decade or so have been around for about as long as I've had them so the advice has to be that you might find you enjoy doing a range of things during your career which might not yet have been put together into a job role. I think it will be people who have made the most of their education, have an interest in lifelong learning and are creative, flexible and able to work with others who can have good chances like I have had to make the most of opportunities when they arise.

REFERENCES

1. Pinker, S. (1995) *The Language Instinct: How the Mind Creates Language: The New Language of Science and Mind*. Penguin.
2. Diamond, J. (1998) *Guns, Germs and Steel: A short history of everybody for the last 13,000 years*. Vintage.
3. Jensen, E. and Buckley, N. (2014) *Why people attend science festivals: interests, motivations and self-reported benefits of public engagement with research*. Public Understanding of Science, Volume 23 (Number 5). pp. 557–573. ISSN 0963-6625.

25

A Lifetime's Fun and Interest with Teaching and Allied Matters

It's hard to pinpoint when and how I became a biologist and scientist.

I was an only child of two parents, both of whom had limited education. Both had good school reports and were clearly bright but left school to pursue a career which is what you did in those days. My mother worked as a booking office clerk on the railways and my father, originally from Kent, ran a soft furnishing department in a store in Worksop, Nottinghamshire. The family background on my mother's side was women at home and the men working down the pit. My grandmother's birth certificate bears a cross, the 'mark of Mark Lee' as my great-grandfather couldn't write his own name!

My mother stopped work when I was born and she returned to work when I was fourteen.

They were from a generation where opportunities for social mobility and aspiration were limited but they put all their energies into me and my development. They didn't have a car and their child didn't have siblings so Sundays were a walk in the woods and fields. How to entertain and engage your kid? Buy him *I-Spy* books! I still have my books, *I-Spy* flowers, trees, birds, farms, garden plants and others.[1]

When I was around four I pulled all of the flowers off the thrift plants in the garden and got slapped on the leg for my effort. Then my folks re-thought the punishment because my actions clearly weren't malicious – I simply didn't realise I'd done anything wrong. So I was given my own 'garden', a small rectangular plot. Each year when my

---

[1] Children's guides in the 1950s and 1960, relaunched in 2009 by Michelin.

Successful Careers beyond the Lab, ed. David Bennett and Richard Jennings.
Published by Cambridge University Press. © Cambridge University Press 2017.

dad went to get his tomato, pea and broad bean seeds, I got my packet of clarkia. I loved sowing my seeds in my garden and seeing my plants grow. I was soon a proficient gardener helping my dad in the greenhouse and the garden.

I didn't know it but I was becoming a naturalist. By the age of ten I could identify lots of plants and animals and tell people something about them. We couldn't venture far from Worksop but there is an important message here. Nature is on your doorstep wherever you are. I may not have seen lions and tigers, mountains and fens but my eyes were opened to what was around me. In the vein of Gilbert White, an 18th-century parson-naturalist, I was observing and absorbing the 'Natural History of Worksop'.[2]

The natural progression from I-Spy books was Observer books.[3] Three-and-a-half by six inches (no fancy metrics in those days!), a pocket book and a goldmine of information. I still have them all and still use them; larger British moths, lichens, birds, butterflies, wild flowers, geology and many more. And organisms had fancy names; Nymphalidae, Falconidae, Sphingidae, Leguminosae. My awakening to taxonomy had begun.

So at the age of eleven I went to Henry Hartland Grammar School in Worksop and discovered that not only was I a naturalist; I was a biologist. The school was brand new and I was in the first year. The teachers were great and took a real interest in us, especially my biology teacher, Miss Pam Carter. I guess I was a bit of a favourite as I was so enthusiastic about her subject and she did everything to encourage my interests.

Whenever I visit the systematic beds in the University of Cambridge Botanic Garden, I'm reminded of our systematic beds at school. Pam (I can call her that now) set up six beds and we were invited to volunteer to look after them. With two mates, we were in charge of Leguminosae. The rest of the groups soon got bored with the project so we ended up looking after all six beds, further enhancing my taxonomic skills.

There were so many opportunities given to us: snail surveying, heronry surveying, dissecting a shark (donated by a local fishmonger after it had been on display in their window and had begun to get a bit ripe), an afterschool biology club and looking after the school pond. I was in my element!

---

[2] Gilbert White's The Natural History of Selbourne was first published in 1789 and has been continuously in print since then.

[3] A series of small, pocket-sized books from 1937 to 2003 on a variety of topics including hobbies, art, history and wildlife.

By this time I was collecting and breeding butterflies and moths as well as doing lots of bird watching. My fourth-year school project was 'Butterflies and birds as a hobby' and I still have it, all handwritten of course. There was no Internet in those days so research meant libraries and books. The town library was my home away-from-home as it was for all my friends. I recall a 19th-century work, *The Birds of Nottinghamshire*,[4] which was basically a catalogue of all of the species seen in the county and duly shot and stuffed! Thankfully the only shooting today is with a camera.

Mr Inger, the head librarian, knew of my interest in butterflies and moths and showed me the small collection the library had and asked me to curate an exhibition.

I still have my nature diary that I wrote when I was fourteen. I was learning not only to observe but record, although I admit it was a bit anthropomorphic:

> I looked out and there was a juvenile song thrush bathing in the pond and it was really enjoying itself fluffing out its chest feathers and looking like a furry barrel.

> I looked out of my bedroom window and saw a blue tit on the nut-holders. It pecked a bit and then flew onto my catapult which was suspended from the clothes line. It hopped up and down the elastic but on finding no food it flew off in disgust.

I was good at art so my diary and project were fully illustrated. In the shed at home I had a fish tank which I'd stock with pond life and spend hours sitting there drawing water boatmen, caddis fly larvae and sticklebacks.

I did well in my Ordinary levels, top grades in almost everything except for languages. I was rubbish at languages, they didn't interest me, I'd never been abroad and, to me, France could have been Mars. Aspiring to be a scientist, I chose biology, chemistry and physics for Advanced level. In retrospect, physics was not a great choice as I didn't enjoy it and wish I'd followed my other strong suit – geography.

Field trips in the sixth form to Suffolk and Devon were real highlights for me. My love of natural history was developing into a love of ecology, a passion which has never left me.

And so minds turned to what to do after sixth form. I knew I wanted to go to university, study zoology and then do research.

---

[4] https://johnknifton.com/tag/the-descriptive-list-of-the-birds-of-nottinghamshire/

None of my friends had families who were familiar with university so we relied on guidance from school. The head, Mr Bulley (unfortunate name for a head because he wasn't a bully, the deputy head was Mr Power!), told my parents that the school would certainly support me for university, even Oxford or Cambridge. We discovered that at that time, an Ordinary level in a modern language was needed for Cambridge and two languages for Oxford. This was a bit of a concern given my Ordinary levels so the decision was to apply to Cambridge and resit French; fortunately, I scraped a pass.

The school knew nothing about Cambridge, not even that you had to apply to a specific college. The next decision was to decide which college. The only guidance they could give (which was clearly outdated) was 'Peterhouse has good food, Selwyn is full of foreigners and King's is a bit of an odd place', so I chose Corpus Christi for no better reason that it had a nice-sounding name. Only after applying did I discover that it was the smallest college – maybe not a wise choice. I did well enough in the entrance exams and interview but Corpus couldn't offer me a place and I went into the pool. Then a stroke of luck. King's, the 'odd place', has always been progressive and at the time was keen on what is today called widening participation. They saw my application and decided that, given my background, I was worth offering a place to study natural sciences.

Adjusting to Cambridge was surprisingly easy. There were plenty of types I'd not encountered before – public school backgrounds, the air of confidence that tends to develop, posh accents – but behind it all were normal people. I realised early on to just be myself and I'd be fine – and I was. I made friends easily, played rugby and football for the College and was successful in my studies. Being awarded a senior scholarship at the end of the second year was a real confidence boost.

In my first year I studied Biology of Cells, Biology of Organisms and Physiology, in the second year Zoology, Physiology and Experimental Psychology and in the final year Part II Zoology. When we reflect on our careers, we recognise key people who made a difference. I was lucky to have Professor John Treherne and Professor Sir Pat Bateson for inspiration and as mentors. John had infectious enthusiasm, a terrific sense of fun and a genuine interest in students. Having spent a day failing to pierce snail neurones with a microelectrode, he just laughed and said it was all character-building. I remember Pat saying that research was all about asking the right questions.

In the final year I had to decide what to do next; my desire was still to do research. I felt very comfortable in Cambridge and secured a place at the Sub-Department of Animal Behaviour (part of the Zoology Department in Madingley, a village four miles out of town). My research area was visual preferences in birds supervised by Professor Nick Humphrey. I had a fantastic three years, had lots of fun and made great friends but in all honesty the research never really grabbed my enthusiasm. I wasn't the best of research students and must have been a bit of a frustration to Nick.

What I was most successful at, and what I enjoyed most, was supervising undergraduates. I taught zoology, experimental psychology and some physiology for eight colleges, more supervising than I should have done but the money came in useful. I was in demand by directors of studies to supervise their students and got excellent reports from the supervisees. I like to think that this was for the quality of my teaching but, if truth be known, it may also have been for the cider I supplied to lubricate discussions!

As the three years neared their end, again the question arose of what to do next. I had to see an application for my research, not just research for its own sake, and I became interested in what birds don't like with a view to bird scaring. I could see applications for scaring birds from crops and around airfields. I explored options, a research post in Canada, another in Botswana and one at the Ministry for Agriculture and Fisheries. But was that what I really wanted? Research hadn't enthused me as much as I'd hoped. What was I good at? What did I enjoy? Teaching.

So the big decision was to forget about a career in research and apply to University of Cambridge Department of Education to do a Post Graduate Certificate in Education (PGCE). Having been offered a place starting in September 1975, by chance I saw an advertisement in the *Cambridge Evening News* for a biology teacher at Hills Road Sixth Form College (usually abbreviated to 'Hills Road' locally as I shall refer to it from now on). It sounded perfect, teaching sixth formers and still living in Cambridge. I applied as an unqualified teacher and was given the job – and here I am, 41 years later, still at Hills Road. Over the years I've been Exams Officer, Head of General Studies and, for 25 years, Head of Biology.

Maybe this sounds unadventurous, but believe me, it isn't. The last 41 years have been full of opportunities to indulge my three passions: teaching, biology and public engagement.

Most jobs have their routine and I get asked whether it gets tedious teaching the same old thing year on year. The answer is a simple 'no' and for one main reason – the students. They are ever-changing in a sixth-form college, new characters every year, each with their own personalities, strengths and weaknesses, aspirations and needs. There is nothing more rewarding than getting to know them, helping and guiding them to academic success, enthusing them in biology and following their progress to university or a career and beyond.

Many good friends are former students stretching back to the early years of my career. Recently I contacted several of them and asked for a photograph and brief biography including memories of their time at Hills Road. 25 of these are now displayed in my department as examples to current students of what careers former biology students have followed. They make heart-warming reading and truly are job satisfaction. There are few jobs where someone is fortunate enough to play such an important role in so many lives.

Over the years I must have taught thousands of students and many have gone on to careers in biology; doctors, nurses, vets, researchers, company executives, pharmacists, conservationists, dentists, university lecturers, teachers, physiotherapists, forensic scientists and many others. Wherever I go in Cambridge – university departments, research institutes and companies – I come across former students. On a visit to the Sanger Institute, a research group leader Dr Ben Lehner bounced up and said, 'It's all your fault I'm here!'

Teaching bright, motivated, interesting students never gets dull. They ask great questions, keep me on my toes, are lots of fun to be with and teach me so much.

I guess my research days showed me that I didn't want to follow a narrow path specialising in one area of biology. I love every aspect of the subject. In a single day I can be teaching ecology, gene technology, muscle action and photosynthesis. Teaching Advanced level means there are opportunities to enrich and extend beyond the confines of the syllabus and students respond. There are ample ways in which the subject can be brought to life and made relevant, and I could give so many example which have arisen recently: the challenges of Zika virus, a vaccine for malaria, use of stem cells, genome sequencing, transgenic organisms – the list goes on.

Working in Cambridge with its rich biology community provides many different opportunities. Each year I organise a visiting speaker programme for my students. This includes twenty speakers ranging from PhD students to doctors, professors and Nobel laureates covering a wide variety of topics such as regenerative medicine, virus plagues, science and politics, body clocks, organ transplantation, genetic counselling, breast cancer, colour in plants, conservation, food security, genes and obesity, and use of animals in research. When I show my programme to other teachers, the response is often, 'Wow, how on earth do you get all of these people?' It's not difficult, I just ask them and they almost invariably say 'yes'. Having been in Cambridge for so long, I've built up a very large number of contacts in the universities (Cambridge and Anglia Ruskin), research institutes and biology-related companies. In many cases I've taught the speakers or I've taught their son or daughter so it's hard for them to say 'no'!

Using my contacts, I organised twilight lecture series for local sixth formers, not just my own students. In partnership with Cambridge Infectious Diseases, we held a series of talks on aspects of infectious disease and with Cambridge Neuroscience a series of talks on neuroscience.

I've partnered with several institutions on collaborative projects for my students. These have included Medimmune, University of Cambridge Departments of Pharmacology and Biochemistry, Medical Research Council (MRC) Cancer Unit and its Mitochondrial Biology Unit, Napp Pharmaceuticals, Sainsbury Laboratory, GlaxoSmithKline and the Babraham Institute (we were given Working with Schools Awards for the last two collaborations). Sometimes they approach me with an idea, sometimes I approach them, and there is a real appetite for these types of collaborations. My students benefit but so do the institutions and their staff.

To enable networking and raise awareness of STEM (science, technology, engineering and mathematics) in the region and beyond, I organised four STEM conferences attended by teachers, research workers, university lecturers, companies and STEM organisations. These facilitated links which have led to many collaborations within the biology and wider STEM community.

In all of these activities, I've been fortunate in having the support of Hills Road. They see the benefit not only for the college and its students but more widely and I get ready access to all of the college facilities and any support I need from colleagues.

Teaching has enabled me to share my enthusiasm for ecology with my students and hopefully open their eyes to the natural world. Visits to Wicken Fen and Hayley Wood in Cambridgeshire, sand dune ecology in Norfolk and conservation work at East Pit in Cambridge are all part of what we offer our students and it has influenced them. Tom Hugh-Jones is a producer of BBC natural history programmes. At the end of a week-long field course in Norfolk I clearly remember Tom saying, 'I've really enjoyed it and I've learnt so much without even realising it'. This is teaching by exposure and stealth. Gareth Dalglish works for Natural England, Chris Bowden works in India on vulture conservation and Paul

Turkentine is a boat skipper as part of a Welsh Assembly Marine Monitoring Team involved with bird, cetacean and seal surveys.

Teaching has also given me the opportunity to write. In the late 1980s, HIV/AIDS hit the headlines and schools had a need for teaching materials. A colleague at Hills Road, (now Professor) Michael Reiss and I wrote a set of materials to use with our students and in the process met a local publisher who asked us if we'd be interested in developing a teaching resource; we agreed and *Aidsfacts* was published. Over the next few years we wrote *Health Assessment, Understanding Drugs, Health Issues, The Biology of HIV and AIDS, AIDS and HIV for Healthcare Professionals, STD facts* and *Understanding Cancer*. Additionally I contributed to *PHSE Drugs* (personal, health, social and economic education) and *The Biographical Dictionary of Biologists*.

Beyond my teaching and management role at Hills Road I've been able to employ other skills and interests to contribute to the life of the college. I was elected as staff governor in 2000, a position I have held since. This means being able to participate in shaping the college mission, strategy and direction in an ever-changing landscape and is a hugely rewarding and important role. In the earlier years of my teaching career there was much more time for staff to join in college activities and I acted in numerous plays, participated in college sport and ran a variety of enrichment activities for students. Sadly those days are gone, and rugby, *My Fair Lady* and puzzles and problems have been replaced by numerous meetings, writing annual departmental reports, appraisals and lesson observations. This has diminished the fun of the job but I know that this is true of many other professions and is not unique to education.

Being a teacher and biologist in Cambridge has offered me so much beyond Hills Road. For ten years now I've been a Patron of the Cambridge Science Festival (described by Nicola Buckley in Chapter 24 of this book) working with a brilliant team at the university in delivering an annual fortnight of public engagement in science. This is the largest free science festival in the United Kingdom and attracts more than 30,000 visitors each year. To be part of it is a real buzz both as an event organiser and as a visitor to some of the hundreds of activities.

Amanda Burton and I established Cambridge Biologists in 2006 with the aim of facilitating co-operation between educational establishments and the biological community and organising events. In 2012 we organised the first Big Biology Day, a public engagement partnership event with Cambridge Science Festival and hosted at Hills Road. This is now firmly established as one of the biggest, free annual public engagement biology events in the country with 30 exhibitors (university departments, learned societies, research institutes, schools and colleges and companies) and attracting more than 2,000 visitors. Its success has spawned similar Big Biology Days around the country.

I involve my students in the public engagement events and they never fail to impress. Hesitant at the start of the day, they're soon in full swing talking to everyone they meet with enthusiasm and passion. They are the science communicators of the future.

My personal favourite activity is owl pellet dissection, something which never fails with young and not so young. I've run the activity at Big Biology Days, the Cambridge Science Festival, Royal Society for the Protection of Birds (RSPB) public days, Open Farm Sundays, Cambridge and Ely Bioblitz and primary schools. The latter are particularly rewarding. There is nothing better than a group of 30 seven-year-olds excited when they discover a skull and identifying it as a field vole – a true scientific investigation. It's a joy to hear them say, 'That was the best lesson EVER'. One girl asked her teacher, 'Is that science? Because if it is, I want to be a scientist.' My crowning glory was a lad who came up after the session and asked for my autograph! Capturing the imagination of the young is so important to me; they may become the career scientists of the future.

Other opportunities to contribute to biology and science in Cambridge have arisen. I'm a trustee of STEM Team East and a lay member of the Animal Welfare and Ethical Review Bodies (AWERBs) at the Babraham Institute and the Agricultural Development Advisory Service (ADAS), reviewing and commenting on applications for Home Office licences for working with animals.

Beyond Cambridge, I've been able to engage with biology at a national level. I joined the Education Committee of the Institute of Biology in 2004 and as the society morphed into the Society of Biology and then the Royal Society of Biology (RSB) I've served on the Education, Training and Policy Committee. It's enabled me to bring a teacher's perspective to discussions surrounding educational issues. Back to the local level, I was member of the RSB East Anglia Branch Committee from 2003 until 2015, serving as Vice-Chair from 2011 and Education Officer from 2010. This mainly involved organising events for members and schools and, again, the local network proved invaluable.

In addition to the RSB committee, I'm a member of the Biochemical Society Education Committee, Microbiology Society Communications Committee and The Physiological Society Education Committee.

From 1980 until 2012, I also worked for the Open University (OU) as a tutor-counsellor on the Science Foundation Course, tutor for both biology, brain and behaviour and human biology courses as well as 15 years as tutor on science summer schools. Teaching for the OU was incredibly rewarding and I really felt I was helping adults to change their lives. Most had missed out on education first time around and the OU gave them a new opportunity. Continuing education is important; no-one is too old to learn. I taught all ages from 19 to 89, some doing it for career enhancement, others for the pure pleasure of learning.

Between 2013 and 2015 I designed and delivered an Access to Bioscience course at Hills Road with a colleague, John McCann. Ten adult students studied with us and six have used their success on the course as an entry to university.

No-one seeks recognition for what they do but it's rewarding when it happens. In 2014 I was named as one of the top 100 practicing scientists in the United Kingdom by the Science Council and in 2015, I was given the Royal Society of Biology President's medal. In 2008 I was given the Open University teaching award. Was I pleased? Of course I was as these were the gifts of respected colleagues and professionals.

From my experience, what advice would I give to a scientist contemplating a career beyond the lab?

- Take all opportunities presented, be open-minded and listen to good advice
- Keep your horizons wide and follow your instincts
- Use networks, create new ones and engage with people
- Don't be afraid of taking initiatives even if they fail, learn from experience and move forward
- Do what you enjoy and what plays to your strengths

Do I regret moving from the lab? Not for one minute. I truly value all of my contacts and friends who are engaged in research, I learn a lot from them and incorporate what I learn into my teaching. Vicariously, I still feel as though I'm engaged in research, just not my own. My career in teaching has been so rich, rewarding and fulfilling with so many opportunities which I've embraced and thoroughly enjoyed. Much is said today about work-life balance but I'm not sure what that is or where the dividing line lies. If I attend a committee meeting in London for one of the learned societies, if I put my energies into supporting the Science Festival, if I visit labs to talk to the researchers – is that work? I don't think so.

Would I recommend teaching? Unreservedly yes; you can have as much fun as I've had!

26

In Search of the Ethical Path

EARLY INSPIRATIONS

Science and technology have held a fascination for me since childhood. I liked number puzzles, I enjoyed building things out of kits like Lego and Meccano, I watched science and nature programmes on TV and I read science fiction. Then for Christmas 1981 my grandfather gave me a micro-computer – a Commodore Vic-20 with just 5 kilobytes of memory! – and confidently told me that these machines would become very important in society. I soon taught myself how to programme it and had a lot of fun creating simple video games. When it came to choosing Advanced level subjects I went for maths, physics and statistics – together with a newly available option in computer science. I thrived studying the conventional subjects but the computer science was mainly orientated towards business applications rather than science so I lost interest in that area.

FIRST CAREER STEPS

When it came to choosing a degree subject I was excited by the idea of studying astrophysics or astronomy but my grandfather convinced me there were many more career options in his own field, electrical and electronic engineering. He also encouraged me to apply for places on university courses sponsored by industry. I followed his advice and obtained a place studying physics and electronic engineering at Lancaster University. The course was sponsored by one of the subsidiaries of

Successful Careers beyond the Lab, ed. David Bennett and Richard Jennings.
Published by Cambridge University Press. © Cambridge University Press 2017.

General Electric Company (GEC), at that time, the United Kingdom's largest arms corporation.

I enjoyed studying the physics modules of the degree but some of the engineering modules did not inspire me. There were too many of what I felt were arbitrary 'rules of thumb'. I much preferred the more solid theoretical underpinnings found in physics.

But there was another, deeper problem which became increasingly clear during my year out undertaking industry placements. One such placement involved carrying out some research and development on image intensifiers. These are clever pieces of equipment which amplify the light entering them allowing the user to see in the dark. The application of the particular devices I was working on was in a rifle-mounted night-sight which would allow soldiers to shoot people in low-light conditions. At first I didn't think much about the ethics of the work but then a colleague told me that, as well as a contract to supply the British military, our company also had contracts with governments with poor human rights records. He left soon after and then my placement ended but I was left with a distinctly less favourable view of the company from then onwards.

FROM ENGINEERING TO ENVIRONMENTAL SCIENCE

I returned to university for my final year questioning not only whether to stay with GEC after graduation but also whether to remain in engineering at all. At that time the main opportunities for electronic engineers were still in military industry despite the fall of the Berlin Wall and other signs that the Cold War was ending. The other career options I saw in the physics and engineering press seemed narrow and uninspiring so I started to look more widely.

My attention was caught by environmental issues. Climate change had just begun to enter the public consciousness following on from concerns about acid rain, the hole in the ozone layer, the Chernobyl nuclear disaster and major losses of tropical rainforest. So I decided to investigate career options in these areas. I didn't get much joy from talking to the university careers office so, on the recommendation of a friend studying environmental science, I just starting asking staff in that department about research posts that someone with my background and skills might be suitable for. Through this I was directed to one professor who was an engineer turned environmental scientist. He had recently obtained funding for a PhD studentship on mathematical modelling of climate change and was looking for someone with a strong background in maths and physics to carry it out. Based on my predicted grades he offered me the post – I was very pleased!

I started the PhD in autumn 1990. I found the work interesting and challenging. I learnt about the many fluxes of carbon in the environmental system and how these were leading to increased warming in the climate system. I learnt about data quality, different techniques of measuring and managing uncertainty, and the sometimes acrimonious scientific debates about the reliability of different modelling approaches. I also gained an appreciation of the political context of the issue at a conference at the Royal Society where I first heard a climate sceptic scientist present his provocative views.

There were difficulties, however. Two I remember distinctly. One was the experimental 'parallel' computer that I used for much of the mathematical modelling. At the start of my PhD it seemed like this hardware would be the 'next big thing' yielding large jumps in processing power. I learnt a specialist computer language to use it but had to deal with huge bugs in the software making progress slow. And, unfortunately for me, the processing gains of the parallel computer were soon outstripped by those in conventional microprocessors meaning that despite all my efforts I was at a growing disadvantage compared with others in the field. The other main problem was that I was the only mathematical modeller in my environmental sciences department who was working on global climate change. This left me somewhat isolated.

As I started to write academic papers the debates over different modelling approaches came back to haunt me. While mathematical journals were interested in publishing our work, climate science journals were less enthusiastic – and it took a lot of effort and rewrites to get the papers accepted.

After submitting my PhD thesis in autumn 1994 I decided I needed some time to think about my longer-term career options so I took some time out to travel and do voluntary work.

TAKING TIME OUT

Over the course of the next few months I worked on two volunteer projects: one in the former East Germany and another in India. In Germany I joined an international group of volunteers carrying out environmental work – specifically clearing litter out of a town's river system. In India, I joined another group of volunteers working on human development projects around the country.

My experiences in India, in particular, had a major impact on the way I saw the world. Through the project work I met many people living in considerable poverty in rural areas but I was struck by how friendly and generous they were to a (comparatively) wealthy Westerner like myself. And they smiled more often than most people in Britain seemed to! They were generally very capable – as small-scale farmers, crafts-people, traders etc. – but their main problem was the major, and often unwelcome, change in their lives imposed by very powerful corporations in co-operation with government bodies. For example, some changes were due to the expansion of mining or plantation projects in the area restricting the land available for farming. The local community organisations would try to help villagers get a good deal but it could be a real struggle. This led me to start to question my conventional ideas of 'progress'. During my PhD I had started to become involved with environmental campaigning at the university – out of concern for climate change, forest destruction and the like – and my experiences in India helped to impress on me the links between environmental and social problems.

A NEW RESEARCH FOCUS

I returned to the United Kingdom unsure of whether I wanted to return to research. I had enjoyed applying mathematical modelling to climate change problems but had found many aspects of the research process frustrating. Furthermore, my PhD supervisor had been looking into research funding for post-doctoral work following on from that covered by my thesis but there was little available unless you were working for one of the big climate research groups such as the Hadley Centre – part of the government's Met (short for meteorology) Office – or the Climate Research Unit at the University of East Anglia. I also wanted to be more proactive believing that environmental problems were not being taken seriously enough by the government or society. I considered campaign work but I had fairly limited skills in this area. I continued to do voluntary work in the United Kingdom while applying for any research jobs that seemed to utilise at least some of my skill set.

After several interviews I was offered the post of research fellow at the Centre for Environmental Strategy (CES) at the University of Surrey in 1996. I was to work on two projects. The main project was to examine the potential effectiveness of what would become known as 'carbon trading' as a way of helping to reduce emissions. The second project was using lifecycle analysis to investigate the environmental benefits of recycling mobile phones.

In the carbon trading project I was to use energy-economic models to explore the effectiveness of different technology and policy options for reducing carbon emissions. I spent a lot of time learning how to use various existing models in the field and how to modify some of them for use in our project. All the issues of uncertainty and complexity that I had encountered before with climate science models were present in this field – but the situation here was complicated by a heavy dose of politics. I found that different political views could affect the choice of which model to use for assessing the costs of action or inaction on climate change – and this was often not made explicit when presenting the results. I found that the large uncertainties in the model results were frequently downplayed or simply not stated in research papers. I was generally disturbed by what I saw as a lower quality of research in the field. I discussed my concerns with my co-workers and we resolved to be much clearer in our work about political assumptions and uncertainties.

As we began publishing our results and conclusions we started to try to input our work into policy-making discussions especially via UK government advisors on climate change and international development. This led to some of our recommendations being implemented – in particular a number of operating safeguards for the carbon trading mechanisms agreed under the Kyoto Protocol, the main climate treaty in force at the time. Given our growing concerns about whether the mechanisms would be effective in providing environmental and social benefits as frequently claimed, we felt that we had at least made the system 'less bad'.

As our research progressed we also began working with the Intermediate Technology Development Group (now Practical Action) carrying out research examining whether transfer of carbon emissions reduction technology – such as renewable energy projects – could be successfully combined with development objectives such as poverty alleviation. We found that programmes of community-scale projects could be particularly beneficial for both aims. Our work was funded by the Department for International Development and again our findings were fed into policy-making processes.

During this time I also became an expert reviewer for the Intergovernmental Panel on Climate Change (IPCC). This gave me a first-hand insight into the workings of high-level scientific bodies and their interactions with the policy arena.

CORPORATE ENTANGLEMENTS

A significant aspect of my research at CES was the relationship with corporate funders. As a research centre which had grown out of collaborative work between engineering academics and those in industry there was rather more contact with the business world than I was used to. There were advantages and disadvantages to such collaboration. On the one hand we obtained data from industry that would have been difficult to access in any other way and then we could feed back any research findings direct to users. On the other hand, there were restrictions on the publication of results and disagreements over interpretation of results.

In the research project on mobile phones we used lifecycle assessment to estimate a range of environmental impacts including contributions to climate change and toxicity in the environment. However, some of the data we were given to analyse was regarded by the corporation in question as commercially confidential. To publish it in the open academic literature, they argued, or even publish certain analyses based on it risked giving an advantage to competitors in the sector. But, of course, a central tenant of academic science is openness about data and assumptions. Hence there had to be careful negotiations about the data that could be included in the published work.

The most disturbing episode of my time at CES came, however, during some consultancy work on carbon trading which our research group carried out for a major oil and gas corporation. At the time, this company was investigating the potential value of the fledgling carbon-trading mechanisms as vehicles for helping to fund energy projects. Some of their proposed projects used renewable energy technologies, some were focused on energy efficiency and some were focused on natural gas – due to its lower carbon content than of coal or oil. It was the latter that became a focus of disagreement between us and the corporation. I remember clearly taking part in a very uncomfortable meeting with company managers and another consultant from within the industry in which they all tried to talk me into endorsing an interpretation of the proposed guidelines that I thought would create a major loophole. I felt this was a step too far but, as a stalling tactic, said that I would think about it. After the meeting I wrote them a detailed e-mail explaining why I thought their interpretation to be wrong – a position which my project supervisor backed. Soon afterwards the consultancy contract with the corporation came to an end and was not renewed but the whole episode had coloured my perceptions of industrial collaboration.

LEAVING ACADEMIA

Although I enjoyed much of my time at CES and learnt a huge amount about environmental issues I decided to look further afield in 2001. I had become demoralised by a range of factors. Obviously, some of the negative experiences I have outlined in the preceding section – especially those concerning industrial collaboration – were significant, but my disillusionment ran deeper than that. My five years at CES had been characterised by a succession of short-term contracts (sometimes as short as three months) which led to a constant battle between trying to carry out the current research project while having to write applications for the next one. My group's research, which was often very policy focused, was also difficult to fund from traditional academic sources and we found ourselves increasingly at odds with the university bureaucracy over budget issues. In addition, national ratings of the 'research excellence' of university departments led to an emphasis on the volume of academic publication which I felt at times actually undermined the quality of our output and its value to end-users such as policy-makers. A further factor was the expectation to travel by air to international academic conferences and to attend as many as possible. Given the very high carbon footprint of air travel, this was increasingly at odds with my motivation for carrying out the research. I argued that we should be using options like video-conferencing much more but the technical and bureaucratic obstacles to this were high. In the end, when an opportunity to leave presented itself, I took it with both hands.

The post I successfully applied for was programme manager for environmental justice at Friends of the Earth and was a one-year contract covering sabbatical leave. The job was broad in nature, coordinating the organisation's emerging work linking environmental issues with concerns about social justice. Some work was research-orientated, working with academics to document the evidence of linkages and there were pathways to feed this to policy-makers in areas such as transport, climate change and food. Some of the work had more of a campaign focus – especially that on climate change. The largest part of the post, however, was orientated towards community work, working with grassroots campaigners – both inside and outside the organisation – to research poor public transport provision and help campaign to improve it.

There was quite a steep learning curve involved in taking this post. For example, within a few weeks of starting I spoke at the parliamentary launch of a new report on environmental justice written by the colleague whose post I was covering and his academic co-authors. Furthermore, although the post was based in the organisation's Policy and Research Unit, the research side turned out to be quite limited and mostly centred on helping local transport campaigners.

There were two aspects of the post that I especially enjoyed. The first was the education work – giving talks to campaigners and others, explaining the concepts behind environmental justice and highlighting the large body of evidence that demonstrated that low-income communities suffer much more from environmental problems than do high-income communities. The second aspect was the work on climate injustice – working with campaigners to get the message out that climate change is one of the strongest examples of injustice related to environmental problems. The wealthy do indeed emit the lion's share of global greenhouse gas emissions and the poorest in society are the most vulnerable to its effects.

Another aspect of working for Friends of the Earth that I enjoyed was the team spirit. While there had generally been a good level of camaraderie among the staff in my university research centre, I had often felt that relations with other parts of the university were less than cordial. This was very different from working for a campaign organisation.

MOVING TO SCIENTISTS FOR GLOBAL RESPONSIBILITY

While working at CES I had joined a membership organisation called Scientists for Global Responsibility (SGR).[1] This was a group of natural scientists, social scientists, engineers and others from related professions which carried out research, education and campaign activities focused on ethical issues in science and technology. SGR had evolved from several groups which had been educating about and campaigning against nuclear weapons during the Cold War. In the early 1990s these organisations had merged and broadened their focus to include wider peace, environmental and social justice issues. This was an organisation which encompassed both an interest in robust evidence and a deep concern that misuse of science and technology was a serious problem in society. I immediately felt that I had found a group which reflected my concerns about the world.

I quickly became more involved. I went to the annual conference and soon after joined the national co-ordinating committee. Unfortunately, the

---

[1] www.sgr.org.uk/

organisation was small with the only paid staff being a part-time administrator. Nevertheless, I helped on a voluntary basis for several years. We obtained some grant funding for a project on ethical careers in science and technology. The aim of the work was to provide information to university science and engineering students on the ethical issues involved in choosing a career. We employed a project worker to carry out some research and commissioned scientists to write about the ethical issues in their field and how this could affect career choice. Eventually in 2001 we published an introductory booklet on ethical careers. We distributed printed copies via stalls at university careers fairs and electronic copies via the fledgling World Wide Web. The booklet is still available on our website and has remained popular to this day, with about 10,000 copies distributed to date.[2]

Our experiences with this and other SGR activities at this time led to the conclusion that we needed to attract larger grant funding and work to expand our income from membership subscriptions and donations so that we could employ more staff. By late 2002 we had raised enough to employ a part-time director. This coincided with the end of my contract at Friends of the Earth so I also resigned from the SGR co-ordinating committee – to prevent a conflict of interest – and applied for the post. Given my background in dealing with ethical issues during my career connected with both military and environmental issues, and my detailed knowledge of the organisation, I was awarded the post and started work in early 2003.

The job has been an exciting mix of activities. One of the main focuses has been to carry out policy-relevant research in areas where it has been lacking. We have published a series of reports over the last ten years critically examining military involvement in science and technology, especially in the United Kingdom. The first, *Soldiers in the Laboratory*,[3] gave an overview of the extent of that involvement within government, the corporate sector and universities, and questioned the ethical basis for these activities. Coming as it did during the early years of the so-called War on Terror and launched at a parliamentary event, it attracted a lot of interest especially from the media, peace campaigners, security analysts and scientists. It highlighted that 30% of the United Kingdom's public R&D budget was spent on military projects – a very large proportion. Among our recommendations was a call for this

---

[2] See www.sgr.org.uk/projects/ethical-careers
[3] www.sgr.org.uk/ArmsControl/Soldiers_in_Lab_Report.pdf

to be quickly reduced by one-third to one-half and the money spent instead on civilian R&D. Notably by 2010 government statistics showed that the changes in public R&D spending had been in line with our recommendations. Now we are making the case for further reductions and an increased focus on work that helps to tackle the roots of conflict.

We have also published policy-orientated reports on other issues including corporate influence on science, shale gas and fracking, and nuclear weapons. On each occasion the lead author has been a researcher in the area in question and I have co-authored and/or edited in line with my expertise. Our reports have helped to bring a stronger evidence base to debates on these issues but also highlighted the importance of ethical issues in decisions over the role of science and technology in our society. Our 2015 report – on the United Kingdom's nuclear weapons[4] – has attracted an especially high level of interest. This is largely due to the political debate over the replacement of the Trident system and the latest scientific evidence on devastating effects should they ever be used.

We also obtained funding for extending our ethical careers programme. Consequently, in the mid-2000s we published nine briefings and booklets. Each one focused on a different issue or sector in science and technology, including climate change, cleaner technology, animal experiments, space technology and the chemicals industry.[5] We took advantage of the rapid expansion of the Web to distribute thousands of these briefings each year to students. This was complemented by other Web-based material such as an 'ethical employers' index.[6]

In 2013 SGR moved its office into a new eco-development just outside Lancaster. This development includes 41 high-specification eco-homes and an eco-renovated office and workshop space. Electricity is provided by a combination of small-scale hydro and solar panels while heat energy is provided by a wood-chip-fired boiler and solar hot-water panels. The wood chips are sourced locally from sustainably managed forests. Hence in our day-to-day operations we are now 'walking the talk' of environmentally sustainable working practices.

Our location has provided the basis for our newest activity: Science4Society Week.[7] One of our concerns in recent years has been the continued sponsorship of science education events for young people by major arms and fossil fuel corporations, and the limited availability of

---

[4] www.sgr.org.uk/resources/uk-nuclear-weapons-catastrophe-making

[5] See www.sgr.org.uk/projects/ethical-careers-project-main-outputs

[6] See www.sgr.org.uk/projects/ethical-employers-contacts-list

[7] See www.sgr.org.uk/resources/announcing-science4society-week-2016

alternatives. Hence in 2014 we ran a pilot for a class of local school children including a tour of our development and a workshop on making model water turbines. This was very successful and we have since expanded our activities funded by several small grants. In 2016 we ran tours, provided downloadable material for teachers to run structured classroom activities and ran an environmentally themed science competition. Several hundred young people took part and we have bigger plans for the future.

In addition to this focused project activity I manage the regular activities of the organisation with financial and administrative support coming from SGR's office manager. The regular activities apply the expertise of our staff, co-ordinating committee and members, and include an annual conference, newsletter, blog and invited lectures/talks promoted through our website and social media. All these activities are funded by membership subscriptions and grants which we work hard to maintain. The post is very demanding, requiring a wide range of skills and knowledge, but, by being able to contribute to some of the key debates in society, it is also very fulfilling.

FOLLOWING IN MY FOOTSTEPS?

I cannot pretend that my career path has been conventional or that the steps I took after I decided to leave academia can be easily repeated. For a start, SGR does not fit neatly into commonly used categories of organisations. It is part campaign organisation, part think tank and part education provider. It works on peace issues, environmental issues, science policy and questions of professional standards. Hence my suggestions for how to follow in my footsteps must be taken with this in mind.

Perhaps it is best to start with the question of steps that can be taken to move to a research post in campaign organisation working on, for example, environmental or peace issues. First, such jobs are rare and generally not as well paid as academic posts. However, they do offer the opportunity to be more outspoken on the urgent issues facing human societies. If this is attractive then there are a number of steps you can take. To begin with you will need to familiarise yourself with which organisations are working on the issues on which you have expertise and (obviously) for which you have strong ethical concerns. Making personal contacts is often important. Sometimes you can meet people working in these areas at conferences or sometimes just sending them an e-mail or making a phone call can be the starting point. Increasingly social media networks such as LinkedIn can be the way in. Helping the organisation in a voluntary capacity is also an important way of getting a foot in the door. This need not be directly in your area of academic expertise: it could simply be in an administrative or IT role, for example. And don't forget to demonstrate your support by becoming a paid-up member!

Another option that is sometimes available, especially if the campaign organisation is small, is to offer to help write grant applications for projects focused on policy-relevant research.

Independent think tanks are another option and there tend to be more research opportunities with such organisations than with campaign groups. Think tanks tend to be privately funded so you will have to check that the funding and any political leanings are consistent with your ethical views. Many of the suggested actions listed above for campaign groups also apply when looking for opportunities at think tanks.

The other relevant option is to look for opportunities working for an independent science education organisation, often referred to in the jargon as an STEM (science, technology, engineering, maths) education provider. Obviously these are mainly in teaching rather than research. Some of these organisations are not-for-profit while others are not. This sector is expanding quickly as the UK government seeks to involve the private sector more in education – and there is a whole debate about the extent to which that is a good thing. If you are interested in this sector I suggest doing your research carefully, as most employment options in the United Kingdom are either in for-profit companies or ones that are at least partly funded by weapons-manufacturing and/or fossil fuel corporations.

CONCLUDING THOUGHTS

When I was younger I saw universities as places where you could carry out exciting and valuable research which would unquestionably help inform society and lead to better choices for the world. My view has become somewhat more jaded in the years since, especially as universities have developed much closer relationships with large corporations and taken on some of the negative aspects of corporate behaviour. I still feel they play an important and largely positive role but there needs to be reform and society needs other organisations to take on more of the critical roles that are increasingly being neglected. This is where I feel ex-academic researchers and educators can play an important role – by working with (for example) independent think tanks and campaign groups to help counterbalance the negative trends within the universities. This is the path I have taken and it is one I have not regretted.

27
_____

Environmental Policy, Politics and Science – Not Always an Easy Ride

The only labs I have been in are ones I have visited. They include labs genetically modifying plants and animals, labs analyzing the constituents of incinerator ash, labs checking that the right trace elements are in a slab of aluminium. I also had the honour of visiting Dolly the sheep, the first cloned mammal, although she was in a rather comfy enclosure rather than a lab as such. Some labs have had the feel of the future, shiny with cutting-edge technology; some have been freezing cold in Portakabins, performing the necessary but unromantic tasks of ensuring that wastes are 'in conformance' with environmental regulations. All have been fascinating but in all cases I have been glad to leave.

That is because I am a scientist by disposition but insufficiently diligent to be a scientist by profession. I admire, and am drawn to, the enterprise of reasoned argument followed by painstaking, long investigation. Most of all I admire the leap of imagination that draws it all together, then yet more detailed exploration to confirm that what started as a hunch really is scientific fact. But I couldn't do it day-to-day. What I like much more is seeing the big picture and using science to inform and shape it. That is how I have tried to forge my career.

I would like to think that my commitment to being a polymath started with my Advanced level choices – art, biology, maths and English literature. In those days (late 1970s) the idea was to do three arts or three sciences, so my combination was considered unconventional, if not irresponsible. I enjoyed the orderliness of mathematics and I loved the incredible insights biology gave into the nature of life but I couldn't see myself in a lab or wielding numbers as a career. I wasn't good

Successful Careers beyond the Lab, ed. David Bennett and Richard Jennings.
Published by Cambridge University Press. © Cambridge University Press 2017.

enough at art to take it further so I settled on a degree in English and art history at the University of Leeds which offered a combination of excellent departments, fashionable Northern grittiness and a great nightclub scene. I chose philosophy as a third subject, found the module on history of science much more interesting than the art department's module on the history of photography (important as that is) and ended up with a joint honours degree in English and philosophy. Of the subjects I covered, I found political philosophy the most compelling, decided that I wanted to be a political journalist and went on to do a Master's degree in the government and politics of Western Europe at the London School of Economics.

By now it was the mid-1980s, the era of Mrs Thatcher, the 'me' generation and the rise of London as a centre of financial activity. It was a great time to be a journalist but unfortunately no-one offered me a job so I set about finding some interim work. I had always suspected that notwithstanding my two degrees, the fact that I'd learned typing and shorthand at sixteen would be one of my greatest assets. Alongside temping at a range of legal and accountancy firms (a helpful way to discover that I didn't want to be a lawyer or an accountant), I was offered a job helping to organize a conference in Rome.

It sounds very glamorous but only the last week or so was to be in Rome; the rest was organized from Kilburn in North London. A pioneering journalist, Robin Sharp, convened the conference to draw attention to the decade that had passed since the UN World Food Conference in 1974. There, Henry Kissinger, US Secretary of State, declared that within ten years no child should go to bed hungry. Of course that wasn't realized. The World Food Assembly 1984 was convened to bring peoples' organisations together to get closer to that goal given the failure of international governments to address poverty and hunger. It was an unprecedented gathering of activists from charities and grassroots organisations from all over the globe and it was the first time I heard the term 'sustainable development'.

My job was to get the delegates to Rome from cities all over the world – no mean task without the benefit of the internet. This seems an appropriate moment to pay tribute to the wonderful Terence Khushal, an independent travel agent operating out of a tiny flat in Kilburn, without whom my job would have been far more difficult.

The World Food Assembly expanded my horizons both geographically and politically. I had a crash course in global injustice, environmental pressures and the inequality of women. I was uplifted by accounts of people in the most difficult of physical and economic circumstances coming together to form businesses, grow food, establish healthcare and resist large-scale and insensitive schemes imposed from outside in the name of 'development'. I met charismatic leaders, men and women. I was hooked on this thing described as 'sustainability' – letting people find solutions that would not compromise the future which suited their environment and culture, and which they could sustain without the help of global institutions and businesses.

My enthusiasm endured but that particular organization did not. Looking around for something similar, I happened on Green Alliance,[1] another tiny outfit in a tiny office, this time in the slightly more salubrious setting of London's Covent Garden. It was above a café and you could tell the time by the aroma from downstairs – bacon for breakfast, Bolognese at lunchtime, bleach at the end of the day. Green Alliance was run by the inspirational and indefatigable Tom Burke and Tessa Tennant with just me as support. I made coffee, cut up newspapers to make press cuttings files, typed letters to MPs and stuck bits of Hansard together to make parliamentary newsletters. No word processors, internet or email in those days, of course – spray glue was as high-tech as it got. The secret of my success, such as it was, was to try not to mind the relatively menial tasks but to ask for more interesting things to do.

Green Alliance's mission, then and now, is to get decision-makers to make the environment a priority. When I started in 1985 the global environment was barely on the political radar. My press cuttings files were dominated by parochial planning and land issues – the effect of this or that road on the British countryside, the problems faced by farmers, the odd river pollution incident. The plight of the rainforests featured occasionally but global warming was considered the fevered imaginings of a few fringe scientists, something might have been happening to the ozone layer but it was not quite clear what, and acid rain was not our fault. Over the next decade that situation changed dramatically. I saw acceptance of the damage chlorofluorocarbons (CFCs) were doing to the ozone layer, comprehensive legislation on pollution and chemicals enacted by the European Union and the setting up of an international scientific process to examine the phenomenon of climate change.

And so started a journey that blended my fascinations with science and politics as scientific advances increasingly informed both public environmental awareness and international political action. My

---

[1] www.green-alliance.org.uk/

relatively competent execution of the routine administration meant that I graduated to organizing meetings and conferences. Green Alliance built a reputation as an expert convener of government bodies, businesses and non-governmental groups, and so I was involved in staging an important London meeting on the Montreal Protocol[2] (which limited the use of chlorofluorocarbons - CFCs), convened an unprecedented coalition of groups calling for better regulation of pesticides and organized a speaking tour for the leading American opponent of genetic engineering, Jeremy Rifkin.

The last example illustrates how, for environmentalists, science can be both friend and foe. Genetic engineering, or genetic modification (GM) as the UK government encouraged us to call it (in the mistaken belief that it would sound less threatening), galvanised my colleagues and people at large like few subjects did before or since. Some viewed the ability to change the genetic make-up of plants and animals as the key to more efficient food production and the eradication of diseases; others saw it as an unnecessary and risky interference with processes we barely understand.

I tried to keep an open mind but, the more I learned about genetic modification of crops, the more concerned I became. A Royal Commission on Environmental Pollution report[3] in 1989 urged caution, particularly because of the possibility of GM crops upsetting the ecological balance of areas outside of farmland. As a consequence, when the Environment Protection Act[4] was introduced as a bill late in 1989 I expressed an interest in lobbying on the section that would enact European Union rules on the scrutiny of genetic modification and had the support of colleagues in other environmental groups. I found myself conversing with politicians in both the Houses of Commons and of Lords, and sitting in public galleries passing notes to them with suggested amendments to strengthen the legislation. I played a part in securing improved access to information about how government committees would judge GM crops in an era when most scientific committees worked under the constraints of the Official Secrets Act prior to the United Kingdom's comprehensive Freedom of Information laws.

---

[2] http://hansard.millbanksystems.com/commons/1990/jul/02/ozone-layer-london-conference

[3] http://webarchive.nationalarchives.gov.uk/20110112040753/http:/www.rcep.org.uk/reports/20-transport/documents/1997-20transport.pdf

[4] www.legislation.gov.uk/ukpga/1990/43/contents

My involvement had an unexpected result. Speaking to a conference of policy-makers about environmentalists' concerns about GM, I was approached during the break by two of the key people involved in the regulatory process. They wondered if I'd consider sitting on one of the very scientific committees I'd been critiquing as a 'lay' member – someone without specific scientific expertise who could comment on the overall process. 'Lay' did not seem unfair – although I had taken a certificate in ecology to augment my Green Alliance role, it was hardly on a level with the professors and doctors on that committee. It was not a difficult decision ('better inside the tent' came to mind) although conducting the role in a way that did not compromise my concerns was clearly going to be a challenge. Having clarified that to be a member of the Advisory Committee on Releases to the Environment (ACRE)[5] I would *not* be subject to the Official Secrets Act, which I could not have signed, and that I would be able to communicate the essence of the proceedings to my colleagues, I agreed.

That was the beginning of more than a decade of participation in the world of scientific regulatory scrutiny and its relationship to political and public debate. It was not an easy ride. The rigour and dedication of the men and women on ACRE was never in doubt and I was happy with every decision we made on experimental use of genetically modified organisms (GMOs). But when we got to the decision to allow the first commercial GM crop I had to register my dissent – I just didn't feel that all the implications had been fully considered. Colleagues in the environmental groups encouraged me to be outspoken which didn't make me popular inside the committee.

I was not alone. Other leading organizations such as English Nature and the Royal Society for the Protection of Birds (RSPB) were voicing doubts about GM and public controversy was increasing. Most of the public concern was around the consequences of eating genetically modified food but there was also a groundswell against releasing GM crops into the environment and some activists destroyed experimental crops. Rather than voice blanket opposition to the technology, my stance towards those in the scientific and industrial communities concerned with GM was that while the first uses of the technology might not pose immediate threats, there was considerable uncertainty, and to the wider public it was hard to see significant benefits. Corporate

---

[5] www.gov.uk/government/organisations/advisory-committee-on-releases-to-the-environment

presentations tended to start with graphs illustrating growing global population and point out the need to feed an expanding world. But they ended with an explanation of how the company was going to make tomatoes with a longer shelf life or create crops that enabled greater use of herbicides in already high-input, developed-country agricultural systems. I felt strongly that although the technology might well have potential for good, the rhetoric was running ahead of the reality.

This stance led to my being invited to speak to a range of audiences about public responses to GM, the reasons for the concerns and the kind of policies that might help to address them. High on my agenda were more thorough ecological testing, better articulation of the benefits and full transparency of decision-making. I went to meetings all over Europe (some of them organized by one of the editors of this very volume, David Bennett) and was frequently asked to give views to ministers in the United Kingdom. In 2000, in an attempt to create an institutional answer to these concerns and improve decision-making, the UK government set up the Agriculture and Environment Biotechnology Commission (AEBC),[6] a body with membership from a large range of interest groups including environmental groups, farmers, scientists and companies. I applied to chair it, knowing that it was unlikely that someone from an environmental group would be asked to take that seat. I was considered insufficiently neutral, and the chair selected was Professor Malcolm Grant, a highly respected academic who had not previously been involved in the debate. I was asked to be deputy chair.

Malcolm Grant's chairing was skillful in the extreme and no-one expected such a diverse group to produce three consensus reports. However, the AEBC's conclusions were not in tune with the views of the government at the time and, although it did prompt the establishment of some more thorough ecological trials and a large programme of public consultation, it was closed down in 2004. The AEBC gave me a lot of valuable experience: in digesting scientific information and reproducing it in an accessible form, in trying to make decisions in the face of scientific uncertainty, in listening more than speaking and in the political treatment of science.

Much was going on for me at the same time as being heavily embedded in the GM debate. I became director of Green Alliance, then still only five people strong, in 1992. As well as working on GM issues, we helped the UK government with conferences in the run-up to, and

---

[6] http://webarchive.nationalarchives.gov.uk/20100419143351/http:/www.aebc.gov.uk/

aftermath of, the 1992 Earth Summit[7] in Brazil, so I had the excitement of travelling to Bergen, New York and Rio during that time. In 1993 I helped to organize a large international conference, Partnerships for Change,[8] fulfilling a commitment from the UK government at the Rio summit. Science was never far away. There was the science that informed the debate about climate change including the need to have an international scientific consensus on what was happening to the atmosphere and what the consequences might be. There was also science behind preserving biodiversity from evidence of extinctions to prospecting for new drugs from the rainforests in order to make an economic case for their protection. Much was also, of course, about chemical pollution. All of these were subjects that I had to research and then communicate.

In 1997 I had my first son and decided to stand down as director of Green Alliance. At times it had been a 60-hour-a-week job and I couldn't imagine combining it with parenthood. Stephen Tindale took over, an excellent choice, as he had been an adviser to MP Chris Smith when he was Opposition Spokesman on the Environment in the UK Parliament so he was strongly politically attuned. I negotiated a retainer to be an advisor, and, kept my GM committee posts on the argument that it would take too long to get anyone else up to speed and enjoyed the best part of a year off with my son. After a year I took on a bit more work with Green Alliance as I didn't want to lose the skills but in 1999 my second son was born so I decreased hours again. That made applying to be AEBC chair in 2000 a big decision and in many ways I was glad that I didn't end up with that level of responsibility at that stage in my life.

When the GM work came to an end I thought it time to develop a different specialism if I was going to remain part time but in demand. In the mid-1990s I had been asked to join the advisory group of Shanks, a large waste management company, as the environmental representative. My colleagues were toxicologists, politicians and waste engineers – a great group. My inaugural trip (and there were to be many trips) was to the United Kingdom's largest landfill site at Brogborough in Bedfordshire. This was a new experience and one few of us have – seeing the trucks that trundle our streets to take our discarded stuff out of sight and out of mind arrive at the face of a mountain of waste and disgorge their contents to join the rest. In the multicoloured mess you can see oceans of plastic, a library's worth of paper, ribbons of video and audio

---

[7] www.un.org/geninfo/bp/enviro.html   [8] http://partnershipsforchange.org/

tape, mattresses, nappies, furniture and, of course, a great deal of food. I was over-awed by the scale of this waste.

That began two decades of studying waste. What is waste? Society's answer is that it is stuff we don't want any more. Science's answer is that it is a rich smorgasbord of materials: minerals, plastics, fibres, organic nutrients, all of which could have value. But science also tells us about entropy which means in crude terms that order tends to chaos and restoring order requires us to put energy back in. That is true whether you are running around cleaning up the house or using trucks and machinery to collect waste and trying to extract useful stuff from it. The latter costs money and if landfill is cheap, as it was in those days, rescuing materials is often not 'economic' unless our conscience or regulations require that we recycle. In 2000 the United Kingdom recycled less than 12% of its household waste and probably about 50% of its industrial waste although no-one was very confident about the figures as no money had been spent on data collection.

The picture changed with a government agenda that *did* want to see recycling and no longer wanted to see the United Kingdom near the bottom of every European recycling league table. Policies and regulations came thick and fast, some European Union-led but not all. I was involved in political discussions about the level of landfill tax to set to make alternatives more economic and the most effective incentives for getting electronic goods and packaging back from consumers. I also got to know about more technical topics such as how to capture maximum methane gas from rotting rubbish (it can be turned into energy) and how many layers of protection are needed at the bottom of a landfill to stop it from leaking.

I became fascinated with the many dimensions to 'waste' policy – scientific, technical, economic, social, environmental and behavioural. Waste contains valuable materials that our economy fails to recapture – how could we improve? Our consumption habits drain the planet of resources but, according to the social science, don't always make us happy – can we change that? We have pollution and inequality as the backstory to our obsession with 'stuff'. I wanted to tell this story and so I decided to write a book.

I'd had the title for some time – *The Secret Life of Stuff* [1]. Mike Petty at the Eden Project in Cornwall in the south-west of England helped me with an outline and to my astonishment I secured a publisher on only the second try. Even more astonishingly, they handed me £7,000 to go away and write the book, which I thought was a small fortune. If I ever properly costed my time, it probably should have been ten times that figure but I didn't care then and I don't now. The thrill of being a published author is priceless.

The book was published in 2011 after two years hard work and contributions from three brilliant researchers. My family put up with a lot. Not only did they have to watch me work harder than I'd ever worked before (I was trying to fit the book around non-executive roles at the Eden Project[9] and the Environment Agency for England and Wales[10]), but every dinnertime they had to put up with me telling them everything there is to know about sewage sludge or pointing out the gadgets containing indium or some other obscure substance. But by the end I felt I had the whole story. That for me was the reward. I didn't expect it to be a best seller, and it wasn't, although it generated a 'respectable' few thousand sales but I'd had the benefit of brilliant research by colleagues and students and the insights from many, many experts. I felt equipped to continue this theme well into the future.

But what was going to be the best format for doing that? I didn't want to run an organization again. I'd got too used to not sitting in one office all day, to managing my own time and being able to spend time with the kids. My first board role, at the Eden Project, came about through a chance conversation with the late and much missed Richard Sandbrook, a non-executive director, followed by several interviews. I couldn't believe that I'd been considered useful enough to serve on the board of such an iconic organization. I did so for eight happy years, constantly astounded by the optimism and brilliance of the founder, Tim Smit, and the amazing team that he and his co-founders had assembled. The Eden Project mission is to tell the story of our dependence on plants through regeneration and horticulture set in a series of giant greenhouses and beautiful gardens. It aligned with all my interests, professional and personal. Every visit combined not only contributing to the strategic oversight of the organization in the boardroom but getting a concentrated injection of happiness and inspiration for my garden and for my many art projects.

I also enjoyed three years on the Board of the Environment Agency for England and Wales, a government 'arm's length' body leading on flood prevention and pollution control. That is a much bigger organization than the Eden Project so contributing to governance there

---

[9] www.edenproject.com/visit

[10] www.gov.uk/government/organisations/environment-agency

felt like an even bigger responsibility. Combined with coaching (which I'd recommend to anyone), it developed my board-level skills. It also gave me a lot of knowledge about areas I hadn't touched before including flood defence and water pollution. These came in handy when applying for my third board role with the Consumer Council for Water.[11] This job, which I still have at the time of writing, has been a great education into the water industry and what it takes to ensure that water comes through our taps and the right things go down the drain. My trip down the East London sewer to admire Joseph Bazalgette's far-sighted engineering from the 1860s and marvel at the 'fatbergs' (unfortunate blockages of congealed grease and wet wipes) has to be one of the highlights of my career.

Governance became a specialism alongside my other interests. When I received a call in 2014 asking if I'd be interested in applying to be chair of WRAP, the Waste and Resources Action Programme,[12] I had just enough experience to not feel completely daunted by the idea. It was the subject I felt I had most knowledge about and really wanted to help make a change. I was honoured to be appointed. WRAP has been responsible for some of the key insights in the field – the massive flows of resources that come into our economy, most of which are lost soon afterwards; exactly how much food we all waste and why; how much waste contributes to greenhouse gas emissions; which products have the biggest environmental impacts. Using those insights, WRAP's programmes have helped governments, business and individuals to change the way they view waste and think instead about a 'circular economy' where waste is 'designed out' and resources are recaptured again and again. My role again combines steering strategic direction with gaining knowledge: from talking to leading designers about the products of the future to looking at materials recovery technology.

So where to next? If I could ever find the patience and time again, I'd like to write another book, this time about water. I'd like to travel more. I have spent my career worrying about the fate of the world but I haven't really seen very much of it. Overall, it sounds clichéd but I'd like to make a difference – through whatever means works best. Probably the biggest lesson of my working life is that change is hardly ever achieved by working alone and that convening people with varied views and expertise is hugely powerful. I intend to continue to do that, bringing science to the table wherever possible.

---

[11] www.ccwater.org.uk/   [12] www.wrap.org.uk/

I'd be very flattered if anyone wanted to follow my career path. My main advice is to follow what you're interested in but ensure you do it in depth so that you feel credible. Only if you feel credible will you sound credible. If you want to seek strategic and governance roles alongside expert roles make sure you get training. I didn't do enough of that early on. I learned mainly on the job and I could have saved myself a lot of nervousness by being better prepared. There is always something new to learn and no shame in admitting that you don't know something: I think it strengthens relationships to ask for help. If you're a woman and are tempted to think that it might work against you at higher professional levels, just don't think like that. A strong sense of purpose will help to carry you through any prejudice you might encounter.

Last but absolutely not least, a pre-requisite for such a flexible career is a supportive partner, especially if childcare is a consideration. My partner, John, could not have been more perfect in this regard, staying at home to cover for me when needed and going back to his own work when the picture changed again. Somehow, though, we both managed to spend substantial amounts of time with our children, a result that I see as our joint, and greatest, triumph. Working practices need to change to make this easier for everyone. I strongly believe that both partners in a relationship should be able to have time with their children as well as pursue careers, and there should be no difference for men and women. Only by bringing up our kids in an atmosphere of equality and healthy work-home balance can we hope to create a more equal world, whatever our profession.

REFERENCE

1. Hill, J. (2011) *The Secret Life of Stuff: A Manual for a New Material World*. Vintage.

Further Sources of Information

YOUR INSTITUTION'S CAREERS SERVICE!

Websites

(NB Website URLs and contents may change so search for similar if so)

Association of Graduate Careers Advisory Services. – www.agcas.org.uk/

Association of Graduate Careers Advisory Services – searchable database of higher education careers services members of AGCAS. – www.agcas.org.uk/people/member_services

Association of the British Pharmaceutical Industry – *Pharmaceutical Industry Career information from the ABPI.* http://careers.abpi.org.uk/Pages/default.aspx

Biochemical Society – *Options after a bioscience degree.* www.biochemistry.org/Education/Highereducation.aspx

Civil Service Fast Stream - www.faststream.gov.uk/

Columbia University – *Career Exploration for Ph.D.s in Science, Technology, Engineering, and Math Disciplines.* www.careereducation.columbia.edu/resources/tipsheets/non-academic-career-options-phds-sciences-engineering-and-mathematics

Harvard University Office of Career Services – http://ocs.fas.harvard.edu/

Michigan State University Career Services Network – https://careernetwork.msu.edu/

Microbiology Society – *Careers.* www.microbiologysociety.org/all-microsite-sections/careers/index.cfm

Milkround - *Graduate Career: A guide to your future* http://advice.milkround.com/supplements/20170207_Graduate_Career/index.html?page=1

Milkround - *Graduate Jobs, Scheme and Internships* www.milkround.com/

Milkround – *Graduate recruitment exhibitions.* http://advice.milkround.com/graduate-recruitment-exhibitions

National Careers Service – https://nationalcareersservice.direct.gov.uk/Pages/Home.aspx

National Institutes of Health Office of Career Services – www.training.nih.gov/career_services

National Postdoctoral Association – www.nationalpostdoc.org/

National Union of Students – www.nus.org.uk/

Nature – *Careers & Jobs.* www.nature.com/nature/careers/

Nature – *Culture: Cultivate the muse - Creative writing can enrich scientists' research.* www.nature.com/naturejobs/science/articles/10.1038/nj7641-381a?WT.ec_id=NATURE-20170216&spMailingID=53430881&spUserID=MjA1NzU5M zY1OQS2&spJobID=1102623693&spReportId=MTEwMjYyMzY5MwS2

Nature – *Jobs of the Week.* www.nature.com/naturejobs/science/

Nature – *Open for Business: Postdoc position in industry can teach people skills that they would not learn in academia.* www.nature.com/naturejobs/2016/160915/pdf/ nj7620-437a.pdf

Nature – *Transferable skills: What are scientists good at (other than science?).* http:// blogs.nature.com/naturejobs/2016/08/29/transferable-skills-what-are-scientists-good-at-other-than-science/

Prospects – www.prospects.ac.uk/careers-advice

Royal Society of Biology – *Job Search.* http://jobs.rsb.org.uk/jobseeker/search/results/

Royal Society of Biology – *Make a difference with a career in biology.* www.rsb.org.uk/ careers-and-cpd/careers/make-a-difference

Royal Society of Biology – *Returners' Resources.* www.rsb.org.uk/policy/groups-and-committees/returners-to-bioscience-group/returners-resources?dm_i= I1,4GOCA,GS4EEG,GGQBK,1

Science (American Association for the Advancement of Science) – *Alternative Careers.* http://blogs.sciencemag.org/sciencecareers/category/alternative-careers

Science (American Association for the Advancement of Science) – *Careers.* http:// sciencecareers.sciencemag.org/

Science Council – *10 types of scientist.* http://sciencecouncil.org/about-us/10-types-of-scientist/

Seltek – *Career Alternatives for Scientists.* www.seltekconsultants.co.uk/candidates/ interview-advice-and-tips/career-alternatives-for-scientists/

Stanford Career Education Student Affairs – https://beam.stanford.edu/

Target Jobs – *Beyond science: Alternative graduate careers for scientists.* https:// targetjobs.co.uk/career-sectors/science-and-research/285505-beyond-science-alternative-graduate-careers-for-scientists

Target Jobs – *Job descriptions.* https://targetjobs.co.uk/careers-advice/job-descriptions

Teach First – *Our Careers* www.teachfirst.org.uk/

The Prodigal Academic – *"Alternate" careers.* http://theprodigalacademic.blogspot .co.uk/2010/09/alternate-careers.html

Think Postgrad – www.thinkpostgrad.com/

University and College Union – www.ucu.org.uk/

University of California, San Francisco Office of Career and Professional Development – http://career.ucsf.edu/

University of Cambridge Careers Service – www.careers.cam.ac.uk/index.asp

University of Cambridge Careers Service – *The 2017 Cambridge Careers Guide.* www.careers.cam.ac.uk/guide.asp

University of Cambridge Careers Service – *Haven't got a clue?* www.careers.cam .ac.uk/careerplanning/haventgotaclue.asp

University of Cambridge Careers Service – *Sectors.* www.careers.cam.ac.uk/ Sectors.asp

University of Oxford Careers Service – *Science Alternatives.* www.careers.ox.ac.uk/ science-alternatives/

Vitae - *About the Vitae Researcher Development Framework.* www.vitae.ac.uk/research ers-professional-development/about-the-vitae-researcher-development-framework

Vitae – *Focus on planning ahead to manage your career.* www.vitae.ac.uk/focus-on-current-theme

Vitae – *Realising the potential of researchers.* www.vitae.ac.uk/

Vitae – *Researcher career stories.* www.vitae.ac.uk/researcher-careers/researcher-career-stories

Vitae – *What do researchers do next? 2016.* www.vitae.ac.uk/news/press-releases/new-report-explores-the-occupations-of-former-research-staff-who-move-beyond-academic-research

Vitae – *What do researchers do?* www.vitae.ac.uk/impact-and-evaluation/what-do-researchers-do

Vitae Researcher Development International Conference 2017 www.vitae.ac.uk/events/vitae-researcher-development-international-conference-2017

WISE – a campaign to promote women in science, technology and engineering - www.wisecampaign.org.uk/

Women in Biology – www-bcf.usc.edu/~forsburg/women/bio.html

Women Returners – http://womenreturners.com/

Reports and Surveys

(NB Website URLs and contents may change so search for similar if so)

Council of Graduate Schools (2017) *Professional Development Shaping Effective Programs for STEM Graduate Students* http://cgsnet.org/ckfinder/userfiles/files/CGS_ProfDev_STEMGrads16_web.pdf

Ernst & Young Global Limited (2017) *University students pessimistic about securing their dream job* www.ey.com/uk/en/newsroom/news-releases/17-01-04-university-students-pessimistic-about-securing-their-dream-job

Fiske, P. (2017) *Look before you leap,* Nature, 542, 127-129 (2 February 2017) www.nature.com/naturejobs/2017/170202/pdf/nj7639-127a.pdf

Higher Education Careers Services Unit (2016) *What do graduates do?* www.hecsu.ac.uk/current_projects_what_do_graduates_do.htm   and   www.hecsu.ac.uk/assets/assets/documents/What_do_graduates_do_2016.pdf

Higher Education Funding Council for England (2013) *Trends in transition from first degree to postgraduate study: Qualifiers between 2002–03 and 2010–11.* www.hefce.ac.uk/media/hefce/content/pubs/2013/201313/Trends%20in%20transition%20from%20first%20degree%20to%20postgraduate%20study.pdf

Higher Education Funding Council for England (2015), *Early career researchers.* www.hefce.ac.uk/analysis/staff/ecr/

National Science Foundation (2015) *Survey of Doctorate Recipients.* www.nsf.gov/statistics/srvydoctoratework/

National Union of Students (2013) *Postgraduates who teach.* www.nus.org.uk/Global/1654-NUS_PostgradTeachingSurvey_v3.pdf

Nature (2015) *Graduate survey: Uncertain futures.* Nature 526, 597–600 (22 October 2015). www.nature.com/nature/journal/v526/n7574/full/nj7574-597a.html

Nature (2015) *Make the most of PhDs.* Nature 528, 7 (2 December 2015). www.nature.com/news/make-the-most-of-phds-1.18915

OECD (2015) *Education at a Glance 2015,* OECD Publishing. www.oecd.org/edu/education-at-a-glance-19991487.htm

Research Councils UK (2015) *The impact of doctoral careers.* www.rcuk.ac.uk/innovation/impactdoctoral/

The Times (2016) *Top 100 Graduate Employers.* www.top100graduateemployers.com/ & www.milkround.com/staticpages/12680/the-times-top-100-graduate-employers/

Vitae (2012) *What do researchers want to do? The career intentions of doctoral graduates* Register at www.vitae.ac.uk/acl_users/credentials_cookie_auth/require_login?came_from=https%3A//www.vitae.ac.uk/vitae-publications/reports/wdrwtd-the-career-intentions-of-doctoral-graduates-feb12.pdf

Vitae (2013) *What do researchers do? Early career progression of doctoral graduates 2013* Register at www.vitae.ac.uk/vitae-publications/reports/what-do-researchers-do-early-career-progression-2013.pdf/view

Vitae (2015) *Careers in Research Online Survey UK aggregate results 2015 for CROS Vitae* Register at www.vitae.ac.uk/vitae-publications/reports/vitae-careers-in-research-online-survey-report-2015-for-cros.pdf/view

Vitae (2016) *What do research staff do next?* Register at www.vitae.ac.uk/news/press-releases/new-report-explores-the-occupations-of-former-research-staff-who-move-beyond-academic-research

Welcome Trust (2016) *Monitor Wave 3 Tracking public views on science and biomedical research.* https://wellcome.ac.uk/sites/default/files/monitor-wave3-full-welcome-apr16.pdf

Wise (2014) *Women in Science, Engineering, Technology and Mathematics: The Talent Pipeline from Classroom to Boardroom* www.wisecampaign.org.uk/uploads/wise/files/WISE_UK_Statistics_2014.pdf

Books

Alternative Careers in Science: Leaving the Ivory Tower (Scientific Survival Skills), Cynthia Robbins-Roth (Academic Press, 1998, 2nd ed., 2005), ISBN-10: 0125893760; ISBN-13: 978-0125893763.

Career Opportunities in Biotechnology and Drug Development, Toby Freedman (Cold Spring Harbor Press, 2009), ISBN-10: 0879698802; ISBN-13: 978-0879698805.

Career Planning for Research Bioscientists, Sarah Blackford (Wiley-Blackwell, 2012), ISBN: 978-1-4051-9670-3.

Guide to Non-Traditional Careers in Science, Karen Young-Kreeger (Routledge, 1998), ISBN-10: 1560326700; ISBN-13: 978-1560326700.

Put Your Science to Work: The Take-Charge Career Guide for Scientists, Peter Fiske (John Wiley & Sons, 2001), ISBN-10: 0875902952; ISBN-13: 978-0875902951.

"So What Are You Going to Do with That?" Finding Careers Outside Academia, Susan Basalla and Maggie Debelius (University of Chicago Press, 2007), ISBN-10: 0226038823; ISBN-13: 978-0226038827.

Index